3356A

(575)

Analysis of

HUMAN MOTION

ANALYSIS OF
Human Motion

A TEXTBOOK IN KINESIOLOGY

By M. Gladys Scott
State University of Iowa

2ND EDITION

Appleton-Century-Crofts

DIVISION OF MEREDITH PUBLISHING COMPANY

New York

PREFACE

A LIST OF ALL THE DIFFERENT ACTS one performs in a day certainly reveals the complexity and variety of the movements involved. A similar log of another's activity might show an equally varied but somewhat different set of skills. Even a casual observation indicates versatility, the adaptability, and the apparent ease and efficiency of human motor performance.

Physical education is concerned primarily with activity or motor skills. For that reason practically every curriculum set up for the training of teachers of physical education includes a course in applied anatomy or kinesiology. Such a course aims to analyze the human mechanism, the machinery which the physical education teacher must understand in order to help the student become conversant with the potentials for movement and to become proficient in at least some of those potential skills. The teacher must understand this mechanism just as the engineer has to learn the principles of the machinery with which he must deal.

Professional education in physical education, and in the therapeutic fields which deal with movement, have attempted for many years to integrate the scientific backgrounds of functions and structure, of principles and application. As in all the scientific fields the procedures of teaching have evolved with knowledge of new facts and changing concepts of utilization of factual materials for a specific purpose. These changes have been apparent in the writings and teaching in the kinesiological field.

The twenty-year interval since the first edition of this book was released has been interesting with respect to kinesiology. The science of human movement has in many ways matured as a distinct, integrated body of knowledge rather than a form of "applied anatomy" as it tended to be in much of the professional thinking and teaching of that earlier period. Mechanics have become an inseparable component, recognized more or less by all writers.

Increased research has evoked a more thoughtful and critical view of the whole problem of teaching motor skills. Such research further shows the diversified background which is incorporated into the professional preparation of the physical educator. The physiologists and clinicians

v

have given recognition to the broad field of movement study, and the efforts of all those dealing with biokinetics reinforce each other.

More kinesiology is being taught to our professional students. More teachers are being prepared to teach kinesiology as the theoretical background of our work with students. Likewise they are being prepared to teach the average learner of motor skills the mechanical and physiological "whys" of the skill presented and of those movement patterns we label as poor and inefficient performance.

The purpose of this book remains much like that of the original edition, i.e., to help the physical education teacher be a better teacher of skills, and to help the therapist to be more effective in the selection and use of movement. The background material of Part I has been expanded to bring into one volume more of the related material, drawing from the various subject matter areas that which has greatest bearing on the understanding of human motion and its internal processes. It is hoped that the discussions of the later sections will lead the student to a thoughtful, independent application of principles. Finally, it is hoped that the systematic method of analyzing activities will help him to be methodical and thorough in selecting, teaching or learning activities. Regardless of which particular activity the student is going to teach, the principles are applicable, and the method of analysis is appropriate.

The author wishes to express appreciation to those who have shared their thinking and provided continuing challenge over the years. The stimuli for this presentation of material have been of several types. First there has been the early teaching of Dr. Arthur Steindler. Doubtless, much of the author's treatment of mechanics has been influenced and acquired by studying under this orthopedic surgeon who taught that normal body function and mechanics must be fully understood as a basis for any teaching or treatment of either the normal or the pathological case.

The second type of stimuli for the author has been the many students over the years. They have included future teachers of physical education and therapists in training for both the occupational and physical therapy fields. Almost without exception they have studied eagerly, have shown satisfaction and appreciation of the new perspective on motor performance. Their inquiries have led to more research, new teaching methods, and to this new version of a discussion which it is hoped will be more pertinent to today's students.

And finally there is the great wealth of material, much of it research in highly specific problems, which has been a source of evolving concepts. Recognition is given to many of these throughout the text and via the lists of references. Appreciation is expressed to all who have contributed directly or indirectly.

State University of Iowa   M. G. S.

CONTENTS

Part I. Introduction

Part II. Mechanics

Part III. Analysis of Activities

Part IV.   Applications for the Physical Educator

Part **I**

INTRODUCTION

CHAPTER 1

Movement in Everyday Living

THE UNIVERSALITY OF MOVEMENT

FROM THE TIME we stretch and start to waken in the morning until we lie down again for sleep at night, practically everything we do is the result of changing muscular contractions. Even the thoughts of the inactive man produce changes in the muscular response. The period of rest and sleep is often thought of as one of inactivity, but respiration must continue, heart action slows but never stops, and the body is rolled, turned, flexed, extended during the sleeping period. These are all motor acts. When the individual opens his eyes or speaks, it is by motor acts. Not until a paralysis is suffered does muscular response cease to exist.

Movement is so generally observable in living organisms that it has attracted the attention of man as far back as we have a record of his philosophic and scientific interests in himself and the world about him.

Even the lower animals know that movement is a sign of life and that it draws attention. They are always quick to detect any motion near them, especially if they are fearful of danger. Many will freeze into a position of immobility when aware of danger, so as to avoid discovery. Or they will move very cautiously and slowly to prevent their movement from being conspicuous.

Much of the success of the magician and sleight-of-hand performer is due to the application of these generally known principles. often forgotten by humans. While one hand very deftly and inconspicuously performs the crucial part of the trick, the other hand or some other part of the body is very actively engaged in any movement or manipulation which will keep the attention of the observer.

Man seems to think in terms of movement. A study of the art of nearly all primitive people shows that it deals largely with active participants in war, sports, or routine occupations. Seldom do we find reclining, sitting, or standing figures which are entirely passive in their attitude. Seated figures were occasionally used as part of a pillar or column beside a doorway. In this manner they gave the appearance of being on guard or of ruling over the scene. The gods, in all the art forms, were usually taking part in man's activities. Man and animals, as depicted in carving, sculpture, drawings, and literature, are active creatures. From earliest times, motor skill and human movement had art and religious, utilitarian and militaristic values.

THE SCIENCE OF HUMAN MOTION

The inquiring, scientific mind has always been attracted to human movement, and such scientists have attempted to understand, analyze, and teach skills to others. This understanding has led to some improvement in method of performing certain acts, and regular experience has often led the individual to acquisition of a technique which he perceives to be either more effective or less demanding of energy.

Perhaps, our present-day emphasis on general efficiency and reduction of energy expenditure has increased the interest in investigation of human movement. In the field of physical education one frequently finds courses on movement fundamentals, body mechanics, movement principles, fundamentals of skills, and similar ones designed to help the student become more proficient and adapt more easily to new skills as they are needed. In the field of industry the efficiency expert has become a highly respected member of industrial management in an effort to help the worker as well as improve output.

In the medical field and related sciences, this analysis of motion covers the whole range of rehabilitation. The specialists in orthopedic medicine, physical therapy, occupational therapy, and, to some extent, recreational therapy are all concerned with what normal motion is, how deviations can be minimized, how efficiency can be restored, and what level of co-ordination and efficiency can be re-established within the limits of the handicap.

To the medical expert as well as to the coach and physical educator, physiology of exercise is basic to understanding the effort produced by the muscles, the onset or delay of fatigue, principles of building strength or endurance in the muscles, elasticity of the muscles, normal tonus versus hypertension and relaxation, and numerous other factors in muscular function in relation to effective action and conservation of energy.

Modern science is engaging in reseach to an extent never before known. Some of this is basic and contributes to better understanding of the human organism and physiology of the motor structure. An example is in the chemical and molecular structure of the muscle cell. Other research is of a technological type and is concerned with application to different kinds of muscular response under varying conditions. In the new realm of space science the motor acts of which the astronaut is capable are as important a consideration as the general physiological and mental adjustment to his new environment. Weightlessness creates a new dimension to man's movement, and such research makes us more aware of the mechanics of terrestrial motion.

But not all of this analysis of human motion has been in recent years. Occasional attempts were made by early scientists to analyze human motion. The Greek philosophers believed in the unity of body and mind. Their interpretation of man's activity, based on observation and analysis, was mechanistic, in accordance with their materialistic interpretation of the universe. Hippocrates* recognized the physiological effect of a commonplace activity such as walking. For example, he wrote that walking should be rapid in winter and slow in summer; unless it be under a burning heat; that fleshy people should walk faster, thin people slower. It was Hippocrates, and Aristotle a century or so later, who devised certain empirical theories of anatomical structure and human mechanics. There was much of truth in their ideas, but the beginnings of the scientific approach came much later.

During the Renaissance, German, English, French, and Italian physiologists and physicists attacked the problem of analyzing animal and human movements. These studies form the real beginning of our modern understanding of the problem. Outstanding among these men were Galilei, the Italian anatomist and physician, Descartes, the French physiologist and philosopher, Borelli, the Italian physicist, and von Haller, the Swiss physiologist.

The nineteenth century saw still greater contributions. The basic facts of neuromuscular functioning were revealed by the work of such men as the Weber brothers, Sherrington, and Helmholtz. Additional experimental evidence through successive decades reaffirms the soundness of many of their theories of nervous stimulation and inhibition, and muscular reaction. Scientists such as Braune, Fischer, Duchenne, Marey, and many others studied the problems of muscle mechanics, of body balance, and of graphic representation as related particularly to locomotion. It was in these years that the science of kinesiology was really founded.

KINESIOLOGY DEFINED

The term "kinesiology" is of Greek derivation. *Kine* comes from the Greek word meaning movement or motion. This same stem is found in kinetic, kinesthetic, kinematics, kinetograph, and other similar words. Kinesiology is the science which investigates and analyzes human motion.

As a modern science kinesiology not only must conform to the practices and standards worthy of the name of science, but must make use also of

---

* Hippocrates, *Regimen in Health,* III, trans. by W. H. S. Jones (Loeb Classical Library, Boston, Harvard University Press).

those facts and principles gathered by scientists in other fields which can contribute to a complete understanding of man's movements.

Movement can take place only as normal body functioning proceeds. Muscle contraction is not an isolated process, occurring independently of the rest of the body. The nervous, circulatory, respiratory, digestive, and excretory systems all have their part to play in this phenomenon. The science of physiology has basic contributions to make to kinesiology.

It is obvious that the use to which a machine can be put depends upon the way it is made: its structure, the material of which the parts are composed, and the way they are put together. It is also known that two machines may perform the same or similar function with different degrees of effort and efficiency. This too is the result of structural quality and arrangement. The human mechanism has many of the characteristics of other machines. Complete understanding of the motion of its parts or of the whole necessitates a knowledge of anatomy, both gross and microscopic.

The human mechanism must meet both the static and dynamic demands of extremely diversified activities. These range all the way from the apparently simple processes of sitting or standing erect to the most complicated co-ordinations of a specialized skill used in sports, dancing, work, or other activities. The physical laws governing matter are universal. Human mechanics are but another illustration of these general principles. The physicist gives the answer to *why* and *how* performance is possible. The question of efficiency of the mechanism is also largely dependent upon physics.

Kinesiology is not an isolated science, sufficient unto itself in methods, knowledge, or contribution. It is a composite of several of the sciences. It necessitates wide information and it offers opportunity for application of principles and laws. Man designs the machines he builds as best he can for the purpose he desires. We inherit our biological and physical make-up. But our human machinery is designed just as cleverly, if not more so, for the demands we make upon it. And if the demands continue beyond the scope of the machine, nature makes every effort possible to make the necessary adaptations. The aim of kinesiology is an understanding of this human machine and its processes of motor functioning.

Kinesiology is the basic science of the physical educator. In physical education the teacher deals with motor performance as a means toward the development of the total individual. This approach through physical activity is used comparatively little by most of the other branches of education. The development of motor performance, through acquisition of skills and their use, opens an avenue to other learning and is a unique contribution of physical education. Hence, the physical education teacher must have thorough knowledge of, and ability to analyze, that performance. Only in this way can the teacher become the guide toward the most effective learning and provide the greatest benefit to the physical organism, and perhaps even avoid making mistakes that will be injurious to the organism.

The first purpose of kinesiology should be to organize and make application of the facts and principles learned in the other basic sciences.

The anatomy student knows that the internal structure of the bone shows a very definite pattern, that the gastrocnemius muscle is made up of many sections and the sartorius is long and thin, and other similar facts. Anatomy is descriptive rather than analytical. The physiology student knows that the muscle possesses the properties of contractility and elasticity, that the muscle is always being stimulated, that all muscles possess a certain degree of tonus; but too frequently he does not know the relationship of these and other facts to the problem of posture, to the alteration of postural habits, and to the effectiveness of all motor performance. The student of physics learns the law of gravity, the distinguishing characteristics of the different types of levers, and the law of inertia. However, they are very apt to be applied only to inanimate objects in the student's mind.

From some source the average student has learned that the heart rate is greater in a standing position than in a reclining one. He also knows that the heart beats faster and breathing is deeper when one is going up a long flight of stairs than when one is walking on level ground. Likewise he has learned from experience that the heavier the load he carries the closer it must be kept to the body to be carried easily; and that the greater the range of a given movement, the greater the speed usually developed. The complete explanation of each of these facts can be given only by drawing on two or three of the above mentioned sciences of anatomy, physics, and physiology.

Thus kinesiology attempts to integrate all the contributing fields of information through direct application to the problems of the teacher of swimming, of dance, of correctives, of sports, and of all other physical education activities.

Second, kinesiology makes an analysis and evaluation of activities. If skills are to be taught and poor performances corrected, then the teacher must be able to break the activity down into the parts functioning and the co-ordination of these parts, and must know the physical laws governing them. In order to understand the physiological, developmental, or therapeutic effects of an activity, it must be analyzed and compared with others. It is assumed that the teacher has definite aims and objectives set up; only if he understands the nature and effects of each activity can he choose intelligently the activities which contribute to these aims.

Third, the analysis of activities should make for better and easier teaching. Few students are sufficiently visual-minded or have adequate kinesthetic sense to imitate immediately and accurately a demonstrated skill. Nor can most activities be completely taught as a single unit. At some time during the learning process parts must be singled out for emphasis, perhaps one part for one student, and another part for another student. Then these parts must be brought together in proper sequence as a co-ordinated whole.

Also, many teachers are required or wish to teach activities about which they know very little. The ability to analyze what they read, what they see others do, and what they try for themselves is essential as they branch out into new activities. In short, this analytical ability is what makes possible creative, individualized, and effective teaching of motor skills.

Fourth, it seems impossible to understand the problems of efficiency and economy without becoming more sensitive to poise and grace, or the lack of them, in other individuals. Such qualities are more than a psychological characteristic or a social asset, for they involve problems of physiological cost, energy budgeting, and muscular timing.

Fifth, Kinesiology should give a better appreciation of posture. The first step in that direction is an understanding of the basic principles which determine the standards for sitting, standing, walking, and body carriage in general. "Good posture" is more than an aesthetic ideal, a common mold for all individuals. It is a mechanical problem—a problem related to gravity, stress and strain on body parts, and muscular strength and tonus.

Sixth, the analysis of movement and understanding of standards should make the teacher more aware of irregular and unusual performance, and of abnormal structure. This is necessary for instruction which aims for the greatest development of the individual, and for consideration of individual potentialities and limitations.

Thus this analysis of human movement is an indispensable part of the equipment and knowledge of the physical education teacher. However, it is of value also to those in the medical fields of orthopedics, physical therapy, occupational therapy, and recreational therapy. They must all work with cases having injuries, disease or congenital defects affecting the motor mechanism. They must know or diagnose the extent of the dysfunction, the reaction to expect from the muscles involved, how to re-educate muscles, what forces to oppose, how to provide substitute motions, where and how to fit artificial supports, and the answer to many other problems. All such problems must be solved for the patient with mathematical and technical precision.

The structure and mechanics of human performance are not ignored in the economic world. Many industries employ an efficiency expert, who is usually both a psychologist and an engineer. It is a part of the responsibility of this expert to determine ways and means to secure the most efficient and economical performance of work by the employees. This includes working position, speed, load, and flow of movement as related to both production and fatigue.

The manufacturers of furniture have been forced to consider human anatomy and human comfort. Unfortunately, however, comfort does not always insure the best effect from the use of the article. For example, the big, easy, overstuffed chair may be thoroughly comfortable and desirable for a period of rest and relaxation. Nevertheless, it is not suitable for the constant use of anyone, particularly a growing child or a person engaged in an activity requiring considerable flexion of the spine. However, manufacturers have largely eliminated chairs which give support at the wrong point in the back, or which cut into the thigh because they are too short or too high. Improvements have also been made in the height of tables, desks, sinks, stoves, telephones, and other appliances.

An attempt has been made to provide for the growing child furniture which is comfortable and also encourages good postural habits. This attempt to satisfy anatomical and mechanical requirements has been more pronounced in school seats and desks than anywhere else. But all adult builds are not similar, so the present-day office furniture, cars, and work equipment have been designed for adjustment for individual differences. This throws the responsibility back on the individual to make the proper adjustment for efficiency, minimizing of fatigue, and maintenance of good working postures.

Industry also has an eye on the market for satisfying the demands of a comfort-seeking public. One can purchase a folding and portable "jump seat," a lightweight but substantial "back" to be used in a boat or on bleachers. Probably every student and many older persons have experienced the fatigue resulting from long sitting on bleachers without the accustomed back support. This is a good illustration of the difference in energy cost of an activity done in two different ways.

Automobile manufacturers attempt to build comfort for both driver and passenger and at the same time to arrange for easy driving. Seats adjust not only in the forward-backward position but in height and angle. The individual with long legs finds little comfort in the smaller compact cars, and the inactivity from riding for some time in seat belts causes a fatigue not experienced when the rider is free to squirm around in the seat. This probably accounts for some of the public indifference to recommendations for seat belts. The knowledge of how to minimize this fatigue is part of the science of human motion and efficiency.

The designers of sports clothing have been more alert to the problems of free action than have those of clothing in general. Research in clothing design has approached the problem from various angles. It has been demonstrated that clothing which binds through the arms and shoulders is more fatiguing and reduces speed of action. Research has also shown that clothing can be designed to meet the changes in proportion of growing children and has established general recommendations that all clothing should provide freedom of movement, avoid strain, and avoid weight on shoulders and back. Newer materials are to some extent solving the weight problem; changing styles and designs again throw responsibility back on the individual.

Thus the daily life of the average citizen is influenced by the knowledge and interest which a few persons have in the human mechanism, its structure, and its physiological and mechanical functioning.

PLAN OF THIS BOOK

The approach to the problems of kinesiology is to be based upon three guiding principles:

1. All tissues of the body show a definite relationship between structure and function, adaptations being made to functional demands both normal and pathological.

2. Human motion occurs in accordance with general mechanical laws, as is evidenced by the structure and functioning of the motor system.

3. The individual can perform an endless variety of movements and can develop a type of motor functioning the economy and perfection of which are dependent upon the adequacy of the organism to meet these kinetic demands and upon a complex adjustment of all phases of the performance. These phases include innervation, chemical and mechanical processes of muscle contraction, association of muscles, and application of mechanical laws.

The first three sections of this book are built around these three statements, though obviously there must be some overlapping in sections. The principles stated at the beginning of each of the first eleven chapters are more specific points elaborating the governing idea of the total section. The discussion which follows in each chapter gives facts, background, and explanation necessary to a full understanding of these principles.

REFERENCES

1. Braun, Genevieve L., Kinesiology from Aristotle to the Twentieth Century, *Research Quarterly*, 12, 1941, p. 163.
2. Broer, Marion R., *Efficiency of Human Movement*, Philadelphia, W. B. Saunders Co., 1960, Ch. 1, Efficient Movement.
3. Duchene, G. B., *Physiology of Motion*, trans. and ed. by Emmanuel B. Kaplan, Philadelphia, J. B. Lippincott Co., 1949.
4. Hellebrandt, Frances, Physiology and the Physical Educator, *Research Quarterly*, 11, March 1940, p. 12.
5. Hill, A. V., *Living Machinery*, New York, Harcourt, Brace & World, Inc., 1927, Ch. 7, Physiology as a Meeting Ground of the Sciences.

6. Hirt, Susanne, What is Kinesiology? *Physical Therapy Review*, 35, 1955, p. 419.
7. Licht, Sidney, *Electrodiagnosis and Electromyography*, New Haven, Elizabeth Licht, Pub., 1956, Ch. 1, History.
8. Mainland, Donald, *Anatomy*, New York, Harper & Row, Pubs., 1945, Ch. 1, Anatomy and Education.
9. Metheny, Eleanor, *Body Dynamics*, New York, McGraw-Hill Book Co., Inc., 1952, Ch. 1, Preview.
10. Morehouse, Lawrence E., and Rasch, Philip J., *Scientific Bases of Athletic Training*, Philadelphia, W. B. Saunders Co., 1958, Ch. 1, Historical Introduction, Ch. 2, Kinesiological Facts in Athletics.
11. Rasch, Philip J. and Burke, Roger K., *Kinesiology and Applied Anatomy*, Philadelphia, Lea and Febiger, 1959, Ch. 1, History of Kinesiology.
12. Steindler, Arthur, *Mechanics of Normal and Pathological Locomotion in Man*, Springfield, Ill., Charles C Thomas, 1935, Ch. 1, The History of the Mechanics of the Locomotor System.

2

The Human Skeleton

THE FRAMEWORK OF THE BODY

1. Bone is living tissue.
2. Bone develops according to the stresses placed upon it.
3. Bones vary in shape and structure according to functional needs.
4. Bones serve several functions for the organism.
5. Ossification of bone follows a regular sequence through the individual's years of growth.

THE HUMAN SKELETON is the framework of the body. Bones vary in size according to sex and race[8] as well as among individuals. It is the bones which primarily determine the characteristics of body build: the tall or short stature; the large thorax or small one; big ankles, knees, or wrists; small, slender feet or broad, chubby ones; spreading and large hands or slender, delicate fingers. These factors are important in the movements of the person as well as in the way he appears to the observer.

The bones serve a number of purposes. Probably the most important is that associated with the movement and work of the organism. They provide not only the dimension of the levers for work but also the axes on which these levers turn. Each bone must be rigid and strong to withstand both the force of the muscles which pull upon it and also the stress of the load which the lever bears. These are referred to as tension and compression forces respectively. Likewise, it must be rigid to protect other tissues such as the vascular center within the long bone or the heart and lungs enclosed by the thorax. This service is challenged infrequently but through the daily stress of motor action, the bone acquires the strength to meet these demands.

INTERNAL STRUCTURE OF BONE

The most obvious differentiation in internal structure is between a structure. The former is referred to as compact bone and is either a thin solid, dense, ivory-appearing portion and a porous, meshed or weblike

a–compact ring from
shaft of long bone

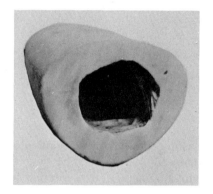

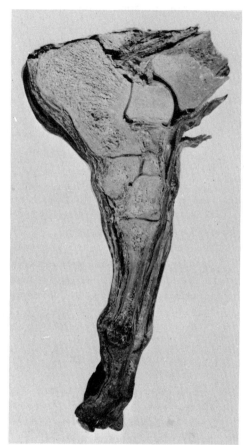

b–cross section of
cancellous interior
of tarsal bones

FIGURE 1: Bone Structure

shell around the bone or a thick heavy tube forming the shaft of a long
bone, appearing as a ring if a cross section is taken. The second type
of structure is _cancellous_ bone, or spongy bone, so named because of
its appearance, not its pliability.

To get at the basis for understanding that bone is living tissue, one
needs to examine the bone microscopically. This reveals a systematic,
almost geometric arrangement of parts. The center of the structural unit
is a tiny canal (Haversian canal) through which extends a capillary
supply of blood for metabolic needs. Around this central canal lie concentric rings of calcification permeated with lesser canals for the branchings of tiny capillaries. These provide columnar units of encrustations.
Such columns do not fit together perfectly, but the spaces between are

filled with layers of a similar type, so that the compact bone appears uniform and solid. The cancellous bone shows the same basic system of calcium deposit around the circulatory canal, but these units are not as nearly parallel in arrangement. If stress on the area is great, as in the condyle of a bone, there the bone is substantial and the holes are smaller and more widely spaced. As stress diminishes in other parts the cancellous bone thins out to mere threadlike structures spaced far apart.

Both compact and cancellous bone respond to the pressure and tension forces acting on the bone. The compact bone may be considered as contributing strength and protection. The cancellous bone is designed to provide strength with economy in weight.

BONE GROWTH

A consideration of the growth and developmental aspects of bone also reveals the living characteristic of the bone. Embryonically the bone is first evolved as a cartilage with similarities in shape and proportion to the ossified, adult bone. The bone changes from this state as a result of activity at *ossification centers*. This process is started before birth and is gradually continued until early in the third decade of life. So systematic is this process of conversion from cartilage to bone that individuals can be compared in structural maturity by comparison of X-ray data on a sample of easily accessible small bones. The carpals and metacarpals are usually used for this purpose, but Clarke[2] suggests a very limited functional segment consisting of capitate, third metacarpal, and phalanges of the third digit.

The ossification centers are scattered through the smaller bones or those of irregular shape. As growth expands around these centers the areas of ossification merge and a unified structure results. In contrast, in the long bones, while the expanded condyles and main shaft grow from centers similar to those in the small bones, the actual extension of the bone on a long axis proceeds at both ends where shaft and condyle meet. These areas are among the last to calcify, remaining throughout childhood and youth as a line of residual cartilage, very active, and very responsive. This area is known as the *epiphyseal line.* (Until its ossification is completed it is an area of lesser strength.) Particularly in the elementary age child, (epiphyseal separation is probably more common than fractures of the shaft) In the upper extremity the epiphyses near the elbow are the first to cease marked growth, but in the lower extremity it is in the knee area where they persist longest and produce the most growth.

[Another point of evidence with respect to bone growth and life is in the normal repair of fractures. The cracks or separated ends first fill in with cartilage and later exhibit the same transformation into bone and renewed rigidity.]

The blood supply to both the marrow and the bone itself is very profuse. This means there is ample supply of elements for metabolism, for bone absorption and replacement, and for production of red cells. The bones reflect nutritional deficiencies, general health status, and pubertal onset.

GROSS BONE STRUCTURE

The bones are classified according to shape and proportions. _Long bones_ (L) consist of a shaft of compact bone filled with marrow which interlaces into the trabeculae of the cancellous portion. This shaft is known as the _diaphysis,_ and the expanded ends are the _epiphyses._ (The line of demarcation during childhood and youth is the _epiphyseal line_ or _disk._) The articular part of the epiphysis is covered with hyaline cartilage. The outside of the epiphysis is covered with a membrane, the periosteum. The muscle or its tendon attaches directly into the periosteum, (and in some cases the tendon fibers are even rooted deeper into the bone.) In areas of muscular attachment the periosteum becomes very fibrous or even cartilaginous, and the bone becomes more or less protuberant. The fibers of the periosteum interweave with the fibers of the joint capsule, thus giving firm attachment to the capsule.

Short bones (S) are of irregular shape but each relatively equal in its diameters, frequently six-sided like a cube. They too have cartilage covering for the articulations and periosteum covering the bone otherwise. They are mostly cancellous bone with a thin outer layer of compact tissue.

Irregular bones (I) are of highly variable shape, usually with different parts or projections. They always contain compact bone as a shell or at articular points, but if of any thickness, they are filled with cancellous bone.

Flat bones (F) are thin but seldom flat. For example, the ribs or cranial bones are classed as flat; they are thin but curved. They are usually made up of outer compact layers or plates with a cancellous layer in between for strength. The entire cross section resembles the cross section of a side of a paper box with the corrugated layer between sheets of paper.

In the skeletal system can be found numerous examples of the interrelationships of structure and function. The lower extremity is far better adapted to weight bearing than is the upper one. The pelvic girdle is a complete ring and relatively solid in the pubic and the two sacroiliac articulations. The condyles of the tibia are broad and flat for the superimposed segment. The foot projects both forward and back from the ankle to provide a better base of support.

Conversely the incomplete and mobile pectoral girdle gives great freedom of motion, and the radius swinging freely around the ulna carries the hand through a wide excursion for placement or use of hand or fingers.

The central or axial portion of the skeleton is comprised of

Skull		
	frontal	F
	parietal	F
	temporal	I
	occipital	F
	sphenoid	I
	ethmoid	I
	malar	I
	maxilla	I
	lacrimal	F
	nasal	F
	palate	F
	mandible	I
	inferior turbinates	I
	vomer	F
Vertebrae	7 cervical	I
	12 thoracic	I
	5 lumbar	I
	5 sacral	I
	4 coccygeal	I
Thorax	sternum	F
	ribs (12 pairs)	F

The extremities have analogous structure as shown by the following outline.

Upper extremity		Lower extremity	
clavicle	L	os innominatum	I
scapula	I	sacrum	I
humerus	L	femur	L
ulna	L	tibia	L
radius	L	fibula	L
navicular	S	os calcis	S
lunate	S	talus	S
triangular	S	1st cuneiform	S
pisiform	S	2nd cuneiform	S
greater multangular	S	3rd cuneiform	S
lesser multangular	S	scaphoid	S
capitate	S	cuboid	S
hamate	S		
5 metacarpals	L	5 metatarsals	L
14 phalanges	L	14 phalanges	L

The trochanter, the tuberosities, and the tubercles not only represent sites of muscle pull, but in most instances provide a mechanical advantage for the muscle. The landmarks on bones are named according to type and association. For example, the deltoid tuberosity relates it to the deltoid and tells the size of the prominence. These landmarks are usually the site of muscular or ligamentous attachment.

The terms are generally used according to the following definitions.

Prominences	crest—sharp ridge
	line—small, elongated ridge
	spine—sharp-pointed projection
	lip—line on the margin of another structure
	tubercle—small bump
	tuberosity—large, rounded prominence
Depressions	foramen (foramina, pl.)—hole
	fovea—deep pit
	fossa—broad, shallow concavity
	groove—long, ditchlike hollow
	sinus—cavity or chamber inside bone

Other terminology used with reference to the bones or body segments follows:

distal—away from the median line of the body
proximal—nearest the median line of the body
inferior—below or under side
superior—above or upper side
deep—buried or internal
superficial—on the periphery or outside

The anatomical position is an erect standing position with maximum elongation of body and legs, feet flat on the floor, head erect, arms hanging straight at the sides with palms forward. This is not the natural relaxed position for the forearm, but it does place the entire length of the radius on the side of the ulna rather than crossing it.

REFERENCES

1. Bayer, Leona M., and Bayley, Nancy, *Growth Diagnosis*, Chicago, University of Chicago Press, 1959, Ch. 9, X-ray of Hand and Wrist.
2. Clarke, H. Harrison, and Hayman, Noel R., Reduction of Bone Assessments Necessary for the Skeletal Age Determination of Boys, *Research Quarterly*, 33, May 1962, p. 202.
3. Evans, F. Gaynor, *Stress and Strain in Bones*, Springfield, Ill., Charles C Thomas, 1957.
4. Gardner, Ernest, Gray, Donald J., and O'Rahilly, Ronan, *Anatomy*, Philadelphia, W. B. Saunders Co., 1960.
5. Mainland, Donald, *Anatomy*, New York, Harper & Row, Pubs., 1945, Ch. 3, Bones.

6. Morehouse, Laurence E., and Rasch, Philip J., *Scientific Basis of Athletic Training*, Philadelphia, W. B. Saunders Co., 1958, Ch. 2, Kinesiological Factors in Athletics.

7. Morton, Dudley J., *The Human Foot*, New York, Columbia University Press, 1935.

8. Piscopo, John, Skinfold and Other Anthropometric Measurements of Pre-adolescent Boys from Three Ethnic Groups, *Research Quarterly*, 33, May 1962, p. 255.

9. Rasch, Philip J., and Burke, Roger K., *Kinesiology and Applied Anatomy*, Philadelphia, Lea & Febiger, 1959, Ch. 2, Framework and Joints of the Body.

10. Steindler, Arthur, *Kinesiology of the Human Body*, Springfield, Ill., Charles C Thomas, 1955, Ch. 2, Physical Properties of Bone.

CHAPTER 3

Articulations of the Body

THE LOCATION OF MOTION

1. Movement takes place in the articulations, hence their structure will determine primarily the type and range of movements of which the body and its parts are capable.
2. The type and range of movement are very similar in all subjects, although some individual differences may be found.
3. Ligaments limit joint range.

CHARACTERISTICS OF ARTICULATIONS

THE ARTICULATIONS OF THE BODY are the sites of motion just as the hinge on the door or the axle of the wheel is the point of action for these two objects. If a hinge of a different type is put on a door, it will result in a different use of the door. The revolving door, the swinging door, and the ordinary door with the one-way hinge behave differently because of the differences in their attachments to the adjoining door frame.

The modern engineer is called upon to build two types of structures. One type must withstand the stress and strain of superimposed parts but there is little or no need for movement of component parts and therefore for segmentation, facilitation or limitation of action, alignment or counterbalance. The problem is rather for strength and permanence of the connecting parts and a firm base for the superimposed parts. The second type of structure is a moving one; the requirements are for controlled freedom, variety in potential action, efficiency in operation, and interrelating action in the various parts. Such a structure calls not only for a firm base but for centers of prescribed motion that are protected against the forces of action. It must meet the demands of a firm, static edifice and also those demands created by its own force and the forces of external origin that tend always to make its parts and its total structure move in various ways.

The human frame must achieve this dual demand. The joints are fitted together or tied together as firmly as possible but are always left free for certain dynamic functions. In some of the most critical points of stability or for protection of internal functions, movement is sacrificed and we find the rigidity and fixation characteristic of the static structure.

The articulations of the body are named according to the structure of the articulating parts. The names are thus somewhat descriptive. In order to analyze the actions of various joints of the same type it is necessary to know the differences in size, the range which is made possible by the articulating surfaces, and the limitations established by surrounding capsule, ligaments, and muscles. A knowledge of the classification is, therefore, merely the beginning in an understanding of the joint; each joint must be studied further in detail.

All the articulations of the body belong to one of three classes depending upon the amount of motion each permits. Movement varies from none in the sutures of the skull to extreme freedom in the shoulder, which is probably the freest joint in the body. These three classes, in order of decreasing movement are:

diarthrodial—freely movable
amphiarthrodial—slightly movable
synarthrodial—immovable

The synarthrodial connections are such as to be little recognized in a consideration of articulations. They include such structures as the junction of the ilium, ischium, and pubis in making a single unified os innominatum; the cranial sutures uniting those bones into a firm enclosure for the brain; or the union of the sacral vertebrae making up the sacrum.

The amphiarthrodial articulations are of little more significance in motor functions than the synarthrodial. Some of the characteristic aspects of articulations are more apparent, i.e., ligaments, capsule, cartilage, but the joints are protected against movement. Examples can be found at the symphysis pubis and sacroiliac junctions.

Action of the body and its parts take place in the diarthrodial articulations. This class of articulation subdivides itself structurally, and hence functionally, into six types. The six are:

arthrodial—gliding joint
condyloid—joint formed by a convex prominence gliding over a more or
              less flat, broad surface
enarthrodial—ball-and-socket joint
ginglymus—hinge joint
reciprocal reception—saddle joint
trochoid—pivot joint

The movements of the body segments will be described, for the present, in the following terms. It should be noted how these relate to the joints as they are identified above.

Gliding is the simplest form of action, but permits only limited motion and is not widely distributed over the body. There is no definite axis of motion but the contour of one surface is such that it slides more or less freely over the cartilaginous covering of its neighbor.

Rotation is a movement around an axis which runs longitudinally through the segment. It is usually described as medial or lateral (inward or outward) according to the direction which the anterior aspect of the segment is moved.

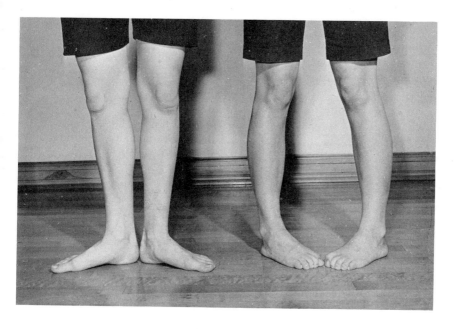

FIGURE 2: Rotation of leg at hip joint
Left–outward rotation; *Right*–inward rotation

Angular movement takes place around a transverse axis. If the two adjacent segments are moving from the anatomical position and are approaching each other, the joint is being *flexed*. Another interpretation of flexion is that the total segment is being folded up or shortened. If the part is being returned to its starting position, it is being *extended*, but if it continues beyond straight alignment it is said to be *hyperextended*. In Table I, extension is used in the sense of hyperextension, as extension is always possible to the normal. This is in agreement with a common practice to use the term extension when the segment starts in the anatomical position and then moves directly into a hyperextended position.

Abduction is a lateral movement away from the anatomical position and away from the central plane of the body. *Adduction* is a movement inward toward that central plane.

Circumduction occurs in all joints which permit the four forms of angular motion. It is a movement in which the extremity of the segment describes a more or less perfect circle. The circle may be large or small, but the larger the circle the more nearly that circle will approach the plane in which the articulation is located. The segment as a whole describes a cone, the base of which is the circle formed by the distal point, and the apex of which is in the joint where the movement takes place (Fig. 4).

The gliding type of joint is best exemplified by the articular processes of the vertebrae and by the carpal and tarsal bones. The amount of movement between any two surfaces is usually slight but the apparent range of action is considerable due to the summation of movements of several vertebrae or tarsal bones.

The ball-and-socket joint is perfectly described by its name. It has an indefinite number of axes of motion and planes of motion. Limitations which exist are due primarily to capsular or ligamentous obstructions rather than to structure of the articulating surfaces. This type permits all forms of angular motion, circumduction, and rotation.

The condyloid type of articulation is in many respects similar to the ball-and-socket and permits all the freedom of the ball-and-socket, with the exception of rotation. The articulations between the metacarpals and the first segment of the fingers are of this type.

The hinge joint should be clear from its name. The range of flexion is usually checked by contact of muscle masses of the two segments, and extension by the limitations of the articulating surfaces and by ligaments. In a true hinge joint, motion is possible in only one plane.

The saddle type is a special arrangement found only in the thumb, which again permits all the freedom of the ball-and-socket type except rotation. This action permits the apposition of thumb to finger tips or palm or spread to grasp a large or small object.

The pivot type is designed to permit rotation. This rotation is around a longitudinal axis, which may be represented by an actual projection, as in the tubercle on the axis, or by an imaginary axis, as in the head of the radius.

The various articulations will be discussed briefly. At the end of the chapter is Table I showing the classification, movements, and range of most of the articulations. The figures quoted for range of each movement are approximate average performance. Without doubt, there are individual variations showing markedly increased or decreased flexibility. Experimental data are available from various sources (see references at end of chapter). These sources do not agree on what normal range is.

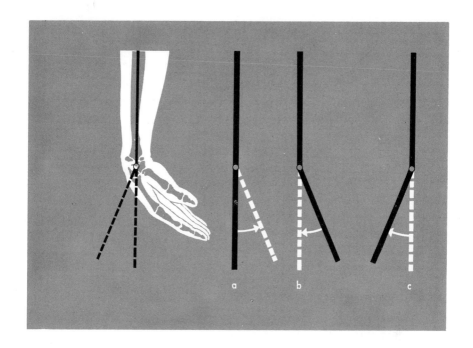

FIGURE 3: Diagram of angular movement in the joints
a–flexion; b–extension; c–hyperextension

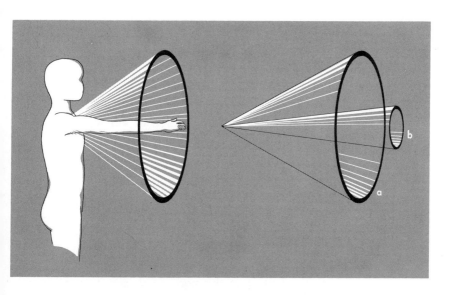

FIGURE 4: Diagram of circumduction
a–wide movement; b–narrow movement

It must be remembered that some of these data are on voluntary movements, others on passive manipulations; some are on one age level and some on another. Some of these individual variations and those of different age and sex groups will be discussed in a later chapter in connection with the means of increasing flexibility.

SPINE

Movements of the spine are the result of motion between the articular facets, some gliding between the bodies of the vertebrae, and compression of the intervertebral disks. Movement between any two vertebrae is very slight, but summations of all joints gives the apparent flexibility.

The articular facets of the *cervical* vertebrae are small and the plane between their surfaces lies approximately horizontally. Motion takes place as a result of sliding of the articular surfaces, but because of the horizontal alignment of the facets movement is more or less free in all directions. The bodies of the vertebrae are small and the processes are short. This further facilitates movement. The so-called movement of the head is either a rocking in the occipito-atlantal junction or distributed further down the cervical vertebrae.

The movements of the head and neck are described as flexion, extension, abduction, and rotation. Flexion (forward) of the cervical region is free, limited usually by contact of the chin on the sternum. Hyperextension is also free, limited largely by the mass of muscle on the back of the neck and by tension of the anterior muscles, ligaments, and other structures of the neck.

Rotation also occurs throughout this region but is more pronounced between the axis and atlas. The atlas does not have a distinct body as the other vertebrae have, and instead the odontoid process projects upward from the body of the axis. This process serves as the hub for the circular atlas. Movement at this point is limited to somewhere around 160° by the ligaments binding the vertebrae and skull together. Differences in shortness of ligaments and fascia produce the individual differences in rotation.

The articular facets of the *thoracic* region are a little larger and broader and lie approximately in a frontal plane. The bodies and intervertebral disks are larger, the processes longer, and the spinous processes point downward, each overlapping the one below. Each rib has dual attachments, one between two adjacent vertebral bodies and the other from the transverse process of the vertebra just above the rib. All these factors affect the movement taking place in this region. Flexion is moderate in amount, being checked by the rigidity of the thoracic cage. Hyperextension is decidedly limited due to the overlapping of the spinous processes. It is ordinarily only about enough to eliminate the normal convexity of this region and make the spine approximately straight. Abduc-

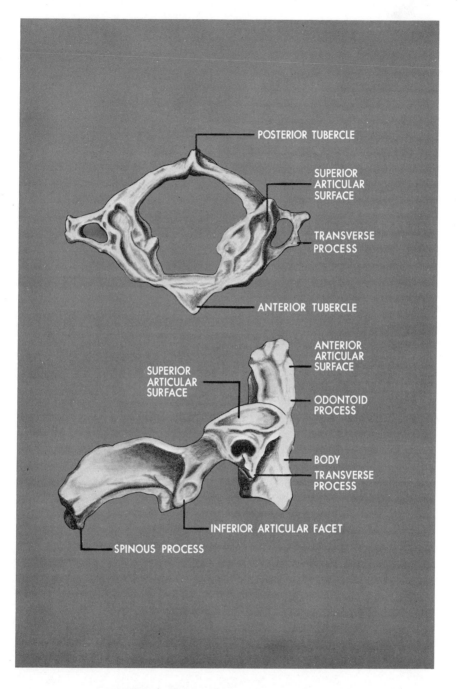

FIGURE 5: First and second cervical vertebra
Top–superior view of the atlas; *Bottom*–lateral view of the axis

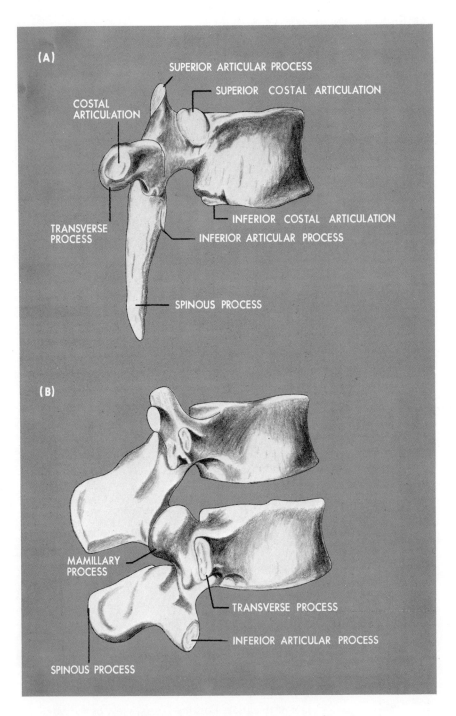

FIGURE 6: Spinous processes of vertebrae
a–seventh thoracic vertebra; b–first and second lumbar vertebrae

tion and rotation are also very limited because of the thoracic cage and attachment of the ribs to the spine.

In the *lumbar* region, which is the third and last of the movable regions of the spine, the vertebrae are more massive. The bodies are large, the neural arch more heavily encased, and the processes shorter but broader. The articular facets are vertical pillars with their contacting surfaces approximately in a sagittal plane. Movement in the lumbar region is again freer, more nearly matching that of the cervical. The actual extent of flexion is difficult to determine because it is almost invariably accompanied by hip flexion. Its check consists usually of limitation of abdominal compression. Hyperextension is also free, resulting in a pronounced increase in the line of lumbar concavity. It is finally limited by contact of the fan-shaped spinous processes and tension of the anterior longitudinal ligament. Lateral bending or abduction is only slightly less free than hyperextension, and is limited by the contact of the fan-shaped spinous processes and tension of the anterior longitudinal ligament. Lateral bending or abduction is only slightly less free than hyperextension, and is limited by the contact of the transverse processes. Rotation is impossible in this region because the articular facets lock against each other. Summation of rotation in the lumbar joints would not exceed 5° to 10°. The lowest source of any appreciable amount of rotation in the spine is the twelfth thoracic and first lumbar articulation. Below that, when rotation is apparently taking place, it is a rotation in the hip joint; hence it is a change in the plane of the pelvis.

The movements of the total spine are represented diagrammatically in Figures 7 and 8. These are represented with the pelvis remaining fixed. This, of course, seldom occurs in actual activity. Such movement gives a slight increase of spinal freedom, and is also helpful in maintaining balance, as will be discussed later.

The sacrum, while it evolves as five vertebrae, each with separate centers of ossification, is completely fused into a single unit. This fusion is a gradual one and is not completed before the twenty-fourth or twenty-fifth year. The lowest point of movement in the spine is the lumbosacral joint. There is considerable rocking of the fifth lumbar on top of the sacrum with all movement characteristic of the lumbar region, but to a limited extent. The angle formed by these two surfaces is a rather large one, though it varies in different individuals from about 10° to 25°. The result of this large angle is at least threefold, and tends to increase whenever the angle is increased. There is a constant sheering effect, which causes an enlarging and strengthening of the sacrum, requires a reinforcement of the ligaments at this joint, and requires greater tension from the muscles in this area.

The sacrum varies considerably in shape and curvature. The differences in angle of the top and in the shape affect somewhat the size of the pelvic cavity as well as the angle between the sacrum and the pelvis. If the sacrum is placed rather high and far forward in the ilia, the angle with the fifth lumbar is usually small and the lumbar curve is somewhat flattened. On the other hand, if the sacrum is lower and farther back in the ilia, the angle is usually larger and the lumbar curve more pronounced. The variations in angle of pelvis will also affect the relationship between pelvis and femur and the muscle tension over that joint.

The sacroiliac articulation is classed as amphiarthrodial. However, it is not important in body dynamics as a moving joint. But the sacrum and the two sacroiliac articulations are important because they form a link in the otherwise rigid pelvic girdle. The importance of this complete girdle will be evident later. As an articulation it is of interest to those treating abnormalities and injuries, since it is subject to strain.

The coccyx is a rudimentary structure and is unimportant functionally in the problem of body mechanics.

There are certain ligaments which run the full length of the movable regions of the spine. Two of these are on the bodies of the vertebrae. The anterior longitudinal or common ligament almost surrounds the body anterior to the pedicles and extends from axis to sacrum. The posterior longitudinal or common ligament is inside the neural arch and connects the posterior borders of the bodies. The remaining long ligaments connect the neural arches and processes. The ligamentum flavum is also inside the neural arch connecting the laminae or posterior portions of the arch. The supraspinous ligament connects the ends of the spinous processes as a heavy cordlike structure except in the cervical region, where it becomes an extended membrane known as the ligamentum nuchae with superior attachment on the occipital bone of the skull. Shorter ligaments, repeated at each successive level, include the capsules around the articular facets and the interspinous and intertransverse ligaments.

Specialized ligaments are found in addition at the base of the skull, connecting primarily the occipital bone to axis and atlas. All are important in protecting the neck at this level, but the greatest restriction in motion probably comes from the alar ligament.

RIBS

The movement of the ribs is a rotary one. The axis of motion is a line extending between the two articulations of the ribs, one with the head of the rib and the side of the vertebra and the other with the tubercle of the rib and the transverse process. Because of the shape of the rib, this rotation causes an elevation or depression of the anterior end of the rib and, hence, of the whole thoracic cage, since the upper ten pairs of ribs are all fastened together. The cartilaginous union between the ribs and the sternum permits only very limited motion. The result of rib movement is

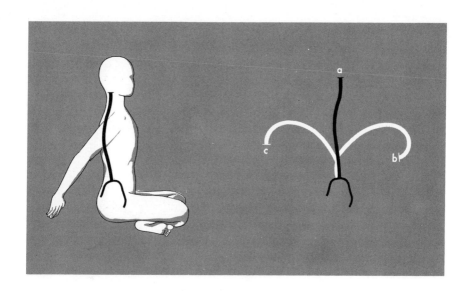

FIGURE 7: Movement of the spine in an anteroposterior direction
a–upright position of the spine; b–complete flexion of the spine;
c–hyperextension of the spine

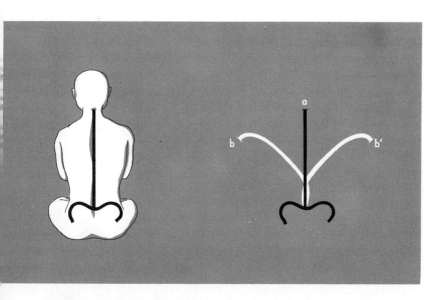

FIGURE 8: Movement of the spine in a lateral direction
a–upright position of the spine; b, b'–complete abduction of the
spine to right and left

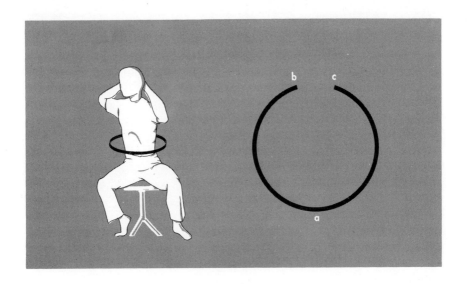

FIGURE 9: Movement of the spine in rotation around the longitudinal axis
a–direction of the face at normal position; b–direction of the face at complete rotation to right; c–direction of the face at complete rotation to left

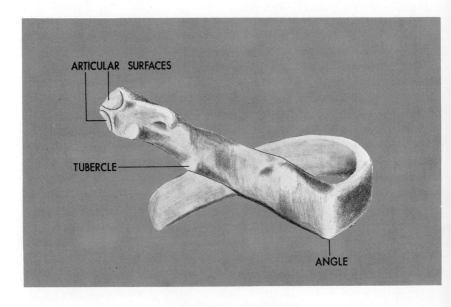

FIGURE 10: Seventh rib

the typical chest elevation in deep breathing or even in the assumption of a very straight and erect body position.

The main ligament at the articulation of the head of the rib is the radiate on the anterior aspect. At the articulation with the transverse process the main protection comes from the anterior and posterior costo-transverse ligaments.

SHOULDER GIRDLE

The junction of the clavicle and the sternum is the only articulation between the trunk and the shoulder girdle, and in fact between the trunk and the whole upper extremity. The posterior portion of the shoulder girdle is free and has only muscular attachments to the spine and thorax. The upper extremity articulates with the scapula and not with the trunk directly.

The movement of the clavicle around its sternal attachment is in many respects similar to that found in a ball-and-socket joint, though much more limited in extent. That movement is best understood in terms of movement of the acromial end of the clavicle. From the normal position, this acromial end may be elevated almost three inches in the typical shoulder shrugging motion. Depression from the normal is possible but only through some 5° to 10°. The acromial extremities may also be moved in anterior and posterior directions. The latter decreases the width from shoulder tip to shoulder tip. The former first increases that width slightly and then decreases it. This forward movement is the chief characteristic of the postural defect "round shoulders." With movement taking place in both the vertical and horizontal planes it is obvious that circumduction may take place. This circling of acromial point accompanies many arm movements.

The scapula and clavicle, being bound together by both ligaments and muscles, must move together. With movements of the clavicle forward and backward, the scapula moves back and forth across the posterior aspect of the thorax. It is referred to as abduction or adduction depending upon its direction away from or toward the line of the spine. Straight elevation of the scapula may occasionally take place through a short range. However, when the acromial end of the clavicle is elevated there is usually a rotation of the scapula. This rotation is referred to as upward or downward, depending upon which way the glenoid cavity is turned. This takes place as a slight sliding movement between clavicle and scapula and as movement in the clavicular joint. It is obvious that the muscles moving either scapula or clavicle will reinforce the action of the others as each bone has comparatively little motion independent of the other.

The reinforcements at the sternoclavicular joint include the anterior

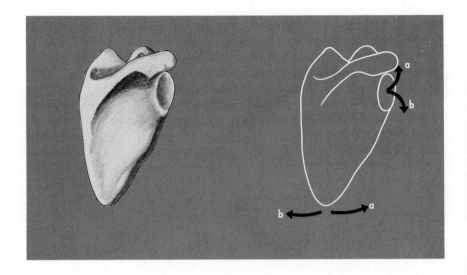

FIGURE 11: Rotation of the scapula
a–upward rotation; b–downward rotation

and posterior sternoclavicular ligaments and the costoclavicular connecting clavicle and rib. The two bones of the girdle are bound together by
the superior and inferior acromioclavicular ligaments, and this junction is
further strengthened by the trapezoid and conoid ligaments, which connect the coracoid process and the clavicle.

SHOULDER

The two articulating bones of the shoulder joint are the scapula and
humerus. The articulating surface of the head of the humerus is about
one half of a nearly perfect sphere with a corresponding shallow pocket
on the scapula. The capsule and ligaments surrounding the joint are
rather loose, so loose in fact, that to one muscle, the supraspinatus, is
assigned as a definite function the task of pulling the superior portion of
the capsule out of the joint in all arm elevations. This looseness of the
capsular structure facilitates wide excursions of the arm. Movement is
limited in front only by contact of the arm with the thorax. Posteriorly
it is checked largely by muscular tension. In other words the circle of
circumduction swings in across the front of the body and is flattened out
somewhat to the rear. Rotation on the longitudinal axis is approximately
180°.

While the capsule is loose, it is strengthened anteriorly by the gleno-
humeral bands and above by the coracohumeral ligament.

ELBOW

The elbow joint is a complex unit permitting two independent actions. The contact of humerus and ulna is most important in the mechanism of flexion and extension. Flexion is limited by contact of muscle masses on the front of the arm and in some cases perhaps by locking of the coronoid process on the front of the humerus. Extension is checked by locking of the olecranon process in the fossa on the back of the humerus, and usually takes place when the humerus and forearm are in direct alignment. The head of the radius also rides over a small circular surface on the lateral condyle of the humerus, but affords neither the check to motion nor the stability to the joint which is furnished by the ulna.

The rotation of the radius takes place around an axis running approximately through the center of its head. Thus the upper end of the radius merely turns in place. The distal end, however, rotates around its point of attachment to the ulna, describing about a 180° arc around that bone. The palm turns with the rotation of the radius, resulting in various positions from complete pronation to complete supination. Thus this movement of the hand really centers at the elbow.

The ligaments of the elbow are the anterior and posterior and the ulnar and radial collaterals. The radius and ulna are connected almost the full length by the interosseous membrane, while the head of the radius is held in place by an annular ligament and the distal end is connected by the anterior and posterior radio-ulnar ligaments.

WRIST

The shallow concavity presented by the lower end of the radius and ulna is filled in by the first row of four carpal bones, although the pisiform does not function in the articulation with the two bones of the forearm. The eight carpals, arranged neatly together into a quadrilateral mass, fit at the top between the styloid processes of the ulna and radius and flare slightly at the distal end to make attachment with the five metacarpals. They are arranged to form a shallow concavity on the ventral surface, thus furnishing a groove to carry the tendons, nerves, and blood vessels to the hand and fingers and somewhat facilitating flexion of the wrist. The flexion-extension movement of the wrist is a summation of gliding between the distal surface of radius and ulna with the first row of carpals, between the first and second rows of carpals, and between second row and the metacarpals. The first of these, however, is most pronounced in its range, and also provides most of the leeway for abduction.

The attachment of the first metacarpal to the trapezium is unique. The reciprocal or saddle arrangement between the two bones permits a movement of the thumb in any plane. This flexibility, combined with flexion of the thumb itself, permits a touching of the distal segment of the thumb to each of the other four fingers and to approximately one half of the

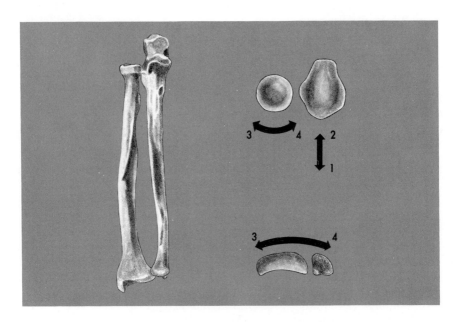

FIGURE 12: Bones of the forearm
1—flexion of elbow; 2—extension of elbow;
3—supination of forearm; 4—pronation of forearm

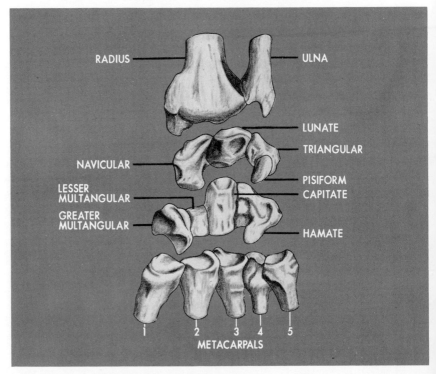

FIGURE 13: Anterior view of the right wrist

a—flexion of hip and spine

FIGURE 14: Hip movement accompanied by spinal movement

b—attempted hip extension
producing lumbar
hyperextension

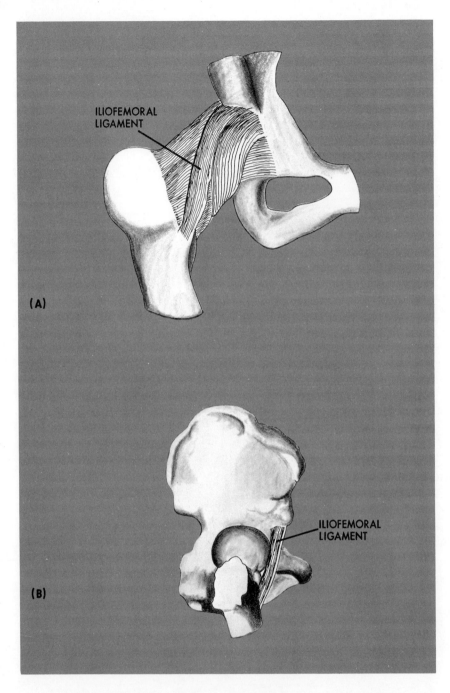

FIGURE 15: Ligamentous limitation on hip movement

palmar surface. This contributes greatly to the skillful use of the hands and is a distinguishing feature between man and most animals, including the ape and monkey, which are nearest to him in structural points.

The wrist is crossed on all four aspects by a series of ligaments: anterior and posterior radiocarpal and the radial and ulnar collaterals. The anterior and posterior and interosseous continue between carpals and between carpals and metacarpals.

HAND

The slight movement between metacarpals allows for cupping or flattening the palm. This cupping of the palm is accentuated by the apposition of the thumb and flexion of the fingers and is used in much of the manipulation performed by the hands.

The condyloid structure of the metacarpals and phalanges gives relative freedom. Flexion and extension are limited by tension of the tendons of antagonistic muscles, and medial-lateral movement is limited by contact of the fingers and by fascia and skin between the fingers.

The two phalangeal articulations are of the simple hinge type designed to function over a range of approximately 90°.

HIP

The acetabular cavity is formed in part by each of the three bones comprising the pelvic girdle. It is made deeper by a cartilaginous cup. Into this cavity the head of the femur is fitted. The head of the femur is nearly two thirds of a complete sphere and extends almost uniformly in all directions beyond the point of largest circumference. The bony structure of the joint would permit almost as much freedom as is found in the shoulder but the capsule, the ligaments, and the muscles make this impossible.

Flexion is usually possible until thigh and abdomen are in contact. The ease with which the final range of that movement takes place depends upon the position of the trunk and the knee and the amount of muscle tension.

The amount of hyperextension is so small as to be practically insignificant. The Y-ligament, or iliofemoral band, cuts directly across the top and front of the joint in such a way that the pelvis and femur lock when in alignment. This ligament is nonelastic, as all ligaments are. When tension is placed on it with the leg either moving or supporting the body weight the result is a tilting of the pelvis forward, with an increase in extension of the lumbar spine. This gives an outward and superficial appearance of hyperextension of the hip. It is also often accompanied by knee flexion which helps to add to that illusion. This limitation of movement is of considerable significance, as will appear in the discussion of the stability of the lower extremity.

Abduction is considerably freer than hyperextension, probably approaching 45° in most cases, but its apparently wider range is explained in the same way as the false hyperextension. The joint reaches the limit of its articular surface on the head of the femur, and the adductor muscles reach a point of considerable tension as abduction nears 45°. In order to get the same effect as a wider excursion of the femur would give, a lateral bending takes place in the lumbar region of the spine.

Pure adduction is possible, of course, only to contact with the opposite thigh, but if the opposite thigh is flexed, or if the leg in motion is slightly flexed, the range increases somewhat until the abductor muscles become taut.

With movement taking place in these two planes at right angles to each other, circumduction is possible. The circle described by the foot

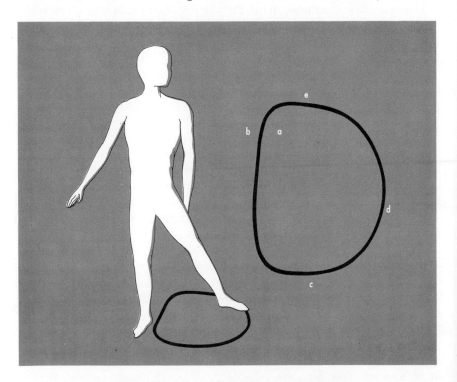

FIGURE 16: Path of circumduction of the left leg
a—normal position of the leg; b—medial position; c—anterior position;
d—lateral position; e—hyperextension

will always be flattened in the rear. As it approaches its widest limits, this flattening becomes more pronounced. It is also flattened on the medial side because of the other leg. In general, this path resembles that in Figure 16. The head and neck of the femur are attached to the shaft of the bone at an angle of about 120°, and the long axis of the bone stands at an angle varying from 20° to 30° with the vertical and with the line of the lower leg. This also will be discussed later in its effect upon the functioning of the leg in support and in locomotion.

Rotation in the hip is limited to about 45° in each direction by tension of the ligaments and muscles.

The capsule includes three ligaments, the iliofemoral anteriorly, the pubocapsular inferiorly, the ischiocapsular posteriorly. Internally the ligamentum teres connects the head of the femur to the acetabular margin much as a string connects beads, and the transverse ligament reinforces the lower, anterior part of the cavity where the glenoid cartilage is incomplete. In the zona orbicularis an unusual type of annular ligament is found that makes a sling encircling the neck of the femur and suspending it from the posterior margin of the acetabulum.

KNEE

While the knee has only two bones involved in the joint proper and the action is fairly simple, it is one of the more complex articulations structurally. The articular surfaces on the condyles of the femur project posteriorly to permit free flexion of the joint. Similarly they end very abruptly in front as one means of checking motion in the opposite direction.

The upper end of the tibia is almost flat, but the two menisci which rest upon it furnish the concavities within which the condyles work. Part of the complexity of the knee is due to the fact that these crescent-shaped cartilages are fastened rather insecurely at their extremities to the tibia and in the flared part to the tibia and capsule of the joint. Within the joint are the two cruciate ligaments, located in the groove between the two articular condyles of the femur, and these ligaments along with the eminence on the center of the superior surface of the tibia divide the tibia into two distinct portions matching the condyles of the femur. The joint is further controlled by the fibular collateral ligament on the lateral side and the tibial collateral on the medial side. The collaterals are external to the capsule of the joint. Posteriorly, the oblique popliteal ligament gives some support. The menisci are attached very lightly to the margins of the tibial condyles by a few scattered bands of ligamentous type fibers.

The tendon of the quadriceps extensor muscle passes anteriorly to the joint and makes up the anterior part of the capsule. At the extreme range of flexion, the tension of these muscles often serves as a check before

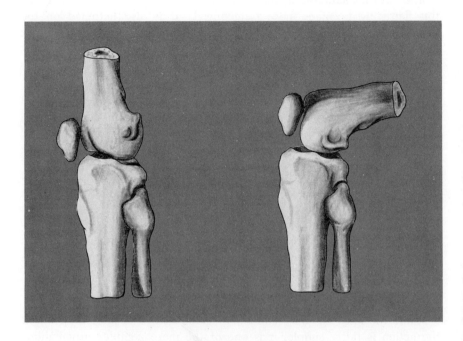

FIGURE 17: Articulating condyles of the knee joint
a–standing position; b–flexed position

the periphery of the articular surface is reached. The patella is located
in the tendon of the quadriceps muscles. This is a sesamoid bone which
has developed there to give mechanical advantage to the muscle. This
is the largest of the sesamoid bones, but the function of mechanical aid is
similar wherever they are found. The quadriceps tendon has a large
bursa interposed above the patellar level over the femur and another
below the patellar level over the proximal end of the tibia. These too are
important mechanically. The patella, as a movable wedge, plays a part
in the functioning of the joint, although it is outside the joint structure
proper.

Thus, the knee is reinforced on all four sides and within so as to give
strength to the joint which must also have freedom. The position of the
knee in normal standing is approximately vertical alignment of femur
and tibia in an anteroposterior direction. As was pointed out before,
the lower end of the femur is inclined inward and the angle between
femur and fibula, or the lateral aspect of the lower leg, is almost always
a little less than 180°. This difference in axis of femur and tibia is partially
compensated for by the larger condyle on the medial side and partially

by the thicker meniscus on the medial side. This difference does, however, result in a slight thrust at the knee which explains part of these
reinforcements.

When the knee is in normal extension the position of the condyles in
the menisci and the tautness of the ligaments lock it against rotation.
However, when the knee is flexed nearly 90° and beyond, the lower leg
may be rotated through some 20° to 25°.

ANKLE

The articulation between the lower leg and the foot involves three
bones—tibia, fibula, the talus (astragalus). Unlike the bones of the
forearm, the tibia and fibula permit no motion, being bound together at
each extremity by ligaments and for most of the length of the shafts by
a strong interosseous membrane. The medial side of the lower end of the
tibia has a long projection known as the internal malleolus. This is the
inner prominence of the ankle. The fibula also projects down to about
the same length and there is thus formed a square boxlike cap to fit over
the top of the talus. The articular surfaces on the three sides of this box
are rather limited, which means that range of motion in the joint must
also be limited.

The top of the talus fits snugly into this arrangement made by the tibia

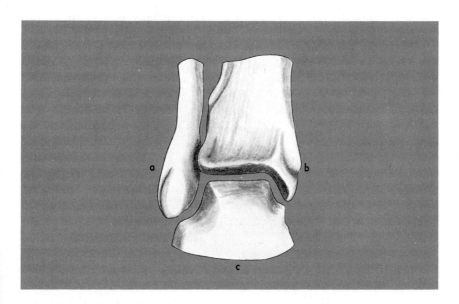

FIGURE 18: Anterior view of the right ankle joint
a—fibula; b—tibia; c—talus

and the fibula. The result is a perfect hinge action, through about 75° to 80° in its total range. Lateral movement and rotation are obviously impossible.

Capsular reinforcements are good. The deltoid ligament is on the medial aspect, the anterior and posterior talofibular ligaments on the lateral side, and the calcaneofibular ligament more posteriorly. The usual designation of movement interprets the ankle action as *flexion* when the foot moves upward toward the front of the tibia, and *extension* when the foot is moved downward more or less in line with the lower leg. These movements are sometimes designated as dorsal and plantar flexion, respectively, to indicate which direction the movement is occuring.

FOOT

The main part of the foot is made up of twelve bones and about half again as many articulations. However, the major articulations group themselves into three functional units (see Fig. 19). Movement in all of these cases is a slight gliding of adjacent surfaces.

The two transverse lines of articulation (*ab* and *cd*) add slightly to the flexion-extension movement which centers in the ankle. They are also the location of much of the elevation and depression of the longitudinal arch of the foot. The posterior one, and to a small extent the anterior one, contribute to the inversion-eversion movement of the foot. A secondary line of articulation lies between these two, but only partly crosses the foot. The navicular (scaphoid) is behind and the three cuneiforms are in front of this line. It functions in the same way as the other two but is more dependent than the others upon the longitudinal line.

The longitudinal line of articulation (*ef*) is a more complex one. The posterior portion is really in more nearly a horizontal plane between the calcaneus and the superimposed talus. Through the central section it turns out laterally and still maintains somewhat of a diagonal plane, so that the inner part of the foot is partially supported on this lateral segment. The anterior section again turns so that it passes almost directly forward between the third and fourth metatarsals. Along this line much of the eversion-inversion movement of the foot takes place.

The foot is thus divided into two longitudinal segments. The medial longitudinal arch is considerably higher than the lateral one. It is also more flexible, and part of its support is derived from the bony beam of the lateral segment rather than solely from muscles and ligaments. It is also supported by the sustentaculum tali, which projects inward under the talus.

In the pronated foot, the medial segment slides downward along this longitudinal axis; and it extends, or the arch elongates, at each of its three transverse lines of motion.

The support of the foot depends to a considerable extent upon the

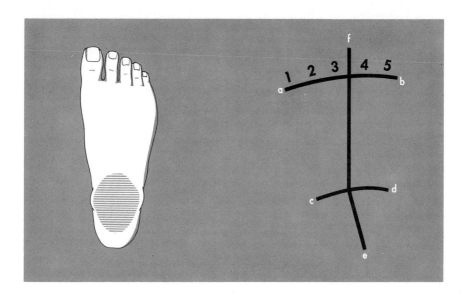

FIGURE 19: The functional lines of articulation of the right foot
ab–tarsal-metatarsal articulations; 1-5–metatarsals; cd–calcaneocuboid,
talonavicular articulations; ef–longitudinal line of articulation

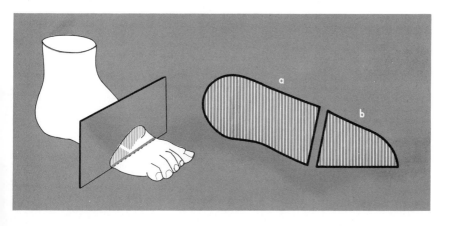

**FIGURE 20: Cross section of the two longitudinal segments of
the right foot**
a–three inner metatarsals; b–two outer metatarsals

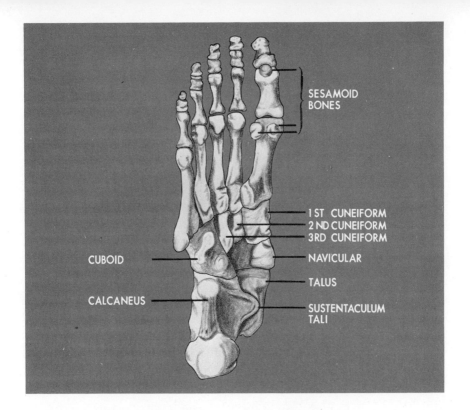

FIGURE 21: Plantar surface of the right foot

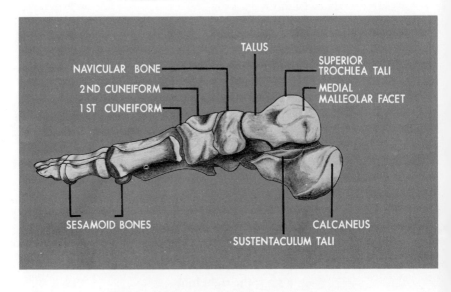

FIGURE 22: Medial view of the right foot

ligaments of the plantar surface. The plantar fascia is very heavy, the long plantar ligament spans the foot from calcaneus to metatarsals; the short plantar ligament goes from calcaneus to cuboid and the calcaneo-navicular extends from the sustentaculum tali of the calcaneus to the navicular.

The articulations of the toes are almost identical with those of the fingers. Hyperextension at the metatarsal-phalangeal joint is usually a little greater than hyperextension at the corresponding joint in the hand. Otherwise the apparent limitations on toe movements are due to lack of use of the toes. Inability to localize and move each toe independently is due to this same lack of practice rather than to limitations of structure.

OTHER ARTICULATIONS OF THE BODY

In both of the other classes of joints, the amphiarthrodial and synarthrodial, movement is entirely lacking or of such a nature that it is unimportant in a study of motor activities. The sacroiliac and symphysis pubis, described in Table I as "elastic," are essentially nonmoving. Usually the joint would give or suffer strain before the bones would fracture. The sutures of the cranium, the union of the pelvic bones, and other fixed articulations are not included in this table.

REFERENCES

1. Billig, Harvey E., and Loewendahl, Evelyn, *Mobilization of the Human Body*, Stanford, Calif., Stanford University Press, 1949, p. 1–13.
2. Clarke, H. Harrison, Body Position and Movement of Joints, *Archives of Physical Medicine*, 31, 1950, p. 81.
3. Gardner, Ernest, Gray, Donald J., and O'Rahilly, Ronan, *Anatomy*, Philadelphia, W. B. Saunders Co., 1960, Ch. 3, Joints.
4. Hupprich, Florence L., and Sigerseth, Peter O., The Specificity of Flexibility in Girls, *Research Quarterly,* 21, March 1950, p. 25.
5. Kendall, Henry O., and Kendall, Florence P., Normal Flexibility According to Age Groups, *Journal of Bone and Joint Surgery*, 30, 1948, p. 690.
6. McCue, Betty F., Flexibility of College Women, *Research Quarterly*, 24, October 1953, p. 316.
7. Mainland, Donald, *Anatomy*, New York, Harper & Row, Pubs., 1945, Ch. 4, Joints.
8. Rasch, Philip J., and Burke, Roger, *Kinesiology and Applied Anatomy*, Philadelphia, Lea & Febiger, 1959, Ch. 2, Framework and Joints of the Body.
9. Steindler, Arthur, *Kinesiology of the Human Body*, Springfield, Ill., Charles C Thomas, 1955, Ch. 4, Physical Properties of Cartilage, Muscles, and Fascia; Ch. 5, Mechanics of Joint and Muscle Action; Ch. 9, Mechanics of the Spinal Column; Ch. 10, Dynamics of the Normal Spine; Ch. 16, Mechanics of the Hip Joint; Ch. 19, Mechanics of the Knee Joint; Ch. 22, Mechanics of the Foot and Ankle; Ch. 26, Mechanics of the Shoulder-arm Complex; Ch. 28, Mechanics of the Elbow Joint.

TABLE I: Motion in the Articulations of the Body

Articulation	Type [a]	Planes or [b] Axes of Motion		Type of Motion	Degrees of Motion
Hip (femoral-acetabular)	enarthrodial	3	(1)	flexion extension [c]	90°–135° very slight, 5°–10°
			(2)	abduction adduction	45°–50° contact with other leg
			(1 & 2)	circumduction	complete
			(3)	rotation [d]	80°–200°
Knee (tibio-femoral)	ginglymus	2	(1)	flexion extension	90°–130° 0
			(2)	rotation	25°–75°
Knee (patellar)	arthrodial	1		gliding up and down	5°
Tibiofibular	syndesmosis [e]	0			
Tibiofibular-talar	ginglymus	1		flexion extension	30°–35° 40°–45°
Intertarsal	arthrodial	3		gliding	very limited in all joints
Metatarsal-phalangeal	condyloid	2	(1)	flexion extension	25°–35° 80°–90°
			(2)	abduction adduction	15°–20° contact with other toes
Toes (inter-phalangeal)	ginglymus	1		flexion extension	90° 0
Sternoclavicular	arthrodial	3	(1)	elevation depression	45°–50° 5°
			(2)	forward backward	10° 10°
			(3)	rotation	20°–25°
Acromioclavicular	arthrodial	3	(1)	abduction of scapula adduction of scapula	5° 5°
			(2)	rotation of scapula	60°–70°
			(3)	elevation of scapula	5°–10°

TABLE I: (cont'd): **Motion in the Articulations of the Body**

Articulation	Type [a]	Planes or [b] Axes of Motion		Types of Motion	Degrees of Motion
Shoulder (humero-scapular)	enarthrodial	3	(1)	flexion extension	180° 50°–60°
			(2)	abduction adduction	150°–180° contact with trunk
			(1 & 2)	circumduction	complete, flattened in the back
			(3)	rotation	180°–190°
Elbow (humero-ulnar)	ginglymus	1		flexion extension	130°–160° 0°–5°
Superior radio-ulnar	trochoid	1		rotation (gliding)	190°–210°
Wrist (radio-ulnar-carpal)	condyloid	2	(1)	flexion extension	90°–95° 60°–70°
			(2)	abduction adduction	20°–25° 55°–65°
Metacarpal-phalangeal	condyloid	2	(1)	flexion extension	90° 20°–30°
			(2)	abduction adduction	15°–20° 5°–10°
Thumb (metacarpal-carpal)	reciprocal reception	2	(1)	flexion extension	80°–90° 20°–25°
			(2)	abduction adduction	40°–50° 0°–10°
			(1 & 2)	circumduction	complete
Fingers (inter-phalangeal)	ginglymus	1		flexion extension	90° 0°–10°
Sacroiliac	syndesmosis	0			"elastic" [f]
Symphysis pubis	symphysis [g]	0			"elastic" [f]
Intervertebral (cervical)	arthrodial	3	(1)	flexion extension	freely movable [h] freely movable
(atlas and axis)	trochoid		(2)	abduction adduction	freely movable freely movable
			(3)	rotation	freely movable

TABLE I: (cont'd): Motion in the Articulations of the Body

Articulation	Type [a]	Planes or [b] Axes of Motion		Type of Motion	Degrees of Motion
Intervertebral (thoracic)	arthrodial	3	(1)	{ flexion	some, limited by ribs
				extension	very little, limited by spinous processes
			(2)	abduction	little, limited by ribs
			(3)	rotation	little, limited by ribs
Intervertebral (lumbar)	arthrodial	2	(1)	{ flexion	freely movable
				extension	freely movable
			(2)	abduction	freely movable
Intervertebral (bodies in all regions)	symphysis				very little
Costovertebral	arthrodial	1		rotation	10°–15°
Sternocostal	synarthrodial	0			

a. See classification in Chapter 3

b. Planes of motion indicate primary directions of movement. For example, flexion-extension is in one plane. In a plane at right angles to it is abduction-adduction. Rotation takes place around an axis but it is considered as a direction of movement. The number in the left hand side of the column is the total number of planes; the number in the right hand side indicates the plane of motion described in the following column.

c. Extension is used in this table in the sense of hyperextension.

d. Range of rotation is considered from one extreme to the other rather than in each direction from a starting position.

e. A type of slightly movable joint with a membrane between the two bones.

f. Subject to strain and injury but not movable.

g. A type of slightly movable joint with a cartilage between the two bones.

h. Since all movement of the spine is a summation of movement in adjacent articulations, no attempt will be made here to state the movement in quantitative terms. The descriptive terms give a basis for comparing movement in regions of the spine.

4

The Muscles of the Body

THE SOURCE OF MOTION

1. The human body is a self-propelling machine, the power for which comes from muscular contraction.
2. The location of the muscle with respect to the joint determines its effect on the joint.
3. The muscles are arranged in antagonistic pairs or groups.
4. The functions of the muscles may be considered as primary and secondary, or as dominant and indirect.
5. The larger muscles are located where the greatest force is needed.
6. Muscles can only pull, they can not push.

ALL MOVEMENTS of the segments of the body are the result of muscle contraction, of muscle tension, or of the application of some external force, gravity being the most common one. It is in the first, active muscular contraction, that energy is expended to create movement. In the case of muscle tension and of force outside the muscle-producing action, the movement is more or less a passive one, and the energy cost is very different.

Active contraction is often given the credit for all movements. There is no doubt that the majority of movements can be attributed to it. The fingers close over the doorknob or a ball because the flexors of the fingers are acting. One opens the door by flexion of the elbow and pushes it closed again by the extensors. Likewise, it is the muscles of the neck which turn the head to look at something over the shoulder, muscles of the back which contract to lift the trunk after bending forward to tie one's shoes, and flexors of the leg which lift the leg to make it easier to reach the shoes to be tied. In short, muscle contraction is the source of all movements in which the arms, leg, and body are raised or held in position against the pull of gravity.

Muscle tension around a joint varies according to several factors, including the position of the joint, the tonus of the muscle, the normal

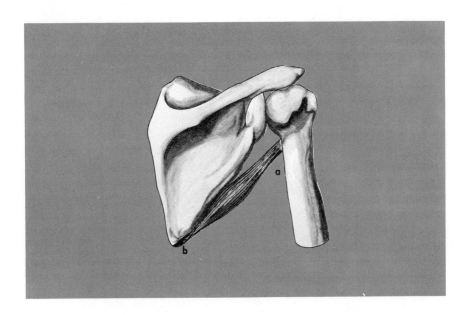

FIGURE 23: A muscle pulls on its two attachments
a—insertion; b—origin

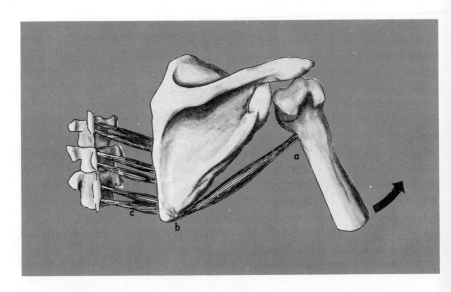

FIGURE 24: A muscle may be stretched by action of other muscles
a—insertion; b—origin; c—rhomboids which can stretch the teres

resting length of the muscle, and the weight or momentum of a body segment or external object controlled by it. Thus when action of a muscle occurs at one joint, action may also occur in another joint much as the arms and legs of a "jumping jack" move by pull of the strings with which the various parts are strung together. For example, when the trunk is bent forward, the knees also tend to flex because of the tension in the hamstring muscles. When the wrist is hyperextended the fingers usually flex because the flexors are being stretched, and conversely when the wrist is flexed, the fingers tend to extend because of the stretch applied to the extensors. When a muscle contracts, the antagonist is always stretched more or less. The amount of stretch possible increases with the range in the joint and decreases with the cross section of the muscle and the amount of tonus or contraction in these antagonists.

The tonus of the muscle and the normal resting length are closely associated. In the healthy person who uses the muscles even moderately, tonus is maintained in the muscle. The length of the muscle is near that required for the customary position of the segment. For example, if the person wears high heels constantly, the muscles of the ankle adjust them-selves to this extended position of the foot; but the state of tonus may be the same as in another person accustomed to low heels. The difference is the development of a different resting length of the gastrocnemius and soleus, and with a shortening of the latter this process of change produces tension or stretching of the anterior ankle muscles. Obviously, increased or lowered tonus of a given muscle group affects the normal position of the joint and the tension on the antagonistic muscles.

The effect of the weight of the body part or the momentum of its movement may be simply illustrated by forward bending of the trunk and the resulting tension in the back extensors. Likewise, a weight carried in the hand and then swung forward with a full swing of the arm produces stretching of the posterior muscles.

Whenever there is nervous stimulation, it causes contraction or causes the muscle to resist relaxation. This results in muscular tension, which tends to increase the resistance offered antagonistic muscles, and to slow up or actually check movement.

Gravity is a constant force pulling vertically downward on all objects at all times. Whenever the body or one of its parts is moved upward, the force must be sufficient to overcome the downward pull of gravity. On the other hand, whenever gravity can produce the desired movement, we soon learn in the interest of muscular economy to let the muscles relax and allow gravity to do the work.

Every muscle has its two ends attached to different bones. In most cases these are adjacent bones; that is, the muscle extends across a single joint. Such muscles are called *uniarticular* muscles. In a few cases the muscle has a two-joint span and is designated as a *biarticular* muscle.

The tension produced on the latter is even more pronounced than that on the uniarticular ones. The most common illustration of this is the difficulty which most individuals experience in flexing the hip to 90° and maintaining the knee in its normal or extended position. A very few muscles are *multiarticular,* i.e., they cross several joints. This is true of the longissimus dorsi and iliocostalis portions of the erector spinae and the tibialis posticus in the foot.

A further consideration of the location of muscles is necessary for an understanding of their action. Usually, the muscle lies very close to the joint. This produces the smoothness and compactness of contour, particularly around the joint, which is considered as one of the marks of beauty in the human form. This fact is of extreme significance in considering the efficiency and effectiveness of effort expended in moving the respective parts and will be discussed in detail in Chapter 10.

It must be remembered that a muscle can only pull; *it never pushes.* And that pull must be in the direction in which the muscle lies. Therefore, to know the effect of a muscle upon a joint, one must know exactly across which aspect of the joint it passes: anterior or posterior, superior or inferior, medial or lateral. This is the first and most important clue to the action of the muscle. In a joint permitting rotation on a longitudinal axis it is similarly necessary to locate the point of attachment and direction of pull with respect to the axis of rotation. These situations are both exactly the same, however. The ordinary flexion-extension or abduction-adduction types of movement are also rotatory ones, i.e., the joint represents the hub of the wheel, the part moved is the spoke, which makes only a partial revolution. Visualize the muscle as a sheet, or cord, depending upon the shape of the particular muscle. Then locate it properly with reference to the joint. Its action is thus greatly simplified.

In the latter part of this chapter the muscles have been grouped as nearly as possible according to their location with respect to the articulation concerned. This puts them into functional units, though in some instances it may necessitate the separation of some muscles which are frequently discussed together, but usually only because they have a common name. Examples of this are the teres major and teres minor, and the pectoralis major and pectoralis minor. In each of these pairs, the two muscles have distinctly different lines of pull and hence different actions.

Only as each individual muscle is fitted into its place with those adjacent to it and co-operating with it is a true concept possible of how that muscle functions.

It is also important to remember that functionally the origin and insertion may be reversed. For example, the abdominal muscles may act in one case with the pelvis fixed and effect a movement of the thorax. In another instance the thorax may be the fixed point of attachment, the result of abdominal contraction being a fixation of or an elevation of the anterior portion of the pelvis.

MUSCLES OF THE TRUNK

It is obvious that the muscles on the anterior aspect of the trunk must be the flexors of the spine. Since the abdominal muscles are arranged in pairs, symmetrically on each side of a medial plane, they will flex the trunk in that plane if the pair works together with uniform force. It is also obvious that since these muscles are working on a somewhat flattened cylindrical trunk and are located laterally from the plane passing from sternum to spine, a single muscle working without its partner will produce a combination of lateral bending and of rotation. The exact location of the muscle determines which will be the more dominant. For example, the external oblique gives more rotation; the iliocostalis part of the erector spinae, flexion backward and sideward.

The line of pull of the external oblique muscles together forms a letter "V." That of the internal obliques forms an inverted "V" (Fig. 25). Either pair produces the same result, flexion of the spine, and adds to the effectiveness of the other, or of the rectus abdominus. However, in twisting of the trunk unsymmetrical action is necessary. Those muscles which have parallel lines of pull are synergistic, i.e., *ab* and *ef* or *de* and *bc*. The other half of each pair is antagonistic to the contraction in progress.

All of the abdominal muscles are made up of a thin flat sheet of relatively long muscle fibers. The rectus abdominus has the greatest thickness but is much narrower than the others. The wide origin and insertion of the obliques and the transversalis make possible the parallel arrangement of the fibers throughout the sheet.

The action of the posterior muscles of the trunk is as apparent as that of the anterior ones. The left and right units again balance each other to give symmetrical results and pure extension. Or with independent action they produce lateral bending and rotation. Also, working with the anterior muscles, they serve as antagonists to each other in flexion and extension and thus make possible straight lateral bending or rotation. Figure 27 shows how the right erector spinae completes the belt around the trunk to the right.

The erector spinae is made up of many different sections, often named as separate muscles. The iliocostalis covers the lumbar and thoracic regions by connecting the ilium and ribs. It continues up as the accessorius and cervicalis. The longissimus lies medial to the iliocostalis and covers a similar range, connecting the sacrum and lower lumbar vertebrae to the transverse processes of the thoracic vertebrae. A continuation of this longissimus arrangement up the spine is designated as the trans-

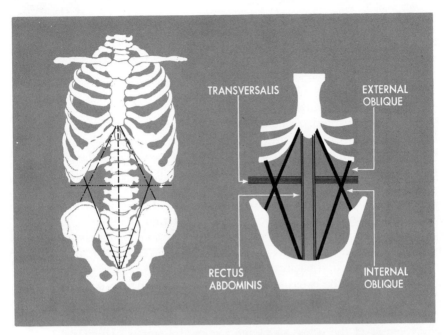

FIGURE 25: Diagram of line of pull of abdominal muscles

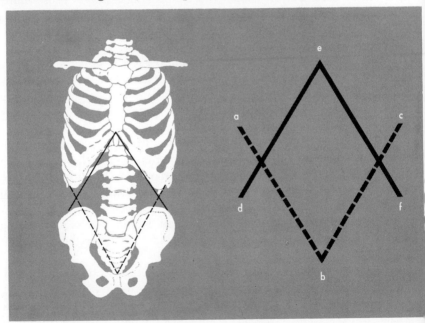

FIGURE 26: Diagram of synergistic and antagonistic action of
abdominal muscles
ab, bc–external obliques; **de, ef**–internal obliques

versalis cervicis and trachelomastoid. The most medial portion, the spinalis dorsi, is made up of shorter parts but extends from the sacrum up through the thoracic region. The multifidus is a deeper muscle also covering the length of the lumbar and thoracic spine. Within these sections are subdivisions made up of many rather short fibers.

The oblique rotators are found only in the thoracic region and connect the vertebrae and ribs. The quadratus lumborum is a flatter sheet more like the abdominals and connects the ilium and twelfth rib. Any of the muscles of the back when working in pairs produce extension of the spine. When working without their partner on the opposite side they produce lateral bending or rotation depending upon their distance from the medial line of the trunk.

The splenius and the sternocleidomastoid are similar in alignment to the muscles of the lower regions of the spine. The scaleni connect the cervical vertebrae and the first and second ribs. They are chiefly muscles of inspiration but can assist in lateral bending or flexion of the neck.

MUSCLES OF THE SHOULDER GIRDLE

The anterior muscles of the shoulder girdle have three areas of attachment so arranged as to make for very effective movement of the girdle. The subclavius attaches to the clavicle and acts at short range to guide the forward and downward movement of the clavicle as it swings around its sternal articulation. The pectoralis minor with its insertion on the coracoid process of the scapula pulls forward and downward on that bone. The serratus anterior attaching to the vetebral border of the scapula pulls the posterior portion of the girdle forward around the thorax or tilts it upward. The unified action spread over the full length of the girdle gives perfect control.

The posterior muscles of the girdle attach almost entirely to the scapula. The line of pull of the levator scapulae is so nearly in line with the center of the bone that the effect is practically a straight movement of the bone in an upward and medial direction. Of course, this may be affected by the tension of other muscles. It is most apt to be influenced by the weight of the arm and the tension of the shoulder muscles, so that there will be a slight downward rotation. However, the levator is practically always assisted by the trapezius, which counteracts this effect and may even be sufficient to cause upward rotation.

The trapezius may be divided functionally into as many divisions as there are varying directions of its fibers. It is ordinarily considered in four parts, however. The first is that attaching to the clavicle and is relatively weak. Its effect is slight elevation of the acromial end of the clavicle, or it may assist in abduction or rotation of the head. The second portion has a medial and upward direction. The effect on the scapula is very similar to that of the first portion but is considerably stronger. The

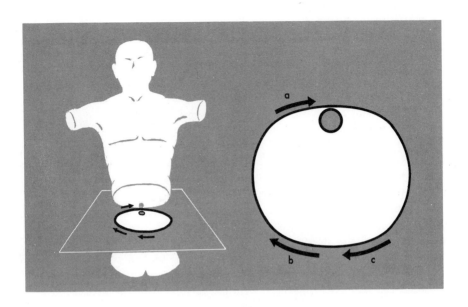

FIGURE 27: Diagram of a cross section of the trunk
with the muscles used in trunk rotation to the right
a–right erector spinae; b–right internal oblique; c–left external oblique

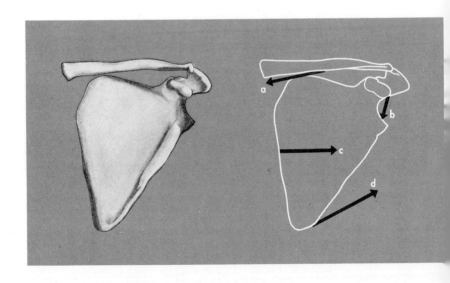

FIGURE 28: Anterior muscles of the shoulder girdle
a–subclavius; b–pectoralis minor; c–upper part of serratus anterior;
d–lower part of serratus anterior

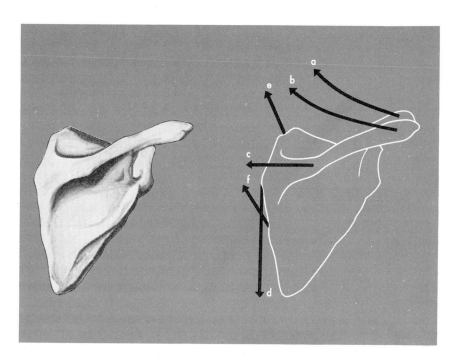

FIGURE 29: Posterior muscles of the shoulder girdle
a, b, c, d–first, second, third and fourth parts of the trapezius;
e–levator scapulae; f–rhomboids

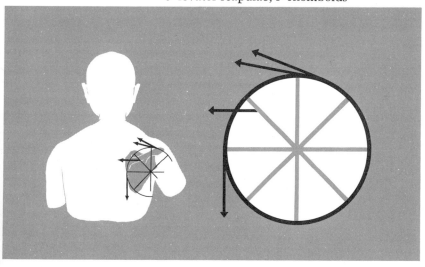

FIGURE 30: Diagram of a wheel being turned by four forces
comparable to the four parts of the trapezius

third portion is approximately horizontal in its pull and the result is almost entirely adduction of the scapula with a slight tendency toward upward rotation because it attaches a little above the center of the bone. The fourth portion pulls downward and slightly inward on the vertebral border, and therefore also produces an upward rotation. Figure 30 illustrates the analogy between this situation and one in which four forces are applied to a wheel in such a manner that the wheel revolves. Each of the four forces would add to the effectiveness of the other three. Any of the four portions may work independently or in combination with any other portion, and the result is upward rotation or adduction or a combination of the two movements.

The rhomboid major and rhomboid minor are functionally one unit, i.e., they are uniform throughout in size and direction of fibers. Since that direction is medial and upward and the attachment is on the vertebral border, the result is adduction and downward rotation.

Movement of the shoulder girdle acccompanies all movements of the shoulder joint except those of very limited range around the anatomical position. This facilitates arm movements by turning the glenoid cavity in the proper direction and gives greater range of motion.

MUSCLES OF THE SHOULDER JOINT

The muscles moving the humerus are divided into four groups according to their location with respect to the axis of the joint. These four groups are as follows:

Anterior	*Posterior*
pectoralis major	teres minor
coracobrachialis	infraspinatus
biceps	triceps
anterior deltoid	posterior deltoid

Lateral-superior	*Medial-inferior*
supraspinatus	teres major
middle deltoid	latissimus dorsi
	subscapularis

The deltoid covers three aspects of the articulation and, therefore, is divided here into three parts. The pectoralis major divides into two divisions, the upper and the lower. The fibers of the upper part lie approximately at right angles to those of the lower. The anterior deltoid and the upper pectoralis are very nearly parallel in direction and hence are synergists in arm flexion and adduction. The lower part of the pectoralis major assists in adduction of the arm and in arm depression. In the latter action it may be an assistant of the latissimus dorsi and teres major in certain instances.

The biceps assists with shoulder flexion, particularly if the elbow is fixed in an extended position. The coracobrachialis runs nearly parallel with the humerus but assists in flexion and adduction, thus co-operating with the other muscles of this group.

The middle deltoid passes directly over the superior aspect of the joint and gives only abduction of the arm. It doubtless assists in arm elevation in all planes, with the possible exception of very easy and limited movements in an anterior and posterior direction. The supraspinatus is immediately beneath the middle deltoid and assists it in every movement. It is equally important in taking up the slack in the upper part of the capsule of the joint. Otherwise, the capsule might interfere in arm elevation.

The posterior deltoid is similar in direction to the anterior one but is directly antagonistic to it because they are on opposite sides of the joint. For this reason if all three parts function together for strong movement the effects in an anterior or posterior direction are neutralized and the result is simple abduction.

The teres minor and infraspinatus are almost parallel to each other and lie almost in a horizontal plane. They are effective in arm extension only when the arm is abducted through at least 30° to 35°.

The long head of the triceps, which originates on the scapula, assists in extension of the arm and is most effective when the elbow is flexed.

The teres major and latissimus dorsi are also nearly parallel in direction, though the latissimus is the longer muscle. Their action may be either adduction or extension or both, depending upon the starting position of the arm. The subscapularis, which belongs to this group by location, may assist slightly in arm adduction or scapular abduction, but will be seen to be more important in arm rotation.

The muscles for rotation of the arm can be illustrated by a cross section of the humerus, with the muscles attaching around the periphery and and the axis of motion being the center of the circle (Fig. 31). While the muscles do not all apply at the same level on the humerus the result is the same. It is observed immediately that the muscles of the anterior and medial group, which attach on the anterior border of the humerus, pull that border medially and hence produce inward rotation. The two muscles of the posterior group, which attach on the lateral border, pull it backward and hence produce outward rotation. The deltoid, coracobrachialis, biceps, and triceps all have such a large vertical component that their rotatory effect is insignificant.

MUSCLES OF THE ELBOW AND FOREARM

The muscles around the elbow joint are located in four groups—anterior, lateral, posterior, and medial. These muscles not only operate the elbow hinge, but also produce most of the rotatory movements of the forearm and to a considerable extent the movements of the wrist.

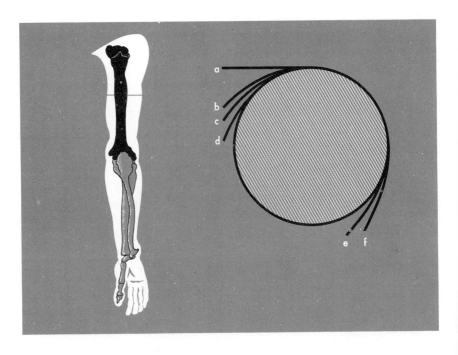

FIGURE 31: Diagram of a cross section of the humerus
with the muscles used in rotation of the arm
a–pectoralis major; b–latissimus dorsi; c–teres major;
d–subscapularis; e–infraspinatus; f–teres minor

Anterior

biceps
brachialis
pronator teres

Lateral

brachioradialis
supinator
extensor carpi radialis longus
extensor carpi radialis brevis
extensor communis digitorum

extensor minimi digiti
extensor carpi ulnaris

Posterior

triceps
anconeus

Medial

flexor carpi radialis
flexor carpi ulnaris
palmaris longus
flexor sublimis digitorum

The anterior and posterior groups produce flexion and extension, respectively. They are unassisted in this function by the medial and

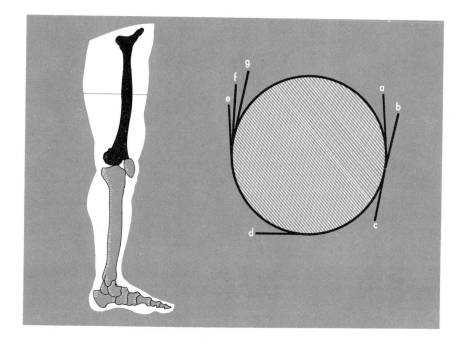

**FIGURE 32: Diagram of a cross section of the femur
with the muscles used in rotation of the leg**
a–tensor fasciae latae; b–gluteus medius; c–gluteus minimus;
d–outward rotators; e–pectineus; f–iliopsoas; g–sartorius

lateral group with the exception of the brachioradialis, which passes far
enough anterior to the axis of the joint to assist in elbow flexion.

The rotation of the radius is commonly referred to as pronation and
supination of the hand. Pronation is effected largely through the pronator
teres and the pronator quadratus. Supination may be produced by the
supinator or in a stronger fashion by the biceps. In pronation the tendon
of the biceps is wound around the radius, and contraction of the muscle
unwinds that tendon, bringing the bicipital tuberosity again facing forward. The brachioradialis is so situated that it may assist in either
pronation or supination if the starting position is at full range of the
opposite movement.

The medial group of the elbow, some of which also have attachments
on the upper forearm, are very similar in direction to the anterior muscles
of the forearm. These two groups work together in flexion of the wrist,
hand, and fingers.

The same may be said of the muscles from the lateral condyle, excepting the brachioradialis and supinator. The remaining five muscles have some attachments on the upper forearm, are similar in direction to the shorter muscles on the posterior aspect of the forearm, and assist them in extension of the wrist and fingers.

Anterior forearm muscles	*Posterior forearm muscles*
flexor profundus digitorum	abductor longus pollicis
flexor longus pollicis	extensor longus pollicis
pronator quadratus	extensor brevis pollicis
	extensor indicis

The anterior muscles produce flexion of the wrist or fingers or both, depending upon the strength of the contraction and antagonistic action. The posterior muscles similarly effect extension of the wrist or the fingers.

MUSCLES OF THE HIP JOINT

The muscles around the hip joint are likewise located in four fairly distinct groups.

Anterior

iliopsoas
rectus femoris
sartorius

Lateral

gluteus medius
gluteus minimus
tensor fasciae latae

Posterior

gluteus maximus
semitendonosus
semimembranosus

biceps femoris
pyriformis
quadratus femoris
obturator internus
obturator externus
gemellus superior
gemellus inferior

Medial

pectineus
adductor magnus
adductor brevis
adductor longus
gracilis

The anterior muscles are primarily flexors of the joint. The iliopsoas is made up of the two parts which are identical in effect on the hip. However, the psoas portion has a slight effect in flexion of the lumbar region of the spine and hence tends to counteract somewhat the tendency of the pelvis to tilt forward in hip flexion. While the main mass of the whole muscle runs downward and forward, it passes across the front of the pelvis with a pulley effect and turns backward to its insertion. This accounts for its forward pull.

The rectus femoris, being a biarticular muscle is influenced in its effect by the position of the other joint. It tends to produce extension of the knee at the same time as it produces hip flexion. However, if the knee is fixed in at least partial flexion the muscle is more effective at the hip, because it is then being stretched and does not approach its limit of contraction so quickly.

The sartorius is also biarticular, but gives flexion of both joints. This double flexion occurs more frequently than the combination of hip flexion and knee extension.

The contraction of these muscles may produce a flexion of the thigh on the trunk or of the trunk on the thigh. In either case there is a tendency for both attachments of the muscles to approach each other. Therefore, in all hip flexion of any significance the abdominals also must be used to support and fix the anterior border of the pelvis.

In the lateral group the gluteus medius and minimus are practically parallel, directly over the axis of the joint and attached at a short distance from it to the greater trochanter. The result is straight abduction.

The tensor fasciae latae lies between the anterior and lateral groups and hence assists in both flexion and abduction.

The gluteus maximus and the hamstring muscles (semitendonosus, semimembranosus, and biceps femoris) are the extensors of the hip. The gluteus maximus is so thick that all fibers do not attach to the femur at the same angle. The fibers are also of such a length that they are under no tension in the ordinary erect standing position. Only when the hip is flexed some 30° to 40° are they stretched sufficiently that they can give any outward effect from their contraction. The hamstring muscles are biarticular, producing hip extension and knee flexion. Most of our natural activities combine simultaneous hip and knee extension. Knee extension is favorable to more effective hip extension by these muscles. The hip extensors may tilt the pelvis backward to the point where the iliofemoral ligament locks the joints. Beyond that point hyperextension must take place in the spine.

The six other muscles on the posterior aspect are outward rotators of the femur. They have a horizontal direction instead of a vertical one.

The medial group consists of the five adductor muscles. The adductors magnus, brevis, and longus coincide almost exactly with the long axis of the femur. The gracilis and pectineus are somewhat toward the anterior aspect and hence help with flexion as well as with adduction.

Rotation of the hip may be illustrated in the same manner as that of the shoulder (compare Figs. 31 and 32). The iliopsoas, pectineus, and sartorius attach on the posterior and medial borders and pull them forward, producing outward rotation. The six outward rotators attach on the posterior border and pull it medially, producing outward rotation. The tensor fasciae latae draws the lateral border forward, hence inward rotation occurs. The gluteus medius, because of its fan-shaped origin and slight spread on top of the trochanter, can produce opposite results. The anterior fibers have a forward component to their force, thus assisting in inward rotation. Likewise, the posterior fibers are on such an angle that they can assist in outward rotation.

MUSCLES OF THE KNEE JOINT

The muscles located at the knee fall into only two groups, the anterior and the posterior.

Anterior	Posterior
vastus internus	semitendonosus
vastus externus	semimembranosus
vastus intermedius	biceps femoris
rectus femoris	sartorius
	gracilis
	gastrocnemius
	popliteus

The four anterior muscles are often considered as a single muscle, the quadriceps extensor. This is because they have a tendon of insertion common to all and function so frequently as one unit. The fibers of the vastus internus and externus insert into the tendon at a slight angle, but they each counteract the effect of the other so that the result is a straight pull or extension of the knee. The rectus femoris assists in this extension only when it occurs at the same time as hip flexion. The total contractile force of this combined group is extremely large.

All of the posterior muscles, with the exception of the popliteus, are biarticular muscles. They all assist in knee flexion, but in every case have their best leverage at the other articulation that they cross.

The gracilis and sartorius both assist, as secondary functions, in flexion of the knee. The gracilis is less effective because it has a straighter line down the length of the thigh. The popliteus is a short and small muscle and is most important in starting the knee into flexion from the fully extended position which is common to so many activities.

Rotation of the lower leg is very limited and possible only when the knee is flexed. It is in rotation that the division of the hamstrings is significant. The biceps, attaching on the lateral side of the fibula, gives outward rotation. The other two, attaching on the inner condyle of the tibia, produce inward rotation.

MUSCLES OF THE ANKLE AND FOOT

Anterior to the ankle	Dorsal surface of the foot
tibialis anticus	extensor brevis digitorum
peroneus tertius	dorsal interossei
extensor longus digitorum	
extensor longus hallucis	

Posterior to the ankle

gastrocnemius
soleus
tibialis posticus
peroneus longus
peroneus brevis
flexor longus digitorum
flexor longus hallucis

Plantar surface of the foot

flexor brevis digitorum
flexor brevis hallucis
flexor brevis minimi digiti
accessorius
adbuctor hallucis
abductor minimi digiti
adductor hallucis
adductor transverse hallucis
lumbricales
plantar interossei

The tibialis anticus and peroneus tertius lift on the inner and outer borders of the foot, respectively. The result is a strong dorsal flexion. The extensors of the toes assist a little in this flexion when a maximum effort is made to extend the toes and to bring the top of the foot to the front of the lower leg.

On the posterior aspect the gastrocnemius and soleus function together through their common tendon of insertion. The tibialis posticus, the peroneus longus, and peroneus brevis assist in this plantar flexion. However, each of these latter muscles is far inferior to the gastrocnemius and soleus in effectiveness of action. The flexors of the toes have a slight tendency toward plantar flexion in their most pronounced flexion of the toes.

The lateral movements, or the inversion and eversion of the foot, are partly due to action of the muscles already discussed and partly to the shorter muscles located in the foot itself. Inversion is due almost entirely to the action of the tibialis anticus, assisted slightly by the tibialis posticus and the flexors, whose effect is an increase in height of arch and cupping of foot rather than actual inversion. Eversion is due chiefly to the peroneus longus and tertius, with a little help from the brevis.

The major responsibilities of the small muscles within the foot are maintenance of the arches, the slap of the foot in walking, and the drive from the toes for propulsion. These all require strong contraction on the plantar surface, and it will be noted that most of the muscles are on that aspect. They are definitely assisted in these functions by the tibialis posticus, peroneus longus, and the long flexors of the toes.

REFERENCES

1. Gellhorn, Ernst, Patterns of Muscular Activity in Man, *Archives of Physical Medicine,* 28, 1947, p. 568.
2. Holmer Robert Martin, *An Electromyographic Study of the Actions of Selected Muscles of the Upper Extremity,* Microcard PH35, 1954.
3. McCloy, C. H., Some Notes on Differential Actions of Partite Muscles, *Research Quarterly,* 17, October 1946, p. 254.

4. Mainland, Donald, *Anatomy*, New York, Harper & Row, Pubs., Ch. 5, Muscles and Fasciae; Ch. 9, Upper Limb; Ch. 10, Lower Limb; Ch. 14, The Back.

5. Merrifield, Homer H., *An Electromyographic Study of the Gluteus Maximus, The Vastus Lateralis and the Tensor Fasciae Latae*, Microcard PH72, 1960.

6. Morton, Dudley J., *The Human Foot*, New York, Columbia University Press, 1935, Ch. 9, Muscles of the Leg; Ch. 10, Intrinsic Muscles of the Foot.

7. Reitman, Richard, *An Electromyographic Study Relative to Movements of the Leg and Thigh*, Microcard PE362, 1957.

8. Sigerseth, Peter O., *Electromyographic Study of Selected Muscles Involved in Movements at Scapulohumeral and Sternoclavicular Joints*, Microcard PH37 1955.

9. Snowberger, Campbell, *An Electromyographic Study of the Multiple Function of the Deltoideus and the Teres Major Muscles in a Selected Group of Skilled Subjects*, Microcard PE301, 1956.

10. Sorochan, Walter D., *An Electromyographic Study of Selected Superficial Muscles Involved in the Movements of the Femocracetabular Joints*, Microcard PE302, 1956.

11. Spalteholz, Werner, *Hand Atlas of Human Anatomy*, Philadelphia, J. B. Lippincott Co., 1933.

12. Walters, C. E., and Partridge, M. J., Electromyographic Study of the Differential Action of the Abdominal Muscles during Exercise, *American Journal of Physical Medicine*, 36, 1957, p. 259.

13. Williams, Marion, and Wesley, Wallace, Hip Rotator Action of the Adductor Longus Muscle, *Physical Therapy Review*, 31, 1951, p. 90.

14. Wolbers, Charles P., *Electromyographic Study Relative to Movements of Thigh at Hip Joint*, Microcard PE309, 1956.

TABLE II: Principal Muscles of Movement and Locomotion

MUSCLES OF THE TRUNK—ANTERIOR GROUP

Muscle a, b	Origin	Insertion	Line of Pull c	Action
Rectus abdominis	(1) xiphoid process (2) cartilage of the 6th, 7th, and 8th ribs	(1) crest of the os pubis	straight upward or downward	(1) together, flexion of the trunk (2) singly, lateral flexion
External oblique	(1) outer border of lower 8 ribs	(1) anterior half of outer lip of iliac crest (2) Poupart's ligament (3) linea alba	downward and medial	(1) together, flexion of trunk (2) singly, lateral flexion and rotation of trunk
Internal oblique	(1) outer half of Poupart's ligament (2) anterior half of middle lip of iliac crest (3) lumbar fascia	(1) costal cartilage of 7th to 10th ribs (2) linea alba	downward and lateral	(1) together, flexion of the trunk (2) singly, lateral flexion and rotation of the trunk
Transversalis	(1) lower 6 costal cartilages (2) transverse processes of lumbar vertebrae (3) anterior half of inner lip of iliac crest (4) outer third of Poupart's ligament	(1) linea alba (2) crest of os pubis	lateral and backward, in a horizontal plane	(1) compression of the abdomen and fixation of the linea alba

a. Muscles are listed in more than one group if they extend into both groups and are functionally part of each group.
b. Some of the muscles have been marked with an asterisk. These are muscles which the student may omit learning without being handicapped in understanding later discussions.
c. The line of pull is given as the direction in which the insertion is moved with contraction of the muscle.

TABLE II: (cont'd): Principal Muscles

Muscle	Origin	Insertion	Line of Pull	Action
Sternocleidomastoid	(1) upper border of sternum (2) sternal end of the clavicle	(1) mastoid process of the temporal bone	downward and forward	(1) together, flexion of the head and neck (2) singly, rotation of the head
Platysma	(1) fascia of the pectoral, deltoid and trapezius muscles	(1) lower portion of mandible (2) fascia of muscles around the mouth	downward and lateral	(1) lateral flexion of the head (2) depression of the mandible

MUSCLES OF THE TRUNK—POSTERIOR GROUP

Muscle	Origin	Insertion	Line of Pull	Action
Erector spinae (iliocostalis, longissimus dorsi, spinalis dorsi)	(1) posterior iliac crest (2) lower posterior surface of sacrum (3) spinous processes of all lumbar and of last 2 thoracic vertebrae (4) transverse processes of all the thoracic vertebrae	(1) posterior portion of ribs (2) transverse processes of vertebrae the full length of the spine (3) base of the occipital around as far as the mastoid process	downward and medial	(1) together, extension of the spine, either localized or full length of spine (2) singly, lateral bending of spine, either localized or full length of spine (3) singly, aids in rotation of the trunk
Splenius (capitis and cervicis)	(1) spinous process of the 7th cervical and of the upper 6 thoracic vertebrae (2) ligamentum nuchae and supraspinous ligament	(1) lateral portion of the base of the occipital bone, and the mastoid process (2) transverse processes of upper 3 or 4 cervical vertebrae	downward and medial	(1) together, extension of the head and neck (2) singly, bends the head sideward and backward (3) aids in rotation of the head

TABLE II: (cont'd): Principal Muscles

Muscle	Origin	Insertion	Line of Pull	Action
Latissimus dorsi	(1) spines of the last 6 thoracic vertebrae (2) posterior portion of last 3 ribs (3) lumbar aponeurosis	(1) bottom of the bicipital groove on the humerus	downward, backward, and medial	(1) depression of the humerus (2) adduction of the humerus (3) inward rotation of the humerus (4) rotation of the trunk backward when the arms are fixed overhead
Quadratus lumborum	(1) posterior portion of the inner lip of the iliac crest	(1) lower border of last rib (2) transverse processes of the lumbar vertebrae	downward and slightly lateral	(1) together, extension of the lumbar spine (2) depression of the ribs (3) singly, lateral flexion of the trunk
° Serratus posticus inferior	(1) spines of last 2 thoracic and upper 3 lumbar vertebrae (2) lumbar fascia	(1) lower border of last 4 ribs	medial and slightly downward	(1) depression of the ribs
° Serratus posticus superior	(1) spine of 7th cervical and upper 2 thoracic vertebrae (2) lower part of ligamentum nuchae	(1) upper border of 2nd, 3rd, 4th, 5th ribs	medial and upward	(1) elevation of the ribs

MUSCLES OF THE SHOULDER GIRDLE—ANTERIOR GROUP

Muscle	Origin	Insertion	Line of Pull	Action
Subclavius	(1) cartilage of the 1st rib	(1) middle third of inferior surface of clavicle	downward and medial	(1) depression of clavicle

TABLE II: (cont'd): Principal Muscles

Muscle	Origin	Insertion	Line of Pull	Action
Pectoralis minor	(1) outer surface of 3rd, 4th, and 5th ribs	(1) coracoid process of scapula	downward and slightly forward	(1) downward rotation of scapula (2) elevation of ribs if scapula is fixed
Serratus anterior	(1) 8 digitations from the outer surface of upper 8 ribs (along the side and front of thorax)	(1) upper 3 digitations on ventral surface of whole vertebral border of scapula (2) lower 5 digitations on ventral surface of inferior angle of scapula	forward around the thorax in a horizontal line	(1) abduction of scapula (2) upward rotation of scapula

MUSCLES OF THE SHOULDER GIRDLE—POSTERIOR GROUP

Muscle	Origin	Insertion	Line of Pull	Action
Levator scapulae	(1) transverse processes of upper 4 or 5 cervical vertebrae	(1) vertebral border of scapula between superior angle and spine	upward and medial	(1) elevation of scapula (2) slight adduction of scapula
Trapezius	(1) base of occipital bone (2) spinous processes of all cervical and dorsal vertebrae (3) ligamentum nuchae	(1) outer third of posterior border of clavicle (2) top of acromion (3) upper border of spine of scapula	first part, upward and medial; second part, medial and slightly upward; third part, medial; fourth part, downward and medial	(1) upward rotation of scapula (2) adduction of scapula (3) depression of scapula
Rhomboid (major and minor)	(1) spinous processes of 7th cervical and upper 4 thoracic vertebrae	(1) vertebral border of scapula from spine to inferior angle	medial and slightly upward	(1) downward rotation of scapula (2) adduction of scapula

TABLE II: (cont'd): Principal Muscles

MUSCLES OF THE SHOULDER JOINT—ANTERIOR GROUP

Muscle	Origin	Insertion	Line of Pull	Action
18 Pectoralis major	(1) medial half of anterior surface of clavicle (2) anterior surface of sternum (3) cartilage of upper 6 ribs (4) aponeurosis of external oblique	(1) lateral lip of bicipital groove of the humerus	first part, medial and upward; second part, medial and downward	(1) adduction of the humerus (2) flexion of the humerus or depression of humerus, depending upon starting position of arm (3) inward rotation of humerus (4) elevation of the ribs, if the arm is fixed above the head
19 Anterior deltoid	(1) outer half of anterior surface of clavicle	(1) deltoid tubercle on humerus	upward and medial	(1) flexion of the humerus (2) helps other parts in abduction of humerus (3) forward movement of the arm through a transverse plane when arm starts in abducted position
20 Coracobrachialis	(1) coracoid process of scapula	(1) middle of medial surface of humerus	upward and slightly medial	(1) adduction of humerus (2) flexion of humerus if arm starts at side (3) depression of humerus if arm starts in elevated position

TABLE II: (cont'd): Principal Muscles

Muscle	Origin	Insertion	Line of Pull	Action
Biceps	(1) supraglenoid fossa on the scapula (2) coracoid process of scapula	(1) bicipital tuberosity on radius	upward	(1) flexion of forearm (2) supination of hand (3) flexion of the humerus

MUSCLES OF THE SHOULDER JOINT—LATERAL GROUP

Muscle	Origin	Insertion	Line of Pull	Action
Middle deltoid	(1) acromion process of the scapula	(1) deltoid tubercle on the humerus	upward	(1) abduction of the humerus
Supraspinatus	(1) supraspinous fossa of the scapula	(1) top of capsule of shoulder (2) superior portion of the greater tuberosity of the humerus	medial	(1) abduction of the humerus (2) pulls capsule out of the joint

MUSCLES OF THE SHOULDER JOINT—POSTERIOR GROUP

Muscle	Origin	Insertion	Line of Pull	Action
Infraspinatus	(1) infraspinous fossa of the scapula	(1) middle portion of the greater tuberosity of the humerus	medial	(1) outward rotation of the humerus (2) extension of humerus backward in horizontal plane when arm starts in an abducted position
Teres minor	(1) dorsal surface of the upper two thirds of the axillary border of the scapula	(1) inferior portion of the greater tuberosity of the humerus	medial	(1) outward rotation of the humerus (2) extension of humerus backward in horizontal plane when arm starts in an abducted position

TABLE II: (cont'd): Principal Muscles

Muscle	Origin	Insertion	Line of Pull	Action
Triceps	(1) infraglenoid fossa of the scapula (2) posterior surface of the humerus above and below the musculospiral groove	(1) olecranon process of the ulna	upward	(1) extension of the forearm (2) long head, slight extension of the humerus
Posterior deltoid	(1) lower border of spine of scapula	(1) deltoid tubercle on humerus	upward and medial	(1) extension of the humerus (2) helps other parts in abduction of the humerus (3) backward movement of the arms through a transverse plane when arm starts in abducted position

MUSCLES OF THE SHOULDER JOINT—MEDIAL GROUP

Muscle	Origin	Insertion	Line of Pull	Action
Teres major	(1) dorsal surface of lower third of axillary border of scapula	(1) medial lip of bicipital groove of humerus	downward, backward, and medial	(1) depression of the humerus (2) adduction of the humerus (3) inward rotation of the humerus

TABLE II: (cont'd): Principal Muscles

Muscle	Origin	Insertion	Line of Pull	Action
Latissimus dorsi	(1) spine of the last 6 thoracic vertebrae (2) posterior portion of the last 3 ribs (3) lumbar aponeurosis	(1) bottom of the bicipital groove on the humerus	downward, backward, and medial	(1) depression of the humerus (2) adduction of the humerus (3) inward rotation of the humerus (4) rotation of the trunk backward when the arms are fixed overhead
Subscapularis	(1) ventral surface of the scapula	(1) lesser tuberosity of the humerus	medial	(1) inward rotation of the humerus

MUSCLES OF THE ELBOW—ANTERIOR GROUP

Muscle	Origin	Insertion	Line of Pull	Action
Biceps	(1) supraglenoid fossa on the scapula (2) coracoid process of the scapula	(1) bicipital tuberosity on radius	upward	(1) flexion of forearm (2) supination of hand (3) flexion of the humerus
Brachialis anticus	(1) middle of the anterior surface of the humerus	(1) anterior surface of coronoid process of the ulna	upward	(1) flexion of the forearm
Pronator teres	(1) inner condyle of humerus (2) medial border of coronoid process of the ulna	(1) middle of the outer surface of the radius	upward and medial	(1) pronation of the hand (2) flexion of the forearm

TABLE II: (cont'd): Principal Muscles

MUSCLES OF THE ELBOW—LATERAL GROUP

Muscle	Origin	Insertion	Line of Pull	Action
Brachioradialis	(1) upper portion of lateral epicondylar ridge on humerus	(1) styloid process of the radius	upward	(1) flexion of the forearm (2) helps to start either supination or pronation depending upon the starting position of the forearm
Supinator	(1) lateral condyle of humerus (2) upper lateral surface of the ulna (3) ligaments of the elbow	(1) upper portion of posterior and lateral surfaces of the radius	upward and medial	(1) supination of the hand
Extensor carpi radialis longus	(1) common tendon from the external condyle of the humerus	(1) base of the 2nd metacarpal	upward	(1) extension of the wrist (2) abduction of the hand
Extensor carpi radialis brevis	(1) common tendon from the external condyle of the humerus	(1) base of the 3rd metacarpal	upward	(1) extension of the wrist (2) abduction of the hand
Extensor communis digitorum	(1) common tendon from the external condyle of the humerus	(1) by 4 tendons to the bases of the 2nd and 3rd phalanges of each of the 4 fingers	upward	(1) extension of the fingers (2) extension of the wrist
Extensor carpi ulnaris	(1) common tendon from the external condyle of the humerus (2) middle third of the posterior border of the ulna	(1) base of the 5th metacarpal	upward	(1) extension of the wrist (2) adduction of the wrist

TABLE II: (cont'd): Principal Muscles

Muscle	Origin	Insertion	Line of Pull	Action
° Extensor minimi digiti	(1) common tendon from the external condyle of the humerus	(1) 2nd and 3rd phalanges of the 5th finger	upward	(1) extension of the 5th finger

MUSCLES OF THE ELBOW—POSTERIOR GROUP

Muscle	Origin	Insertion	Line of Pull	Action
Triceps	(1) infraglenoid fossa of the scapula (2) posterior surface of the humerus above and below the musculospiral groove	(1) olecranon process of the ulna	upward	(1) extension of the forearm (2) long head, slight extension of the humerus
° Anconeus	(1) posterior surface of the outer condyle of the humerus	(1) posterior surface of the upper ulna and olecranon	backward	(1) extension of the elbow

MUSCLES OF THE ELBOW—MEDIAL GROUP

Muscle	Origin	Insertion	Line of Pull	Action
Flexor carpi radialis	(1) common tendon from the inner condyle of the humerus	(1) base of the 2nd metacarpal	upward and slightly medial	(1) flexion of the wrist (2) slight pronation of the hand (3) abduction of the hand
Flexor carpi ulnaris	(1) common tendon from the inner condyle of the humerus	(1) pisiform (2) unciform (triangular) (3) base of the 5th metacarpal	upward	(1) flexion of the wrist (2) adduction of the hand

TABLE II: (cont'd): Principal Muscles

Muscle	Origin	Insertion	Line of Pull	Action
Palmaris longus	(1) common tendon from the inner condyle of the humerus	(1) annular ligament (2) palmar fascia	upward	(1) flexion of the wrist (2) tightens fascia of the palm, causing the palm to cup
Flexor sublimis digitorum	(1) common tendon from the inner condyle of the humerus (2) coronoid process (3) anterior oblique line of radius	(1) by 4 tendons each of which split to attach on the sides of the bases of the 2nd phalanges of the 4 fingers	upward	(1) flexion of the 2nd phalanx of each finger (2) flexion of the wrist

MUSCLES OF THE WRIST—ANTERIOR GROUP

Muscle	Origin	Insertion	Line of Pull	Action
Flexor profundus digitorum	(1) upper two thirds of the anterior and lateral surface of the ulna (2) interosseous membrane	(1) by 4 tendons into the base of the 3rd phalanx of each of the 4 fingers	upward	(1) flexion of distal phalanx of the fingers (2) flexion of the fingers and of the wrist
Pronator quadratus	(1) lower anterior surface of the ulna	(1) lower portion of the anterior and lateral surface of the radius	medial	(1) pronation of the hand
Flexor longus pollicis	(1) upper two thirds of the anterior surface of the radius (2) interosseous membrane	(1) base of the 2nd phalanx of the thumb	upward	(1) flexion of distal phalanx of the thumb (2) flexion of thumb

MUSCLES OF THE WRIST—POSTERIOR GROUP

Muscle	Origin	Insertion	Line of Pull	Action
Extensor longus pollicis	(1) upper posterior surface of the ulna	(1) base of the last phalanx of the thumb	upward	(1) extension of the thumb (2) abduction of the thumb

TABLE II: (cont'd): Principal Muscles

Muscle	Origin	Insertion	Line of Pull	Action
Extensor brevis pollicis	(1) upper posterior surface of the radius (2) interosseous membrane	(1) base of the first phalanx of the thumb	upward	(1) extension of the thumb (2) abduction of the thumb
°Abductor longus pollicis	(2) middle posterior surface of the radius	(1) base of 1st metacarpal	upward and medial	(1) abduction of the thumb (2) abduction of the hand
Extensor indicis	(1) posterior surface of the ulna (2) interosseous membrane	(1) tendon of the extensor communis digitorum to the index finger	upward	(1) extension of index finger

MUSCLES OF THE HAND—LATERAL GROUP

Muscle	Origin	Insertion	Line of Pull	Action
°Flexor brevis pollicis	(1) transverse carpal ligament (2) ulnar side of 1st metacarpal	(1) base of 1st phalanx of thumb	medial	(1) flexion of the thumb across the palm (2) flexion of 1st phalanx of thumb
°Adductor transversus pollicis	(1) anterior surface of 3rd metacarpal	(1) base of 1st phalanx of the thumb	medial and upward	(1) adduction of the thumb (2) flexion of 1st phalanx of thumb
°Opponens pollicis	(1) anterior surface of the carpals	(1) lateral surface of 1st metacarpal	medial and upward	(1) flexion of the thumb
°Abductor pollicis	(1) lateral surface of the carpals	(1) lateral surface of 1st phalanx of the thumb	lateral	(1) abduction of the thumb

MUSCLES OF THE HAND—MEDIAL GROUP

Muscle	Origin	Insertion	Line of Pull	Action
Palmaris brevis	(1) palmar fascia and transverse carpal ligament	(1) skin and fascia of palm	upward	(1) assists in flexion of the palm

TABLE II: (cont'd): Principal Muscles

Muscle	Origin	Insertion	Line of Pull	Action
° Flexor brevis minimi digiti	(1) transverse carpal ligament	(1) first phalanx of little finger	upward	(1) flexion of the little finger
° Abductor minimi digiti	(1) pisitorm (2) tendon of flexor carpi ulnaris	(1) medial surface of base of 1st phalanx of fifth finger	upward	(1) abduction of the little finger
° Opponens minimi digiti	(1) transverse carpal ligament	(1) ulnar border of 5th metacarpal	upward	(1) flexion of the little finger (2) adduction of little finger when it is in a flexed position

MUSCLES OF THE HAND—DEEP PALMAR GROUP

Muscle	Origin	Insertion	Line of Pull	Action
° Lumbricales	(1) tendons of the flexor digitorum profundus	(1) radial side of the 1st phalanx of each finger (2) tendon of extensor communis digitorum	upward	(1) abduction of the fingers (2) flexion of 1st phalanx, extension of 2nd and 3rd
° Palmar interossei	(1) anterior surface of metacarpal bones	(1) base of 1st phalanx of each finger (2) tendon of extensor communis digitorum	upward	(1) adduction of the fingers (2) flexion of 1st phalanx, extension of 2nd and 3rd of 2nd, 4th, and 5th fingers

MUSCLES OF THE HAND—DEEP POSTERIOR GROUP

Muscle	Origin	Insertion	Line of Pull	Action
° Dorsal interossei	(1) sides of metacarpals	(1) tendon of extensor communis digitorum	upward	(1) abduction of the fingers (2) flexion of the 1st phalanx and extension of the 2nd and 3rd phalanges of 2nd, 3rd, and 4th fingers

TABLE II: (cont'd): Principal Muscles

Muscle	Origin	Insertion	Line of Pull	Action
MUSCLES OF THE HIP JOINT—ANTERIOR GROUP				
Iliopsoas	(1) sides of the bodies of the 12th thoracic and all the lumbar vertebrae (2) upper half of the anterior surface of the ilium	(1) lesser trochanter of the femur	forward and upward	(1) flexion of trunk on thigh, or thigh on trunk (2) outward rotation of femur
Rectus femoris	(1) anterior inferior spine of the ilium (2) anterior margin of the acetabulum	(1) tuberosity of the tibia	upward	(1) flexion of trunk on thigh, or of thigh on trunk (2) extension of the knee
Sartorius	(1) anterior superior spine of the ilium	(1) medial surface of the inner condyle of the tibia	upward and forward	(1) flexion of trunk on thigh, or of thigh on trunk (2) flexion of the knee (3) outward rotation of the femur
MUSCLES OF THE HIP JOINT—LATERAL GROUP				
Gluteus medius	(1) upper lateral surface of the ilium	(1) lateral surface of the greater trochanter	upward	(1) abduction of the femur (2) inward rotation of femur by the anterior fibers (3) outward rotation of femur by posterior fibers
Gluteus minimus	(1) middle of lateral surface of the ilium	(1) superior surface of the greater trochanter	upward	(1) abduction of the femur (2) inward rotation of femur by anterior fibers

TABLE II: (cont'd): **Principal Muscles**

Muscle	Origin	Insertion	Line of Pull	Action
Tensor fasciae latae	(1) aponeurosis just off the crest of the ilium behind the anterior superior spine	(1) fascia latae half way down the thigh	upward and slightly forward	(1) abduction of the femur (2) flexion of the femur (3) inward rotation of the femur
MUSCLES OF THE HIP JOINT—POSTERIOR GROUP				
Gluteus maximus	(1) lateral posterior surface of the ilium (2) posterior surface of the sacrum and coccyx (3) greater sacrosciatic ligament	(1) gluteal line of the femur (from the greater trochanter to the linea aspera)	upward and medial	(1) extension of the femur (2) outward rotation of the femur
Semitendonosus	(1) lower surface of the tuberosity of the ischium	(1) upper medial surface of the shaft of the tibia	upward and backward	(1) extension of the hip (2) flexion of the knee (3) inward rotation of the lower leg
Semimembranosus	(1) upper and lateral surface of the tuberosity of the ischium	(1) inner surface of medial condyle of the tibia	upward and backward	(1) extension of the hip (2) flexion of the knee (3) inward rotation of the lower leg
Biceps femoris	(1) lower surface of the tuberosity of the ischium (2) full length of linea aspera	(1) lateral surface of the head of the fibula	upward, medial, and backward	(1) extension of the hip (2) flexion of the knee (3) outward rotation of the lower leg
Pyriformis	(1) anterior surface of the sacrum	(1) superior surface of the greater trochanter of the femur	medial and slightly backward	(1) outward rotation of the femur

TABLE II: (cont'd): Principal Muscles

Muscle	Origin	Insertion	Line of Pull	Action
Quadratus femoris	(1) lateral surface of the tuberosity of the ischium	(1) intertrochanteric crest of the femur	medial	(1) outward rotation of the femur
Obturator internus	(1) inner surface of ilium and pubis from foramen to iliopectineal line (2) inner surface of the obturator membrane (3) inner surface of the rami of the pubis and of the ischium	(1) inner border of greater trochanter of the femur	medial	(1) outward rotation of the femur
Obturator externus	(1) outer surface of lower half of the obturator membrane (2) outer surface of the rami of the pubis and of the ischium	(1) in the fossa between the greater trochanter and the neck of the femur	medial and slightly forward	(1) outward rotation of the femur
Gemellus superior	(1) spine of the ischium	(1) inner border of greater trochanter of the femur	medial and slightly backward	(1) outward rotation of the femur
Gemellus inferior	(1) upper lateral surface of tuberosity of ischium	(1) inner border of greater trochanter of the femur	medial and slightly backward	(1) outward rotation of the femur

MUSCLES OF THE HIP JOINT—MEDIAL GROUP

Muscle	Origin	Insertion	Line of Pull	Action
Pectineus	(1) ascending ramus of the os pubis (2) iliopectineal line of the ilium	(1) pectineal line of the femur (from the lesser trochanter to the linea aspera)	forward and upward	(1) adduction of the femur (2) flexion of the femur (3) outward rotation of the femur

TABLE II: (cont'd): Principal Muscles

Muscle	Origin	Insertion	Line of Pull	Action
Gracilis	(1) anterior surface of the body of the os pubis (2) descending ramus of the os pubis	(1) medial surface of the tibia just below the condyle	upward and slightly forward	(1) adduction of the femur (2) flexion of the femur (3) inward rotation of the leg
Adductor magnus	(1) lateral surface of the body of the ischium (2) lateral surface of the rami of the pubis and of the ischium	(1) entire length of the linea aspera (2) adductor tubercle	medial, upward, and slightly forward	(1) adduction of the femur (2) slight flexion of the femur when leg starts in a fully extended position (3) slight extension of the femur when leg starts in a fully flexed position (4) slight outward rotation of the femur
Adductor longus	(1) descending ramus of the os pubis	(1) middle third of the linea aspera on the femur	medial, upward, and slightly forward	(1) adduction of the femur (2) slight flexion of the femur when the leg starts in a fully extended position (3) slight outward rotation of the femur
Adductor brevis	(1) anterior surface of the body of the os pubis	(1) upper third of the linea aspera on the femur	medial, forward, and slightly upward	(1) adduction of the femur (2) slight flexion of the femur when the leg starts in a fully extended position (3) slight outward rotation of the femur

TABLE II: (cont'd): Principal Muscles

(handwritten margin notes: "vastus medialis locks knee"; "Quadriceps"; "Ham strings"; "1150 Strongest"; "Sunday"; 86, 87, 88, 89, 90, 91, 92)

Muscle	Origin	Insertion	Line of Pull	Action
MUSCLES OF THE KNEE—ANTERIOR GROUP				
Vastus internus	(1) medial lip of the linea aspera	(1) tuberosity of the tibia	upward and medial	(1) extension of the knee
Vastus externus	(1) lateral lip of the linea aspera	(1) tuberosity of the tibia	upward and lateral	(1) extension of the knee
Vastus intermedius	(1) anterior surface of the femur	(1) tuberosity of the tibia	upward	(1) extension of the knee
Rectus femoris	(1) anterior inferior spine of the ilium (2) anterior margin of the acetabulum	(1) tuberosity of the tibia	upward	(1) flexion of the trunk on the thigh or of the thigh on the trunk (2) extension of the knee
MUSCLES OF THE KNEE—POSTERIOR GROUP				
Semitendinosus	(1) lower surface of the tuberosity of the ischium	(1) upper medial surface of the shaft of the tibia	upward and backward	(1) extension of the hip (2) flexion of the knee (3) inward rotation of the lower leg
Semimembranosus	(1) upper and lateral surface of the tuberosity of the ischium	(1) inner surface of medial condyle of the tibia	upward and backward	(1) extension of the hip (2) flexion of the knee (3) inward rotation of the lower leg
Biceps femoris	(1) lower surface of the tuberosity of the ischium (2) full length of linea aspera	(1) lateral surface of the head of the fibula	upward, medial, and backward	(1) extension of the hip (2) flexion of the knee (3) outward rotation of the lower leg

TABLE II: (cont'd): Principal Muscles

Muscle	Origin	Insertion	Line of Pull	Action
Sartorius	(1) anterior superior spine of the ilium	(1) medial surface of the inner condyle of the tibia	upward and forward	(1) flexion of the trunk on the thigh or of the thigh on the trunk (2) flexion of the knee (3) outward rotation of femur
Gracilis	(1) anterior surface of the body of the os pubis (2) descending ramus of os pubis	(1) medial surface of the tibia just below the condyle	upward and slightly forward	(1) adduction of the femur (2) flexion of the femur (3) inward rotation of leg
Gastrocnemius	(1) posterior surface of the condyles of the femur	(1) lower posterior surface of the os calcis	upward	(1) extension of the ankle (2) flexion of the knee
*Plantaris	(1) lower, lateral extension of the linea aspera (2) oblique popliteal ligament	(1) lower posterior surface of the os calcis	upward	(1) flexion of knee (2) extension of foot
*Popliteus	(1) lateral surface of the lateral condyle of the femur	(1) upper posterior surface of the tibia	upward and lateral	(1) flexion of the knee (2) inward rotation of the lower leg

MUSCLES OF THE ANKLE AND FOOT—ANTERIOR GROUP

Muscle	Origin	Insertion	Line of Pull	Action
Tibialis anticus	(1) upper two thirds of the lateral surface of the tibia	(1) medial surface of the inner cuneiform (2) base of 1st metatarsal	upward and lateral	(1) flexion of the ankle (2) inversion of the foot
Peroneus tertius	(1) lower anterior surface of the fibula (2) interosseous membrane	(1) base of the 5th metatarsal (2) fascia over metatarsals	upward	(1) flexion of the ankle (2) eversion of the foot

TABLE II: (cont'd): Principal Muscles

Muscle	Origin	Insertion	Line of Pull	Action
Extensor longus digitorum	(1) upper two thirds of the anterior surface of the fibula (2) interosseous membrane (3) lateral condyle of tibia	(1) 4 tendons, each to the 2nd and 3rd phalanges of the 4 toes	upward	(1) extension of the toes (2) flexion of the ankle *dorsi*
Extensor longus hallucis	(1) middle of the anterior surface of the fibula (2) interosseous membrane	(1) base of the last phalanx of the 1st toe	upward	(1) extension of the 1st toe (2) flexion of the ankle *dorsi*

MUSCLES OF THE ANKLE AND FOOT—POSTERIOR GROUP

Muscle	Origin	Insertion	Line of Pull	Action
Gastrocnemius	(1) posterior surface of the condyles of the femur	(1) lower posterior surface of the os calcis	upward	(1) extension of the ankle (2) flexion of the knee
Soleus	(1) posterior surface of the head of the fibula (2) oblique line of the tibia	(1) lower posterior surface of the os calcis	upward	(1) extension of the ankle *plant.*
Tibialis posticus	(1) posterior surface of the tibia (2) interosseous membrane (3) upper posterior surface of the fibula	(1) inferior surface of the inner cuneiform (2) tuberosity of the navicular (3) bases of the 2nd to the 4th metatarsals	backward under inner malleolus, upward	(1) extension of the ankle (2) slight inversion of the foot
Flexor longus hallucis	(1) lower two thirds of the posterior surface of the fibula (2) lower surface of the interosseous membrane	(1) base of the last phalanx of the 1st toe	backward under inner malleolus, upward	(1) flexion of the 1st toe (2) extension of the ankle

TABLE II: (cont'd): Principal Muscles

Muscle	Origin	Insertion	Line of Pull	Action
Flexor longus digitorum	(1) lower posterior surface of the tibia	(1) base of the last phalanx of each of the 4 toes	backward under inner malleolus, upward	(1) flexion of the toes (2) extension of the ankle
Peroneus longus	(1) upper two thirds of the lateral surface of the fibula	(1) base of the 1st metatarsal (2) 1st cuneiform	lateral and backward under the foot, under external malleolus, upward	(1) extension of the ankle (2) eversion of the foot
Peroneus brevis	(1) lower third of the lateral surface of the fibula	(1) tuberosity of the 5th metatarsal	backward under external malleolus, upward	(1) extension of the ankle

MUSCLES OF THE DORSAL SURFACE OF THE FOOT

Muscle	Origin	Insertion	Line of Pull	Action
Extensor brevis digitorum	(1) outer surface of the os calcis (2) lateral talocalcaneal ligament	(1) 1st phalanx of great toe (2) tendon of the extensor longus digitorum to 2nd, 3rd and 4th toes	backward	(1) extension of the first 4 toes
* Dorsal interossei	(1) double head from adjoining bases of the metatarsals	(1) base of 1st phalanx of the 2nd, 3rd, and 4th toes	1st, backward and medial; 2nd, 3rd, and 4th, backward and lateral	(1) abduction of the toes (2) flexion of 1st phalanx of the 2nd to 4th toes

MUSCLES ON THE PLANTAR SURFACE OF THE FOOT

Muscle	Origin	Insertion	Line of Pull	Action
Flexor brevis digitorum	(1) inner surface of the os calcis (2) plantar fascia	(1) 4 tendons, each to 2nd phalanx of the 4 toes	backward	(1) flexion of the toes
Flexor brevis hallucis	(1) plantar surface of the inner cuneiform (2) tendon of the tibialis posticus	(1) base of the 1st phalanx of the great toe	backward	(1) flexion of the 1st toe

TABLE II: (cont'd): Principal Muscles

Muscle	Origin	Insertion	Line of Pull	Action
Flexor brevis minimi digiti	(1) sheath of the peroneus longus (2) base of the 5th metatarsal	(1) base of the 1st phalanx of the 5th toe	backward	(1) flexion of the 5th toe
Accessorius	(1) inner and plantar surface of the os calcis	(1) tendon of the flexor longus digitorum	backward	(1) flexion of the toes
* Abductor hallucis	(1) inner surface of the os calcis (2) plantar fascia	(1) inner surface of the base of the 1st phalanx of the great toe	backward	(1) abduction of the 1st toe
* Abductor minimi digiti	(1) plantar surface of the os calcis (2) plantar fascia	(1) lateral surface of the base of the 1st phalanx of the 5th toe	backward	(1) abduction of the 5th toe
* Adductor hallucis	(1) base of the 2nd, 3rd, and 4th metatarsals (2) tendon of the peroneus longus	(1) base of the 1st phalanx of the great toe	backward and lateral	(1) adduction of the 1st toe
* Adductor transverse hallucis	(1) transverse ligament of the metatarsals (2) inferior metatarsophalangeal ligament	(1) lateral surface of the 1st phalanx of the great toe	backward and lateral	(1) adduction of the 1st toe
* Lumbricales	(1) tendons of the flexor longus digitorum	(1) base of the 1st phalanx of 2nd, 3rd, 4th, and 5th toes	backward	(1) flexion of the 1st phalanx of the toes
* Plantar interossei	(1) inner side of bases of 3rd, 4th, and 5th metatarsals	(1) bases of the 1st phalanx of 3rd, 4th, and 5th toes	backward	(1) adduction of the toes (2) flexion of the 1st phalanx of the toes

CHAPTER 5

Physiology of Movement

THE PROCESSES OF MOTION

1. Normal functioning of the muscular system is dependent upon normal functioning of all other systems of the body.
2. Stimulation of a muscle produces contraction and usually shortening of the muscle.
3. The motor unit is the functional unit of the muscle.
4. The strength of the muscle contraction depends upon the strength of the stimulus.
5. Tonus is a characteristic of a healthy muscle.
6. Muscle activity takes place through the regular processes of metabolism.
7. Co-ordination or co-operation of muscle groups is dependent upon the proper sorting of stimuli within the central nervous system.
8. Fatigue decreases the efficiency of muscle action.

CELL STRUCTURE

THE MUSCLES OF THE BODY are of three types—smooth, cardiac, and skeletal. Each of these three has distinguishing characteristics of structure, innervation, and function. The skeletal muscle, sometimes called striated or voluntary muscle, is the one directly responsible for motor activity. Therefore, it is the type to be considered here.

An understanding of the microscopic structure of the muscle increases an understanding of muscular performance. The structural unit of the muscle is the cell, usually designated by the name "fiber." In common with other types of cells, the muscle fiber has an outer membrane enclosing the protoplasm, known as the sarcolemma and sarcoplasm, respectively. Running lengthwise through the protoplasm are the myofibrils. The transverse bands of the fibrils give the skeletal muscles their characteristic striated appearance, and hence the name "striated muscle."

The fibrils are the unique structure of the muscle cell. Characteristic properties of the muscle are elasticity, irritability, and contractility. Elasticity makes it possible for the muscle to be stretched and then return to its original length. Irritability is its capacity to respond to stimuli. Contractility is its ability to exert tension on its origin and insertion. These properties are shown during movement of the body segments. Movement is always effected by the contraction of certain muscles and usually the stretching of their antagonists.

It has been known for a long time that the fibril is the site of the contractile capacity of the muscle. Relatively recent research has begun to reveal the process of this contraction and to yield significant information concerning this function. Physiologists and biochemists have provided, and are continuing to provide, information about the internal processes of the muscle cell. This information is fundamental to the kinesiologist's full appreciation of the complex function of movement.

The knowledge of gross anatomical structure of muscle has had a relatively unsophisticated origin. The student of anatomy worked with specimens available to him, and dissected and divided one muscle from another. He found where each attached, where it lay with respect to other muscles in the segment and with respect to the articulation which it operated, and saw how it differed in texture and appearance from other tissues. The gross anatomist could also detect the line of fibers in the muscle and so identify the internal arrangement and conjecture regarding their varying lengths. This information has been valuable.

The microscope made it possible to look inside the cell and determine the differentiated structure—the nuclei, the protoplasm, and the myofibril —and even to see the striations on the tiny fibrils. This information, plus other facts learned about neural connections to the skeletal muscle, led to an understanding of these muscles as specialized cells designed to move the segments in definite ways.

The development of the electron microscope made it possible to magnify the tissue 400,000 times, more or less. In this close-up and enlarged view the cell and its contents take on new perspective. It is very much like seeing the stripes and plaids in a piece of fabric, but not until one sees the individual threads of warp and woof does one really perceive the true color and texture of the individual threads.

Muscle fibers vary considerable in size. Some are as small as 10 to 15 microns, others may exceed 100 microns[3] (a micron is $\frac{1}{1000}$ mm.). There is an approximate proportionality between cell diameter and size of muscle. However, there is variance in the same muscle in a series of subjects and in the state of muscle conditioning. The myofibril is 1 micron or less in diameter and the cross striations of the fibril are clearly visible. This is accentuated in the cell by the fact that these striations on different fibrils in the cell are aligned so as to give a straight stripe across the cell, rather than a "checkerboard" or "salt-and-pepper" pattern.

Study of the cross section reveals that the fibril is made up of two kinds of filaments. One of these filaments is about half the diameter of the other and longer than the larger one. These will be referred to as the S and L filaments, meaning simply small and large in diameter. These two filaments are arranged in alternating and regular pattern which is highly consistent in all fibrils. The arrangement approximates a hexagonal one rather than a true cylindrical form for the fibril, with each S filament in the center of a triangle formed by L filaments (see Fig. 33) and each larger one in turn is surrounded by 6 S filaments in a hexagonal pattern (Fig. 33b). These filaments are in the general dimension of 50 and 100 angstroms (an angstrom is $\frac{1}{10,000}$ of a micron). The regularity of geometric pattern is almost startling in structures so small. Nevertheless, it apparently is an arrangement to bring the two filaments, with their two types of protein, into juxtaposition. Such an arrangement appears to be necessary for contraction. A corresponding regularity of relationship between the two filaments can be observed in the striations of the fibril.

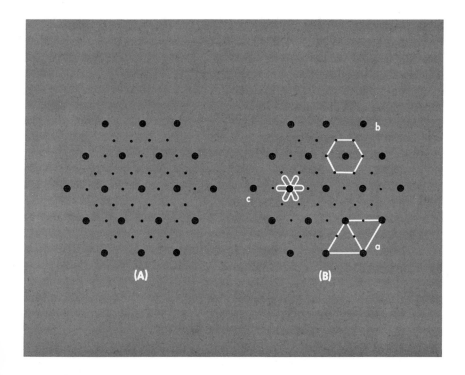

FIGURE 33: Diagram of arrangement of protein filaments in fibril
a–triangular arrays of L filaments with central S filament;
b–hexagonal arrangement of S filaments round an L filament;
c–bridges from L filaments

longitudinal arrangement of the filaments. Again the analogy of the plaid fabric applies. There is a repeated pattern in which each unit is identical with each successive one as the eye moves along the length of the fibril. The unit extends from one Z-line to the next one and is called a sarcomere (see Fig. 34). Between these two Z-lines are stripes of dark, gray, and light. The Z-line is the darkest stripe. Immediately adjacent to it is a light stripe referred to usually as the I-band. Next is a somewhat darker stripe called the A-band. In the center of the unit is a rather narrow stripe of intermediate color, called the H-zone. Then is repeated the A-band and the I-band, with the termination of the unit in the next Z-line.

The difference in dark-light quality of the striations is apparently due to the difference in protein substance (actin and myosin) found in the two filaments and the way in which the light used in microscopic study differentiates these proteins. The filaments are arranged in the fibril in an interlacing pattern as shown in Figure 34b. The S or actin filaments are apparently continuous through the Z-line and into adjacent sarcomeres. There may be even more minute threads connecting them through the H-zone. This would mean they are continuous for the full length of the fiber. The L or myosin filaments are short units located in the middle portion of the sarcomere (Fig. 34b). It is these filaments which act in contraction, apparently sliding past each other in an intermeshing pattern.

As contraction takes place, the S filaments move medially in the sarcomere meeting in the center of the sarcomere and forming a more compact mass by either overlapping or compression of oncoming ends. This collision of S filaments is followed by compression of the ends of the L filaments on the Z-line restraining band (see Fig. 34d). It has been found that the A-bands remain constant in length during contraction but that the length of the I-bands changes, and likewise the H-band changes directly in relationship with the I-bands. In other words if one considers the distance from the margin of H to H this remains practically constant regardless of whether the muscle is contracting (Fig. 34d) or being stretched (Fig. 34c).

Further examination of the L filaments shows that each has a series of projecting arms or bridges which extend out to the S filaments. These bridges are arranged in units of six in a spiral fashion around the filament and each projects toward one of the six S filaments which invariably surrounds the larger one (Fig. 33c). More is known of the structural detail of the myofibril than is known of the reasons behind the process of response in the sarcomere. It is known that there must be neural stimulus to elicit contraction; that both types of protein—actin and myosin—represented in the two filaments must be present in relation to each other; and that the myosin bridges on the L filament are the site of some

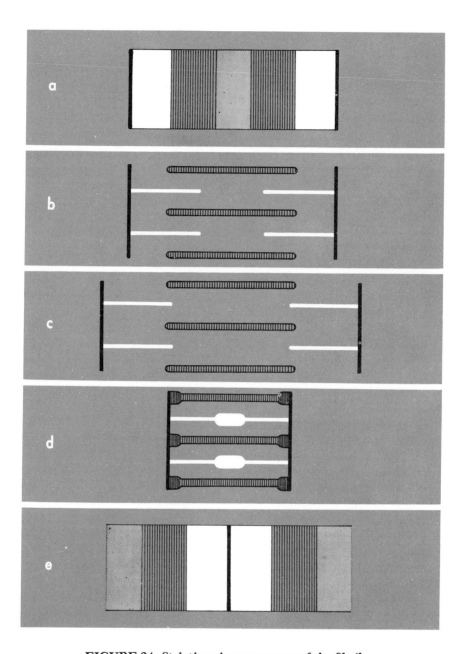

FIGURE 34: Striations in sarcomeres of the fibrils
a–fibril at rest, differentiated bonds; b–filaments in the fibril;
c–sarcomere when stretched; d–sarcomere when contracted;
e–parts of two sarcomeres

type of molecular action. Hypotheses of physiologists differ on this physiochemical process and remain to be studied further.

FUNCTIONAL ARRANGEMENT OF CELLS

The muscle fibers vary considerably in length. In most of the shorter muscles, apparently the fibers extend the entire length of the muscle from one attachment to the other. In longer muscles of both the upper and lower extremities, fibers have been found to extend the full length of the muscle. However, in a muscle such as the sartorius and the gracilis many of the fibers terminate in the belly of the muscle, to be continued by another cell in the more distal part of the muscle. The identification of the terminal cuff of attachment of the fiber has facilitated very recent studies[3] of fiber length. A regular termination of cells might readily account for the segmentation of a metameric muscle such as the rectus abdominus.

The fibers are arranged in different patterns in the various muscles. The details of arrangement will be discussed in Chapter 8. In general, they are bound together by a fascia which covers the entire muscle and which often divides the muscle into subdivisions. The fibers usually attach to a tendon of origin and one of insertion. The myofibrils attach into the cuff formed at the end of the cell by the multiple folding of the sarcolemma. The fibers of the tendon attach into the outside folds of this cuff thus making a substantial junction of these contractile and noncontractile structures. Apparently in those muscles which attach directly into the periosteum there is a similar linking of epithelial cell membranes into the extremity of the muscle cell. In those few muscles in which part or all of the muscle attaches directly into an aponeurosis (example, oblique abdominals) the junction is the same as the musculotendinous ones.

It can be observed that some muscles appear darker in color than others. Muscles are, therefore, sometimes referred to as red and light. The red fibers have more plasma and granular content and more muscular hemoglobin. These fibers are found in muscles which are used for continued or repeated action and may actually be able to store some oxygen in this myoglobin. The light fibers appear to be better suited to quick contraction. In general, human muscle is a mixture of light and red fibers, but extensors of the lower extremity, which must be in almost constant use, have a larger proportion of red fibers than most other muscles. Since this is a quality which appears to differ with the use which is made of the muscle, it may be a factor associated with the process of conditioning of the organism.

The cell or fiber is the structural unit of the muscle, but the motor unit is actually the functional unit. The motor unit is made up of a motor neuron coming into the muscle and the fibers to which the branchings of this neuron attach. The number of fibers in a motor unit is highly variable, but estimates of the average are usually around 150. The fibers in this motor unit are not situated in a compact structural unit but are somewhat distributed through the muscle. The distribution of fibers enables an apparently more general response of the total muscle when only a few motor units are working than would be possible in a more localized arrangement.

The capillaries permeate the muscle and each fiber is thus provided with a supply of blood. The muscle cell is absolutely dependent upon both the blood supply and the nervous stimulation for its life and functioning.

CONTRACTION PROCESSES

When a stimulus is relayed to a muscle it results in contraction of the muscle, provided the stimulus is adequate for the physiological condition existing in the tissue at that time. If the stimulus involves only a few motor neurons and reaches only a few motor units, the contraction is weak. If the stimulus affects all the motor units in the muscle synchronously, the contraction of the muscle is at its maximum.

The all-or-none law is related to the differential action of the motor units in a muscle. The law states that when an individual muscle fiber is stimulated sufficiently to produce action, it contracts to its fullest extent. Since the cells in a motor unit function in response to stimuli from a given neuron, then a stimulus will produce maximum contraction of all the motor unit. However, this law refers to action of the motor unit only and not the entire muscle. The number of units stimulated and the rhythm with which they function account for variations in strength. The determination of the number of motor neurons to be affected is made in the central nervous system.

The neural impulse arriving at a muscle cell causes a depolarizing of the cell membrane and ion changes within the cell. The resultant biochemical change produces the interaction of the actin and myosin filaments (S and L) mentioned earlier. The complete understanding of this process of actomyosin linkage awaits further research on the various explanatory hypotheses. The actual beginning of contraction occurs slightly after the depolarization effect. This interval is referred to as the latent time of the muscle and is approximately .003 second. The cell is not immediately receptive to additional stimuli, there being an interval of approximately .005 second before the cell membrane returns to its resting state.

Directly related to the phenomenon of contraction is that of the tonus of the muscle. Nervous impulses arriving in a muscle may not be adequate to produce a contraction that will cause the body part to move. However, they may affect the tonus of the muscle. All muscles with intact nerve supply in a conscious individual maintain a continuous state of slight contraction. This mild contraction is accounted for by the fact that only a few motor units contract and do so in continual rotation. Tonus is greater in states of excitement and positions of readiness, lowers in normal standing or sitting, and becomes progressively less in relaxed resting positions and in sleep.

Tonus serves a dual purpose. Movement takes place more quickly when a stimulus comes because there is already slight tension in the muscle. The movement also takes place more smoothly as a result of that tension. Tonus gives the same results that are obtained when towing one car behind another if the rope is made taut before the first car starts. It eliminates the time required to take up the slack in the rope and avoids the jerk which occurs when it starts pulling.

Tonus of the human muscle normally helps to give the smoothness which is desirable in most movements. This is partially dependent upon the action of the antagonistic muscles, whose tonus serves as a resistance or check to the action of the opposite muscles when movement starts. During movement, relaxation of the antagonists contributes to economy of muscular action.

When relaxation occurs the stimuli are subminimal, or the state of the muscle resists stimulation. When a certain muscle or group of muscles is stimulated, the antagonists of those muscles are ordinarily allowed to relax. This process of maintaining relationship between two sets of stimuli is referred to as *reciprocal innervation*. Certain exercises or activities in which the person engages may require a rigidity of position or tenseness of movement. Such actvities require stimulation and action of both muscle groups.

The substances providing the source of energy for contraction, as well as oxygen, are brought to the muscle by the blood supply. There is an adequate supply of both in the muscle at all times for very brief bouts of muscular effort. Then the muscle becomes ineffective in the absence of a proper blood supply.

There are certain by-products of this process of contraction. Perhaps the most conspicuous is the production of heat. The process which produces the heat provides the basis for action or mechanical work, but the heat represents actual energy loss. Though it serves to warm the body it is lost from the body. Heat serves to make the person feel comfortably warm; after extreme exertion or prolonged effort it may exceed the comfort level. The heat appears to facilitate also the chemical processes within the muscle and to facilitate contraction, perhaps by reducing the viscosity of the cell.

Other by-products of the contractile process include carbon dioxide and lactic acid. Ordinarily the carbon dioxide is removed promptly by the blood supply. The lactic acid accumulates primarily in cases of continuing contraction of the muscle where reduction in available oxygen is occurring. At first the lactic acid seems to have little effect, perhaps even increases muscle irritability slightly. Later, it is associated with fatigue and may have a contributory effect.

When a muscle which has been at rest is first brought into action, there is a gradual increase in the extent of contraction in response to what are apparently identical stimuli. This gradual increase to optimum working conditions is known as the *treppe* phenomenon. During this state, there is a reduction in the period of relaxation between contractions and a shortening of the period of resistance to later stimuli. The results of this state include greater mechanical efficiency and probably greater safety in many activities.

As fatigue sets in, the muscle contracts over a shorter and shorter range but in its period of relaxation does not return completely to normal length. If only a part of the muscle is needed for sustained action, fatigue is delayed. If all the muscle is needed for rapidly repeated contractions, fatigue comes sooner. In very strong movements where the muscle is used to its limit, it may cease functioning in a state of strong contraction which persists for some time. This state is called *contracture* and is one of the conditions of "muscle cramp."

When the muscle contracts against a resistance less than the force in the contraction, the part to which it is attached is thereby permitted to move. The tension within the muscle remains relatively constant and the contraction is therefore referred to as an *isotonic* one. The movement may continue after the actual contraction ceases because of the momentum of the moving part, but the tension within the muscle is constant through the period of muscular contraction.

When the muscle contracts against a resistance greater than the force which the muscle can produce, the muscle remains the same length though the tension within the muscle mounts in proportion to the motor units activated. This contraction is called an *isometric* one. In terms of mechanical work nothing is being accomplished, but in terms of events within the muscle cell, the muscle is engaging in all the processes of contraction. Tension within the muscle may reach its highest point in this situation and may even be uncomfortable.

When the muscle is working against gravity to control the rate and range of the downward motion, the strength of the contraction must be geared to the size of the load. But it is kept at a point just less than the load so that movement takes place. The movement requires an elongation of the muscle, but the control requires contraction. This is *eccentric* contraction. It may be followed by relaxation of the muscle, in which case the part would drop passively; it may be followed by a matching of effort and load, and the part will stop; it may be followed by greater effort than the load, and the part will reverse direction. These represent progressive changes from eccentric, to isometric, to isotonic contraction.

TABLE III: Types of Muscle Response and Internal-External Evidence

	Isotonic	Isometric	Eccentric
EXTERNAL EVIDENCE			
Action	Overt movement	Fixation	Retardation
Resistance/force	Less	Equal	More
Visual Appearance	Bulging	Bulging	Streamlined
Palpation	Hard	Hard	Subsiding
Position of insertion	Moving toward origin	Stationary	Moving away from insertion
$W = F \times D$	Positive	None	Negative
INTERNAL PROCESS			
Energy used	Dependent on load	Dependent on time held	Dependent on load and time
Heat	Yes	Yes	Slight
Tremor	None	Increasing with time held	Seldom
Fixators	Moderate	Strong and diffused	Decreasing
Myofibril action	I-bands shorten		Lengthening of S filament
EXAMPLES			
Knee action while on feet	Extending	Holding flexed	Slow flexing
Shoulder action, weight in hand	Abduction	Holding abducted	Slow adduction
Trunk extensors while on feet	Extending	Holding in forward bow	Slow forward bending

Table III presents a comparison of the various aspects of these respective reactions and examples of muscle groups which perform each of these types of contraction under different circumstances. Observation of one's own movements will help to clarify the relationship between purpose of the movement and the demands upon the muscle. Understanding of the common elements in these types should help to explain why analysis of energy cost of activities must be based on physiological costs as well as on the mechanical end result.

A load may be applied to a muscle in various ways. These variations are important considerations in an understanding of its performance. If the load is so placed that it does not affect the muscle until contraction starts, the extent of contraction possible for the muscle varies inversely with the size of the load. By increasing the load, a point is soon reached where the muscle is incapable of moving it. But if a load is so placed that it causes the muscle to be stretched while it is resting, the muscle behaves differently. As long as the load is reasonable for the muscle, the contraction is approximately the same in extent for each load, though the movement may start from a different point. In this condition, the muscle can move a load which it could not move by the first type of loading. When it is being stretched, the chemical processes liberating energy are proceeding at a higher rate. The result is a better contraction. The use which a performer can make of this fact is shown by the bending of the knees before a jump, or arm extension preparatory to a throw. The load may, of course, be increased beyond the point where the muscle can function. If the load is such that it produces nearly the maximum range of safe elongation, and the muscle attempts to move the weight but is unable to do so, then tension in the muscle reaches its maximum. It is in a situation of this type that strains and muscle injuries occur, particularly if the muscle is not warmed up.

It is known, also, that a muscle does not do the most work with a very small load or with one near maximal size. The optimum load is somewhere between these two extremes, usually approximately one-half the maximum load. It is the point where the muscle does the greatest amount of work for each contraction.

It is apparent that the muscle varies in length at different stages of its functioning. If the load is heavy or if the pull of antagonists moves the joint through a considerable range, the muscle is elongated. The amount of elongation from a given force varies directly with the original length of the muscle and inversely with its cross section. It also varies directly with the size of the stretching force. The elasticity of the muscle is such that it may normally be stretched from one-third to one-half of the normal resting length without injury to the muscle; and the muscle still remains capable of contracting. On the other extreme, the muscle is still effective up to complete contraction of the entire muscle. This range from maximum elongation to maximum contraction is the amplitude of the muscle's action (Fig. 35).

However, before the muscle reaches either extreme of its amplitude, it loses some of its effectiveness. The optimal range of functioning is, therefore, somewhat narrower (D' to C') than its amplitude. Greatest efficiency is in the range B to D' with gradual decrease on the contractile side of B.

The efficiency of the human machine is considered in the same way as that of any other machine. Its efficiency rating is the ratio of substances used to external work produced; or, as frequently stated, it is the output divided by the intake. Most machines have a low percentage of efficiency.

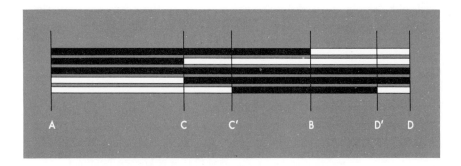

FIGURE 35: Amplitude of the muscle's action
AB–resting length of the muscle; **AC**–length at maximum contrac-
tion; **AD**–length at maximum elongation; **CD**–amplitude;
C'D'–optimum range within the amplitude

The human machine is no exception, though it is not inferior in efficiency
to most man-made machines. This low efficiency is due to a number
of things, such as production of heat, removal of lactic acid, viscosity of
the muscle cell, internal resistance of fascia and skin, mechanical disadvantage of the muscles and the levers, antagonistic muscle action,
inertia, gravity, and the large amount of internal work necessary.

If a muscle is deprived of its motor nerve, it exhibits certain changes.
It is incapable of response, i.e., it cannot contract or maintain tonus. If the
nerve supply is intact but the muscle is not used over a period of time,
the muscle becomes flaccid, probably will decrease in girth, potential
strength capacity is reduced, capillary function is decreased, and the
muscle cells take on more of the characteristics of the light cell rather
than the red muscle cell. This state of deterioriation is called *atrophy*.
On the other hand, regular systematic use of the muscle will produce
hypertrophy, in which each of the characteristics just noted will progress
in the opposite direction, thus making a muscle capable of very efficient
action.

CIRCULATORY SYSTEM

The outgoing channels of the circulatory system are the arteries,
arterioles, and capillaries; their responsibility is distribution of the blood.
The venules and veins have the opposite function, that of collecting the
blood from the diverse parts of the tissues. The medium of transportation
through these channels is the blood, and the central organ responsible for
its dispersion is the heart.

The heart behaves like the skeletal muscles in some respects, although there is automatic nervous stimulation with a regulatory mechanism. Contraction of the right side of the heart forces the blood into the pulmonary artery, leading to the lungs for aeration. Contraction of the left side of the heart forces the blood into the aorta, leading to the various tissues of the body.

The arteries and arterioles are elastic, allowing for increased pressure with each heart beat, and in turn adding pressure to help force the blood along. The capillaries carry the blood directly into the muscle tissue. Each capillary has comparatively few fibers to supply; the substances for the tissue pass from the blood into the lymph spaces around the fibers. This is a process known as transudation—a combination of filtration, osmosis, and diffusion. The amount of blood in the capillaries is controlled by the precapillary sphincter and is related to the ease with which substances pass from them into the tissues. The removal of materials from the tissues occurs by transudation back into the venous portions of the capillaries.

The blood is made up of at least two important parts from the standpoint of muscular activity—the fluid portion and the red corpuscles, which are carried in suspension. The red corpuscles contain hemoglobin. As they pass through the lungs the hemoglobin takes on oxygen in an unstable combination, from which the oxygen may be released in the tissues. On the other hand, the carbon dioxide is carried back to the lungs, partly in the hemoglobin of the red cells and partly as a carbonate in the plasma. It is discharged in the lungs in exchange for oxygen.

The plasma carries the glucose as it comes from the intestinal cavity. It is taken to the tissues if it is needed there, to the liver where it is stored until needed, or it may be converted into fat and stored as a still more stable reserve. The plasma also carries the various products of the endocrine glands, some of which have an effect on muscle growth, on the state of muscular stimulation and irritability, and on the process of metabolism in the muscle.

The white corpuscles are also carried in the blood. They are the protectors of practically all tissues of the body, and attack foreign organisms wherever found. They have no relationship to muscle contraction.

RESPIRATORY SYSTEM

The respiratory system is made up principally of the lungs; they connect with the buccal and nasal cavities which lead to the exterior. The alveoli constitute the main portion of the lungs and, because of their structure, present a large surface area for gaseous exchange with the blood. The bronchioles, trachea, and larynx connect the alveolar portions of the lungs and the upper cavities.

The epiglottis helps to prevent the entrance of anything except air into the lungs. When either liquid or food starts down the throat, the larynx rises, the base of the tongue is depressed, and the passageway into the trachea is closed.

Respiration is normally rhythmical and automatic, though to a certain extent it can be controlled by the will. When the carbon dioxide content of the blood reaches a certain point, it results in stimulation of the respiratory center in the medulla and the pulmonary ventilation is increased.

The aeration of the blood takes places through the walls of the alveoli into the blood stream. As the air is taken into the lungs, it has the dust and foreign substances filtered out; it is also warmed and humidified. There is a constant exchange of oxygen and carbon dioxide between the lungs and blood, because there is always some air remaining in the alveoli even after forced expiration. The rate of diffusion of these gases through the walls of the alveoli depends primarily upon the amount of each in the blood stream. This, in turn, depends upon the activity of the person at the time, the exchange being much greater in an active person than it is in an individual at rest.

Inspiration is brought about by contraction of the diaphragm, which lowers the thoracic floor, and by the contraction of muscles of the thorax which lift and rotate the ribs. The enlargement of the thoracic cavity allows the air to flow in. This is usually done slowly, although it may be fast, until the thorax feels fully distended.

Expiration may be quiet or forced. If quiet, the elastic recoil or the pressure of the ribs as they drop, and the abdominal pressure on the diaphragm as it relaxes, is sufficient to force the air out. When the expiration becomes very strong, the ribs are forced down by muscular action and the diaphragm is forced up by abdominal action. The rate and depth of respiration is usually dependent upon the activity of the individual and the needs of the tissues.

REFERENCES

1. Bangerter, Blauer L., and Barney, Vernon S., Comparison of Three Programs of Progressive Resistance Exercise, *Research Quarterly*, 32, May 1961, p. 138.
2. Brouha, Lucien, and Radford, Edward P., The Cardiovascular System in Muscular Activity, in *Science and Medicine of Exercise and Sports*, Warren Johnson (ed.), New York, Harper & Row, Pubs., 1960, p. 162.
3. Coërs, Christian, The Motor Unit, in *Therapeutic Exercise*, 2nd Ed., Sidney Licht (ed.), New Haven, Elizabeth Licht, Publisher, 1961.
4. Dubuisson, M., *Muscular Contraction*, Springfield, Ill., Charles C Thomas, 1954.
5. Fischer, Ernst, Physiology of Skeletal Muscles, in *Electrodiagnosis and Electromyography*, Sidney Licht (ed.), New Haven, Elizabeth Licht, Pub., 1960.

6. Guyton, Arthur C., *Textbook of Medical Physiology*, Philadelphia, W. B. Saunders Co., 1956, Ch. 5, Function of Skeletal and Smooth Muscle.
7. Hellebrandt, Frances A., Application of the Overload Principle to Muscle Training in Man, *American Journal of Physical Medicine*, 37, 1958, p. 278.
8. Hubbard, Alfred, Homokinetics: Muscular Function in Human Movement, in *Science and Medicine of Exercise and Sports*, Warren Johnson (ed.), New York, Harper & Row, Pubs., 1960, p. 7.
9. Huxley, H. E., The Contraction of Muscle, *Scientific American*, 199, 1958, p. 66.
10. Karpovich, Peter V., *Physiology of Muscular Activity*, Philadelphia, W. B. Saunders Co., 1953, Ch. 2, Skeletal Muscle.
11. Mommaerts, W.F.H.M., *Muscular Contraction*, New York, Interscience Publishers, Inc., 1950.
12. Morehouse, Laurence, and Miller, Augustus T., *Physiology of Exercise*, St. Louis, C. V. Mosby Co., 1948, Ch. 2, Contraction of Muscle.
13. Podalsky, Richard J., The Mechanism of Muscular Contraction, *American Journal of Medicine*, 30, 1961, p. 708.
14. Rasch, Philip J., and Burke, Roger K., *Kinesiology and Applied Anatomy*, Philadelphia, Lea & Febiger, 1959, Ch. 4, Physiology of Muscular Contraction.
15. Riedman, Sarah R., *The Physiology of Work and Play*, New York, Holt, Rinehart and Winston, Inc., 1950, Ch. 2, Muscular Contraction in Exercised Muscles; Ch. 4, Intrinsic Properties of Muscle; Ch. 5, Chemical Basis of Motion; Ch. 7, Muscles as Work Machines.
16. Riley, Richard L., Pulmonary Function in Relation to Exercise, in *Science and Medicine of Exercise and Sports*, Warren Johnson (ed.), New York, Harper & Row, Pubs., 1960, p. 162.
17. Szent-Györgyi, A., *Chemical Physiology of Contraction in Body and Heart Muscle*, New York, Academic Press, Inc., 1953.

CHAPTER **6**

Neural Bases of Movement

1. Conductivity is the primary characteristic of the neuron.
2. A synapse conducts impulses in one direction only.
3. The rate of conduction through the cell is dependent upon the diameter of the cell.
4. The neuron possesses a threshold below which a stimulus will not excite. This is variable with the condition of the cell.
5. A synapse will either facilitate or inhibit passage of an impulse.
6. Action potential indicates the strength of muscle action at that time.
7. A neuron may grow a replacement for an axon which is severed.

CELLULAR STRUCTURE

THE NERVOUS SYSTEM, like all other parts of the organism, is constructed of cells. These cells are unique in structure as a result of the function they must serve. The nervous system is a communication system and is required to connect with every tissue in every part of the body, no matter how great the distance from the brain. Early scientists theorized that the neural mass was a continuous filament from brain to finger or toe, on the assumptions that contiguous cells could not transmit impulses. However, this cellular unit is now well understood, and new evidence on the details of structure is rapidly accumulating from electron miscroscopic investigations.

The nerve cell is known as a *neuron*. It has the same component elements of any cell, i.e., plasma, nucleus, and membrane. The body of the cell is highly variable in size and shape, apparently dependent upon location in the nervous system. The smallest cells are no more than 4 or 5 microns in diameter while the largest may be nearly 100 microns. The characteristic aspect of the neuron is its multiple processes, extending from the cells in more or less opposite directions. These may vary in length from 2 or 3 microns to several feet.

The processes of the cell are classified according to the function which they serve. Those which conduct impulses to the cell body are called *dendrites*. Each cell usually has several dendrites, and each dendrite has multiple branchings, thus increasing the potential connections with other neurons. The dendrites contain Nissl substance the same as the cell body.

The second type of process is the *axon*, which transmits impulses to adjacent cells. Each cell has one axon. It is usually very long in comparison to the dendrites, and it lacks the Nissl substance found in the rest of the cell. The axon also has many branchings, and these are located near the end of the axon, which is much reduced in diameter at this point. It is the branches of the axon, sometimes called teladendria, that make contact with the dendrites of other cells. Where contact is made, the axon connection usually undergoes a slight swelling; this may be terminal or a contact as the axon passes a particular neuron.

The contact made between cells is called a *synapse*, a term given this junction by Sherrington. The membranes of the cells are not fused; they are not even completely in contact as shown by electron microscopy. Nerve impulses "jump" these synaptic spaces from axon to dendrite. Each axon may connect with many other neurons, and each neuron may receive impulses from hundreds of axons. The synapse is a one-way passage between the contiguous membranes.

There are two types of adaptations of these processes which are worth noting with respect to motor function. There are the receptor endings found in muscles, tendons, ligaments, and articulations. They are either free nerve endings or specialized corpuscles in which the nerve processes are embedded. These are specialized endings of the afferent nerves. They will be discussed in the chapter on kinesthesia.

The second adaptation is the motor ending. The skeletal muscle receives impulses from axons of motor neurons whose cell bodies are located in the spinal cord or brain. This myoneural junction is known as the *motor end-plate*. This motor nerve, sometimes designated as an alpha fiber, extends its axon into a muscle. The branches extend to many muscle fibers where the terminal branch is emplanted on the cell membrane. Each axon may connect with a few muscle fibers (less than 100) or with many (approximately 2000) depending upon the muscle and its use. The motor neuron, its axon and end-plates, and the muscle fibers activated by this motoneuron constitute the *motor unit*. The motor units with the smaller number of fibers are found in muscles such as those of the fingers where fine manipulations are possible, while the multicelled, larger unit is found in muscles such as those of the lower extremities where strength and gross movements are usual.

PROPERTIES OF NEURONS

The chief characteristic of the neuron is conductivity. This is a capacity found to some extent in most cells of the body. However, the neuron is particularly adept in this respect. The impulse is an electrochemical process which traverses from dendrite to axon terminal and across the synapse in serial fashion through the neural chain. The impulse is carried along the neuron without loss in magnitude of the impulse.

A neuron may be stimulated by an electrical impulse. This is the most common method of experimentation for study of nerve and muscle function. However, it may also be excited by chemical, thermal, or mechanical stimuli. Whatever the source of stimulus the impulse traveling the neuron and its resultant action are always the same.

The rate at which the impulse travels depends upon the size of the neuron and the location of the neuron. In general the larger the diameter of the axon the faster it conducts the impulse. It appears that nonmyelinated fibers have a lower conduction rate; there is lack of evidence for the cause of this difference. It is possible that the myelin sheath prevents spread and loss of impulse but more probable that it actually accelerates the impulse by the effect of its nodular arrangement.

After an impulse has been put into a neuron for transmission, there is a very brief interval in which no additional impulse may be initiated in the cell. This is followed immediately by another short interval in which only a stimulus which is stronger than the preceding one can be initiated. This is the refractory period (absolute and relative for the respective parts). This means not only that the nerve impulses are traveling as rapid-firing repetitions rather than as a continuous flow, but also that the maximum rate of firing in any particular neuron is determined by its dimensions.

There is a threshold in the neuron which sets the lower limits for strength of a stimulus necessary to excite the cell. A stronger stimulus produces the same results in the neuron as the minimal one which excites. Neurons vary in their excitability or threshold, and a particular one may vary from time to time. An example in the latter part of the refractory period was cited above. High frequency currents may be too brief to initiate a neural impulse, but likewise a continuous stimulus raises the threshold of excitability. In general the stronger the stimulus the shorter the time interval necessary for excitation. However, this is far from a rectilinear relationship.

A neuron which is destroyed has no capacity to restore itself from the fragments of the cell. However, in peripheral nerves, a severed axon does not always result in death of the cell, though the axon is absorbed and lost. In fact, many peripheral nerves rebuild an axon by slow growth out from the cell body. Such a regenerated axon may be of different length than that of its predecessor and connect with different muscle cells.

THE NERVOUS SYSTEM

The nervous system is divided into two parts—the central system and the peripheral system. For purposes of understanding differences in structure and function this classification is very helpful. However, it must be remembered that the two parts work together with continuous and highly complex control of the channels of impulse transmission.

The two divisions of the nervous system are composed of parts according to the following outline:

Central	*Peripheral*
Cerebrum	Cranial nerves 12 pairs
Cerebellum	Spinal nerves 31 pairs
Brain stem	Plexuses
Spinal cord	

The above outline represents extreme simplification. Some of the detail will be discussed briefly. The cerebral components make up most of the mass of the brain, and exhibit two distinct hemispheres, the right and the left. The cerebrum is a highly convoluted structure; some of the folds are particularly deep and distinct and are referred to as fissures. A thin, outer cortex is made up of the cell bodies, in contrast to the interior which is made up of the processes of the neurons in the cortex, and certain aggregates of cell masses which are referred to as ganglia. In study of excised tissues the cell bodies appear darker in color than the processes and connective structure in the interior. Hence, the terminology usually applied is descriptive. Gray matter is found in the cortex and ganglia and white matter in the remainder of the tissue. There is great similarity in detail from one subject to another.

The cerebellum is similar in many respects. It is fissured and convoluted, has a gray cortex, and islands of gray in the interior. It occupies the lower posterior portion of the cranial cavity. It is concerned with automatic control of posture and movement. It has areas for specific muscles and their control just as the cerebral hemispheres have highly specialized areas functionally. The cerebellum has neurons linking directly with parts of the cerebrum.

The brain stem is composed of several highly differentiated parts. It consists of a mixture of gray and white material built into pathways or tracts passing upward and downward. The brain stem connects the cerebrum, cerebellum, and the spinal cord for the diverse functions served by cranial nerves, reflex control of circulorespiratory action and visceral activities, motor action, and sensory information.

The spinal cord is a slightly oval structure in cross section but basically a cylindrical mass extending from the foramen magnum at the base of the skull down the neural arch of the vertebral column into the area of the upper lumbar region. Attached to the cord are pairs of nerves at successive levels, known as the spinal nerves.

A cross section of the cord shows that the gray matter is interiorly located in a butterfly-shaped pattern, two wings with a body between. The "tips of the wings" are designated as ventral and dorsal *horns* according to their direction. In general the ventral horns contain descending tracts and the dorsal horns the ascending tracts. The ventral horn contains bodies of neurons leaving by the anterior root to skeletal muscles or to automatic ganglia outside the cord.

The white matter of the cord surrounds the gray and contains both ascending and descending tracts and connecting fibers within the cord. A central fissure divides the white matter into right and left halves and therefore into six distinctive tracts—dorsal, lateral, and ventral on each side.

The neurons of the central nervous system have shorter processes in general than the peripheral ones. Arborization is greater, and axons are mainly unmyelinated. Further, the neurons are suspended on a connective tissue frame made up of special nonconducting cells, *neuroglia cells*. These are largely responsible for giving the structure and some protection to the very fragile neuron mass.

Further protection is afforded the central nervous system by the meninges, which form successive linings for the cranial and vertebral cavities and cover the brain and cord. A second protective factor is found in the cerebrospinal fluid, in which the brain and cord are more or less suspended. And finally, additional protectiveness is afforded by the bony structure of the cranium and vertebrae and by their respective articulations.

The components of the peripheral nervous system are divided in various ways usually determined by the use which a particular investigator, author, or teacher wishes to make of the categorization. This writer will then exercise the same privilege and use a very crude classification: sensory, motor, autonomic. The sensory neurons are afferent ones; the motor and autonomic are efferent. The autonomic nerves are not directly associated with motor performance so will not be considered further here.

Neurons are seldom situated alone. They lie more or less parallel to others. A nerve, such as a cranial or spinal nerve, is made up of hundreds of neurons. They are bound together by a connective tissue envelope. The fibers from the connective tissue run into the nerve and bind some of the neurons into smaller units, providing a more or less distinct sheath for each neuron. This connective tissue not only gives strength and support to the nerve but bears the capillary supply for the neurons. It is such a bundle of neurons that we will refer to now as nerves.

The cranial nerves are of lesser significance in gross motor function than are the spinal nerves. They are named in Table IV with motor functions

TABLE IV: Cranial Nerves Classified and Motor Functions Listed

Cranial Nerve	Type*	Motor Function
1. Olfactory	S	
2. Optic	S	
3. Oculomotor	M A	Movements of eye
4. Trochlear	M	Movements of eye
5. Trigeminal	S M	Movements of mandible
6. Abducens	M	Movements of eye
7. Facial	S M A	Facial movements
8. Acoustic	S	Equilibrium (and hearing)
9. Glossopharyngeal	S M A	Movement in throat
10. Vagus	S M A	Movements in throat (swallowing and breathing)
11. Accessory	M	Movement in throat, and of head and shoulder
12. Hypoglossal	M	Movement of tongue

* S = sensory, M = motor, A = Autonomic.

designated where motion occurs. Thus their relative nonapplicability will be noted. There are 12 pairs.

The spinal nerves are arranged in 31 pairs. Each single nerve is made up of a ventral and a dorsal root which emanate from the respective horns of the spinal cord. The ventral roots contain motor neurons which run to the skeletal muscles. All nerves above the mid-lumbar region also contain preganglionic cells of the autonomic system. The posterior root includes sensory fibers from skin, superficial or deep tissues, or even viscera. The posterior root includes a ganglion just outside the cord. Thus it is seen that a spinal nerve usually contains the three types of cells: sensory, motor, and autonomic. There are differences in the make-up of these nerves.

Table V at end of chapter lists the principal muscles of gross motor movements and the afferent and efferent nerve tracks. For the physical educator who deals with handicapped students and for the therapists, this should be an important reference.

The spinal nerves are classified in sequence down the spine.

Cervical	1–8
Thoracic	1–12
Lumbar	1–5
Sacral	1–5
Coccygeal	1

There is some variation in nerve supply to some muscles. This is further complicated by the fact that the spinal nerves unite with some five or six adjacent nerves to form a plexus. There are five of these plexuses, each named for the five regions of the spine but each drawing fibers from more than the nerves in the particular region of the spine.

PHYSIOLOGY OF NEURAL FUNCTION

A stimulus enters the nervous system through a receptor. The receptor may be either in the sensory organs, such as the eye or the ear, or in the motor system. The impulse thus initiated flows through the cell or sequence of cells to some part of the central nervous system. It may be carried into the brain, where cortical integration enables the individual to make a deliberate, considered response to the sensation. Or it may involve action of cerebellum and cerebral cortex in understanding disturbances of balance and learning to control the movement. Or it may be a stimulus which elicits a reflex response, and it is then channeled through the spinal cord by a single neuron connecting afferent and efferent neurons and thus action is prompt and automatic.

The excitation wave involves movement of ions in the cell and this can be traced by an action potential. Within a single cell the excitation wave spreads throughout the cell, i.e., it may travel in any direction in the cell, though normally it arrives in a dendrite and flows through the cell body and on through the axon. The synapse is a "one-way thoroughfare" for the impulses. The process of crossing a synapse can take place only in the presence of acetylcholine. This process is not too thoroughly demonstrated at present, but the acetylcholine appears to be produced by the synaptic ending of the excited neuron. It fills the gap between the two cells, causing increased permeability of the adjacent neuron so that an impulse is initiated in the next cell.

The action at the end-plate and muscle fiber is apparently of the same type as synaptic passage. Acetylcholine has been found present here also, and impulse flow in the muscle cell has also been demonstrated. It is much slower than in the nerve cell.

A single stimulus in a motor neuron produces a single, brief muscle twitch. A stronger stimulus reaches more muscle fibers and produces a stronger contraction. Stimuli repeated at a rapid rate result in prolonged contraction or tetanus in the motor units involved. Sustained positions are possible through sequential firing of stimuli in which different motor units work in rotation but maintain approximately the same amount of effort against the resistance.

A muscle response to a stimulus may be involuntary and is called a reflex. These may be very simple, with connections at the cord level as mentioned above. Some of these appear to be inherent in the organism and apparently associated with safeguarding the organism or some part of it. For example, the knee jerk in response to tapping (sudden stretching) of the quadriceps, the flexor reaction to pain in the hand or foot, or blinking in response to something moving quickly toward the eyes, are all involuntary and noncerebral-connected. These are spinal reflexes.

On the other hand, responses which are more or less reflex in type may have cortical connections based on associations and previously guided or selected responses. Repetition of the experience has established channels through which the impulse will travel in the future. Through such a process we achieve *learned responses* and ability to perform skills of even a complex nature in the same way time after time. This is a conditioned reflex.

It has long been recognized that as a given muscle is stimulated to action its antagonists are inhibited. Theories have varied on this process and therefore methods of study have varied. At present it appears probable that certain neurons produce an inhibiting substance which raises the threshold of the postsynaptic cell membrane, just as others produce the acetylcholine which promotes the transmission of the impulse. Further studies point to the cerebellum, the spinal cord, and spinal ganglia as sites in which inhibitory effects are produced and the resultant reciprocal innervation is promoted.

The point at which a motor nerve enters the muscle is known as the motor point of that muscle. Since at this spot there is a concentration of nerve impulses, and since the electrical potential of the nerve cell is essentially the same as that which travels into the muscle cell on stimulation, it is the preferred point at which to pick up information on muscle action. In studies of muscle action and co-operation, the electrodes are placed over (or in) the motor point. The process of electromyography picks up the action current, amplifies it, and records it. Such studies are adding considerable information on muscle functions and integration of effort of various muscles in a given act.

We are prone to assume that fatigue occurs in neurons just as it does in muscles. Actually the neuron seldom, if ever, becomes unable to transmit impulses as a result of continued use. The same is probably true of the myoneural junction. Passage of repeated stimuli may make the synapse more resistant. This is particularly true in the ganglia. Here the threshold increases and the rate of transmission decreases. This fatigue or inhibition of the ganglion cells is a unique characteristic. The level of resistance and the recovery rate vary from one ganglion to another. Each also has its own pattern of response to incoming stimuli. The ramifications of synaptic connections in any ganglion are almost numberless, and each ganglion is a unique entity.

NEURAL BASES OF MOVEMENT SENSATIONS

The special senses of the human organism are frequently referred to as being five in number, i.e., sight, hearing, taste, smell, and touch. There is a sixth which is being recognized much more generally by the various scientific disciplines. It is *kinesthesis,* or sensation of body movement and position. It is a complex function made up of so many contributing parts that it may properly be considered as separate entities rather than as a single sense. The knowledge of morphological and physiological bases of the kinesthetic sense is far more meager than that of the other senses. Nevertheless, some facts are worth noting.

Proprioceptors

A sensation is a recognition of stimuli impinging on the organization. Since the nervous system is the communication system of the body, these stimuli must affect the neurons. Stimuli enter the nervous system through special nerve endings, receptors. If the source of the stimulus is outside the body they are called exteroceptors. If the source of the stimulus is inside the body they are called interoceptors. It is to this latter class that the nerve endings associated with kinesthesis belong. Those located in the motor mechanism, i.e., the muscles, tendons, and articulations, are in a subclass, the proprioceptors. These are of several types.

The muscle *splindle* is a highly specialized structure of fusiform design. It consists of a bundle of smaller (in cross section) cells which are surrounded by a thin connective tissue capsule which attaches in the same manner as does the membrane enclosing the usual muscle fiber. The cells which are within these capsules are variable in number but less than ten, and are referred to as *intrafusal* fibers in contrast to those outside making the bulk of the muscle, the *extrafusal* ones.

The spindle is situated parallel with the extrafusal fibers in that part of the muscle. For the most part they are located in the belly of the muscle, more toward the origin than the insertion.

The intrafusal fibers are more slender on the ends than in the mid-area. These ends are striated and are contractile. The mid-section of the intrafusal fiber is not striated, has a concentration of nuclei and is encased by a connective tissue tube separated from the fiber by a lymph space. It is in this area that the neural connections are found.

To each of the intrafusal fibers there extends a large afferent neuron

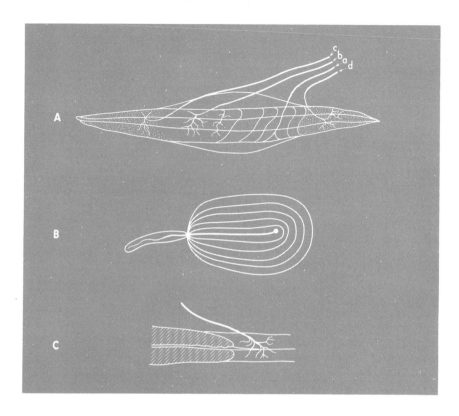

FIGURE 36: Proprioceptive receptors
A–Muscle spindle–a–annulospiral ending, b–flower spray,
c and d–alpha fibers; B–Pacinian corpuscle; C–Golgi ending

which is coiled around the fiber and therefore is commonly called the *annulospiral* receptor. It is invariably found associated with the intrafusal fiber. There is a second ending which is not consistently present. This is called a *flower spray* ending because of its multiple branchings. In addition to these there are small efferent neurons which terminate in neuromotor end-plates in each end of the intrafusal fiber. It will be recalled that each extremity is striated and contractile. These efferent neurons are *gamma efferents*. The efferents to the extrafusal fibers are *alpha fibers*.

The intrafusal fibers through their neural connections in the nuclear area, the annulospiral and the spray endings, are responsive to stretch. Even slight stretch is picked up by the annulospiral ending, particularly that produced by contraction of the muscle. The spray ending, on the other hand, is stimulated by passive stretching of the muscle and is fairly sensitive to minute amounts of stretch. The stretch stimulus is relieved by the contraction of the extrafusal fibers, but after contraction takes place there is corresponding shortening of the intrafusal fibers and so they are again sensitive to stretch.

The second of the stretch receptors is found in the tendon of the muscles in branched neural endings known as the *Golgi tendon organs.* These are distributed most generously near the connection with the muscle fibers, but in the tendon proper. These endings have a much higher threshold, that is, require a much more pronounced stretch than do the spiral endings in the muscle. The Golgi endings are stimulated whether it is a passive stretch of the muscle or it is active contraction.

There is still another proprioceptive ending, the *Pacinian corpuscle.* These are located in the fascia, tendon sheaths, ligaments, joint capsule and articular cartilages. They are essentially of the same form as those found in the dermis, with high frequency in finger tips, palms, plantar surface of the feet, lips, and other areas where there is high discrimination of touch and other pressure.

The afferent neurons connect with others in the central nervous system. The stretch reflex is apparently the only monosynaptic connection. Otherwise these neurons feed stimili into several or many others. For example, it is known that stretching of the muscle will produce positive or facilitating effects on the synergists, as well as the muscle stretched, and an inhibiting effect on antagonists. All participate because of neural transmission.

Many types of control appear to be operating. The annulospiral stimulation activates the intrafusal cells as well as extrafusal to eliminate tension. The annulospiral stimulus can also be triggered by action of either alpha or gamma efferents. As the muscle shortens, the less effective is the gamma-stimulated adjustment and facilitation of muscle contraction, although they do keep the intrafusal cells adjusted in length to varying lengths of the muscle, so that they will remain sensitive. Further the Golgi endings appear to produce an inhibiting effect on the gamma neurons of the same muscle. Granit[6] further summarizes the relationship between alpha and gamma reflexes as "linked, co-excited, and co-inhibited." No real contradiction to this has been cited, though much remains to be studied.

The inhibition which is exerted on certain motoneurons has been recognized for a long time but never fully understood. It is possible that certain neurons facilitate the synaptic firing while others inhibit it. If one accepts the premise that impulses travel from one cell to another with changing tissue potential and with chemical requirements, then this difference might readily be explained by differences in chemical produced. This too needs further study. It is also known that the spinal and supraspinal tracts show both inhibitory and facilitatory effects and doubtless further knowledge of their processes enters into full understanding of the inter-relationship of control.

It may seem contradictory to state that voluntary movement involves sensory or afferent information as well as an intact efferent system. In other words, movement is not just spontaneously originated. This is per-haps another way of saying that a sensation has meaning to the organism only as it is interpreted and acted upon.

The area of the brain long labeled motor area, is a sensorimotor area. The efferent impulses are channeled to the muscles not only from that area but from other cortical areas as well. It appears, in fact, that areas other than the so-called motor area are responsible for the more complex co-ordinations.

In a deeper layer of the motor area are large neurons known as pyram-idal cells. Each connects, apparently directly, with a specific motor unit. These are joined by many smaller neurons, apparently arising from gan-glia in all parts of the brain. These make up the pyramidal tract. These pass into the mesencephalon, the pons, and the medulla and on into the spinal cord. The majority go to the opposite side of the cord into lateral sections and the rest continue uncrossed into lateral or ventral sections. It is known that stimuli traveling down the pyramidal tract to the muscles also spread stimuli into other cortical ganglia, the sensory area, the cerebellum, and the pons. Thus the basis for an integrative function is laid. Too little is known of the nature of these interconnections and their respective functions.

Reflexes make up a considerable number of the responses. A minimum of two neurons is involved, an afferent and an efferent. These would of necessity be concerned with a single segment only. Most reflexes involve several segments of the cord, and there is involvement of one or more internuncial or connecting neurons. These neurons may be short or long and make up a considerable part of the white columns of the cord.

Many of the reflexes serve a protective function. For example, the eye blink avoids entrance of damaging foreign bodies and irritation of the eye. The stretch reflex maintains tonus, especially in antigravity muscles. Likewise, although sudden stretch produces relaxation or release of con-traction, this is probably at cord level and represents controlling action of the internuncial cells. Closely related is the contraction of extensors of the lower extremity from pressure in the plantar surface. This is most obvious with the young child learning to stand. These reflexes may also be responsible for the alternating support and swing characterizing the gait.

While the cord function is largely that of integration and reflexes, the other parts of the central nervous system have other types of control.

The subcortical areas are mainly facilitatory or inhibitory. Facilitation is achieved by cells of the lower portions of the brain acting primarily on the extensor muscles for support against gravital pull. Likewise in part of the medulla and pons is a small inhibitory area, which serves to counter or cancel some of the processes of facilitation. This area is apparently not acting independently but rather as a connecting channel for inhibitory areas of the cortex.

Labyrinth

Another source of movement sensation is situated far from the motor mechanism. It is the labyrinth of the inner ear, located in the petrous portion of the temporal bone. The labyrinth is made up of two tiny chambers; the smaller is the *saccule,* probably not associated with the movement sensation, and the larger chamber is the *utricle.* Opening off the utricle are three bony canals in a half-loop form, the *semicircular canals.* The canals and utricle are also known as the *vestibular apparatus.* This entire area is lined with a very thin epithelial membrane which secretes a small amount of lymphlike fluid that partially fills the labyrinth.

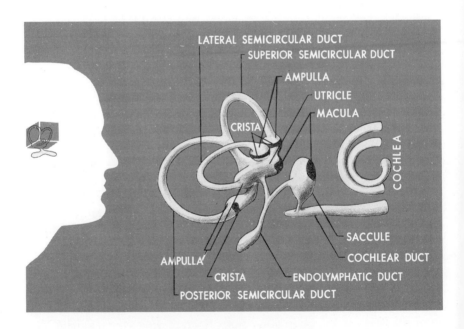

FIGURE 37: Diagram of the ear
From *Three Unpublished Drawings of the Anatomy of the Human Ear,* by Max Brödel, by permission of W. B. Saunders, Publishers.

The canals are three in number in each ear, they lie approximately at right angles to each other, and they correspond in this respect to the three primary planes of the body. Each canal lies in exactly the same plane as its counterpart in the opposite ear. One end of each canal is slightly enlarged, and it is in this area, known as the *ampulla,* that the sensory ending is located.

In the wall of the ampulla the epithelial cells become more columnar and exhibit ciliated projections from their surface. Over these cilia is a slightly gelatinous mass, still leaving them highly pliable. The effect of this total arrangement is a localized mound known as the *crista.* The nerve ending lies beneath the epithelial cell and is attached to its base.

As the head is moved quickly, the lymph in the canals appears to flow through the canal, just as water in a dish spills because it does not move as the dish is moved quickly. The movement over the crista drags on the cilia, and the tension so created in the cell stimulates the receptor. This is thus a source of information regarding angular acceleration of the head or the body.

Suspended in the endolymph of the utricle are very thin calcium concretions known as *otoliths.* In the lining of the utricle are sensory cells similar to those of the ampullae. Gravitational pull keeps the otoliths on these sensory mounds (the maculae) in the bottom of the utricle, whereas an inverted position of the head allows them to rest on different endings. These receptors are then the source of information relative to static positions and linear acceleration.

This area is connected to the central nervous system by the vestibular nerve. Most of the fibers of this nerve terminate in a specific vestibular area near the junction of the pons and the medulla. Other fibers and connecting neurons go to other parts of the medulla and to the cerebellum. It is these portions of the hindbrain that control equilibrium. This is done as a reflex action through the appropriate facilitation and inhibition from efferent neurons leaving the pons and medulla.

REFERENCES

1. Brazier, Mary A., *The Electrical Activity of the Nervous System,* London, Sir Isaac Pitman, 1951.
2. Coërs, Christian, and Wolf, A. L., *The Innervation of Muscle,* Springfield, Ill., Charles C Thomas, 1959.
3. Eccles, John C., *Physiology of Nerve Cells,* Baltimore, The Johns Hopkins Press, 1957.
4. Gardner, Ernest, *Fundamentals of Neurology,* Philadelphia, W. B. Saunders Co., 1958, Ch. 10, Control of Muscular Activity.
5. Guyton, Arthur C., *Textbook of Medical Physiology,* Philadelphia, W. B. Saunders Co., 1956, Ch. 4, Function of Nerves and of the Myoneural Junction; Ch. 7, Neurophysiology.

6. Granit, Ragnar, *Receptors and Sensory Perception,* New Haven, Yale University Press, 1955, Ch. 6, Muscle Receptors and Their Reflexes; Ch. 7, Spinal and Supraspinal Control of Posture and Movement.

7. Henry, Franklin, and Rogers, Donald E., Increased Response Latency for Complicated Movements and a "Memory Drum" Theory of Neuromotor Reaction, *Research Quarterly,* 31, 1960, p. 448.

8. Loofbourrow, G. N., Neuromuscular Integration, in *Science and Medicine of Exercise and Sports,* Warren R. Johnson (ed.), New York, Harper & Row, Pubs., 1960, p. 80.

9. Mainland, Donald, *Anatomy,* New York, Paul B. Hoeber, Inc., 1945, Ch. 15, Brain and Spinal Cord.

10. Nachmansohn, David, *Chemical and Molecular Bases of Nerve Activity,* New York, Academic Press, 1959.

11. Rasch, Philip J., and Burke, Roger K., *Kinesiology and Applied Anatomy,* Philadelphia, Lea & Febiger, 1959, Ch. 5, Neural Control and Motor Learning.

12. Ruch, Theodore C., and Fulton, John F. (eds.), *Medical Physiology and Biophysics,* Philadelphia, W. B. Saunders Co., 1960.

13. Sherrington, Sir Charles, *The Integrative Action of the Nervous System,* 2nd ed., New Haven, Yale University Press, 1947.

14. Tasaki, Ichiji, *Nervous Transmission,* Springfield, Ill., Charles C Thomas, 1953.

15. Walthard, Karl M., and Tchicaloff, Michel, Motor Points, in *Electrodiagnosis and Electromyography,* Sidney Licht (ed.), New Haven, Elizabeth Licht, Pub., 1956.

16. Wiggers, Carl J., *Physiology in Health and Disease,* 5th ed., Philadelphia, Lea & Febiger, 1949, Sec. II, Physiology of Peripheral and Central Nervous System.

TABLE V: Principal Muscles and Neural Supply (Motor)

Muscles	Nerves	Muscles	Nerves
TRUNK ANTERIOR		**SHOULDER—LATERAL**	
rectus abdominis	Th 7,8,9,10,11	middle deltoid	C 5,6
external oblique	Th 7,8,9,10,11	supraspinatus	C 5,6
internal oblique	Th 9,10,11		
transversalis	Th 7,8,9,10,11		
sternocleido-mastoid	11th cranial; C 2, 3	**SHOULDER—POSTERIOR**	
		infraspinatus	C 5,6
TRUNK-POSTERIOR		teres minor	C 5
erector spinae	(Spinal nerves corresponding to successive fasciculi)	triceps	C 7,8
		posterior deltoid	C 5,6
splenius	C 5,6,7,8	**SHOULDER—MEDIAL**	
latissimus dorsi	C 6,7,8	teres major	C 5,6
quadratus lumborum	thoracic 12; lumbar 1,2	latissimus dorsi	C 6,7,8
		subscapularis	C 5,6
SHOULDER GIRDLE —ANTERIOR		**ELBOW—ANTERIOR**	
		biceps	C 5,6
subclavius	C 5	brachialis anticus	C 5,6
pectoralis minor	C 5,6,7,8; Th 1	pronator teres	C 6
serratus anterior	C 5,6,7		
SHOULDER GIRDLE —POSTERIOR		**ELBOW—LATERAL**	
		brachioradialis	C 7,8
levator scapulae	C 3,4	supinator	C 6
trapezius	11th cranial; C 3,4	extensor carpi radialis longus	C 6,7
rhomboids	C 5	extensor carpi radialis brevis	C 6,7
		extensor communis digitorum	C 7
SHOULDER—ANTERIOR		extensor carpi ulnaris	C 7
pectoralis major	C 5,6,7,8; Th 1		
anterior deltoid	C 5,6	**ELBOW—POSTERIOR**	
coracobrachialis	C 7		
biceps	C 5,6	triceps	C 7,8

TABLE V (Cont'd.): **Principal Muscles and Neural Supply**

Muscles	Nerves	Muscles	Nerves
ELBOW—MEDIAL		pyriformis	S 1,2
flexor carpi radialis	C 6	quadratus femoris	L 5, S 1
		obturator internus	S 1,2,3
flexor carpi ulnaris	C 8; Th 1	obturator external	L 3,4
palmaris longus	C 6	gemellus superior	S 1,2,3
flexor sublimis digitorum	C 7, 8; Th 1	gemellus inferior	L 5; S 1
		HIP—MEDIAL	
WRIST—ANTERIOR		pectineus	L 2,3,4
flexor profundus digitorum	C 8; Th 1	gracilis	L 3,4
pronator quadratus	C 8; Th 1	adductor magnus	L 3,4
flexor longus pollicis	C 8; Th 1	adductor brevis	L 3,4
		adductor longus	L 3,4
WRIST—POSTERIOR		KNEE—ANTERIOR	
extensor longus pollicis	C 7	vastus internes	L 2,3,4
extensor brevis pollicis	C 7	vastus externus	L 2,3,4
		vastus intermedius	L 2,3,4
		rectus femoris	L 2,3,4
HIP—ANTERIOR			
iliopsoas	L 1,2,3,4	KNEE—POSTERIOR	
rectus femoris	L 2,3,4	semitendinosus	L 4,5; S 1,2,3
sartorius	L 2,3,4	semimembranosus	L 4,5; S 1,2,3
		biceps femoris	L 4,5; S 1,2,3
HIP—LATERAL		sartorius	L 2,3,4
gluteus medius	L 4,5; S 1	gracilis	L 3,4
gluteus minimus	L 4,5; S 1	gastrocnemius	S 1,2
tensor fasciae latae	L 4,5; S 1		
		ANKLE—ANTERIOR	
HIP—POSTERIOR		tibialis anticus	L 4,5; S 1
gluteus maximus	L 5; S 1,2	peroneus tertius	L 4,5; S 1,2
semitendinosus	L 4,5; S 1,2,3	extensor longus digitorum	L 4,5; S 1
semimembranosus	L 4,5; S 1,2,3	extensor longus hallucis	L 4,5; S 1
biceps femoris	L 4,5; S 1,2,3		

TABLE V (Cont'd.): Principal Muscles and Neural Supply

Muscles	Nerves	Muscles	Nerves
ANKLE—POSTERIOR		FOOT—DORSAL	
gastrocnemius	S 1,2	Extensor brevis digitorum	L 4,5; S 1
soleus	S 1,2		
tibialis posterior	L 5; S 1		
peroneus longus	L 4,5; S 1	FOOT—PLANTAR	
peroneus brevis	L 4,5; S 1	flexor brevis digitorum	L 4,5; S 1,2,3
flexor longus digitorum	L 5; S 1	flexor brevis hallucis	L 4,5; S 1,2,3
flexor longus hallucis	L 5; S 1,2		

Part II

MECHANICS

CHAPTER 7

Motion

1. Motion requires some force to produce it.
2. The location of the point of application of force to an object determines the type of motion resulting.
3. Most human motions are rotatory.
4. The articulations of a segmented object determine the type of motion which can take place.
5. The type of support given any object determines the type of motion which can take place.

MOTION IS USUALLY thought of as an observable change of position. This definition limits motion to that which is perceived by the eye and thereby fails to be all-inclusive. There are certain movements which proceed so slowly that the changing position is not perceived. Likewise, motion in space without a point of reference may not be perceived readily. At the other extreme, motion may take place so rapidly that detail or even the motion itself is not clear. For example, the propeller blade of an airplane turns so rapidly that one sees only the blurred circle, not the moving blade. For observational purposes, fast movement is often reduced to slow-motion film or other pictorial records.

Since motion is a change in position, it must be a term defining change relative to something else. For example, the fingers flex on the palm, the elbow flexes on the upper arm. The pedestrian moves slowly with respect to the sidewalk, but the runner moves quickly around the track. This introduces a qualitative variation in the movement that may be beyond the observable range at both extremes.

Rest is also a relative term. An object is said to be at rest when its position with respect to some point, line, or surface remains unchanged. While these definitions serve a purpose, they may be misleading. For example, one may sit quietly in a chair—a state of rest; but at the same time one could be typing rapidly. The hands are moving with some speed but not in a wide range, merely covering the keyboard. Human motion then varies from many precise movements with little physical work performed to a wide range of heavy work with the total body and heavy resistance involved.

There are two basic types of motion; all movement illustrates one of these two. In one the object is carried as a whole in whatever position it may be—for example, the passenger in a car is carried forward by the vehicle. In the other type, the body or its parts move around a point of contact or around a central point known as the axis of rotation. This point may be within the body or outside it; it does not require a fixed support or contact as shown by the diver on a somersault or twist dive.

In considering the differences between these two types of movement, let us first define them in general terms and apply them to inanimate objects. Assume that an object is moving as a whole, and every point in that object describes a straight line in the direction of the motion. Each of these lines is parallel to every other line so described. The result is a simple progression of the total object and is known as *translatory motion*.

When there is some point that serves as a center, and every point in the object describes an arc about that center, it is known as *rotatory motion*. All points will move in concentric fashion around this axis of rotation. The terms *linear* and *angular* motion are sometimes used as synonyms of translatory and rotatory motion, respectively.

In a freely suspended body, the axis of rotation is at the point that is the center of gravity of the object at that moment. In a supported object, or one in contact with another surface, the axis is at the contact point or in a nearby articulation.

Translatory motion may take place in any of three primary planes, as illustrated in Figure 38, or in any intermediate plane. The plane bb' represents a straight forward or backward motion, cc' a direct lateral one, and aa' a straight vertical or up and down movement. The planes here illustrated all lie at right angles to each other.

Rotatory motion may take place around either of two axes. The longitudinal one runs the length of the object. The transverse one runs across the object at any level in its entire length. The transverse axis may also extend in any direction. Figure 38 diagrams these axes. The line aa' represents the longitudinal axis. The lines bb' and cc' represent two positions of the transverse axis, each located at right angles to the other but at the same level. An indefinite number of positions for the transverse axis might be established between these two or at different levels along the total height of the object.

Rotation around the longitudinal axis may be described as clockwise or counterclockwise. Rotation around a transverse axis is described as forward or backward. Forward is the same as clockwise, assuming the clock used for reference faces the performer's left. Backward rotation is counterclockwise or in the opposite direction in the above situation.

The various segments of the body are attached to each other, and all movements of these segments are rotations around the articulating point in exactly the same sense that the pendulum rotates about its point of

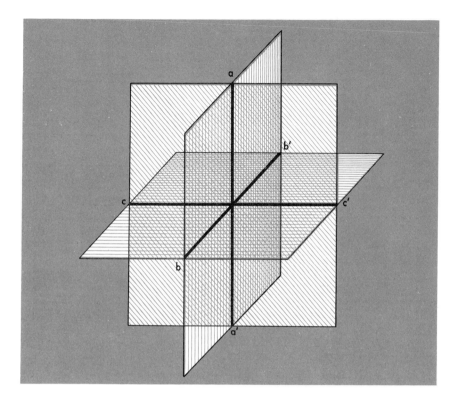

FIGURE 38: Axes of Motion
aa′–a vertical axis; bb′–a transverse axis; cc′–another transverse axis

support. Thus it can be seen that the movements of flexion, extension, abduction, or adduction in any joint are rotatory motions around the axis of the joint.

Almost the only time the human body experiences pure translatory motion is when it is carried by some means, is pushed, is pulled, or glides over a slippery surface. When the whole body is propelled from one place to another, the end-result is translation. After a series of steps forward, the body may appear to have experienced translatory motion. Actually this is accomplished by a series of movements of the segments, each movement being rotatory. Furthermore, there has been contact of the foot with the ground and rotation has occurred at the point of contact. Thus, whether our locomotion is forward, backward, sideward, or vertical, it is the result of rotation at two or more points.

In addition to rotation of the segments, we may experience rotation around either of the two axes of the total body. If movement occurs around the longitudinal axis, there is a spinning or twisting of the body. It occurs around a transverse axis in diving and in some tumbling stunts. In the twist dives there is movement around both axes.

Some force is required to produce all motion. The place at which that force is applied to an object, and the other conditions and forces affecting the object, determine the type of motion resulting. If force is applied to the midpoint of a uniform cylindrical body resting on its side, that body will roll, or if the surface is very slippery and the friction is reduced to a minimum, the body may slide straight forward. The first is rotation around the longitudinal axis; the second is translatory motion. If, however, that force is applied a little nearer one end, than the other, the movement will no longer be straight ahead but will be in an arc with a long radius. As the force is moved nearer the end, this rotation becomes more marked and the radius shortens. When the force is applied at one end, rotation will be around the center of the body.

Thus the farther the force is applied from the center of the object, the greater the effectiveness of that force for rotation about that center. This tendency of a force to produce rotation is called the *moment of rotation*. The moment of rotation, or moment of the rotatory force, may be defined as the force times the radius of application, the radius being at right angles to the force.

REFERENCES

1. Goddy, William, and Reinhold, Margaret, Some Aspects of Human Orientation in Space, *Brain*, 76, 1953, p. 337.
2. Steindler, Arthur, *Kinesiology of the Human Body*, Springfield, Ill., Charles C Thomas, 1955, Ch. 8, Measurement and Computation of Bodily Motion.
3. ————, *Mechanics of Normal and Pathological Locomotion in Man*, Springfield, Ill., Charles C Thomas, 1935, Ch. 3, Relation of the General Laws of Mechanics to Human Motion.

8

Physical Principles of Internal Action

EFFICIENCY OF THE MACHINE

1. The action of a muscle depends upon its structure, i.e., length and cross section of fibers, angle of application, and relative lengths of the lever arms.
2. Physiologically, internal and external work are similar.
3. The relative lengths of lever arms determines the effectiveness of the lever.
4. The location of the axis of the lever determines the way in which the lever functions.
5. Levers differ in value; the first class is primarily for balance, the second for economy of effort, the third for speed and range of motion.
6. Muscle have two components in their pull through most of the range.

WORK

Work IS A WORD that is used to mean many things and has many connotations. For example, under that heading are included physical labor, mental effort directed toward some goal, the earning of a livelihood, and any tedious and boring activity as contrasted with enjoyable occupations. None of these meanings, however, is the same as the technical meaning which must be considered here in its relationship to motion.

In terms used by the physical scientist or the engineer, *work is the overcoming of resistance,* and more specifically in quantitative terms it is *the product of the force exerted times the distance covered* ($W = FD$). Resistance may be of various types but is principally gravity, inertia, and friction.

This definition requires that there be motion in the direction of the force and implies outward results. In this sense the pillars or foundations of a building do no work. They may support a tremendous weight but, since they merely hold it in place, they are not working.

A corollary of the definition of work is that of force. Force is anything which produces motion or change of motion. As applied to work three things must be considered, namely, magnitude, direction, and point of application. Magnitude is usually measured in terms of gravitational units, i.e., pounds, grams, or kilograms. The point at which it applies to an object and the direction with respect to that object are both important. This is often illustrated diagrammatically. The size or amount of the force is shown by the relative length of the lines representing the forces. The force acts in the direction of the arrows which are attached to the line of force and at the point on the object to which the line is attached.

Obviously the distance through which a force works must be expressed in linear units, feet, centimeters, or meters. Carrying the work definition to its finish, the result is a product of force and distance units. Work is thus always expressed in units of foot-pounds, gram-centimeters, or kilogram-meters.

This may be applied to the operation of the human motor system. Movements of any or all parts of the body are work. The force producing the work is in almost all cases contraction of the muscles. The occasional exception will be discussed later. This muscular contraction has already been described as a result of nervous stimulation, made possible and accompanied by a chemical process. This total phenomenon of contraction usually results in a shortening and thickening of the muscle without change in volume. The force with which it contracts and the distance through which it contracts determine the work performed, It is obvious that this process of contraction requires a food and oxygen supply, results in waste products, and may result in muscular fatigue.

Muscles may also serve the same function as the pillars of a building. When the body or any of its parts are held in position, that support must come from the muscles. The process of contraction is exactly the same, except that the muscle does not shorten. Or external resistance may be added till the muscle cannot exert sufficient force to move the resistance. Muscular contraction in that case may be greater than when movement takes place, but there are no external measures of it. When a body part is controlled so that gravity will not cause it to drop suddenly, there is muscular contraction opposing but not producing the movement. In all cases the process in the muscle is identical except for the absence of actual shortening of the distance between the two ends of the muscle.

It is necessary, therefore, to differentiate between internal and external work. Physiologically they are very similar; mechanically they are different.

The work equivalents and the energy costs are frequently of interest to the student of movement. One foot-pound of work is the lifting of one pound of resistance through one foot. In calorie equivalents, one foot-pound equals 0.324 calories, or three foot-pounds equal approximately one calorie. Performance of certain work or sport skills can be translated into work load and calorie expenditure. This was done by many investigators in the early attempts to determine work cost and efficiency. Passmore and Durnin[15] comprehensively reviewed the many studies published on this topic. Their summary of studies on walking rate is of interest. It appears that at rates up to 6.5 km./hr. (approximately 4 m.p.h.) there is a straight line increase in calorie cost in relation to speed increments. However in the range of 7 to 10 km./hr. the cost goes up abruptly, being twice as costly at 10 as at 6.5.

Passmore and Durnin[15] also studied various factors in relation to cost of walking and found that age and sex had no effect, but weight did. Table VI shows the increased cost at each rate for the various weights.

TABLE VI: Energy Expenditure (cal./min.) Variations with Speed of Walking and Gross Body Weight

Speed (m.p.h.)	80	100	120	Weight (lbs.) 140	160	180	200
2.0	1.9	2.2	2.6	2.9	3.2	3.5	3.8
3.0	2.7	3.1	3.6	4.0	4.4	4.8	5.3
4.0	3.5	4.1	4.7	5.2	5.8	6.4	7.0

Walking cost is also known to vary according to the surface on which one walks. Passmore and Durnin[15] present figures on this also. The following are illustrative:

Walking 5.5 km./hr. on asphalt paving = 5.6 cal./min.
Walking 5.3 km./hr. on ploughed field = 7.6 cal./min.

Recent interest in weight control has raised popular interest in energy cost at various sports and other leisure pursuits. The comparative cost of sports is available from several sources.[9, 12, 13, 15] The discrepancies which are found among them are doubtless due to varying conditions such as wind which would affect canoeing, bicycling, and running; surface on which the activity is done; size of the tires and weight of the bicycle; weight of the performers. Passmore and Durnin[15] have pulled together some comparative figures on another type of recreational pursuit —playing of musical instruments. These may also be subject to some variability according to weight of the subject, but since these do not involve gross movement of the total body, that should be less significant. Samples from their table of indoor recreation:

sitting at ease	1.6 cal./min.
sitting, playing drums	4.0–4.2 cal./min.
sitting, playing organ	3.2–3.5 cal./min.
sitting, playing violin	2.7 cal./min.
sitting, playing cello	2.6 cal./min.
sitting, playing piano	2.5 cal./min.
standing, conducting orchestra	2.5 cal./min.
sitting, playing flute	2.2 cal./min.
sitting, playing accordion	2.2 cal./min.

All such studies have been subject to errors of various types, not the least of which is variation in techniques of performing the skills. For example, many of the bicycle studies have been done on the bicycle ergometer where balance is not involved, therefore energy cost is probably not as high as on the road. Much more work needs to be done to determine such things as the extent to which the unskilled and inefficient movement is more costly than the skilled, the fast than the slower movement, and how much higher a price the obese must pay in different activities than the slender person.

The actual energy costs of work are frequently cited as a basis for doubting the efficiency of exercise in weight control. Present estimates of energy costs are not far enough in error to affect that argument. However, such conclusions fail to take into account the effect of exercise on metabolic rate and in establishment of modified habits of exercise and diet.

FIBER ARRANGEMENTS AND WORK OF THE MUSCLE

Since the muscle is the source of force for most of the movements of the body, it is essential to consider some of the factors determining the amount of force the muscle can produce. It is well known that the muscles of the legs can exert more force than those of the arms in most individuals, that a given muscle can exert more force after it has been exercised regularly for a period of time than it could before the exercise, and that there are variations from one subject to another in the strength of a given muscle. There is no simple answer to all of these examples and others like them, for there are many factors affecting the ability of the subject to produce force in a given task. However, there is one factor which is related to all of these examples.

The muscle fiber is the structural unit of the muscle and contracts to its fullest extent when stimulated. The single cell is capable of a certain amount of force, the amount being dependent upon its diameter or fibril content. Functionally, the cell does not act as a separate unit. The motor unit is activated to its fullest extent when stimulated. Therefore, the strength of the motor unit, or the smallest functional unit, is dependent upon the sum of the cross sections of all the fibers in the unit. Thus, the maximum capacity of the muscle must be the sum total of cross sections of all the motor units, or of all the fibers in the muscle.

Studies on strength of the muscle per unit of cross section vary from 6 to 10 kilograms per square centimeter. In pounds this varies from 85 to 142 per square inch. There are many things that could explain this discrepancy. The physiological condition of the muscle affects its strength, particularly disuse which causes loss of strength before outward signs of atrophy occur or cross section diminishes. Recent studies have also shown that the strength of women is about 85 per cent that of men per unit of cross section. Other studies have also shown that psychological factors may either inhibit or enhance the efforts toward all-out contractions. Some of these factors may be interrelated. For example, can cultural influences concerning "ladylike behavior" provide an inhibiting force which accounts for the reduction in strength of women cited above? The 85 pounds per square inch is usually used as representing the capacity in the average person. At best it is an approximation and probably an underestimate.

It might appear that by measuring the circumference of any muscle, or even of an arm or leg, and subtracting for skin, fat, bone, and nonmuscular structures, it would be possible to compute the potential strength of the muscle or muscles concerned. The problem is not, however, so simple. The chief difficulty is that the muscles are not uniform in shape and internal arrangement. It is possible to compute the true cross section of a cylinder by taking the circumference at any point, but the same cannot be done with a cone or other irregularly shaped object.

The different muscles of the body may be divided according to internal structure into two main groups, each of which has several types. The first of these groups has the fibers running longitudinally through the muscle, in a general direction from origin to insertion of the muscle tendons. The second group is the penniform, meaning featherlike. The fibers run diagonally through the belly of the muscle as the fibers of a feather spread from their point of attachment on the central quill.

In the longitudinal group the different types have various performance possibilities. In most cases the fibers are parallel. They may be very short and arranged in thin sheets, as in the intercostals; or a little longer but otherwise the same, as in the pronator quadratus and the rhomboids; and still longer as in the quadratus lumborum. In the muscles with parallel arrangement the fibers attach directly into the periosteum, or into a flat, broad tendon about the width of the muscle, as in the oblique abdominal muscles. At the extreme of length and somewhat thicker are the gracilis and sartorius muscles.

In another type of the longitudinal group the tendon runs in the same direction as the fibers and results in the spindle-shaped muscle which externally may resemble a penniform one. The psoas and teres muscles are examples of this arrangement.

A combination of the above types results in a triangular arrangement. One end has a wide, fan-shaped attachment, as the flat sheet muscles have. At the other end the fibers converge to a tendon or point of attachment, with a piling up of fibers. This is the arrangement in the deltoid and the subscapularis muscles.

In any of the longitudinal muscles a measurement of the cross section would be fairly easy and accurate. The penniform group offers various and complex problems of measurement.

The simplest penniform pattern is found in the peroneus longus. The tendon of insertion begins only a little lower than the origin of the upper fibers and runs parallel to the fibula. The fibers arise down the side of the fibula and run diagonally downward and outward to the tendon, attaching at an angle of about 35° to the tendon. A cross section through any part of the muscle would run diagonally through the fibers and include only a small percentage of them. The rectus femoris is bipennate, the fibers converging from two sides of the tendon, as in an ordinary feather. The triceps and gastrocnemius have many sections. Some muscles are difficult to classify exactly because of the complexity of their structure. The only way to get a true cross section of a complex muscle would be to take various cuts which would include a cross section of all the fibers of the muscle. This will be referred to as the physiological cross section. With this in mind it is now possible to say that the force of which a muscle is capable is directly dependent upon the physiological cross section (Fig. 40, sum of *bb'* and *cc'*).

Various studies have been attempted to establish a means of predicting strength of muscle groups by measurement of the girth of the segment. This is not very satisfactory because it is not possible to measure adipose and connective tissue adequately and to eliminate them from the cross section. The bones of different individuals vary in size, but cannot be accurately predicted from the measures of joint diameters now in use. The internal structure of the muscle makes it necessary to compute norms for estimating rather than to deal with external girths.

The distance through which a muscle contracts is due not to the cross section but to the length of the fibers. Normally the muscle can contract to about one half of its resting length.

It is now possible to examine particular muscles and see that each is built for its specific type of work. The intercostal muscles, for example, have very short fibers but are located where only very slight movement is possible. Hence the fibers are sufficiently long. However, if the cross section of all parts of the intercostals was computed it would show considerable force possible for the compression or expansion of the thoracic cage. On the other hand, with flexion taking place in both the

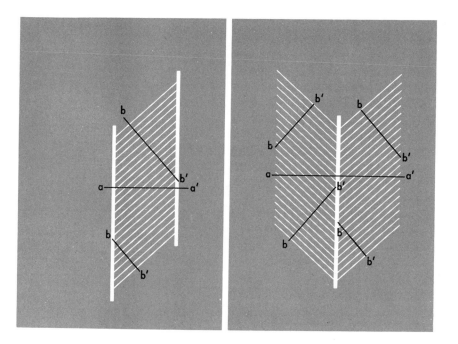

FIGURE 39: Diagram of fiber alignment in penniform muscles
a–a unipennate arrangement; b–a bipennate arrangement

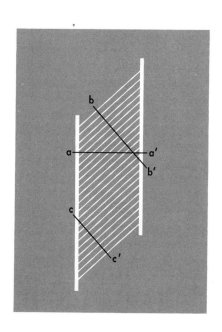

FIGURE 40: Diagram of a simple nniform muscle and cross section
of the muscle fibers
aa'—cross section of the muscle;
bb' + cc'—physiological
cross section of the muscle

hip and the knee, the long fibers of the sartorius are necessary. The triangular arrangement, as in the deltoid, makes possible compactness and application of the force at a single point. This is not so in the true parallel plan.

In general in the longitudinal group the fibers are long or short depending upon the range permitted in the joint which they move. The cross section varies in direct proportion to the strength needed. The same factor holds true in determining the length of the fibers in the penniform group. Tremendous increase in force is obtained by this arrangement while the muscle bulk is kept smaller and distributed over a longer area. The muscle is more compact and streamlined than would otherwise be possible. The gastrocnemius has relatively short fibers, for example, but they are sufficient for the range possible in the ankle. The muscle has, however, a huge physiological cross section which it needs in lifting and projecting total body weight in many activities.

In general, the muscles of the body are built for force or for speed. The significance of the latter will be explained in connection with the problems of leverage. Occasionally a muscle must meet the demand of both force and speed. This is true of the quadriceps extensor muscles.

If the physiological cross section and the length of the fibers are known it is then possible to compute the amount of work of which the muscle is capable.

$$W_{ft.\text{-}lbs.} = \frac{\text{cross section} \times \text{lbs. of force possible} \times \text{½ length of fibers}}{12}$$
$$\text{in sq. in.} \qquad \text{per sq. in.} \qquad \text{in inches}$$

Where W = work in foot-pounds
        85 = pounds of force possible per square inch
        division by 12 reduces inches to feet

Or

$$W_{kilo.m.} = \frac{\text{cross section} \times \text{kilos. of force possible} \times \text{½ length of fibers}}{100}$$
$$\text{in sq. cm.} \qquad \text{per sq. cm.} \qquad \text{in cm.}$$

Where W = work in kilogram-meters
       6 = kilograms of force possible per square centimeter
       division by 100 reduces centimeters to meters

Units of the metric system are often not very meaningful. If the muscular measurements are in the metric system, but it seems desirable to express work in units of the English system, that may be done by the following formula.
      6 kilograms = 13.2 pounds
      30.5 centimeters = 1 foot

Thus:

$$W = \frac{\text{cross section} \times 13.2 \times \frac{1}{2} \text{ length of fibers}}{30.5}$$
$$ \text{in sq. cm.} \qquad\qquad \text{in cm.}$$

In order to further illustrate the work of the muscle the following hypothetical cases will be considered.

(1) 2 sq. in., 2-inch fibers, work = 14.17 ft.-lbs.
(2) 4 sq. in., 2-inch fibers, work = 28.33 ft.-lbs.
(3) 2 sq. in., 4-inch fibers, work = 28.33 ft.-lbs.
(4) 8 sq. in., 2-inch fibers, work = 56.66 ft.-lbs.

These examples indicate facts which have already been stated: namely, (a) the increase or decrease in work is directly proportional to an increase or decrease in cross section of the muscle (examples 1 and 2, 1 and 4, above); (b) the increase or decrease in work is directly proportional to the increase or decrease in length of fibers (examples 1 and 3); (c) work may remain the same in amount but differ in character with differences in muscle structure (examples 2 and 3). In examples 2 and 3 the amount of work is 28.3 foot-pounds, but in one case it is 340 pounds to be moved through 1 inch and in the other it is 170 pounds to be moved through 2 inches. Thus some muscles are constructed internally for force and some for speed and extensive movement.

The measurements of the muscles given in Table VII were made on a cadaver of an adult male. A few muscles were selected which seemed regular enough, for the most part those with simple longitudinal arrangement, to make measurement of cross section approximately accurate. Cross-sectional measurements were fairly easy; the length of the fibers is more of an approximation. Measurements of a single case could not be used as a norm for strength of a given muscle in all cases. These measurements are presented merely to help the student who does not have the opportunity for study of cadavers to visualize better the size of these muscles, and the relative potentialities for work. These measurements may also be used as specific examples for problems in use of the work formulas and computation of work.

Determination of the potential force of a muscle by cross section is a somewhat theoretical question because it fails to consider any factor other than the size of the muscle. As the physical educator or the therapist deals with this problem of the musclar capacity for work, it is in the living organism not the excised muscle. It is obvious that measurement of a given muscle is not possible in the manner discussed above. Some other means must be used, therefore. Several instruments have been

TABLE VII: Measurements Made on a Male Cadaver

Muscle[a]	Width (cm.)	Thickness (cm.)	Avg. length of fibers (cm.)	Work (ft.-lbs.)
Pectoralis major	8.0	1.0	15.0	(To be filled in by the student)
Pectoralis minor	4.2	.7	12.0	
External oblique	23.0	.3	13.0	
Internal oblique	20.0	.25	9.0	
Rectus abdominis	4.5	.4	31.0	
Deltoid	18.0	.65	15.0	
Lumbricales				
5th	.1	.5	2.6	
2d	.2	.3	2.6	
Sartorius	2.5	.65	46.0	
Tensor fasciae latae	3.5	.8	16	

a. All on right side.

developed and are usually referred to under the general term, *dynamometer*.

The first dynamometer was designed for measurement of the strength of hand and finger flexors, and some two or three types have evolved. One of the forms permits an attachment by which strength of arm and shoulder girdle can be measured in pushing and pulling, or a vertical pull similar to that used in chinning may be assessed. The need to measure other muscle groups led to the production of a platform dynamometer, permitting records to be taken on strength of back extensors and leg extensors. These two types were known as manuometer and back-and-leg dynamometer, respectively.

More recent developments have been more diversified in operational principle. Clarke[5] first proposed use of the tensiometer, and has standardized techniques for measurement of practically every muscle which can be isolated to any extent. Others have used this instrument extensively, particularly in research. The force indicator serves a similar purpose but is calibrated for lower values and shorter range than the tensiometers are.

All of the above types register the mechanical force directly in pounds, kilos, or units which can be converted directly by calibration tables into pounds or kilos. The strain gauge dynamometer has been in use for some time and provides an electronic amplification and record of the tension generated in the strain gauge by the subject's efforts. The first adapter was again for grip, but other devices have been used. The chief advantage of this type of instrument is that the duration of effort as well as the maximum amount may be accurately determined. Through the use of this instrument, study of localized muscular endurance has progressed. Localized muscular endurance is another expression of the strength potential and its use.

Strength testing can be done less objectively by other means. Many stunts, fitness tests, or weight training efforts are essentially self-testing in this respect. Most of these have the advantage of dealing with isotonic contractions, while the nature of the various dynamometers usually limits measurement to isometric effort. There is a psychological advantage in the former, if not a physiological one. Too frequently the performer on a dynamometer observes, "I tried but nothing happened." The dial of the dynamometer and tensiometer are seldom where they can be seen by the performer. However, the strain gauge dynamometer does have the recording in view, and work with it has helped to indicate that there is a motivational value from knowledge of results. This further shows that human effort on a particular task is not a product solely of the cross section of the muscle.

With the dynamometer it is possible to measure strength of muscle groups only, not of individual muscles. The dynamometer gives a measure of the force which is effective in moving the segment operated by the muscle group. This force is always less than the total force of which the muscles are capable. In order to understand the reason for this lessened force it will be necessary to understand the problems of leverage.

LEVERAGE

A machine is a device for the execution of work. All complex machines are made up of a series of the fundamental or simple machines. This is also true of the motor mechanism of the human. The simple machines are the lever, pulley, wheel and axle, inclined plane, wedge, and screw. The lever is the form which is found in the body.

All machines are concerned with two forces. One is the force put into the machine. The other is the force opposing the operation of the machine, in other words, the force which the machine is designed to overcome. This is the resistance. The end-result of the operation of the machine is work.

A lever is a rigid bar turning about a fixed point or axis. Its movement is a rotatory one. There must be a force to operate it; there is a resistance to be overcome; and the work resulting is equivalent to the magnitude of that resistance times the distance which it is moved. The leverage arrangements of the body are found in the bones and muscles. Each bony segment is a lever rotating about its attachment to the adjacent segment. The force for operating it is produced by muscular contraction. The resistance may be either internal or external or both.

The effectiveness of a lever depends upon the location on the lever of three points: the axis, the point of application of force, and the point

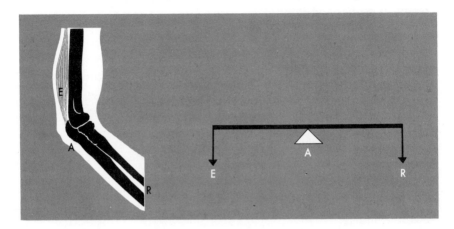

FIGURE 41: Diagram of first-class lever and the forearm as
operated by the triceps muscle
A–axis; E–effort; R–resistance

of application of resistance. Any one of the three points may lie between the other two. The lever is designated as belonging in one of three
classes depending upon which of the three points is in mid-position.

The first-class lever has the axis between the effort and resistance.
The most familiar example of this class and of the way in which it functions is the teeter board. A crowbar is another example, but the axis is
usually placed near the resistance rather than near the middle as in the
teeter board. Also, a pair of scissors is made up of a pair of first-class
levers, the resistance is the material which is being cut by the scissors.
One of the clearest examples in the body is the forearm as extended by
the triceps (Fig. 41). The same is true of the foot in any instance when
there is no weight on it and it is free to flex or extend by movement in
the ankle joint. As it hangs, it moves back and forth much like an inverted teeter. The axis is at the ankle, the two ends of the foot are of
unequal length. In flexion the force is produced by the tibialis anticus
and peroneus tertius and resistance comes principally from the tension
of the gastrocnemius and soleus. In extension the effort and resistance
are in the opposite pairs of muscles. The same arrangement is found in
the support of the head. When the head balances on top of the atlas, it is
pulled either forward or backward depending upon the action of the
anterior or posterior muscles. The tension of the antagonistic muscles and
the inertia of the head are in each case the resistance. Likewise, lower
in the spine, a cross section of the trunk at any given level may be con-

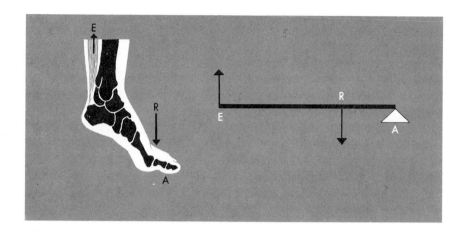

**FIGURE 42: Diagram of second-class lever and the foot as
operated by the gastrocnemius and soleus
A–axis; E–effort; R–resistance**

sidered as a first-class lever. The axis is at the intervertebral articulation; the force comes from either abdominals or back extensors; and the resistance is due to the antagonistic muscles and weight of the trunk. Thus the whole trunk and the head balance just as the teeter board balances, but with the axis located posterior to the center of the board.

The second-class lever has the resistance between the other two points. The classical illustration of this type is the wheelbarrow, with the handles by which the load is lifted projecting well beyond the load. There are very few levers of this class in the body. There is some disagreement among kinesiologists on this point. Most of the discussion centers around the action of the foot when the weight is lifted from its normal standing position with heel down to a position on the ball of the foot.

There are a few points which are necessary to an understanding of this difference of opinion. It was stated before that the foot functions as a first-class lever with the axis at the ankle when the foot is freely suspended. The axis which is necessary to heel raising is, however, no longer at the ankle. The movement which does take place at the ankle is merely an adjustment to facilitate balance of the body. The actual movement is a rotation around the point of contact, the ball of the foot. Thus, it is located at one end of the lever, the metatarsal-phalangeal articulations.

There is no disagreement concerning the source of effort. It comes from the contraction of the gastrocnemius and soleus, and to a lesser extent from the peroneus longus and tibialis posticus. There is no such agreement, however, concerning the resistance. Those who assert that this situation is also one of first-class leverage say that the resistance is that of the supporting surface. Since the resistance of that surface is too great to be overcome it causes a lifting of the axis and hence of the whole body. A more obvious and logical resistance seems to be the weight of the body as held down by gravity. A lifting of the weight is the purpose of this foot movement, not a depressing of the toes or a moving of the contacting surface. The resistance of the support is the same as that expected at any axis; such resistance is necessary for fixation of the axis.

There are still other factors which add to the complexity of the situation and hence to the difficulty of interpretation. One of these is the fact that a part of that weight which is being lifted is also the source of the energy operating the lever. It is, however, a very small part of that weight; and in all levers the point of application of the effort always moves in the direction of its force.

And lastly, the line of body weight or point of application of the resistance shifts. During standing, its position is a short distance anterior to the malleoli; but as the weight is lifted the gravital line approaches nearer and nearer the axis until it practically coincides with it. However, this would not appear to be a major difficulty in analysis. It merely means that the resistance has an ever-decreasing distance from the axis. Hence, the higher the position of the heel the more effective is the action of these posterior muscles although their force is also decreasing to a certain extent.

An exact determination of the points involved in this question is extremely difficult. Due to the complex structure of the gastrocnemius and soleus any estimate of the physiological cross section and potential force is highly inaccurate. The exact length of the force arm and the angle of application of the force must also be approximations.

Data collected by this author reveal certain facts of interest pertinent to this debate and to ankle functions. The force arm of the anterior and posterior muscles of the ankle were found to be essentially the same length on the average, although there were some individual differences in which each force arm had slightly greater measurements for some subjects. The strength of plantar and dorsal flexion was measured in these same subjects (college women). The action was free, i.e., there was no weight on the feet. The dynamometer representing the resistance was applied across the foot at the distal end of the first metatarsal. The ratio between ankle extension and flexion was determined for each case. It varied from 2.7 to 4.1, with an average of 3.3. This seems to indicate greater strength and angle of pull for the extensors.

Another measure of ankle extension was made on these same subjects

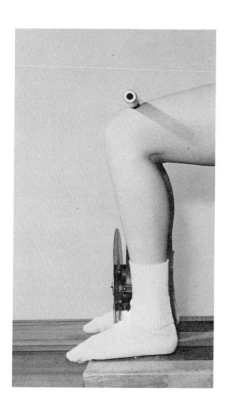

FIGURE 43: Ankle extension with
the subject seated
at the dynamometer

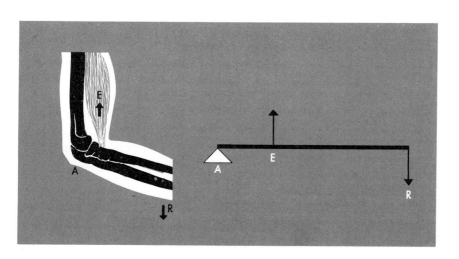

FIGURE 44: Diagram of third-class lever and the forearm as
operated by the biceps muscle
A–axis, E–effort; R–resistance

for purposes of comparison. The subject was seated at a platform dynamometer with the cross bar on top of the knees. The resistance of the machine was located approximately as the weight would fall in standing, i.e., lower leg nearly vertical and weight line just anterior to the external malleolus (Fig. 43). The strength of ankle extension was measured in this position. The ratio was computed between extension in this position and extension when the foot was moving freely against the resistance of the dynamometer at the metatarsal level. The ratios ranged from 1.9 to 3.4, with an average of 2.6 for these subjects. This is in spite of the fact that the gastrocnemius was working at a disadvantage, since the knee was flexed and hence the muscle was shortened. This seems to indicate an axis at the ball of the foot, a longer force arm, and shorter resistance arm; or in other words, the foot is apparently operating as a second-class lever. The change in mechanical advantage would give approximately these results.

The third-class lever has the force between the other two points. A common example is found in the door which is closed by a spring. This also is illustrated in the body by the forearm as flexed by the biceps or brachialis muscles. The axis is at the elbow, the muscles are attached a short distance distal to the elbow. The resistance is the weight of the hand and arm or, to make it more obvious, the weight of an object in the hand. Study of the muscles of the lower extremity reveals the fact that most of the hip and knee muscles are operating these segments as third-class levers.

The total distance from the axis to the point of application of the force is known as the force arm (or power arm); and the distance from axis to resistance is the resistance arm. This is true of all classes of levers, even though the two may coincide. The relative length of the two arms of the lever will determine the way it functions. It was previously stated that the greater the distance from the axis to point at which the force applies, the greater will be the moment of rotation of that force.

In general, the first-class lever is built for equilibrium, the second-class for saving of force, and the third-class for speed and range of movement. These generalizations will be illustrated by the following examples.

Any lever will balance if

the force $\times$ force arm $=$ resistance $\times$ resistance arm.

Let us use teeter boards which are 20 feet long, with a 10-pound weight on one end of each and an arrangement to put the axis at any point we desire along their length. Then resistance = 10, the lever arms will vary, and we are solving for "F," the amount of force necessary to balance the lever. In order to simplify the examples the weight of the board will be disregarded. Table VIII illustrates the results in cases 1 to 8. Cases 10 and 12 in the same table deal with levers of different lengths, but help to illustrate the same principles.

TABLE VIII: Force Required to Balance Levers of Various Sizes

Case	Force arm	Resistance arm	Equations	F
1	2	18	$F \times 2 = 10 \times 18$	90
2	4	16	$F \times 4 = 10 \times 16$	40
3	8	12	$F \times 8 = 10 \times 12$	15
4	10	10	$F \times 10 = 10 \times 10$	10
5	12	8	$F \times 12 = 10 \times 8$	6.6
6	15	5	$F \times 15 = 10 \times 5$	3.3
7	16	4	$F \times 16 = 10 \times 4$	2.4
8	18	2	$F \times 18 = 10 \times 2$	1.1
9	8	12	$F \times 8 = 10 \times 12$	15
10	4	12	$F \times 4 = 10 \times 12$	30
11	12	8	$F \times 12 = 10 \times 8$	6.6
12	12	4	$F \times 12 = 10 \times 4$	3.3

A study of these figures in Table VIII will reveal the following facts:

1. The force required to operate the lever is inversely proportional to the length of the force arm.

2. Only when the two arms are equal in length will the force necessary for balance equal the resistance to be overcome.

3. By adding to the length of the force arm the force may be reduced to almost nothing.

4. The effectiveness of the resistance follows the same rules as those which determine the effectiveness of force.

5. The force necessary to operate the first-class lever depends upon the relative length of the lever arms, i.e., whether the axis is in the center or shifted in the direction of one or the other of the ends.

The question immediately arises whether these facts apply to the other two classes of levers. They do. However, they require special consideration. By definition, the second-class lever has a shorter resistance arm than force arm. The application of the above rules then means that the force required in a second-class lever is always less than the resistance to be overcome. This explains the statement made previously that the second-class lever in the foot has an advantage.

Let us use the previous example, the wheelbarrow, to illustrate this point. If the load is 50 pounds, located in the box at an average distance of 2 feet from the axle, and the ends of the handles are 5 feet from the axle, the equation will read as follows:

$$F \times 5 = 50 \times 2$$
$$F = 20 \text{ pounds}$$

Likewise, in the foot of a given subject the ankle extensors pull at a distance of 6 inches from the ball of the foot; the weight is 100 pounds; and at the start of heel elevation the weight falls 3 inches behind the ball of the foot. Then $F \times 6 = 100 \times 3$ or 50 pounds.

The same rules also hold for the third-class lever. By definition, the third-class lever always has a shorter force arm than resistance arm. Hence, the force required is always greater than the resistance to be overcome. Thus, the door which weighs 20 pounds with the center of its weight at 20 inches from the hinges, will require 80 pounds of force in the spring ($F \times 5 = 20 \times 20$).

All considerations so far have assumed that the force and the resistance were each applying at right angles to the lever. It is apparent from even a very superficial study of the muscles that very few of them are applying force at right angles to the bones which they operate.

Measurements made on a cadaver give an approximation to the condition in the living subject and reveal some interesting information on this point. With the leg straight as it would be in standing, the adductor group of muscles shows a fairly good angle in comparison to some other muscles. The adductor magnus varies considerably from the top to bottom fibers, but on the average is at an angle between 15° and 20° to the line of the femur. The adductor longus is slightly better than 30°, while the brevis which runs much more nearly horizontally, has an angle of nearly 45°. The angle of the pectineus is still more acute, being between 50° and 55°. The sartorius does not exceed 20°.

At the shoulder, a similar state is found. The anterior portion of the deltoid has an angle of 30° to 35°, and that of the posterior portion is a little more acute. The angle of the pectoralis major increases rapidly from upper to middle fibers, but it must also be remembered that as the arm is abducted by the deltoid this angle decreases very significantly. It is in a somewhat abducted position of the arm that the pectoralis is most apt to function.

Many other muscles might be cited which have even smaller angles than those given here. The important point to remember is that a majority of the muscles are located at an angle of 45° or less and a large percentage at 30° or less.

The angle considered here is the angle between the line of pull of the muscle and the lever. This can be noted in the diagram in Figure 45. This angle is the one on the side of the line of pull toward the axis. It is obvious that this angle of pull does not remain the same during the movement of the segment. The two ends of the muscle are fixed,

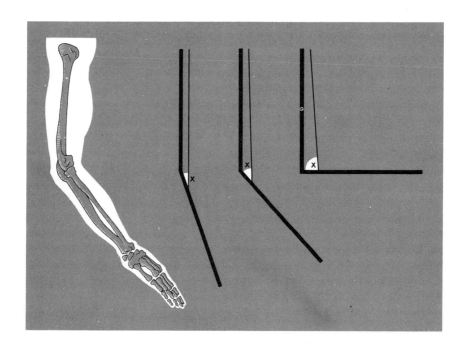

FIGURE 45: Variation in the angle of pull with variation in the position of the segment

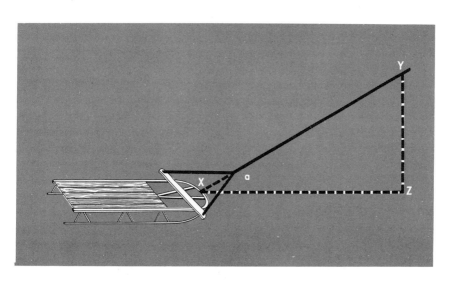

FIGURE 46: Components of force
XY–total force exerted; **XZ**–forward component (**XY** cos angle **a**);
YZ–upward component (**XY** sin angle **a**)

and its contraction merely shortens it in approximately the same line. However, since this contraction moves the lever the angle between the two must change. Figure 45 illustrates this change. In most cases the angle increases as the segment is moved away from its anatomical position. There is also a narrow zone, within the total range, through which the muscle is functioning at or near 90°.

With every change in the angle of pull, there is a change in the moment of rotation; and the total amount of force is effective only when that angle is 90°. If you pull on a sled with a short rope, not only does the sled move forward, but the front end of it is lifted up. When the rope is lengthened or it is held nearly horizontally the sled merely moves forward. In the first case, the sled is actually being pulled in two directions, forward and upward. With the longer rope pulling near the horizontal, the upward pull is reduced to such a small amount that it has no lifting effect on the sled.

Any force applying on an object at any angle other than 0° or 90° has two components, or the same effect as two forces which lie at right angles to each other. The size of each component depends upon the total force in question and the angle between the line of the force and the object.

Since the muscles of the body apply for the most part at an angle considerably less than 90°, they must have two effects on the lever. The rotatory effect is the one necessary for movement. This corresponds to the lifting effect in the example of the sled. The other effect is directly in line with the long axis of the lever. This force is called the *stabilizing* component. This component is waste force in so far as external work is measured. It is, however, highly important in relieving joint strain and in maintaining the joint structure intact. This will be discussed in more detail later.

Some change must now be made in the equation governing the operation of the lever. In addition to the total force and the distance at which it applies from the axis, the angle between its line of pull and the lever must also be considered. It has been demonstrated that as the angle of pull decreases the rotatory effect decreases. A proportional decrease in the length of the force arm would then correct the equation. This shortened force arm is equal to the distance from the axis of motion to the line of pull, when that distance is measured so that it is at right angles to that line of pull. There is thus re-established the same situation as previously considered—a force arm at right angles to the line of force. This new force arm is referred to as the *perpendicular distance* of a muscle.

The perpendicular distance and thus the rotatory effect may be affected by either of two factors, i.e., the distance from the axis at which it attaches to the bone and the angle at which it is pulling at a particular

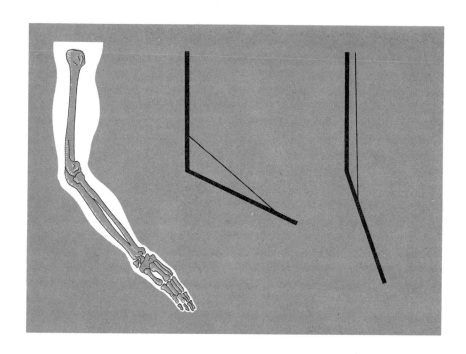

FIGURE 47: Differences in force arm

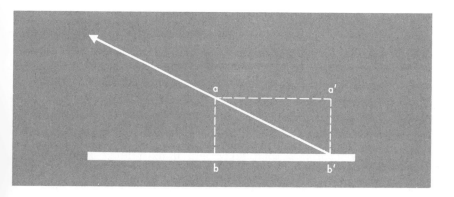

FIGURE 48: Parallelogram of force

instant. The insertion of a given muscle has a fixed distance from the axis of motion. As it contracts it will have a change in angle, producing an increase or decrease in size of angle. There is a corresponding increase or decrease in the length of the perpendicular distance of the muscle. Or, two muscles may have exactly the same angle of pull (Fig. 47), but one inserts farther from the axis than the other. The one with the more distant point of insertion will have the greater rotatory effect.

Another way of considering the loss in rotatory force from small angles of pull is by analyzing the parallelograms of force for different angles. Figure 48 illustrates this point. Select any point along the line of pull of the muscle. A point near the insertion would represent a weak contraction, a more distant point a stronger contraction. From this point drop a line to the lever at right angles to the lever. To complete the parallelogram simply draw two additional lines, one parallel to the perpendicular just drawn but situated at the point of insertion. The second line will run parallel to the lever from the arbitrarily selected point on the line of pull to intersect the second vertical. The sides of the parallelogram represent the two components. AZ or XY indicates the rotatory component and AY or ZX the stabilizing component. The ratio of XY to the total force (AX) is known as the *sine* of the angle and is a function of the size of the angle of pull. The proportion is the same whether you have a weak contraction or a strong one. The table of sines appears in the Appendix. Study of this table will help the reader to understand how small a proportion of force is spent in rotation for the many muscles that apply at the very small angles.

The definition of rotatory motion stated that all points in an object move in an arc about the axis of motion. Points which are located at a distance from the axis describe a longer arc than a point which is closer. The length of the arc described by a given number of degrees of rotation is directly proportional to the distance of the points from the center of motion. Thus, if a lever is desired which will make a wide excursion it must be long.

If a muscle attaches at a short distance from the joint and the lever is considerably longer than this distance, it offers the possibility of a wide range of movement of that segment. The muscle may contract only a very short amount; but the extremity, being removed from the axis n times as far as the muscle, will move through n times as great an arc.

Moreover, the lever is a solid piece and it must move as a single unit. Thus, the point which is moving n times as far will move n times as fast. The extremity of the longer lever will then have not only a wider excursion but it will also move more rapidly. Numerous examples of this are found in either the upper or lower extremity. In many activities the arm functions as one long lever. The deltoid may cause the arm to swing and may contract through only one inch in so doing. But the hand which is approximately five times as far from the shoulder joint as the deltoid tubercle will move five times as far and cover that distance in the same time that the deltoid tubercle is moving its shorter distance.

It is apparent then that a lever must be built either for speed and range of motion or to secure the best results from the force applied. This is merely another example of the familiar law of conservation of energy: that which is lost in speed and distance is gained in force, and vice versa. A study of the formula for the operation of the lever will also demonstrate this fact.

Either speed and range or force may have potential value for our activities, sometimes both may be essential. The most common arrangement in the extremities is a short force arm and a long resistance arm. The short force arm sacrifices force for compactness and streamlined contour around the joints. A long force arm would make a very bulky mass and give a distorted outline to the joint unless the muscle was bound down to conform to the line of the bone. This is true in a very few instances, particularly at wrist and ankle. This, however, reduces the angle of application to such an extreme point that most of the advantage gained by distance is lost. Even with the short force arms most of the muscles are held rather close to the joint which means that they have both factors present which make for a short perpendicular distance. The long resistance arm makes possible a wide range of movement and considerable speed.

So far, very little has been said concerning the resistance factor on the lever. This can be summarized briefly. The effectiveness of resistance follows exactly the same laws as the effectiveness of the force. The two determining factors are the distance of point of application from the axis and the angle of application. The concept of the perpendicular distance as a measure of the working resistance arm is just as sound as when used for the force arm.

The components of resistance are also dual, that opposing the rotation of the lever or at right angles to the lever, and that in line with it. The latter, however, instead of holding the lever in contact with the axis more frequently tends to pull it from its point of contact. This is in opposition to the stabilizing component of the force. The resistance may be inertia of the part, gravity, or resistance of an external object being manipulated. Likewise, the angle at which the resistance applies to the lever may vary. When the angle is not 90°, the resistance has two components; and the effectiveness of the resistance depends upon the "perpendicular distance" of that resistance.

The long resistance arm of the levers in the extremities of the body means a greater effectiveness of that resistance. That in turn requires greater force to operate the lever. The leverage of the upper and lower extremity is thus in favor of speed and range at the expense of force. The force necessary to operate these levers can be gained in only one way, the structure and arrangement of muscles. Several muscles can, and often do, co-operate in almost all movements, making possible a force equal to their total strength. Many of the muscles are of penniform arrangement which increases the amount of potential force. Their fibers are adjusted to the range of the joint and the range of motion of the point of attachment. The shorter the force arm, the shorter is the range of this point. But a large percentage of the force available is spent in stabilizing the joint.

There are some adaptations of muscles which add greatly to the effectiveness of their force. Any structure which increases an otherwise short perpendicular distance is a means of increasing force. The irregularities of the bones are outstanding in this respect. The bulbous ends of the long bones not only make increased articular surfaces, but they change the course of the tendon. The closer the tendon attaches beyond such a condyle or enlargement the greater will be the angle between the tendon and the lever. This is probably more pronounced at the knee joint than anywhere else, though it is of significance in the action of the phalanges and elbow.

Large bony projections are important. The trochanter, as a lateral extension of the femur, gives a distinct advantage to the three gluteals and the outward rotators of the hip. The olecranon process at the elbow serves as a block to elbow hyperextension but, of greater importance, it gives a force arm of fair length. The posterior projection of the calcaneus also serves a dual role. It makes for easier balance of the body weight over the foot and increases the force arm of the tendon of Achilles. The spines on the front of the ilium give slightly greater distance from the sartorius and rectus femoris to the axis of the hip joint. The transverse processes of the vertebrae serve the muscles of the back in the same way. The sesamoid bones also have a relationship to leverage. The patella is the outstanding example of this arrangement. The tendon of the quadriceps extensor muscle must not only curve around the condyles of the femur and tibia, but it is held well out from them by the patella. The sesamoid bones in the plantar surface of the foot are of similar value to the flexor muscles of the first toe.

Structures much less firm than bone are also effective. The bursae inserted under many tendons are cushions for protection and also serve to hold the tendon up at more nearly a right angle. At the knee this type of structure is found above and below the patella, between the tendon and the bone. This is a third factor favoring more effective action of the extensor group of muscles.

Examination of the posterior aspect of the calcaneus shows that it is divided into two halves. The area for attachment of the tendon of Achilles is limited to the lower half of that surface. Between the tendon and the upper half is a bursa. The same is true between the deltoid and the humerus, the gluteus maximus and the femur.

It has been explained that force or speed and range of movement may come from different arrangements of muscles and of leverage. These are combined in different ways in the body. For example, the sartorius is a long, narrow muscle, and has a short force arm and small angle of pull. It can control flexion through a wide range. On the other hand, the gastrocnemius is made up of many short fibers, and has adjustments which give a fair perpendicular distance. The result is a huge effective force over a small range. The quadriceps extensor muscles secure a combination of these results. The short force arm, the long resistance arm, and long fibers in the muscle make the speed and range possible. The total cross section of all four muscles and the various adjustments at the knee give a large effective force for this lever.

The formula for work was force times distance. Either factor might vary; as long as neither was zero, work was being accomplished. The machinery for motion of the body segments is adapted to those two variations. Later analysis of activities will show the use made of them.

REFERENCES

1. Arkin, Alvin, *Absolute Muscle Power, the Internal Kinesiology of Muscle,* Microcard PH45, 1939.
2. Asmussen, Erling, and Boje, Ove, *Body Temperature and Capacity for Work,* Microcard PH1, 1945.
3. Bender, Jay Allen, *Effects of Exercise on Basal Metabolism,* Microcard PH28, 1951.
4. Broer, Marian, *Efficiency of Human Movement,* Philadelphia, W. B. Saunders Co., 1960, Ch. 6, Leverage; Ch. 7, Force.
5. Clarke, H. Harrison, Comparison of Instruments for Recording Muscular Strength, *Research Quarterly,* 25, December 1954, p. 398.
6. _____, Energy Cost of Isometric Exercise, *Research Quarterly,* 31, March 1960, p. 3.
7. _____, Improvement of Objective Tests of Muscle Groups by Cable-Tension Methods, *Research Quarterly,* 21, December 1950, p. 399.
8. Goldman, R. F., and Iampietro, P. F., Energy Cost of Load Carriage, *Journal of Applied Physiology,* 17, July 1962, p. 675.
9. Hearn, George R., *Variation in Energy Cost of Certain Standard Exercises,* Microcard PH14, 1948.
10. MacConaill, Michael A., Mechanical Anatomy of Motion and Posture, in *Therapeutic Exercise,* Sidney Licht (ed.), New Haven, Elizabeth Licht, Pub., 1961, p. 47.

11. Malhotra, M. S., Ramaswamy, S. S., and Ray, S. N., Influence of Body Weight on Energy Expenditure, *Journal of Applied Physiology,* 17, 1962, p. 433.

12. Mayer, Jean, Exercise and Weight Control, in *Report of University of Illinois Colloquim on Exercise and Fitness,* Chicago, Athletic Institute, 1960, p. 110.

13. _____, *Key to Lasting Slimness,* San Francisco, J. Richard Collins, Pub., 1960, p. 19.

14. Morton, Dudley J., *Human Locomotion and Body Form,* Baltimore, Williams and Wilkins Co., 1952, Ch. 12, Gravity and Muscle Action.

15. Passmore, R., and Durnin, J. V. G. A., Human Energy Expenditure, *Physiological Reviews,* 33, October 1955, p. 801.

16. Rasch, Philip J., and Burke, Roger, *Kinesiology and Applied Anatomy,* Philadelphia, Lea & Febiger, 1959.

17. Steinhaus, Arthur H, Physiology at the Service of Physical Education, *Journal of Health and Physical Education,* 2, 1931, p. 40.

18. Steindler, Arthur, *Kinesiology of the Human Body,* Springfield, Ill., Charles C Thomas, 1955, Ch. 9, Mechanics of the Spinal Column.

19. _____, *Mechanics of Normal and Pathological Locomotion in Man,* Springfield, Ill., Charles C Thomas, 1935, Ch. 6, Dynamics of Muscle Action; Ch. 30, Rationalization of Work in Locomotion.

20. Wiggers, Carl J., *Physiology in Health and Disease,* 5th ed., Philadelphia, Lea & Febiger, 1948, Ch. 3, Bioenergetics.

CHAPTER **9**

Physical Principles of Total Body Action

1. Gravity is a constant force acting on all bodies.
2. The human body is unstable when in a standing position.
3. Equilibrium in all activities is an active muscular process to control the center of gravity of the body and its parts with respect to the base of support.
4. Inertia is a property of all objects.

LAWS OF MOTION

MOTION AND REST have been defined as relative and contrasting terms. A body at any given time must be either at rest or in motion. Some factor or factors must determine which state is present. The principles governing this situation were first stated and discussed three centuries ago by Sir Isaac Newton, and have since carried his name. These laws are—

1. (a) A resting body remains at rest if no external force operates upon it, or
   (b) A body moving with uniform motion retains this state of uniform motion as long as there is no external force operating upon it.
2. Acceleration is
   (a) directly proportional to the force producing it,
   (b) inversely proportional to the mass of the body, and
   (c) in the same direction as the force producing it.
3. Every force which meets resistance has an equal and opposite counter-force.

The first of the Newtonian laws is usually referred to as the *law of inertia*. This law explains the necessity for an external force to act on a body and is the basis for the definition of force which was given in the preceding chapter. By this law, rest and motion are both states of resistance and in a sense are passive states. The amount of resistance which a body offers to change from rest or motion is dependent upon the mass of the body and varies directly with that mass.

Examples of inertia are familiar to everyone. It takes considerable force to start a car which is at rest, but when the car is once in motion it moves rather easily. The larger the car the more pronounced these effects. A person sitting in a car which starts suddenly is thrown to the back of the seat; or if a moving car stops suddenly, the passenger continues in motion until stopped by the windshield, the top, or other obstruction. Inertia makes it difficult for the runner to stop quickly after the finish line. The inertia involved in tossing a shot-put is much more apparent than that in throwing a ball. However, the inertia of a thrown or batted ball is very real in the experience of the catcher. We shall see in the analysis of activities that in some instances inertia may be an advantage and in some a disadvantage, but it is a factor which is always present.

The second Newtonian law, or the *law of acceleration*, is concerned with the quantitative values of the force producing the change. The items to be considered are the amount of the force, the direction of the force, the point of application of the force, and the duration of the force. If an object is in a state of uniform motion, it will cover a definite distance in a given time. This relationship of distance covered to the time consumed is called *velocity*. Thus we say that a car travels at 30 miles per hour or a swimmer swims a certain number of feet per second.

A change in velocity from time unit to time unit is called *acceleration*. Acceleration may be either an increase or a decrease in velocity. If a force opposes the direction of motion a decrease in velocity will result; if the force is in line with the motion, there is an increase in velocity. The size of the object is also a factor. For instance, it is possible to develop a greater velocity on a thrown ball than is humanly possible on a shot, due to the greater mass of the latter.

If several forces act on an object at the same time, each will act independently, but the effect on the object is the resultant of those forces. Again, understanding of the parallelogram of forces will be helpful (see Fig. 48). If the sides and ends of the parallelogram are considered as two forces acting, then the resultant is the diagonal through the figure—the hypotenuse of the two triangular halves.

All objects are subject at all times to at least one force—gravity. Every movement will be a resultant of the force producing the movement and of the force of gravity. This accounts for the arc described by the ball in flight or by the broad-jumper. Most objects are also subject to friction, which has a retarding effect. Wind or air resistance may also be a considerable factor. This is certainly true in throwing, running, skating, and other activities where speed is important.

The third Newtonian law, or the *law of reaction*, is also an essential

part of the explanation of how movement is produced. When force is
applied upon an object, that object is also pushing back on the source
of effort. When one is walking on the ground, force is applied with
the foot by the contraction of the muscles, but the ground resists that
force. It is this resistance, or counterforce, which makes locomotion
possible. When one is walking in soft sand or mud, the force can be
only as effective as the counterforce; in this case the counterforce is
greatly reduced. When one steps on a step, box, ladder, or other object,
one is supported if the counterforce offered is equal to the weight of
the person; the object crashes down if the counterforce is less than the
weight. One exerts greater force when jumping than when walking.
Therefore, the take-off must be from a firmer surface.

If an object is to remain at rest, or in a state where there is no motion,
then there must be either no forces acting on it, or they must act in
such a way that the sum of their effects is zero. However, when an
object is free of support the force of gravity is always present and always
pulls the object downward with a definite acceleration—32 feet per second per second. (Acceleration is change of velocity. Velocity in this
case is changing at the rate of 32 feet per second for each second of
drop.) A resting object must have a supporting force, either a point or
a surface of contact sufficient to match the pull of gravity. If gravity and
the supporting force are the only forces acting on the object, then it is
in a state of rest. In popular terminology this is referred to as a state of
balance. This is a reasonably satisfactory interpretation for rest, and the
two terms may be used somewhat interchangeably, though it will be
pointed out later that balance does involve some additional factors.

All objects do not have the same weight or the same shape or the
same type of support. It is obvious then that they cannot balance in
the same way. It has been stated previously that motion may take place
in any plane and around either of the two axes, a vertical or a transverse
one. The resting object must be balanced around these axes in such a
way as to prevent any movement. The structure of the object is the determining factor.

The mass of an object or the quantity of matter which makes up an
object has already been given as a measure of inertia. The larger, heavier,
denser object will offer greater resistance to loss of balance; or, if poorly
balanced, it will move more easily.

One concept of mass which is particularly helpful to an understanding
of this problem is that an object is made up of an infinite number of
tiny particles. Assuming that there is the same substance throughout
the object, then all these particles will be of the same size, shape, and
weight. They will also have an equal gravitational attraction, and the
line of pull for each particle will be vertically downward and parallel to
the pull of every other particle.

If the object is to be balanced around a vertical axis to prevent movement in an anterior-posterior direction, there must be a plane of balance located somewhere within the object. The object may be thought of as a first-class lever or as a series of superimposed first-class levers. The plane of balance which is being determined is the axis of the lever or levers. Every particle in the object has an equal downward force, but at a different distance from the axis. According to the laws of leverage the effectiveness of each particle is dependent upon its distance from the plane or axis. In a uniform and symmetrical object it is clear that the plane of balance is in the exact center of the object in an anteroposterior direction. In an unsymmetrical and nonuniform object the axis is shifted in the direction of the heavier and most distant particles.

Movement may also take place around this vertical axis in a lateral direction, or at right angles to the direction already discussed. This plane of balance is determined in the same manner as the first. Each particle has an effectiveness equal to the product of its weight times its distance from the plane. (The plane of balance is located where the sum of the products on one side equals the sum of the products on the other.)

These two vertical planes intersect at a line which determines the vertical weight center of the object. For convenience this line will be referred to as the _gravital line_ of the object (Fig. 49).

Movement also occurs around a transverse axis. The plane of balance between the two ends is located in exactly the same way. There are thus three planes, each located at right angles to both of the others. They intersect at a point. In a symmetrical and uniform object this point is the exact center of the object (Fig. 50). In an unsymmetrical, nonuniform one it may not be the center by linear measurement, but it is the weight center of the object, the point around which it balances in every direction. This point is called the _center of gravity_.

Movements around any of these planes are rotatory movements. A loss of balance usually results in a movement to a position in which balance is possible.

We know that some objects balance more easily than others. This property of easy or difficult balance is known as stability. There are certain factors in the structure of the object which determine the degree of its stability. The one which is most easily recognized is the size of the base of support. The second factor can hardly be separated from the first. The second is the height of the center of gravity. The two are often dependent upon each other. An increase in the size of the base, while the height of the object remains the same, usually lowers the center of gravity. Likewise, a decrease in base raises the center, all other things remaining equal. Also, two objects may have the same size of base, and same height, but one may be smaller at the top. It

FIGURE 49: Planes of balance

FIGURE 50: Center of gravity in symmetrical objects

will then have a lower center of gravity. Loading the base also lowers
the center. In general, the larger the base the lower the center of gravity,
and the greater the stability of the object; conversely a small base and
high center of gravity reduce stability.

The third factor is the location of the gravital line with respect to the
base of support. The object with low center and large base, which has
been described as stable, should also have the gravital line falling inside
the area of support. The nearer it falls to the center of this area the more
stable it is. As the line shifts toward the periphery of this supporting
area, the greater becomes the tendency for the object to rotate around
this edge and to fall. Any time the gravital line falls outside the base of
support, the object falls unless there is some other force holding it in
place.

Weight is the fourth factor. The heavier an object is, all other things
being equal, the greater the stability. This is largely a question of inertia. A lightweight object can be blown over by a little push or gust
of wind that would not affect a heavier one in the least.

All discussion so far has assumed an object made up of a single, unified
whole. If, however, an object is made up of superimposed segments,
there may be a tendency for the object to move at any or all the junctions
of these segments. If a column of children's building blocks is set up, it
will stand easily if the blocks are placed squarely one over the other.
If they deviate to one side, the column becomes unsteady. It will stand
only if the gravital line of each block falls inside the area of contact with
the block below and also inside the base of support of the bottom block.
The more nearly the centers of gravity of superimposed segments fall in
a vertical line, the more stable will the stack be. The alignment of centers
over the base, accomplished often by a shifting of the base, is the secret
of many of the tricks of the juggler and circus performer.

Different combinations of these factors produce varying degrees of
stability. The range and relative status of stability can be defined and
illustrated. A cone in its various positions illustrates this point. If you
attempt to stand it on the point, it is impossible for it to stand alone.
The base is small, the center of gravity is relatively high, and it is
impossible to keep the gravital line in this point. The cone falls and
eventually comes to rest on its side. In this process of falling the center
of gravity moves downward in an arc. Any object is unstable if the
center of gravity moves in this downward direction as the object moves
from its designated position (see a, Fig. 51).

In the position to which the cone has fallen on its side, it can be rolled
about, but it will remain on its side unless the point is raised and placed
in a vertical position. The center of gravity remains at a constant height
from the supporting surface. This is a neutral state of stability.

If the cone is raised so that it rests on the circular base, it will stand there easily. A force may be applied to it, causing it to rock over toward one edge of the base. If that force is small and is discontinued, the cone will drop back into position on the base. As it rocks onto the edge, the center of gravity is moved upward in an arc. As long as the center of gravity falls inside the base or behind the edge on which the cone is turning, the cone will fall back into position and stand. Whenever the center of gravity passes beyond that edge, it starts downward on the arc and the cone falls. Any object is stable if any displacement from a position of balance causes the center of gravity to travel upward in an arc.

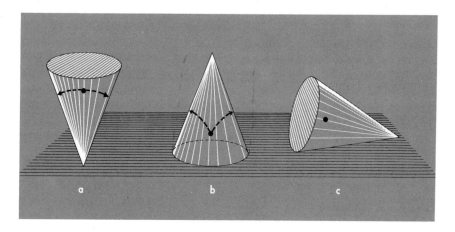

FIGURE 51: Comparison of stable and unstable objects
a–unstable; b–stable; c–neutral

The greater the upward or downward arc described by the center of gravity, the greater is the degree of stability or instability. The degree of stability necessary for an object is entirely dependent upon the function of the object, the forces which it must withstand, and the forces which it may have either within or without to support it. The reader is familiar with objects of stable and unstable characteristics.

These facts concerning balance apply to all objects, including the human body. It is subject to loss of balance or to movement in many directions. The plane of balance for movement in an antero-posterior direction divides the body into front and back weight halves and is known as the *primary frontal plane.* If the person is standing in an erect position without any load, the external landmarks through which the frontal plane passes are approximately as follows: (1) a little anterior to the external malleolus, (2) the anterior portion of the knee joint, (3) the hip joint, (4) the acromial prominence of the shoulder, and (5) the lower point of the ear.

The plane of balance for movement in a lateral direction divides the body into right and left halves. This is called the *primary sagittal plane.* In the erect standing position it will bisect the skull, run directly down the row of spinous processes, and between the legs and feet. On the front of the body the plane would pass through the center of the nose, bisect the mandible, sternum, and the symphysis pubis.

Balance around a tranverse plane results in a division into upper and lower weight halves. The division between these halves is known as the *primary transverse plane.* The point of intersection of these three planes, or the center of gravity, has been determined in various ways for different positions. This was one of the earliest points of interest in nineteenth-century investigations of the human body and its movements. Calculations of the center located it for man, in an erect military position, at 2 to 3 cm. anterior to the second sacral vertebra, and the vertical line through it fell 3 cm. in front of the ankle joint. The location of the center still appears to be fairly accurate, the gravital line is a little too far back for the "at ease" standing position. These early experiments indicated that the center was located upward at about 57 per cent of the total height from the soles of the feet to the vertex. This is the basis for the common placement of the center at five-ninths of the height.

The above figures were all established on men. The exact position varies slightly with the position of the body and the build of the individual. In women it is usually slightly lower because of the comparatively narrower shoulders and wider, better-padded hips than men have. On the average these variations are relatively minor and the center can be considered in most cases in the posterior portion of the pelvis at about the second sacral vertebral level.

More recent studies have indicated some of this fluctuation in position of the center. Hellebrandt[3] and co-workers performed a series of studies on women. Their findings place the center of gravity for this group at 55 per cent of the total height above the soles of the feet. Individual variations were found, as high as 59 per cent and as low as 53 per cent. The total number of cases involved was 445, which is far above any previous number studied.

The anteroposterior weight line was found in this same series of experiments to be on the average 5.08 cm. anterior to the external malleolus. Fox[2] also found on college women that on the average it lies 1 cm. anterior to the anterior border of the malleolus, which location corresponds very closely with the anterior border of the tibia near ankle level. The variation in position was considerable in different individuals. The longer foot usually carries the weight farther in front of the malleolus. However, the proportion of the foot in front and behind the line was approximately the same. In general it was located midway in the weight-bearing part of the foot, which is from the calcaneal tuberosity to the distal end of the metatarsals.

Another interesting fact concerning the Hellebrandt study was that most subjects, when allowed to assume a comfortable stance, shifted the weight well to the left. When asked to stand in their "best posture" the weight was shifted too far to the right for symmetrical weight-bearing.

The value of this study and some of the other recent ones is further increased by the fact that the data were obtained on living subjects in everyday poses. This was not always true of the pioneering studies in the last century.

Equipment can be constructed easily for determination of gravital planes and their location in the base of support. Determination of this intersecting point in the base will confirm these individual variations, and can be a source of good motivation for work on posture, better working positions, and better weight distribution when on the feet.

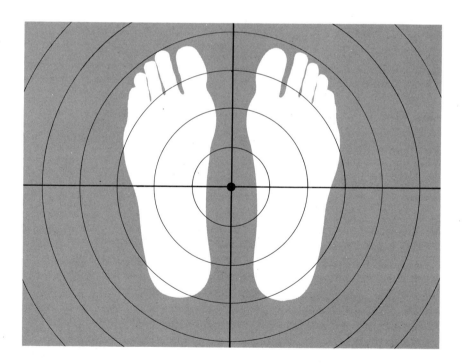

FIGURE 52: Footprints showing position of the center of gravity
while standing

These three planes of balance are the primary planes, or the planes of orientation. A plane parallel to one of the primary planes is called by the same name, i.e., a frontal, sagittal, or transverse plane. This terminology is particularly helpful in describing directions of movement and will be used considerably in discussions in later chapters. For example, it is often confusing and indefinite to describe a movement as flexion or extension of the shoulder. But to define a movement as forward or backward in a sagittal plane through a given number of degrees is clear and concise. This movement takes place around an axis in a frontal or transverse plane. Or a lateral movement of the arm in the frontal plane, through 90° around an axis in the sagittal plane, can leave little doubt as to direction and range of movement.

When the individual carries any type of load, that load becomes a part of the total weight to be balanced, the center of gravity is changed, and adjustments are made in position to keep the gravital line located as centrally as possible. The closer the load can be held to the body, the easier is the balance. If it can be lowered, balance is easier.

In analyzing human structure from the standpoint of stability, we find that all the factors for instability are illustrated, particularly in the standing position. The base varies with the position of the feet but is relatively small in comparison to height. When one is standing with the feet together this base is just the size of the feet. The center of gravity is high, being located slightly more than halfway up from foot to head. These two factors alone would make an unsteady structure. In addition the body is made up of segments, so irregular in shape and placement that they might challenge the expert juggler to keep them so aligned. The lower segment is the foot, a long, flat, articulated unit. Toward one end of this is placed another long, vertical segment, which in turn is topped by a still more massive part, also with a long upright axis. On top of these disjointed stilts the pelvis rests like a rocker so that it may roll back and forth.

The base of the spine is set in the rear of the pelvic girdle. Above this base is a series of twenty-four more segments. No one of these twenty-four vertebrae is placed directly above the one below, and consequently at every intervertebral articulation there is a rotatory force which tends to increase the already existing spinal curves. Because of the firm attachment of the spine to the pelvis every change of position of the pelvis also changes the alignment of the vertebrae. The thoracic cage and all the weight of the abdominal and thoracic viscera are suspended on the front of the spine. Finally on top of this whole structure is the head, balanced fairly well on the atlas but used very frequently in a forward position.

In considering these successive segments we find that the centers of weight of the separate segments do not fall in a straight line, and in many instances the line of gravity falls very near the edge of the

 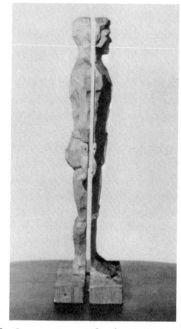

a–Separation at the transverse plane   b–Separation at the frontal plane

c–Separation at the sagittal plane   d–Open at the sagittal plane

FIGURE 53: Primary planes of the body

articulating surface which supports it. This means there is a moment of rotation at every joint.

The weight of the arms must also be borne by the spine. They are used much of the time in a forward position and away from the body. The weight of these long appendages definitely affects balance. If the arms are moving, their reaction on the trunk is a factor in the problem of balance and maintenance of position.

There is no doubt then that the skeletal arrangement of the body is an unstable one. A comparison of the frame of the human and of many of the four-footed animals is about like comparing the bicycle and a four-legged table. It must be remembered, of course, that the four-footed animal is also segmented and therefore tends to collapse. However, from the standpoint of size of base and location of gravital line within the base, the four-footed animals have the advantage. The height of the center of gravity depends upon the length of the legs, and in animals such as the dog and the horse it varies with the breed. It is always somewhere in the trunk, moving anteriorly in animals such as the buffalo and moving caudally in the kangaroo. In every instance, however, it falls well within the base formed by the feet. This base is usually rectangular; but in the case of the kangaroo it is formed by the rear legs and tail, which are used as a tripod when the animal stands. In the various types of monkeys and apes the structure more nearly resembles the human. However, in monkeys and apes the greater development of the pectoral girdle and upper extremity raises the center of gravity. The monkey almost always resorts to four-footed locomotion when on the ground, because his rear legs do not extend completely and his arms are extremely long in proportion to his legs. When attempting to stand he is either on all fours or squatting on the rear legs.

Just as there are variations in stability among the animals, so the human can assume positions for rest which are graded in ease of maintenance. Obviously, the most stable position possible is either a prone or supine one. These are two of the very few positions we assume from which movement in any direction will cause a rise of the center of gravity. Even if we only roll onto the side, the center of gravity travels upward. This side position is unstable because of the narrow base and the tendency to roll forward or backward and let the center of gravity drop down again. It becomes stable only as the legs and arms are spread in some fashion to increase the size of the base and prop the person up.

All the various positions of kneeling and sitting go up the scale toward instability. In all cases the weight is kept rather low. The size of the base may vary from very small, as in a squat-sitting position, to a very large one, as in a long-sitting with hands braced on the floor behind the back. The person may be more subject to loss of position in one direction than in another. For example, in long-sitting (legs extended straight ahead) there is little possibility of loss of balance forward, but a very real one backward. A person in this position usually braces the body with hands on the floor to the rear, thus increasing the size of the base; or inclines the trunk slightly forward if the hamstrings will permit; or allows the spine to flex. Either of the latter two procedures carries the weight line a little farther inside the base.

All standing positions raise the center of gravity further from the floor. Spreading the feet apart lowers the center slightly, but at the same time it contributes to stability by increasing the size of the base. With feet together the base is small and the center rises only during the time that the body rocks to heel or toe. The extreme of instability is on tiptoe of one foot only, with the arms up or holding some heavy object high as if to place it on a shelf.

If, then, our skeletal structure is a collapsible one, and practically all positions that we assume are difficult and require fine adjustments of weight, there must be some force responsible for maintaining balance. The ligamentous connections between the segments do help to some extent, but they cannot do more than check the rotation at a given articulation. Usually this limitation in turn transfers that rotation to neighboring articulations. The only force capable of maintaining alignment of segments is muscular contraction. In the maintenance of every position that the body assumes, with the exception of prone and supine and some of the semireclining positions with complete support of body, there is muscular activity. Studies on energy cost of activity usually estimate the cost of sitting in a relaxed fashion as requiring about 15–20 calories per hour above the basal metabolic rate. This would seem to indicate the value of these reclining positions in avoidance or overcoming of fatigue. There is also more to the progressively increasing heart rate in sitting and standing than merely the necessity of forcing the blood through vertical channels. Muscular activity is greater and the heart must work faster to carry its responsibility in that metabolic process. It is this inactivity or avoidance of motion which accounts for internal work. Internal work is almost always in progress, but varies in amount from moment to moment.

There are, however, certain structural arrangements which facilitate the maintenance of the erect position. The body is not as poorly designed as the above discussion might indicate. Probably the greatest factor is the strength of the extensor muscles. The body is tending always to collapse because of gravity and the rotatory force at the articulations. The extensor muscles of the legs and back are the ones to prevent this collapse. The total strength of all the extensors of the ankle, the knee, the hip, and of the spine is considerable. If the flexors and extensors of the various joints are compared, the extensors are found to be more numerous, or larger, or have a better perpendicular distance. Sometimes all three conditions are found, as at the ankle. The strength of the extensors is sufficient to support not only the whole body weight but also additional weight carried by the body, and sufficient to check motion of the body.

The foot extends both forward and backward from the ankle joint. This increases the base and gives a little leeway in both directions for shifting the center of weight and still keeping it within the base of support. Morton[6] has a formula for distribution of weight in the standing position. Half is on each foot if weight is centered. The weight on each foot is divided equally between the calcaneal point of support and the line represented by the distal end of the metatarsals. That carried by the metatarsals is one-third on the first metatarsal, and the other two-thirds is distributed equally over the remaining four. This illustrates still further how the weight is centered over a medial band running antero-posteriorly through the median line of the base.

The knee is checked against hyperextension, which limits movement to one direction. Hyperextension is likewise absent in the hip joint. This keeps the trunk from rocking too far back. The firm attachment of the spine to the pelvis in the sacroiliac joint also helps in trunk alignment. The range of movement possible between each two vertebrae is very slight. Limited movements are more easily controlled, and the erector spinae is arranged in short parts to control these localized movements. The head is reasonably well balanced with strong muscles at the rear to support the head in a forward position.

The above factors all help to prevent loss of position in an antero-posterior direction. There are other points which are advantageous to holding position in a lateral direction. The symmetry of the body helps to keep it balanced. The natural spread of feet and legs and width of the hips make possible a lateral transfer of weight with relative ease. The broader base is firm because of the fact that there is no lateral movement in the foot, except that of rocking from one border to the other; also the ankle and knee are locked against lateral bending.

On first consideration the body structure may seem a surprising combination of good and poor points, functioning inefficiently. Actually, however, there is a marvelous adaptation of structure to function. Functional demands are dynamic as well as static. The segmentation of the body allows freedom and variety of movement which would be impossible with a more solid object. The articulations are suited to the needs and are controlled by articular structures and the muscles.

The height of the body gives an increased range of vision and movement of the head. That height is also used sometimes in developing speed in the handling of other objects. The base is small as is necessary for a mobile and active being, but it permits adjustments which increase stability very materially. Sufficient muscular strength is provided to control the body over this base.

The long free appendages make possible the varied and skilled forms of locomotion and manipulation. They permit movements of either small or large range, close to the body or at full extension, delicate movements or strong ones. The lower extremity is designed primarily for forceful movements, the upper one for variety of movement and fine manipulation.

In every respect the interrelationship between structure and function is demonstrated. By trial and error one soon learns something of the potentialities and limitations of one's own motor system. The skilled movements of man are the result of his attempts to apply his intellect to motor activity, to vary and improve his skills and coordination, to make his body an expressive and creative instrument of performance.

REFERENCES

1. Bachman, John C., Motor Learning and Performance as Related to Age and Sex in Two Measures of Balance Coordination, *Research Quarterly*, 32, May 1961, p. 123.

2. Fox, Margaret, and Young, Olive, Placement of the Gravital Line in Antero-Posterior Standing Posture, *Research Quarterly*, 25, October 1954, p. 277.

3. Hellebrandt, Frances, The Location of the Cardinal Anatomical Orientation Planes Passing Through the Center of Weight in Young Adult Women, *American Journal of Physiology*, 121, 1938, p. 465.

4. Metheny, Eleanor, *Body Dynamics*, New York, McGraw-Hill Book Co., 1952, Ch. 7, The Balanced Posture: Standing.

5. Morton, Dudley J., *The Human Foot*, New York, Columbia University Press, 1935, Ch. 12, The Center of Body Weight; Ch. 13, The Foot in Stance.

6. ————, *Human Locomotion and Body Form*, Baltimore, Williams and Wilkins Co., 1952, Ch. 2, Organic Interaction with Gravity; Ch. 3, Gravity a Designing Factor.

7. Rasch, Philip J., and Burke, Roger, *Kinesiology and Applied Anatomy*, Philadelphia, Lea & Febiger, 1959, Ch. 8, Center of Gravity and Equilibrium.

8. Scott, M. Gladys, *Kinesiology Handbook*, New York, Appleton-Century-Crofts, 1947, Lesson 27, Determination of Gravital Line.

9. Steindler, Arthur, *Kinesiology of the Human Body*, Springfield, Ill., Charles C Thomas, 1955, Ch. 7, Body Balance and Body Equilibrium.

10. ————, *Mechanics of Normal and Pathological Locomotion in Man*, Springfield, Ill., 1935, Charles C Thomas, Ch. 4, Center of Gravity.

CHAPTER **10**

The Motor System in Operation

1. Rotation of the body or its parts on the longitudinal axis presents the minimum of resistance.
2. The human machine has a low degree of efficiency.
3. The most economical movement is one which uses the minimum of muscular force in relation to the work produced.
4. Momentum of one part of an object may be transferred to the whole, and conversely, momentum of the whole imparts momentum to the parts.
5. The standards of skill in a performance are based on economy of effort and effectiveness of results.

THE LITTLE BOY may take the alarm clock apart bit by bit and see how many pieces there are, how each part is made, and how they were assembled. Someone may explain to him what each piece is for and why it is made as it is. However, he probably will not know much about how it actually runs, why winding makes it run, or why the alarm goes off, unless he watches it being reassembled and running again.

And so it seems best, after tearing the human machine apart, scrutinizing its build, and analyzing the performance of its parts, that we review it in its entirety and as it performs some of its various duties.

Let us consider again the question of muscular contraction. It has been described as having a stated amount of force per unit of cross section, varying somewhat with the physiological condition of the muscle. The primary factors in the physiological condition are fatigue, source of food substance, and removal of waste substances from the tissue. The position of the lever at a given moment is also a determining factor in potential force. When a joint is in its mid-position all muscles may be nearest a relaxed condition. The length at this time is commonly defined as the normal length of the muscle, or its resting length. For example, when the arm is hanging easily at the side, all muscles of the shoulder joint are at rest and the muscles have a certain length. If the arm is raised and carried across the chest, it is because the pectoralis major, anterior deltoid, and coracobrachialis are contracting. Their length will be correspondingly shortened. On the other hand, if the arm is swung backward these muscles will be placed in tension, and they will be stretched longer than their resting length. This range from maximum contraction to maximum stretch has been defined as the amplitude of the muscle.

From the discussion of tonus it was learned that when a muscle is taut it will go into quicker and smoother action. Also, it has been found that when an excised muscle is loaded so that it is stretched it can lift heavier loads than it can otherwise. The same effect is obtained when the articulation is moved so that the muscle is stretched. But the muscle may be stretched so far that it no longer contracts easily. Conversely, it may be contracted so near its maximum that it is no longer capable of much movement of the lever, and, of course, it fatigues very easily in that state.

The relative degrees of tension and contraction affect the way the muscle functions. It works best through a range somewhat less than its total amplitude, and has its greatest contractile power in the elongated phase of that range. If the elbow and shoulder are extended, the biceps is stretched and can go into action quickly and effectively. If the upper arm drops forward and the elbow is near complete flexion, the biceps is too short to be very efficient.

This advantage of muscular tension is utilized in almost everything we do. It is one of the major purposes of the preliminary movement in all acts. Throwing or striking without a back swing, or jumping without leg flexion would all be very weak. Muscle tension accounts for part of the difference in force. The rest is due to the difference in the distance over which the force is applied and hence the speed developed.

Most muscles cross only one joint and attach to adjacent bones. Other muscles are longer and cross two joints. This difference in structure of the muscles results in variations in tension. The biarticular muscles, or those which cross two articulations, behave somewhat differently from the one-joint muscles. Because of their tension they have a tendency to keep the two joints in about the same position of flexion or extension.

If the one-joint flexors of the hip, such as the iliopsoas or pectineus, contract, the hamstring muscles are stretched on the back of the leg. If the knee is not fixed, the lower leg also flexes on the thigh sufficiently to keep the muscles at approximately their normal length. Likewise, when the hip is extended, tension on the rectus femoris causes the knee to extend. That extensory effect may even carry as far as the ankle, because of the arrangement of the gastrocnemius.

In general, the articulations are moved to about the same extent. The trunk and the lower leg are usually parallel in leg movements; at least, that is the natural position. This will be observed in the leg flexion occurring preparatory to most forms of the jump. The opposite effect is required in some gymnastic exercises and stunts. In these cases the purpose is either to stretch muscles or to develop a sense of balance in a different and perhaps unnatural position.

Few people find it easy to sit on the floor with back erect and legs straight out in front. If the knees are forced to the floor there is more or less pain at the back of the knee. Practically everyone has experienced this, but the cause is not always known. This position is a definite strain on the insertion of the hamstrings. In trying to assume it one usually finds that either the knees bend or the back flexes, sometimes both. Either movement shortens the distance between the two points of attachment and hence relieves the strain.

The strength for most movements comes from a combined action of one- and two-joint muscles reinforcing each other. The two-joint muscles acting alone will extend the legs. This is because they are strong, because the leverage is favorable, and because they make a complete system exerting tension down the full length of the leg. This is extremely important from a practical standpoint. We are constantly using the extensors of the legs to hold the upright position, to lift weights, or to provide driving power in locomotion. Muscle tension acts as an ally to muscle contraction, and in favor of extension. Seldom is strong flexion necessary. The list of regular activities in which flexion is the most essential and most vigorous part of the movement is extremely brief. Flexion, when it occurs, is usually in the direction in which gravity can be used as the principal force.

The extensor muscles of the legs are larger than the flexors; this is partially due to the fact that they are used more. The greater strength of the extensor muscles is due to more than the fact that the extensors are larger and more numerous. At the hip, the flexors fit very closely over the front of the hip joint. This means a very small perpendicular distance. This situation is improved considerably by the fact that two of the muscles turn sharply backward and attach toward the posterior aspect of the femur. Their angle of application is thereby greatly improved. The hamstrings have a longer distance than the flexors, and one which is larger at the hip than at the knee. Their action, therefore, tends first of all to produce extension of the hip rather than knee flexion. The extensors of the knee are aided by the various arrangements over the joint and at their point of attachment. The advantage is in their favor. The gastrocnemius also fits very closely over the knee but is adjusted to work quite effectively at the ankle. On the anterior aspect of the ankle, the tibialis anticus, peroneus tertius, and the extensors of the toes are all held in close contact with the bone by the annular ligament. This very small angle results in a small rotatory component in their force.

The arrangement of the muscles and levers, therefore, favors extension. As the segments move into flexion the angle is almost invariably improved, thus compensating somewhat for the reduced efficiency of the muscle. Again it must be recalled that the extensory apparatus of the legs is in almost constant use, but strong flexion is a very exceptional occurrence.

The isolated lever moves around its axis, which is fixed; and it moves independently of all other parts or levers. This is not the case with the levers of the body. The ends of the segments are joined together and each moves with respect to its neighbor. But when the hand or foot is fixed movement of one segment necessitates movement of the next one and so on until the position of the whole body is shifted. In this sense a given muscle or group of muscles may cause movement of distant parts and produce very unexpected results.

One of the simpler examples of this is seen if one leans against the wall facing it, palms on the wall at shoulder height with elbows projecting sideward, the toes about two feet from the wall. If the person pushes against the wall, the hand cannot move, the arms extend, and the body is moved back until it is in an erect standing position. The two segments of the arm work as a unit. Action centers at the elbow where the triceps is pulling it into extension. Extension of the elbow also results in extension of the wrist and forward movement of the humerus. The two groups of muscles capable of producing each of these movements can assist the triceps in moving the body.

The elbow dip, or push up, is exactly the same action but in a nearly horizontal plane. Therefore, more of the body weight is supported by the hands and the action must be stronger. Only by the co-operation of all muscles affecting the three joints, each group indirectly affecting the other two joints, can this movement be performed. All pushing movements are done in very much the same way.

The same type of thing is seen in the lower extremity. When climbing stairs one's weight is lifted by extension at the three articulations. Extension cannot naturally take place at any one of the articulations without also occurring at the other two. Thus the gastrocnemius, soleus, and peroneus directly affect the ankle, and indirectly the knee and the hip. The vasti extend the knee directly, and the ankle and hip indirectly. The hamstrings and the gluteus maximus indirectly assist in knee and ankle extension because hip extension produces tension on the rectus femoris. The latter tends to extend the knee, which in turn puts tension in the gastrocnemius. The same thing is true in the alternate flexion and extension in riding a bicycle. Flexion is largely passive and produced by the force of the pedals. Extension is stronger and serves as the propelling power of the bicycle.

There is yet another factor we must review in considering the performance of the levers of the body. Any muscle pulling at less than right angles has some stabilizing effect. Practically all the muscles pull at less than 90° most of the time, and many of them at very small angles. When the angle is small most of the force is stabilizing. This is not wasted force, however, since it relieves strain and stress on the body. It is necessary to hold the articulations intact and to prevent ligaments from being stretched. Ligaments lack the resiliency of the muscles. Some protective force must be exerted to counteract the weight of the parts, the weight of external objects handled by the body, and centrifugal force. The latter tends to tear the body apart, particularly in fast swinging movements and when some weight is being carried in that swing.

For example, a fast tennis stroke with the racket in the hand tends to cause the racket and hand to go off at a tangent to the swing. This is an example of centrifugal force, a tangential pull carrying detached parts outward during spinning action. It is really an example of moving inertia, i.e., the part continues moving in a straight line when the restraining force (centripetal) is no longer effective. The tennis player feels the effects of this pull at the elbow or at the shoulder. Usually, however, it is transferred to the whole body, which is pulled off balance, and the player steps forward. The sensation in the shoulder and the lifting effect of the swing is more pronounced in the tennis service than in the drives, probably because the arc is a little larger and more speed is developed. The contraction of the muscles maintains the normal contact of the articulating surfaces. The stabilizing component is, then, an essential part of performance; it is a form of internal work; but it is loss in terms of external movement.

Occasionally a muscle may pull at an angle greater than 90°. An illustration of this is seen in the forearm as it nears complete flexion. The angle between the biceps and the radius has changed from a very small one to more than a right angle. The nonrotatory component is, therefore, in the opposite direction, or has a negative effect. In this particular case, the biceps is assisted very definitely by the other elbow flexors, which do have a considerable positive force. Also, the structure of the olecranon process is helpful in preventing separation of the joint, and it is assisted in this by the tension of the triceps. When such an obtuse angle is reached, the tension of antagonists and the positive parallel component of the synergists must be relied upon.

When inertia was discussed in the last chapter it was considered only in relationship to movements of the whole body. It applies, of course, to movements of parts in exactly the same way, and to translatory or rotatory motion. When an object rotates around a central axis the most distant point from the axis has the greatest inertia, the nearest point the least. The average distance of the mass particles is the determining factor. Inertia increases with the square of that average distance. When an object rotates around a central axis the average distance is at a mini-

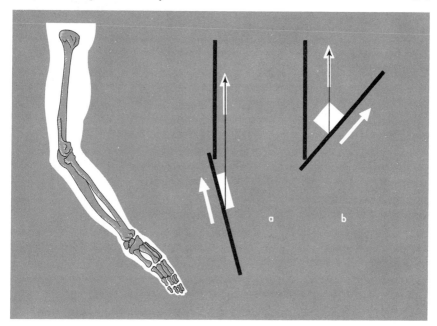

FIGURE 54: Components of force of the biceps
a–elbow near extension; b–elbow near full flexion

mum. When it rotates about a transverse axis at one extremity it becomes relatively larger. In rotation of a given segment, such as the forearm, the inertia is very small because all points are near the axis of rotation. In flexion of the elbow, however, it is considerably greater because of the length of the arm and hand. The same is true of all segments, including the trunk. With rotation around the longitudinal axis of the part, inertia is at a minimum; but with rotation around an axis at the end, it is much larger.

The muscles are adapted to this requirement. In every case the so-called rotators of a joint are small in comparison to the other muscle groups, or rotation is performed as a secondary function of the other muscles. At the hip, the outward rotators are very small in comparison to either flexors, extensors, or adductors. The difference between abductors and rotators is less marked, but ordinarily a large part of the apparent abduction is really trunk abduction. Inward rotation is a secondary function of some of the muscles of the other groups. Rotation at the knee is a secondary function of the flexors. At the shoulder joint the other muscle groups co-operate in various ways to give rotation.

There are many activities in which this principle is used effectively. In all types of throwing, whether simple ball throwing or a specialized throw such as a discus throw or shot-put, and in all types of striking, whether in chopping wood or pounding a stake, making a golf or tennis stroke, or in boxing or handball, rotation on the longitudinal axis of the trunk or whole body is used to add speed and momentum. This rotation is ordinarily combined with a transfer of weight, or the use of body momentum in the direction of the movement. Both serve as substitutes for muscular contraction in gaining force and speed.

Momentum of one part of the body may be used to accelerate another part, and thus gain force or speed. For example, when the arms swing upward on a jump they help to lift the body into the air because of their upward momentum. Likewise, momentum of the trunk of the discus thrower sets the arm and hand in motion. Of course, the hand also has the advantage of being extended at some distance from the center of rotation. It gains momentum from both. On the other hand, vigorous arm action may react on the trunk to draw it toward the arms. In a jump, if the arms are brought down forcefully while the body is in the air, they draw the trunk upward. This technique is used to gain height on a vertical jump or to gain distance in a broad jump. Similar effects may be obtained by use of the legs in jumping, diving, tumbling, and other activities.

It is common observation and experience that movements differ greatly in such points as force, speed, and range, as well as in freedom, precision, and smoothness—what we sometimes refer to as quality of movement. All these factors are dependent upon the way in which the muscles work together. The galvanometer, the oscillograph, and the electromyograph are all devices to record the presence and extent of muscular activity in a given movement. The recording is of the electrical phenomenon occurring in a contracting muscle. This is referred to as the action potential. Studies of this type are increasing in number. They have aided in understanding the synergistic pattern of action in complex skills and in the economy of muscular activity in certain types of movement.

The simplest form of voluntary movement occurs in an easy, natural, to-and-fro swing. The speed and range depend upon the same factors as in the pendulum, i.e., the length of the swinging part, the location of the center of gravity of the part along its total length, and the amount of force imparted to the swing. It is a slow, easy, and economical movement, but one very seldom found in human motion. The action potentials indicate a very short contraction at the beginning of the swing. It is sufficient only to overcome inertia. There is no antagonistic action; the momentum is spent against the force of gravity, the elasticity of the muscles, and the tension of joint structures. The opposite swing is accomplished in exactly the same way, and once the part is set in motion there is practically no effort necessary to keep it going. Some of the movements of the very small child are of this type, or in any easy natural walk the arm swing of the adult may approach this. Usually, however, the adult movement, if not varied in any other way, is increased in rate till it is no longer executed with such economy.

Merely increasing the speed of a swinging movement requires more force from the muscle, though the contraction is still quite short and at the beginning of the swing. However, stopping is no longer a passive affair. The antagonists must start contracting before the swing is completed. This serves to check the movement and reverse direction. Without this antagonistic action all fast movements would have a wide amplitude. Furthermore, many of our fast movements are fairly restricted in range and the greater the restriction the greater the loss. The fast movement is then an uneconomical one in exactly the same way that it is uneconomical to accelerate a car to a high rate of speed and then quickly to apply the brakes.

In many types of activities other than the swinging type discussed above, gravity is utilized to conserve muscular effort. Many of our movements are against gravity, and gravity is relied upon to furnish the check. In lifting, force is judged accordingly. In lifting a box or suitcase which is thought to be heavy, but is actually empty, one lifts it very high. Sufficient force has been applied to overcome the weight but there are no antagonists ready to check the resulting speed.

Whenever a movement is downward, gravity is almost invariably allowed to do the work. If muscular effort is used it comes from the antagonists which check the movement. For example, arm lowering may be accomplished by merely allowing the arm to relax and fall. But if it is lowered very slowly the deltoid must control the drop. The form occurring most frequently is probably a relaxed drop with control just at the end to keep the arm from hitting the body too hard. On the other hand, if the rate of descent must be greater than falling time, or there is resistance to the movement, then the depressors of the arm are used. These facts can all be demonstrated by the electromyographic technique.

Fast movements vary in quality and in economy. This is most apt to occur when the performer has developed skill in the act and is able to practice differential relaxation. He then develops the ability to produce the strength to impel the segment into action and to then let the muscles relax so that the part moves freely by its own momentum. The antagonistic control can be kept out of the action under certain circumstances. If the ballistic action carries the segment toward the limits of the elasticity of the antagonists and no need for limiting the range of motion exists, then the action is stopped "passively" and economically by inelasticity of the antagonistic muscles and the inertia of the rest of the body mass which is at the other end of the antagonists. For example, in a ballistic swing such as a tennis drive, the anterior shoulder muscles may cease to contract before the racket actually reaches the ball. The follow-through brings the arm forward until the posterior muscles are taut and the momentum is slowed by the resistive drag of the body, which is moving forward much less rapidly. This type of action is more apt to be used in a tennis serve than in a drive.

The ballistic swing is also used in skills which by their very nature end against resistance. An example is observed in pounding of stakes with a heavy hammer. More force is needed than just that resulting from dropping the hammer head to contact the stake. Muscular contraction provides the initial acceleration, and gravity and momentum are allowed to finish the swing with no brakes applied even though the performer knows that he must rhythmically and repetitively lift the hammer and drop it.

In such movements there is a continuity, smoothness, and rhythm that we are apt to associate with forceful, skilled movement, and describe as good quality of movement. Not only is the beginner seldom able to achieve this effect, but it is possible that some individuals are never able to acquire it.

Few of our movements are as simple as this; and in many instances external objects are being handled, which means increased resistance. The precision of speed, direction, and range that is necessary can be accomplished only by the co-operation of many muscles. In many cases agonists and antagonists both work with alternate dominance.

Postural balance, or any position when the body is poised for an activity, requires alternation of opposite muscle groups. In some instances this may resolve itself into a muscular rigidity in order to maintain a practically immobile state or to control external resistance. The action potentials of the two sets of muscles are in this case somewhat alternating but less rhythmical, and the impulses are less dependent upon each other.

Speed and resistance are the factors which determine the number of muscles used and the strength of their contraction. Fast movements produce a momentum which must be controlled. Resistance may vary from passive resistance of the part—i.e., tension of muscles, friction, and inertia—to muscular contraction in states of rigidity, and to various forms of external resistance.

The neuromuscular system is very sensitive to these demands and makes the adjustments necessary. The proprioceptors are stimulated by pressure and tension caused by muscular contraction and movement of parts. The individual becomes aware of movement and position. The semicircular canals and the eyes both receive stimuli concerning position and movement. These stimuli set off the mechanism for adjustment or control. Perception and intellect enable the individual to understand and meet problems of resistance and to translate them, often unconsciously, into motion and its control. The accuracy of all movements depends, then, upon the sorting of stimuli and the adjustments made to them.

Few if any of the complex movements can be performed by a single unified group of muscles such as flexors or extensors. These movements must often be guided by others. When a given muscle produces flexion it may also tend to produce outward rotation. In order to counteract this rotation or to control it to the desired degree an inward rotator must contract to the exact amount. This second muscle may also produce flexion, so an adjustment must be made between the two to give only the necessary amount of flexion. Also, the direction or type of movement may change when part way through the act. Introduction of the new muscles may cause a completely new adjustment in the muscles already acting. In any movement complete co-operation is necessary. In the unskilled performance there is usually an excess of muscular effort. Tenseness results from an attempt to secure accuracy; and rigidity may result when rigidity is unnecessary or when it may even be a hindrance.

Many movements also require a fixation or adjustment of one part not actually involved in the external motion. For example, the scapula is always moved when arm movements of any extent occur beyond a minimum range. Or, as more frequently happens, the point of origin for the acting muscles must be fixed. Without control, action of the hip flexors will move the pelvis onto the thigh as well as flexing the thigh toward the pelvis. In all leg flexion the abdominals hold the front of the pelvis firm so that the effect of the flexors will be only on the leg. Likewise, fixation of the thorax and abdomen may occur in any strong movements of either upper or lower extremities. The triceps may be used to prevent flexion in strong supination of the forearm, and the extensors of the neck and head may be used to prevent flexion with a rotation of the head. Proper co-operation of these assisting muscles is an essential part of such acts.

The sequence in which the muscles act and the relative timing of each to every other one is important. This is true not only because of the visible effect on the movement but also because the kinesthetic sensations of one part are often the stimulus to a later part. This is evident in such activities as basket shooting, the football punt, many tumbling stunts, and the golf drive. This dependence upon kinesthetic feeling and its place in learning was illustrated in an early study of Griffith's[3] on the learning of the golf drive. One group learned by the usual method of watching the ball and receiving the verbal instructions. The other group was blindfolded, was told what to do and what happened to the ball on each swing. The latter group made greater errors at first but eventually secured superior results by depending only upon the feeling of the performance. The amount of the superiority was small while the blindfold was retained; the amount increased in the two weeks following its removal. The ultimate results are not known.

The actual rate at which the act is performed is also important. An increase or decrease in rate affects the timing between different muscles. This is the reason for learning a skill at approximately the speed at which it is to be used. It is a familiar occurrence in games to see a player make a poorly executed hockey drive, shot at the basket, or football punt, because he is having to work at a rate faster than the one to which he is accustomed. In another experiment Griffith[4] demonstrates this and also shows that for each player there is an optimum speed for basket shooting.

In every case proper co-operation of muscles results in a graceful, easy, skillful, and economical movement. The stiff, awkward, jerky performance has usually too much muscular force, is uneconomical and ineffective. Antagonistic action may be a part of the control. Movements without antagonistic control may be easier and more economical movements; but the right amount of power of the agonists will help determine the extent of antagonistic action. Economy of forces is a definite factor in the problem of endurance.

Because of its construction the body, like most other machines, has a low degree of efficiency. There are many factors accounting for this which cannot be prevented. Unskilled, uneconomical movements can be overcome, however.

The first and most outstanding cause of mechanical inefficiency lies in the metabolic process accompanying contraction. Part of the loss is in heat, part in the lactic acid produced. This is the natural process of combustion and waste production. In addition there are various forms of resistance, namely, the viscosity or internal resistance of the muscle fiber, the still greater restraint of fascia and skin surrounding the muscle, the tension of antagonistic muscles, the inertia of the part, the pull of gravity, and sometimes friction. All of these must be overcome before external work is evident. This is characteristic of all reciprocating machines in which part of the force must be used to check or reverse movements of a part of the machine.

Much of our activity involves the maintenance of inactive and stationary positions. But these are unstable positions and require muscular effort. Internal work makes the same demands on fuel but external results are zero. The instability of the total body, and the tendency to rotation at most of the articulations are contributing factors to this constant internal work.

The mechanical disadvantage at which most of the muscles work is of tremendous significance. Most of them have relatively short force arms which gives them a handicap to start with, and their angle of pull is usually so small that most of the force is parallel to the bone. This component is necessary to avoid strain on the joint structures but it is loss in terms of work output.

REFERENCES

1. Bosmajion, John H., Electromyographic Study of Two-Joint Muscles, *Anatomical Record*, 129, 1957, p. 37.
2. Clarke, David, The Correlation between the Strength/Mass Ratio and the Speed of an Arm Movement, *Research Quarterly*, 32, March 1961, p. 12.
3. Griffith, Coleman, R., "An Experiment in Learning to Drive a Golf Ball," *Athletic Journal*, 11, 1931, p. kk.
4. ———, "Timing as a Phase of Skill," *Journal of Educational Psychology*, 23, 1932, p. 204; and "Types of Errors in Free Throws," *Athletic Journal*, 11, 1930, p. 22.
5. Fulton, Ruth E., Speed and Accuracy in Learning a Ballistic Movement, *Research Quarterly*, 13, March 1942, p. 30.
6. Gray, R. K., Start, K. B., and Glencross, D. J., Test of Leg Power, *Research Quarterly*, 33, March 1962, p. 44.
7. Hubbard, Alfred W., *The Upper Limits of Slow Movement and the Lowest Limits of Ballistic Movements*, Microcard PE87, 1950.
8. Steindler, Arthur, *Kinesiology of the Human Body*, Springfield, Ill., Charles C Thomas, 1955, Ch. 25, Lower Extremity as a Whole.
9. ———, *Mechanics of Normal and Pathological Locomotion in Man*, Springfield, Ill., 1935, Ch. 8, Electrophysical Analysis of Muscle Action; Ch. 9, The Coordination of Skeletal Muscle Action; Ch. 10, Fatigue and Recovery; Ch. 22, The Lower Extremity as a Whole.
10. Wheatley, Max, Electromyographic Study of the Superficial Thigh and Hip Muscles in Normal Individuals, *Archives of Physical Medicine*, 32, 1951, p. 508.

CHAPTER 11

Manipulation of Objects

1. Gravity is a constant force acting on all objects.
2. Momentum of one object may be transferred to another object.
3. The effectiveness with which the body moves other objects depends upon the amount, the direction, and speed of the force applied.
4. Receiving objects coming with speed or stopping body momentum on a firm surface necessitates resistance over a distance. This is accomplished by relaxation and flexion of body parts at the time of contact.

MOST OF THE DISCUSSION in previous chapters has dealt with the movements of the body resulting from force applied either within or outside the body. All these principles, of course, apply likewise to all other objects. But a very large part of our activity is for the purpose of producing motion of other objects, of varying that motion, or of stopping it entirely.

Objects of many types may be set in motion. If something is to be merely pushed along on a supporting surface, the force should be applied in line with the center of gravity. However, if the force is distributed around that center so that the effect is the same as if it were applied at the single point, the effect on the object will be the same. If there is friction between the object and its support, the object tends to rotate about that point or line of friction. The force producing the motion should not be at the center of gravity but moved toward the source of friction to prevent rotation around that retarded point.

When a force is applied with the hands and arms it may cause the object to move away from the body or it may cause the body to move away from the object. When the body is erect the trunk may be fixed and thereby resist the latter reaction. If the force required to move the object is greater than can be produced by the arms and resisted by the trunk, the body should be inclined toward the object. This position gives a greater component in the desired direction, and gives an angle which makes use of the leg extensors. It is also easier to hold the position at this angle.

This adjustment is characteristic of all pushing against heavy resistance. Exactly the same things are true of pulling.

Inertia is a property of all objects. Therefore, the first consideration in effecting motion is the inertia of the object. If a ball is thrown, its original inertia must be overcome and a velocity developed sufficient to carry it the desired distance before gravity pulls it to the ground. With a small baseball or tennis ball that is not much of a problem. But as the ball becomes heavier it is significant. A basketball is heavy enough so that children and even some high school girls find it difficult to develop sufficient velocity to carry it from the free throw line to the basket. In this type of throw the arc through which the ball may be carried before release is short. A heavy ball and short arc both contribute to low velocity. The solution in this case is to use an underhand throw which lengthens the arc of the arms somewhat and makes it possible to use knee flexion and extension more effectively. Knee flexion lowers the ball, and therefore increases the range over which the force is applied. The extensors of the legs are then used to give the necessary force. If the ball may be played from a position closer to the basket, the direction is then more nearly vertical and the leg extensors are again very effective.

In a single overhand type of throw of an object which can be grasped by the fingers the arm is whipped back to practically a full reach with weight back and body inclined backward. This gives the maximum range over which force may be applied, which means maximum velocity if force is applied throughout.

There are other factors in this action which make for increased velocity. The lever affecting the ball is no longer just from the elbow to hand, or shoulder to hand, but is the entire body. The whole body rotates over the foot from a position just on balance at the rear to one off balance in front, so that a step must be taken to save the position. The ball being out at the end of this long lever is traveling at considerable speed, estimated at as much as 140 feet per second for a very good thrower. This figure is similar to that given by another source. Kenny* studied the speed of balls covering 60.5 feet from pitcher to plate as delivered by twenty-one players with widely varying years of experience in baseball. He states the average time for the ball to cover that distance, when delivered by an overhand throw, as .58 second. This is equivalent to a velocity of approximately 104 feet per second. However the time for the player with the fastest ball was .49 second; this is approximately 124 feet per second. These figures assume that the speed is constant throughout the flight. Air resistance would affect it to some extent.

There is still another factor which is important in developing this velocity. At the same time that the hand is being brought forward and

* James D. Kenny, A Study of Relative Speeds of Different Types of Pitched Balls, unpublished master's thesis, State University of Iowa, 1938.

the body is rotating over the foot it is also rotating from right to left
(right-handed thrower) around the vertical axis. This rotation or twisting of the trunk adds force with which to whip the ball through its arc.
Such acceleration means added velocity at the moment the ball is
released.

The direction in which the ball is traveling at the instant it is released
is important in determining its line of flight. The acceleration of gravity
is constant. There must be enough upward force in the delivery to
counteract the downward pull sufficiently to allow the ball to remain in
flight until its forward movement is accomplished. Considering that
problem only, one might deliver the ball almost vertically. However in
this case, the forward component of the throwing force is so slight that
the ball almost drops in the thrower's hands. If the purpose of the throw
is distance, such a delivery is ineffective. If the purpose is to get height
or to increase the time the ball is in the air, the vertical delivery is
desirable.

The speed of the ball is obviously related to the angle at which the
ball should be thrown. If the ball has high velocity and goes a short
distance it may be thrown almost horizontally. If it has low velocity it
must be thrown at a greater angle with the horizontal even though it is
to go only a short distance.

Any object which is projected into space is subject to at least two forces
during its flight, namely gravity and air resistance. The downward drop
of all objects is at the rate of 32 feet per second. This means that the
change in velocity of the falling object is at the rate of 32 feet per second for each second it continues. For example, an object starting at
zero velocity attains a velocity of 32 feet per second by the end of the first
second; it will have fallen 16 feet. At the end of the next second it is
falling at the rate of 64 feet per second and it will have fallen 64 feet. Its
acceleration continues at that rate as long as it continues to fall.

Distance fallen $= \frac{1}{2}gt^2$: g $= 32$, t $= 2$ seconds, $\frac{32}{2}(2)^2 = 64$.

Air resistance is dependent upon many factors. The surface, size, and
shape of the object help determine the air flow around it. The velocity
of the object is an important consideration. Resistance increases approximately with the square of the velocity. The rotation of the object and air
currents are related to each other, and both affect the flight of the object.
Air resistance is, therefore, never exactly the same in any two instances.

The force which projects the object must be one which sets up a momentum sufficient to overcome these forces to the desired extent. In a
throw for distance, for example, all factors must be adjusted for maximum effects. The momentum of the projected object depends upon its
mass and its velocity. Since a given individual is capable of only a certain

amount of force, the velocity developed usually varies inversely with the mass of the object. For example, a shot cannot be moved by the hand as rapidly as a tennis ball.

The velocity of a thrown ball is dependent upon the amount of acceleration between starting time and the time of release. This is raised to a maximum in various ways. The first item of significance is an increase in the length of the lever. The inexperienced and untrained thrower often attempts a throw with the axis of the movement in the elbow. A single underhand throw with simple arm swing will carry farther merely because of increased length of lever, plus the fact that the angle of release is usually better. A throw for distance or speed is always made with the longest lever possible, from extended hand to foot. The body then rotates as a whole over the supporting foot. This lengthened lever means an increased arc or distance over which the force may be applied. It also means that the body weight is thrown into the rotation and utilized in developing momentum. Also the leg extensors are used, adding force. In addition, the body is simultaneously being rotated around a vertical axis. It was pointed out previously that this develops speed with relatively little effort.

All of these adjustments make the hand move at a high speed, and this speed is imparted to the object. When the ball is no longer held by the fingers, inertia carries it on until overcome by gravity and air resistance.

Because of centrifugal force the ball tends to go off at a tangent to the arc described by the hand. Because it is difficult to control the direction in that case the arm and hand are often adjusted to a much flatter arc. This is particularly true in an overhand throw, where the hand travels in very nearly a straight line. An underhand throw is much more difficult to flatten and is, therefore, often very poorly directed. Also, a ball which is too large to be held by the fingers and which must rest on the open palm, is more difficult to control at the moment of release. Therefore it is prone to go off on an undesired tangent. This fact is often evident when children or girls throw a basketball. The hands are very small in comparison with the ball and control is more difficult than it is for larger hands.

The angle at which a ball should be thrown is dependent upon the distance it is to go and upon its velocity. While it is in flight it is subject to two factors, its forward velocity and its gravitational acceleration, both of which are constant except for the effect of air resistance. The path which it travels is a parabola. It is the resultant of the velocity in a given direction and gravitational acceleration vertically downward. After being released, the ball continues to rise, but by decreasing amounts for each successive unit of time. The height which it attains is dependent upon the velocity and angle of release. The total distance covered is also dependent upon the same factors. The highest point is theoretically at half the total distance and also at the mid-point in time (assuming that the ball lands at the same height at which it was released). However, this does not take into consideration air resistance which will affect the path more or less, depending upon conditions. Usually there is a very slight decrease in height and a little decrease in total distance. This decrease becomes more significant with high speeds. Also, larger and lighter balls are affected more by air resistance because the surface is greater and the mass is proportionally less.

The problem of air resistance is of still more significance if the projected object is spinning or rotating about an axis through itself. If the object has linear motion the air resistance is constant over all the surface presented for contact with the "air wall." However, when it is rotating, the side which is turning into the "air wall," or in the direction of flight of the object, meets increased resistance. Likewise on the opposite side, which is turning away from the direction of flight, air resistance is slight; in fact the flow of air over this side of the object tends to accelerate the rotation. The effect of this is to change the course of the object. It will curve away from the side of greater resistance to that of lesser resistance. It is this type of spin that causes the curve on the pitched ball or the hook or slice in golf.

It works the same way if the rotation is around a transverse axis, that is, if the ball has top or back spin. This is again seen in the soaring of the ball in a good golf drive, or the drop of the tennis ball on the drive with top spin.

This must be taken into consideration in understanding the course of the ball. The effect is cumulative and will be greater in long flights, in the latter part of the flight at high speeds, or with a ball having a rough surface, as the golf and tennis balls have. Back spin may be used effectively to cause the ball to gain distance in flight and to remain almost motionless on the ground after landing. However, top spin causes the ball to drop sooner and makes it roll after dropping.

A resting object must have its resistance to motion overcome. There are various ways in which this may be done. It may be merely by the gradual application of force until it is sufficient to overcome inertia and also friction, if it is present. Or inertia may be overcome by suddenly applying a great force even though it is of short duration. For example, the body weight can be thrown in as part of the force, thus making it momentarily effective although it could not be used over an extended period of time. However, when the force is applied over a brief period, the effect of gravity and friction are soon apparent. Therefore, if the object is to be kept in motion sufficient force must be continued to counteract the forces of gravity and friction and to secure positive acceleration.

An object which is held in the hand or which is at rest on some other surface may be set in flight by throwing or striking it. The throw has been discussed; the similarities and differences between throwing and striking will be considered. Striking may be with the hand (or the foot if we interpret it loosely to include kicking) or with some tool. Exactly the same adjustments as are made in throwing are usually made to secure force in striking. A long lever which can be moved rapidly is the first essential. Combined use of many muscles helps to secure force. A rapidly moving point at the time of contact, shifting of body weight into the movement, and rotation of the body on the long axis are all means of acquiring momentum. The momentum thus developed in the hand, foot, or tool is imparted to the ball or other object. The ball is given velocity and direction by this act.

Direction is even more difficult to control in this case than in throwing. The angle at which the ball leaves the striking surface is dependent upon the angle at which it hits (Fig. 55). If a ball hits the surface at right angles it bounds directly back but is dropping gradually because of gravity. However, when the ball strikes at an angle other than a right angle, it leaves at an angle similar to the one with which it hits. Let line aX represent the ball which came in at right angles to the surface; it is also the path of the rebound. A ball coming in on path bX rebounds on Xc. The angle bXa is the angle of incidence; the angle cXa is the angle of rebound. They tend always to be the same.

The general line of the stroke may be forward and approximately horizontal but if the striking surface is inclined upward, the ball will assume a similar upward direction. It can be seen very readily that only a slight tilt of the tennis racket upward can give decided elevation to the ball. The amount of tilt needed depends upon the way the ball is bouncing from the ground and the position along the bounce at which the ball is struck, as well as the distance of the player from the net and placement desired beyond the net. Figure 56 shows the effect of a vertical racket face with contact at different parts of the bounce.

Since these movements are rotatory ones, the striking surface is usually traveling in an arc. This means that the striking surface is at every successive instant facing in a different direction. Obviously in that case, if the object is to go in a given direction, there is only one point on that arc which will send it there. This would create an almost impossible problem of timing. This is partly solved by adjusting parts of the body while it is moving so as to flatten the arc of the swing, and by adjusting the striking tool so as to secure the desired direction. Outside of these adjustments, accuracy depends upon correct timing of the contact. This is evident in tennis strokes or baseball batting.

It must be remembered that the reaction of the object hit is just as great on the striking surface as the force which projects it into space. Therefore, the striking tool must not only be of a firm substance, but it must not be allowed to "give," that is, to be moved by the other object. If it does

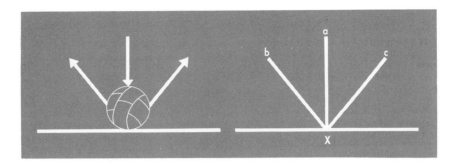

FIGURE 55: Angle of rebound

"give" the projecting force is correspondingly decreased and the direction may be changed.

The striking tool may give because the grip is loose or the wrist is allowed to bend at the time of contact. This is seen in some tennis strokes. Many players use a grip with the thumb up the back of the handle of the racket when making a backhand drive. The purpose is to brace the racket against the impact of the ball. When the racket moves, it decreases the force for the rebound and also changes the direction of the rebound.

The force with which the ball is projected back into space may be reduced because either the ball, or bat, or both "give" when contact is made. Even the most solid ball in use in sports is compressed somewhat when struck. The hard baseball, hockey ball, and golf ball are comparatively firm. Yet flattening of the side of contact is shown by the fast action camera to be very pronounced when these balls are hit forcefully. Softer balls show greater amounts of compression. For example, the softball flattens more than the hard ball. A good tennis ball shows still greater amounts; an old tennis ball offers almost no resistance. The amount of compression, and hence the rebound, of an inflated ball depends upon the amount of air in it. It is for that reason that most sports using inflated balls have a standard or uniform ball, including recommendations for air pressure in the ball.

The striking tool itself may "give" with the impact for the same reason that the ball is flattened. Of course, the "give" is negligible with a baseball bat, a golf club, or wooden paddle or club. It is very real in a strung racket. Good strings in a tennis or badminton racket are firm and have very little "give." As the racket becomes old or worn, the strings loosen. If one uses an old racket on an old ball the rebound is very short. On the

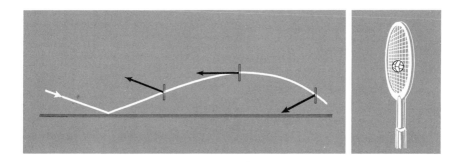

**FIGURE 56: Angle of rebound from a vertical racket face at
different points in the arc of the bounce**

other hand, the loose net is used on the lacrosse stick to trap the ball
and carry it.

In kicking it is usually more difficult to flatten the arc described by the
foot than that described by the hand in striking. Also, as in soccer, the
kick is usually made with the front of the instep, and it is difficult to get
the foot under a stationary ball in the proper position. The adjustment
must be made in the angle of the foot. The course of the ball which is
struck or kicked is governed by exactly the same factors as the thrown
one. It may or may not have spin imparted to it.

Many of our activities involve the stopping of a moving object either to
gain possession of it or to change its motion. In fact most of our sports
require these two skills as much or more than striking stationary objects.
In golf the ball is at rest when played, but that is the exception rather
than the rule.

A ball is struck on the move in exactly the same way as a motionless
one. It is usually moving toward the striking surface and has a certain
momentum in that direction. Its effect on the striking surface is, therefore, greater than that of the stationary ball. However, if the reaction of
the striking surface is sufficient, it is sent back in the other direction. The
momentum of the striking tool into the object is used to create that
counterforce and increase the return flight. This is illustrated in tennis.
The drive has a long forward swing so that the ball may be returned with
the desired speed and distance. But the volley may be made merely by
the racket held firmly in the path of the ball. The two balls might have
come with the same speed but the return by the drive will be long and
fast, that by the volley will be merely a short rebound.

Control of direction is again a major consideration. The arc should be
flattened as near the horizontal as possible. This adjustment is very pro-

nounced in baseball batting. The batter who starts with the bat high and goes down for the ball usually misses it. The stroke must also be adjusted with respect to the direction and speed of the oncoming ball. Increased speed gives it increased momentum. A ball which is either rising or falling will contact the striking surface differently from one which is nearly horizontal in its course. This was illustrated in Figure 56 by a tennis stroke. If the ball has spin it will rebound differently; the angle of rebound becomes greater or smaller depending upon whether the spin is toward or away from the direction of rebound.

A striking surface which is flat and fairly large presents rather few problems. But one which is smaller or rounded is more difficult to use. The ball rebounds from its point of contact, but on a rounded object, such as a baseball bat, the point of contact does not always face out into the field. Also, when one considers that the ball is also rounded, it is surprising that there are not more foul tips and foul grounders than there are.

Balls struck at some point other than the center of the bat and of the ball are usually spinning very rapidly. This spin is developed in the same way as any type of spin or rotatory motion. If an object is struck with a force directed squarely into the center of gravity it results in translatory motion. If that force comes at a point away from that center there results a moment of rotation in that direction. For example, a ball struck below the center of gravity has back spin, builds up increased resistance on its lower surface and less on its upper surface. It will continue to rise longer than it would if it had been hit squarely behind the center.

Also if the striking surface is moving across the face of the ball when it is hit, the ball is rotated in that same direction. This moving of the club across the face of the ball accounts for some of the slices and hooks in golf. It is made use of to gain either top spin or back spin in tennis.

When two objects meet which are moving in the opposite direction the result will be in terms of the difference in momentum of the two objects and in the direction of the greater of the two. It will be remembered that momentum equals mass times velocity. Thus a large object moving slowly may impart to a small one tremendous speed. This is true in most of our ball games where a rather heavy tool gives velocity to a comparatively small ball or shuttlecock. It also explains how, in football, the smaller man with speed can successfully block a larger man who is moving slowly. The smaller man must exert more force and use more energy to develop speed than would be required of the larger man, who relies more upon his mass.

It is due to the differences in speed that the kinetic energy of the smaller man may be the greater. To illustrate this point let us consider players A and B. A weighs 200 pounds and is moving at the rate of 8 feet per second. B weighs 160 pounds and is moving at the rate of 10 feet per second. Kinetic energy° varies with the square of the velocity. The kinetic energy of A is 200 foot-pounds; that of B is 250 foot-pounds. The lighter man has the advantage because of the difference in speed.

The momentum imparted to the ball by the bat or racket is an illustration of the general law of conservation of energy. The total momentum within a system remains constant. The bat and ball represent a system or unit. The bat is moving in one direction (→) with a certain momentum; mass is a relatively large factor in this momentum. The ball is moving in the opposite direction (←) with a certain momentum; velocity is a relatively large factor in this momentum. When the bat and ball meet each reacts upon the other; the momentum is the sum of the momentum of the two. However, the effect of the ball on the bat is a negative one; the velocity of the bat is decreased. The effect of the bat on the ball is sufficient to stop the ball and reverse it. The ball is now traveling at a certain velocity in the same direction (→) as the bat.

There is one other factor in this situation; the elasticity of the ball or its response to compression. The harder ball tends to regain its convexity much more readily than the softer ball. Therefore it leaves the striking tool faster. A good golf ball represents an attempt to build the maximum of elasticity into the ball.

The amount of compression of a ball also affects the angle of rebound. The angle of rebound approximates the angle of incidence for a hard ball. It is somewhat less than the angle of incidence for a softer ball because the decompression tends to make it leave at more nearly a right angle to the implement. The resultant angle is a compromise between the right angle and the angle of rebound.

Some of the same principles governing striking also apply to catching. In catching there is a contacting surface but it should be one which does not cause the ball to rebound and which closes around the ball when contact is made. This contacting surface must be adjusted to the direction of the oncoming ball. It must not be rigid or the ball will rebound. It is either ready to recede with the impact of the ball or is already moving slowly in the same direction as the ball when it makes contact. This is equivalent to saying that resistance must be applied over more or less distance, or that time must be used to produce negative acceleration on the ball. The greater the momentum of the oncoming ball the greater must be the adjustment of the catcher. The momentum of the ball may be great enough that the catcher needs more space for stopping the ball than can be secured by merely allowing the arms to flex. In that case he steps or shifts the weight during the catch, thereby increasing the range and time of the catch.

° Kinetic energy $= \frac{1}{2}mv^2$: mass $= \dfrac{\text{weight in pounds}}{32}$

This relaxation or "give" in catching can be continuous with the preparatory movement for a subsequent throw. The player with this smooth continuity of catch and throw is more apt to avoid fumbling and to be successful and efficient in throwing.

REFERENCES

1. Bowne, Mary E., Relationship of Selected Measures of Acting Body Levers to Ball-Throwing Velocities, *Research Quarterly*, 31, October 1960, p. 392.
2. Selin, Carl Warren, *Analysis of the Aerodynamics of Pitched Baseballs*, Microcard PE364, 1957.
3. Slater-Hammel, A. T., and Andres, E. H., Velocity Measurements of Fast and Curve Balls, *Research Quarterly*, 23, March 1952, p. 95.
4. Steindler, Arthur, *Kinesiology of the Human Body*, Springfield, Ill., Charles C Thomas, 1955, Ch. 32, The Arm as a Whole.

Part **III**

ANALYSIS OF ACTIVITIES

CHAPTER 12

Components of a Skill

THE SKILLS AND ACTIVITIES in which humans engage are varied in type, purpose, and intensity. We have already discussed some of the factors which make a particular activity functional and the mechanics necessary to its effective performance. For any given skill, we tend to teach a precise form to all individuals and carefully coach each into this pattern of action. This form is based on what we know of the best mechanics for use of force, for maximum accuracy, and for conservation of the performer's efforts. There is real merit to this ideal concept of the optimum pattern of these complex skills. Yet we do not always succeed in getting uniformity in a group of students. How much difference does it actually make? And why do we not get what we teach?

It is actually surprising after a brief series of lessons that there is as much uniformity in performance as usually takes place. The author has had considerable experience in going into classes in various sports, for observation and for rating student performance. Within two or three days time classes might be observed and rated which had been taught by five or six different instructors. After completing these observations it was possible to identify the little differences in form which had been taught by the various instructors, the points which had been emphasized and on which time had been spent in drill, and to identify those things in which the students were deficient.

Even if this instruction goes on for some time and skills are developed to a highly proficient level, there will be clearly observable variations in form. These are individual variations, which usually are an improvement for each individual over the basic pattern that was being taught. Individual variations may have developed because of that learner's body build, strength level for the task, endurance, or carry-over from previously learned skills. Even temperament or attitudes may affect the way in which a student goes about the performance. It is to be hoped that the instructor is wise enough to see some of these individual differences and promote suitable variations in the skill to the extent that it is an improvement. The good coach is ever alert to this type of adaptation, and is apt to refer to it as taking advantage of the talent and minimizing the shortcomings within the squad. Is the physical education teacher equally good in this respect?

Even in everyday skills there are individual variations. How many times can one recognize another at a distance by the manner of movement? How many times does the physical education teacher carry a mental image of the student's movement in certain skills long before the name has been sorted out of the total list for association with that student either as a person or as a performer in the class? While some of these individual differences are an asset to that person, others may be a real liability. The good teacher of movement or the therapist dealing with rehabilitation must be able to distinguish between those variations which are good for that person, mechanically sound for that person's capabilities, and those which are mechanically poor, less effective than they might be, and fatiguing and frustrating to the performer.

The repertoire of skills of each person is long. How did he acquire so many? There are those which seem to be almost inborn, to be a product of maturation and developing reflexes. The infant progresses from aimless arm waving to purposeful acts, such as reaching for things he wants, to feeding himself, sitting, crawling, standing, and finally walking. No one really teaches him these things, but rather provides the potential situations repeatedly and a little motivation to accelerate the process.

The young child starts a process of imitation which he continues into adulthood. He sees others around him doing something, and he tries it. He may be a good imitator or a poor one but out of this experience he builds up skills, many of which he continues to use indefinitely. Imitation is a perfectly good method of learning for the young child, and he enjoys it, as evidenced by his interest in "follow the leader" types of activity.

There are many other skills that the child is deliberately taught by someone. This type of learning proceeds from early years in such skills as buttoning and unbuttoning clothes to learning penmanship and later typewriting, from tricycle to bicycle riding, from snowball and rock throwing to kicking and batting and later golf and tennis, and so on for a myriad of work and play skills. The number he acquires will depend largely upon his environment and the comparative incentives for active and inactive pursuits. In any case he will know before adult years a variety from simple to complex patterns, some which he must do and some which he does for the joy of doing them.

In spite of these variations, there are definite similarities in many of the skills. It is possible to group them in certain ways according to similarity of the skill or its purpose or by the mechanics of performance. Because of the complexity and variety of performance, it seems best to follow a regular procedure in organizing the discussion about skills presented in this section of the book.

Almost every activity consists of three phases—the preparatory movement, the act itself, and the follow-through. In some cases there may be only two parts, as in most swimming strokes or in walking. It is hoped that this organization will be helpful to the student as a plan of study.

The preparatory movement is considered as that part of an act which is preparatory to the desired goal. For example, in striking or throwing it is the backswing, in jumping the leg flexion and backward arm swing. The act itself is considered in these cases as beginning with the forward movement or the leg extension. The point between may be an abrupt change of movement or the first may blend imperceptibly into the second. Also the end of the act itself and the beginning of the follow-through may have to be defined arbitrarily. In a throw, the division can very easily be considered to be at the time of release, in a stroke at the time the ball leaves the striking implement, in a jump either at the highest point in the flight or at the moment of contact in landing. The latter seems preferable, since the jump is really completed at that time and the rest of the jump is only the landing and recovery. This situation is further confused because of the fact that transfer of weight is often considered as almost synonymous with follow-through; whereas, it is in reality a continuous process throughout the three phases of the action.

The main thing to consider in an analysis is the complete movement, the sequence and relationship of parts. The exact dividing point in a complex movement may be relatively unimportant from the standpoint of understanding the movement. Convenience in handling or a logical division may be the rule for separation.

Since it is advisable to have a definite idea of what is being discussed the first step should be a brief but clear description of each of the three phases in sequence. The second step is an analysis of each phase in terms of segments moving, parts fixed, and muscles used to produce force, control movement, or secure timing. The last step is to interpret each part in terms of mechanical principles. This means an understanding of the reasons for each phase, the source of force, use of levers, relationship of center of weight, factors in speed or control, antagonistic muscle action, and many other points.

	Description	Muscular Analysis	Mechanical Analysis
Preparatory Movement			
Act			
Follow-through			

This plan provides a framework for the complete analysis. Variations from accepted "form" in any movement may be discussed in terms of differences of purpose or effectiveness, as adaptations to certain situations, or as errors which fail to satisfy certain principles and are not acceptable therefore.

Each of the various activities in sports or in the performance of daily routine almost uniformly includes a preparatory movement and a follow-through. In fact, the few activities where either or both are omitted do so specifically to avoid the results of those phases. This is seen in tennis strokes. The drives have a long backswing and follow-through, whereas the volley usually has a very minimum of each. In the drives maximum power is desirable on the forward swing, in the volley the purpose is principally to provide a surface from which the ball may rebound a short distance.

The preparatory movement serves one or more of several purposes. Usually it stretches the muscles to be used by changing the position of the joint. This is done by movement in the opposite direction from the one in which the act is done. For example, in preparation for a jump the legs are flexed, thus stretching all the leg extensors. In a throw the arm swings backward, stretching the anterior muscles of the shoulder and arm. It was pointed out previously that this stretching puts the muscle at that position in its amplitude where it works most effectively.

Another result of the preparatory movement in almost every act is to increase the length of the arc through which the force is applied, and hence to increase the speed and momentum of the movement. This is very important, whether one is projecting the body as in jumps or imparting momentum to an object as in throwing or striking.

A third result of the preparatory movement is that of directing the force in the desired direction. A long continuous movement gives a chance for an adjustment of line and a co-ordination of all parts in the proper direction. These are not possible in a short thrust, stab, or toss.

In popular terminology, a "transfer of weight" occurs in many activities. This movement is so named because the body is supported first over one leg and then shifted quickly over the other one for support. For example, the thrower starts with the weight back over the right foot. As the throw is made a step is taken forward on the left foot which immediately assumes the support of the body. Likewise, in a forehand drive in tennis the shift is from the right to the left foot, but in this case it is from side to side, or laterally, instead of from the rear forward. "Transfer of weight" implies this shift of support. However, there is much more significance to the movement than is indicated by the term.

Actually the body mass is moving in approximately a horizontal plane; its speed depends upon the force put into the movement. Momentum is implied. For any given performer, the mass being relatively constant, momentum* varies with the speed of that particular act. Therefore, "transfer of weight" is in reality "transfer of mass" and is effective only when the velocity factor is sufficient to produce considerable momentum. The term "transfer of weight" is justifiable only when used synonymously with "transfer of mass" or momentum. The term "transfer of weight" is used in this book interchangeably with the other terms. The reader should interpret the term with its full meaning.

The transfer of mass continues throughout the movement. This transfer and the follow-through usually serve several purposes. First of all, the body mass is often carried through a long arc and thrown into the movement with such force that the momentum adds to the effectiveness of the act. In some activities such as overhand throwing or striking events transfer of mass and follow-through help make possible the use of the maximum length of lever. The lever is the total length of the body, since the point of support becomes the center of rotation around which the entire body moves. Also of significance is the fact that many of the extensors of the body are brought into use. These are the strongest muscles of the body and give the necessary force to develop body momentum.

Perhaps the further advantage can be explained best if we consider what would happen if one attempted to eliminate the follow-through. What would be the effect if the arm and body stopped moving when the ball was released, or the bat contacted the ball? From the standpoint of economy it would be a great waste. Muscular effort would be spent on developing the necessary speed up to a given point, and then further muscular effort would have to be used to check that momentum while it was at its height. It is exactly the same type of loss which occurs when a car is accelerated to high speed and then the brakes are suddenly applied. The driver of the car knows that that procedure not only wastes gasoline, but it is also hard on tires and brakes. The body suffers in the same way. Movements become tense, antagonistic forces are applied, and injury to muscles or tendons can easily result under these circumstances. A movement without a follow-through must be comparatively short and jerky. Most movements demand precision and direction. However, in a short jerky movement, accuracy and direction are difficult to maintain. Thus, the force necessary to stop the movement would decrease momentum before the desired moment, since its effect cannot be instantaneous; it may interfere with direction of the movement; and it may result in injury. It is also an extravagant use of effort.

The relaxation on landing from a jump or in catching a ball is just as much a part of the scheme as is the continuation of a movement begun. Relaxation serves to conserve energy, to avoid injury, and to control the momentum of the body or object involved.

---

* Momentum equals mass times velocity.

How many activities can you think of in which there is no preparatory movement or no follow-through, or in which both are lacking? The list will be short, but there are a few.

It was stated that swimming was more easily divided into two parts. That is merely for convenience. The recovery part is in reality the preparatory movement, the first part of the drive is the act, and the last part of the drive often corresponds to the follow-through, particularly in the arm strokes. The rest on the glide completes the follow-through, giving relaxation and streamlining the body. In some activities this is not so apparent and they may actually consist of two phases.

Working from this basic outline, all activities will be divided into logical parts and analyzed accordingly. Where deviations occur, an attempt will be made to show the reasons for each variation.

REFERENCES

1. McCloy, C. H., The Mechanical Analysis of Motor Skills, in *Science and Medicine of Exercise and Sports,* Warren R. Johnson (ed.), New York, Harper & Row, Pubs., 1960, p. 54.
2. Oester, Y. T., and Licht, Sidney, Routine Electrodiagnosis, in *Electrodiagnosis and Electromyography,* Sidney Licht (ed.), New Haven, Elizabeth Licht, Publisher, 1956, p. 109.
3. Smith, Gwendolyn K., *A Kinesiological Analysis of Selected Phases of the Physical Education Program for College Women,* Microcard PE77, 1946.
4. Steindler, Arthur, *Kinesiology of the Human Body,* Springfield, Ill., Charles C Thomas, 1955, Ch. 1, Aims and Purposes of Kinesiology.

CHAPTER 13

Static Positions of the Body

ANY POSITION in which an attempt is made to hold the body stationary is a static position. The more common ones will be discussed here. They are lying, sitting, and standing. These were introduced in the discussion of stability. Other related problems of significance are the holding of different types of loads, and poses in dance, gymnastics, apparatus work, and diving.

It was pointed out previously that many positions which we assume, and which are commonly considered to be resting positions, do not completely eliminate the need for muscular control. Prone or supine positions on a completely supporting surface permit maximum relaxation. The same is true of a semireclining position in certain types of chairs. In these cases the body is so supported that relaxation will not cause the body to change position, other than perhaps a sliding of an arm to the side, or the characteristic drop and spreading of the feet which occur when one is lying on the back and lets the legs relax.

It must be remembered, however, that assuming one of these positions does not guarantee relaxation and inactivity of the muscles. The person lying on his back may be just as rigid or even more so than someone who is standing. Likewise, there is great individual variation in the amount of rigidity, and hence of muscular activity, shown by different persons, all of whom are in approximately the same position. Those persons who are overly rigid, who are perhaps jerky and awkward in performance, who make a lightning-like response to even a minor stimulus, are said to be in a state of hypertension. This is a state of excessive and constant muscular effort. It is exhausting, and naturally many other ailments appear after a time.

The standing position cannot be a completely relaxed one. The arrangement of segments and the effect of gravity upon them has been discussed. Let us assume a normally erect position with the feet together. The weight line falls anterior to the ankle joint. There is, therefore, a tendency toward forward inclination of the body at the ankle joint, which must be opposed by the ankle extensors. The forward angle of the tibia is not more than 3° to 5° but it is sufficient to produce a moment of rotation eliciting action from the gastrocnemius and soleus muscles.

If a heel of any height is put under the foot, a new alignment of segments must be made. Without such an adaptation the body would be inclined so far forward that balance would be impossible. Most of the adjustment is in the ankle, but there is some in the articulations above the ankle. In every instance the extensor muscles make and hold this adaptation.

In the erect standing position the line of gravity falls in the anterior part of the knee joint, so that the tendency is toward hyperextension rather than flexion. Under these circumstances the knee extensors are usually relaxed. However, if the slightest flexion occurs the extensors spring into action immediately to prevent collapse. When high heels are worn there is a tendency for flexion in the knees, and the vasti must function constantly.

The line of gravity normally coincides very well with the axis of the hip joint. If the spine is well balanced on the pelvic girdle the problem of balance at the hip is slight. If the spine is held erect it must be done by the pull of the erector spinae and by contraction of the abdominal muscles to flatten the lumbar region. If the spine is allowed to slump, the weight falls on the extensors, causing them to be stretched. They usually protect themselves by slight tension to prevent extreme flexion and excessive stretching. The head balances fairly easily if kept upright, but it is allowed to hang forward in many of our activities. Therefore, the extensors must support it.

Thus even the most erect standing position requires muscular action, almost exclusively that of the extensors. Deviations from an erect position create additional demands on the extensors.

The ordinary standing position is not an immobile one, even though we commonly think of it as such. There is always a slight amount of body sway in an anteroposterior direction and it is greater in some individuals than in others. This is due to the alternate dominance of anterior and posterior muscles. For example, the extensors tend to draw the weight backward. This feeling of change, and the perception of movement through use of the eyes automatically causes contraction of the antagonists, and the body sways forward. This sway is likewise a stimulus to the extensors, and so the process continues.

Ordinarily we are not aware of this sway until it is eliminated for some reason. Posing for a picture by time exposure may make one aware of it. Attempts to completely eliminate this sway usually result in discomfort or occasionally in a feeling of faintness.

Skaggs[7] reports a study of body sway which was done with a small group of subjects. The main purpose of the study was to compare body sway when the muscles of the legs were in normal tension with sway when they were in hypertension. The average amount of sway and the variability increased as the period of standing increased. This was true for both conditions. The hypertensive state tended to cause a little greater sway and greater variability for each length period, but the differences were not statistically significant. The differences in amount of sway between subjects with shoes on and the same subjects barefooted were extremely small.

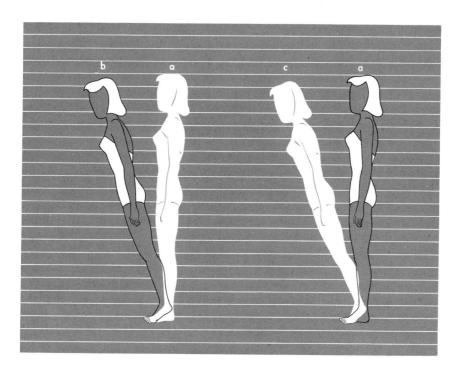

FIGURE 57: Effect of high heels on balance
a–correct alignment barefooted; b–same alignment of segments,
3-inch heels

It is possible to study sway with the same equipment referred to earlier for determination of the gravital lines. The writer has found considerable individual variation in sway. In many instances it is increased when the subject stands with eyes closed, and for some it increases when trying consciously to prevent sway. Fatigue also tends to increase sway, apparently due to sensory fatigue or delay in muscle response.

It is evident that an erect position of the spine is the one in which the moments of rotation between vertebrae are at the lowest. However, when a standing or an unsupported sitting position is maintained for a long time, the extensors fatigue. Flexing the back occasionally permits the extensors to relax or even be stretched, thus affording relief. Also, sitting, leaning back with arm support, or leaning forward with hands or elbows on the knees relieves the muscles of the back and allows those of the arms and shoulder girdle to do the work.

There are many times when one bears the entire weight on one foot. This occurs for a brief period of time on each step. It is also done while kicking, when taking off one's shoe while standing, when doing certain stunts, and in other similar situations. The weight must now be centered over a smaller base, which is very near a triangle in form. The antero-posterior dimension is exactly the same as when on both feet. It is in a lateral direction in which the problem of balance is found. The mid-line for weight bearing purposes would appear to be between the second and third metatarsals. This is apparently true from the dimension of the width of the foot at the metatarsal-phalangeal area of the foot. This is also the center of the foot determined by Morton[5] in his staticometric study of weight bearing. He calls this line from the center of the talus, running distally between the heads of the second and third metatarsals, the "axis of balance."

There must be adjustments made above the foot to bring the body mass over this line. Raising the arm and shifting the trunk are common adjustments when other requirements of the task do not prevent them. When adjustments above the foot do not satisfy the requirements of equilibrium, one of two types of action may be observed in the supporting foot. It begins to invert as the weight shifts laterally or to evert if the weight moves too much medially. This is a subtalar motion which makes a slight adjustment in the axis of the foot. But the strength of these muscles is not great, and the range of action is limited. Of more importance, perhaps, is the fact that the foot movement seems to offer a counteraction against which the weight can be shifted back into line. If the body weight shifts completely out of the base of support, then the person is apt to take a hop in an attempt to re-establish a base under the center of gravity. This may or may not be successful. If it is not successful, then the other foot must be placed on the floor to make a larger base and offer restraint for the body mass which has started to fall. In other words, the person is no longer in a static position.

Many stunts use this one-legged support, the instructions often stipulating that the foot must remain in contact with the floor, sometimes also requiring that the hands remain on the hips, and that the eyes remain closed. These are all attempts to require very precise control of the gravital line over the center of the foot.

When the person holds a load of any type the weight tends to create a stronger moment of rotation at all the lower articulations where such a tendency already exists. This effect is minimized as much as possible by shifting the trunk so that the body may be used to balance the added weight and bring it more closely to the central line.

If the weight is held in front of the body about waist or chest height, the upper trunk is inclined backward. This is the characteristic position in activities such as carrying a loaded tray or holding an infant in the arms. Excessive leaning is usually accomplished by extreme hyperextension of the lumbar spine and by thrusting the hips so far forward that the weight of the trunk is supported principally by the iliofemoral ligament. The need for excessive leaning can be overcome by moving the load close to the body or shifting it up to the shoulder.

Weight is sometimes supported on the back of the shoulders. If it is very great the abdominals are unable to balance it with the trunk erect. Therefore, the individual leans forward, thus shifting responsibility to the spinal extensors. If the load can be placed more nearly in line with the weight line of the body it can be supported more easily. For example, the infant may be placed on the hip or across the shoulder; the tray may be lifted to the shoulder. The head carry of some of the primitive people has a definite advantage in this respect. Of course, similar adjustments must be made laterally, but usually it is not necessary to make as great a shift as in the anteroposterior direction. If such positions must be repeated frequently and maintained for long periods of time they are fatiguing because muscular effort must still be expended. There is also the possibility that after a time there will be a change in tonus and in balance between antagonists, and a kinesthetic feeling for this new position which will make it habitual even though the load is gone.

Weights that are held below the center of gravity are compensated for in the same way as those at a higher level. They are usually held in one hand at the side, although from the standpoint of balance it would be easier to have the load divided. The weight is really applied to the body at the shoulder. Therefore, strong extension of the trunk and legs is just as important as in the previous situations. If the load is carried on only one side, it must be supported by the muscles of that arm and shoulder and by the trunk muscles of the opposite side. The strong downward pull on the wrist, elbow, and shoulder requires muscular pull at all joints of the arm. In this position the force of each muscle is largely stabilizing, and the task is fairly easily accomplished. Such positions are common in daily activities. Among sports, bowling best illustrates this position, although it is not really a static position.

Some positions in pyramids and the base in many couple stunts are stationary positions supporting the weight of another performer. Body mass is frequently used to counterbalance the weight of the top, as in the knee balances. Horse and rider or a standing mount must be supported with back straight to prevent strain on the erector spinae. The ways in which the moment of rotation may be reduced are discussed in the chapter on tumbling.

Most of the poses in modern dance are very brief, at least in comparison with the dance forms such as the ballet. The emphasis is on movement to a position rather than the position itself. However, precise adjustments for balance are always made. If the trunk and arms are extended forward, one leg is extended backward, helping in balance as well as line. If the arms and trunk are bent sideward a wide base is used. If a sitting position is taken, it is usually with one or both knees flexed, or a supported position, either of which lends itself to quick and easy action following.

Many apparatus activities use a hanging position as the starting and finishing point. Hanging may be of two types, active or passive. Passive hanging is the more relaxed form. The finger flexors are used to grip the bar or ring. The performer hangs at arms' length, with shoulder muscles partially relaxed. The weight of the body, therefore, causes extreme abduction of the scapula and elevation of the acromial end of the shoulder girdle. The trunk and legs also hang relaxed. Most of the tension is borne by the ligaments rather than the muscles.

In active hanging there is more muscular contraction, which results in a fixation of the articulations and support of the weight by the muscles. The most pronounced difference is in the position of the shoulder girdle. Posteriorly it is held down more nearly in its normal position by the rhomboids and trapezius, anteriorly by the pectoralis minor and subclavius. The deltoid, pectoralis, and latissimus dorsi are active at the shoulder to prevent strain and stretching of the shoulder joint. The latter two are especially valuable because they connect the thorax and the arm and hence help to avoid displacement of the shoulder joint. The contraction of the latissimus, the fixation of the spine and thorax, and the weight of the legs on the pelvis all tend to produce hyperextension of the lumbar spine, and an accompanying increased tilt of the pelvis. This is counteracted by abdominal contraction which also helps to fix the front of the thorax. The legs may hang relaxed or be actively extended.

The active position is essential as a starting position for other activities. It is also the form to be used in development of strength in the muscles of the shoulder and pectoral girdle, especially if that improvement is aimed at the correction of round shoulders. If the suspension activity is used for stretching the spine in cases of scoliosis, the passive hang is preferable.

The hand stand on the horizontal or parallel bars is identical in form to the hand stand on the floor though the method of getting into the position varies decidedly.

A pose is used as the preliminary part of any dive. In the running dive it is merely a position of attention and is an ordinary or slightly exaggerated erect standing position. In the standing dive, however, it must be a position which will fulfill the standards of good standing and at the same time permit shifting quickly and easily into action. This position is characterized by greater tonus and is truly a position of readiness.

A dive is a variation of the jump, but the standing dive does not permit the usual leg flexion and body lean which is characteristic of the strong and forceful jump. Some adjustments can facilitate the jump and not interfere with the requirements of the pose. For this present discussion we will refer to a standing front dive, the purpose of which is to get height and a relatively close entry.

FIGURE 58: Stance for a standing dive
a—good; b—too far forward; c—too much of a forward thrust

Since the diver is to go up, the toes should be on the board or diving platform rather than curled over the edge. This gives a more nearly vertical push-off instead of a forward one. It also helps slightly to check against body lean. There are two very common errors in body position. In one, the alignment of body segments is correct but the weight is shifted far forward by ankle flexion. This makes it possible to get more force from ankle extensors, and easier to get into the water head first, but it reduces the height of the dive. This results in a backward component which is too great, while the upward component is reduced.

In the second error, when the arms are lifted forward, the shoulders are thrust back and the hips forward. This position has no real advantage, violates the standards of the dive, and reduces the upward thrust. From this position usually the arms are then brought down and back, and this thrusts the trunk forward, with the same results as above. The arms may be lifted to the side and then moved forcefully in and up for a lift without disturbing the body alignment.

A slight knee flexion is necessary when the dive starts, but the trunk should remain in its upright position; and the hips should not protrude backward as they do in the ordinary jump.

The position of the head is important in balance as well as in helping to control the line of flight on the take-off. The same is true of the standing back dive. In the latter dive the position of the arms is helpful in balance.

The first essential for success in archery is the maintenance of an erect, well-balanced standing position, a position which is duplicated for every arrow shot, at least for all from the same distance. In most standing positions the problem of balance is greatest in an anteroposterior direction. This is not true in archery. The resistance of the bow and sideward elevation of the arm tend to pull the trunk sideward in the direction of the bow. In an attempt to counteract this pull the performer often inclines the trunk in the opposite direction. The good archer maintains an erect position by proper muscular control, dependent upon a kinesthetic perception of position. The feet are spread sideward a little as a means of facilitating balance in the lateral direction. The position of the body and the pull and fixation of the arms constitute practically the whole of the actual performance. The position must be one which is exact and also absolutely steady. Any swaying of the trunk or vibration of the arm is destructive of aim.

REFERENCES

1. Brown, Gaydena M., Relationship between Body Types and Static Posture of Young Adult Women, *Research Quarterly*, 31, October 1960, p. 403.
2. Cureton, T. K., and Wickens, J. S., Center of Gravity of the Human Body in the Antero Posterior Plane and its Relation to Posture, Physical Fitness and Athletic Ability, *Research Quarterly*, 6, March 1935, p. 104.
3. Hellebrandt, Frances A., Standing as a Geotropic Reflex, *American Journal of Physiology*, 121, 1938, p. 471.
4. Howland, Ivaclaire S., *Body Alignment in Fundamental Motor Skills*, New York, Exposition Press, 1953.
5. Morton, Dudley J., *Human Locomotion and Body Form*, Baltimore, Williams and Wilkins Co., 1952, Ch. 7, The Feet as a Base; Ch. 8, The Single Foot as a Base.

6. O'Connell, A. L., Electromyographic Study of Certain Leg Muscles During Movements of the Free Foot and During Standing, *American Journal of Physical Medicine*, 37, 1958, p. 289.
7. Skaggs, E. B., Further Studies of Body Sway, *American Journal of Psychology*, 49, 1937, p. 105.
8. Smith, J. W., Muscular Control of the Arches of the Foot in Standing: An Electromyographic Assessment, *Journal of Anatomy*, London, 86, 1952, p. 484.
9. Steindler, Arthur, *Kinesiology of the Human Body*, Springfield, Ill., Charles C Thomas, 1955, Ch. 7, Body Balance and Body Equilibrium; Ch. 14, Mechanics of Posture.

14

Locomotion

WALKING

WALKING IS THE SIMPLEST form of progression. There is a surprising similarity between the gait of different persons, although in certain details individual characteristics appear. Walking is probably the most efficient act in which the human engages. This is doubtless the result both of development of the locomotor pattern and of the individual's practice and relative proficiency in it. Steindler[13] makes this statement, "Automatic movements which from time immemorial have been executed by mankind, such as running, walking, are carried out with a remarkably favorable degree of efficiency, for instance, walking with an efficiency degree of 33.3 per cent."

The individual propels himself forward by a drive or extension of the legs and with the use of gravity. The walk is a process of pushing the body out of balance while it is supported over one leg and of then bringing the driving leg forward in time to save the body from falling. This process is repeated with every step.

Let us analyze the walk as nearly as possible according to the outline set up for analysis of activities. The arms and legs will be considered separately in order to simplify the discussion. The action of the legs is divided into two phases, the swinging phase and the supporting phase.

Description of the Swinging Phase of the Leg

At the end of the drive the leg and foot are completely extended and on an angle backward from the line of the trunk (Fig. 59, position *a*). The forward swing starts immediately after the final moment of contact. The movement originates as flexion of the hip with the thigh moving forward. The knee also starts flexing and the foot returns from its extended position to normal alignment with the leg (position *b*). As the leg passes under the body, flexion at each of these three articulations becomes a little more pronounced; after the foot clears the ground under the body, the lower leg is extended (position *c*). This brings the leg into position for contact with the ground again.

[handwritten marginalia: Cent of gravity / Angle / summation / momentum / Findings / Prime Mover / Forces / Involved]

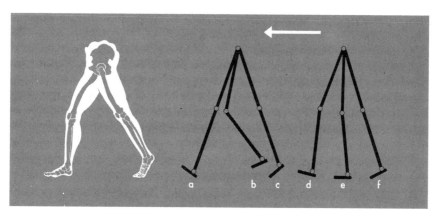

FIGURE 59: Diagram of leg action during walking

Description of the Supporting Phase of the Leg

At the moment of contact the leg is reaching slightly forward. The heel makes contact first; but the weight moves forward very rapidly, carried along the outside border of the foot to the ball of the foot. There is a very slight flexion at the knee at the moment of contact (position c'). The hip and knee then start into extension and so continue throughout the drive (positions d and e). The contact of the foot shifts across to the inside of the ball of the foot and the final push off comes from flexion of the great toe (position a).

Relationship of Action in Both Legs

When one leg is directly beneath the body and supporting it the other is swinging forward. Before the final drive from the first takes place, the second makes contact in front of the body. For a brief period both feet are in contact with the ground and the typical stride position occurs. The first leg finishes its drive and swings forward while the second supports. It also makes contact before the second finishes its drive. So the action of the two legs is normally identical, the walk is rhythmical and is characterized by this period of double leg support at the end of every step with an intervening period of single leg support.

It is evident that the legs cannot perform in this fashion without affecting the position of the superimposed trunk. We will consider first the immediate effect upon the pelvis. The most obvious one is the swing of the pelvis with the legs. As the right leg is carried forward the right side of the pelvis also moves forward. At the same time the left leg is moving backward and the left side of the pelvis is moving with it. This must obviously occur also since the right side is moving forward. With the alternate leg action the pelvis, of course, oscillates in the opposite direction. The step is usually taken with the toes pointing straight ahead, or nearly so; the foot remains in contact with the ground, but the pelvis turns. Some rotation at the hip must result. When the foot is back, the pelvis is back and the leg is rotated inward at the hip. When the leg is forward, the pelvis is forward and the leg is rotated outward at the hip.

The pelvis also moves in the vertical direction. Just as one leg starts its forward swing, that side of the pelvis rises slightly but drops again to reach its lowest point at the end of the swinging phase. Contact of the foot with the ground causes it to rise, and it continues to rise until after the supporting leg has passed is perpendicular direction. That side of the pelvis then drops slightly.

Description of the Arm Swing

The arm swing varies considerably with variations in speed of the walk. This is a description of a fairly slow, easy walk. The arm swings forward from the shoulder with the arm hanging more or less relaxed. It is usually in almost a sagittal plane but may move slightly medialward. There is sometimes a little elbow flexion at the end of the swing. The arm then drops back and on to a position slightly posterior to its resting position. The elbow may lead a little in this movement. The backward path is usually in almost a true sagittal plane.

The movements of the shoulders are similar to those of the pelvis but usually a little less pronounced. The arms swing alternately as do the feet. But the arms swing in opposition to the feet, i.e., the left arm goes forward with the right leg and the right arm with the left leg.

Muscular Analysis and Swinging Phase of the Leg

The hip flexion which starts the swing is produced by the iliopsoas, sartorius, the pectineus, and, at the very beginning of the swing, the gracilis helps a little. The pectineus and the gracilis also help prevent abduction of the leg which might result from the forward swing of the pelvis. They may be assisted in this by slight action of the adductor longus. The sartorius is more important in hip and knee flexion. Easy and quick flexion of the thigh is possible only if the pelvis is fixed. This is done by action of the abdominals.

Knee flexion is at first largely passive due to the tension of the hamstrings. That tension becomes more pronounced with the hip flexion and is aided by the sartorius.

Ankle flexion starts as the result of relaxation of the gastrocnemius, soleus, and peroneus longus. It is continued by contraction of the tibialis anticus and peroneus tertius. They continue until the time of contact resulting in the "heel first" position.

The pectineus and gracilis acting as adductors keep the leg swing in a straight line. The outward rotation of the leg takes place at the same time, and is produced by the pectineus in the early part of the swing, by the iliopsoas, and the six small outward rotators.

The knee extension which comes in the latter part of the swing is partially passive due to the momentum of the leg and the relaxation of the hamstrings. It also involves action of the quadriceps extensor muscles.

Muscular Analysis of the Supporting Phase

At the instant at which contact is made the knee flexes slightly because of a relaxation of the quadriceps muscles and tension of the hamstrings. The latter causes the lower leg to be drawn backward toward the ground in fast walking. The knee is controlled throughout the period of support by the vasti.

Hip extension is taken care of principally by the hamstring muscles. If the stride is long, the gluteus maximus contracts more strongly than it does on a short stride. In extension, as in flexion, the pelvis must be fixed; this is done by the quadratus lumborum and the erector spinae on the same side of the leg which is extending.

Ankle extension comes from the gastrocnemius, soleus, peroneus longus, and tibialis posticus. The peroneus longus and brevis are largely responsible for the slapping action of the foot shown by the shifting of the weight from the outside to the inside of the foot. The final drive comes from flexion of the toes which is produced by action of both the long and short flexors.

During the supporting phase the tensor fasciae latae and the gluteus medius and minimus are acting. The result of their action is to assist in inward rotation of the hip which must take place with the reversal of stride. But of still greater importance is the fixation of the pelvis to prevent the unsupported side from dropping.

The trunk extensors also help by counteracting the effect of the abdominals on the spine and pelvis and by fixing the pelvis to give firmer origin to the leg extensors.

Muscular Analysis of the Arm Swing

In the easy walk which has been discussed the arm swing has very little force put into it. It is rather of a free pendular type. The force for the forward swing is produced by the anterior deltoid and pectoralis major and in a little more forceful swing they are assisted by the coracobrachialis. The slight elbow flexion which sometimes occurs is passive, due to relaxation at the elbow and to the momentum of the lower arm.

The backward swing may be largely passive if the arm drops only to the side or slightly back. As more force is needed for that swing and the excursion of the arm increased the teres major, latissimus dorsi and posterior deltoid act. The triceps speeds up elbow extension and the long head assists in the action at the shoulder.

The oscillations of the shoulders or upper trunk are even more passive and dependent upon arm swing than are those of the hip. In the faster walk the arm actually assists in oscillation of the hip by reaction on the trunk.

Mechanical Analysis of Leg Action

It is evident from the description of the various movements of the walk that each is a rotatory movement of one segment upon another. The walk is then a series of rotatory movements combined in such a way that the end result on the whole body is the same as if translatory motion had taken place. The principle on which this is based is very simple.

If a single lever is rotated around an axis first at one end and then at the other, it will then be in a position exactly parallel to its starting position providing the angle of rotation is the same each time and that the rotation is in opposite directions. A double rotation which meets these requirements gives the same end result as translatory motion (Fig. 60). Two such combinations are found in a complete step.

During the swinging phase the femur swings forward rotating at the hip joint. During the supporting phase it again rotates forward but this time action is at the knee. The same is true of the tibia. The combination of these movements can be traced in Figure 61.

Forward progress is made because of the drive of the rear leg and the angle at which it is working. Throughout the supporting phase the leg is at an angle with the line of weight except for the instant when it coincides with that vertical line. For that brief moment the leg is merely supporting the body against the pull of gravity. At all other times the force of the leg has two components, the vertical one and the horizontal one. The longer the stride and the greater the angle with the vertical, the greater is the horizontal component. The horizontal component, when the leg is to the rear, is the part effecting forward movement. The horizontal component increases gradually from the time the supporting leg passes a vertical position till it reaches the end of its contact.

The force of the driving leg is created by the contraction of the extensor muscles. It can be effective only if it meets with two types of resistance. The supporting surface must be firm, i.e., offer counterforce to the vertical component. The effect of lack of counterforce is demonstrated when one tries to walk in soft sand, mud, or snow. The second resistance necessary is friction. This serves as a counterforce to the horizontal component and without it the foot merely slides back when force is applied. The effect of lack of friction is demonstrated when one tries to walk on ice or on a highly polished floor.

The amount of pressure exerted against the ground is somewhat variable. When a strong, forceful walk is performed by a man the force exerted may exceed the weight of the man by as much as 40 pounds. The slower walk, the short mincing step, and many strides in high-heeled shoes add very little beyond the weight of the body. The expression "walking on eggs" is a very apt one for the gentle walk in which no force is applied. For running and other forms of progression the force increases considerably beyond the 40 pounds.

The forward component of the rear leg pushes the body forward and without some restraint it would fall. After the foot finishes its drive the body continues to ride forward over the supporting leg which in turn is quickly passing into a position in which it gives a forward drive. In the meantime the first foot is swinging forward to make a new base of support and prevent a fall. The foot makes contact in front of the body on an angle, so that the body weight which is placed on it is pressing downward. The supporting surface provides a counterforce for each component and thus provides an upward and backward restraint.

The upward component saves the body from falling. The backward one may check the forward speed of the body but usually there is enough relaxation in the ankle and knee to minimize this check. In the faster walk the knee is flexed enough to bring the foot back toward the ground. Also, the angle of the leg with the vertical is constantly decreasing with a resulting decrease in the backward component. At the same time the trunk is moving forward; hence the period of restraint is only momentary.

The alternation of double and single leg support is one of the things which distinguishes the walk from other types of progression. The proportion of each varies with the rate of walking, the phase of single support increasing rapidly with the speed of the walk. The period of single support increases the problem of trunk balance. Also, due to the fact that the leg drive is not directly in line with the center of the body and that part of the time the opposite side is unsupported, there occurs a slight lateral oscillation. With most people, however, it is relatively insignificant.

The muscular effort expended during the walk is put into various parts of the movement. There is the force spent in moving the swinging leg, the force holding the body up against gravity, and lifting it on each step, the force moving the body forward, the force spent in maintaining equilibrium of the trunk, and the force spent for restraint. Even in its easiest form there is considerable work being done. It is, however, only a very small percentage of what it would be for movement through an equal vertical distance.

The purpose of the arm swing is largely to maintain balance in the trunk, to facilitate the forward swing of the pelvis, and to keep the trunk and head facing straight forward. If the trunk and face rotated with the pelvis it would result in an alternate turning toward the right and left. If the head and shoulders were held firm to resist this rotation, it would

FIGURE 60: Double rotation giving a translatory effect
ab–starting position; bc–second position; cd–third position;
1–first angle, 30° clockwise; 2–second angle,
30° counterclockwise

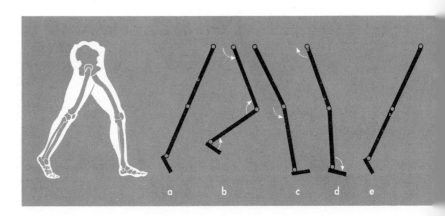

FIGURE 61: Rotatory movements of the leg during walking

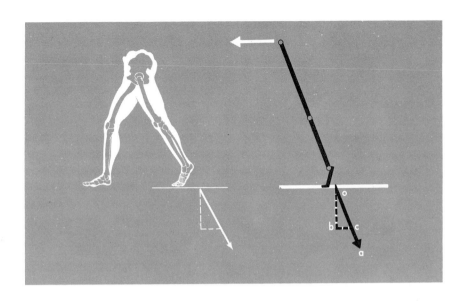

FIGURE 62: Components and counterforce of the driving leg

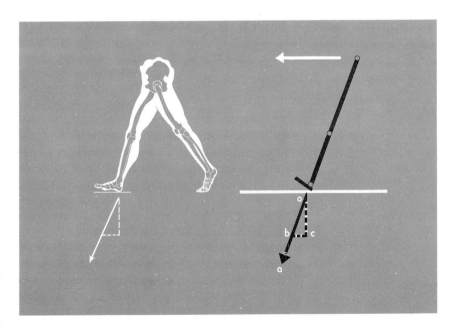

FIGURE 63: Components and counterforce of the restraining leg

result in tenseness and waste of effort. The natural opposition of the arms tends to react on the trunk and to cause the forward oscillation of the pelvis on the opposite side. The result is that the arm and pelvic swings assist the movement of each other and maintain an easy motion without tension.

The body is normally inclined forward slightly, particularly as the speed of the walk increases. This serves several purposes. First, the trunk is more nearly in front of the driving leg or in line with the force. This makes the forward force more effective. Secondly, since the body is kept slightly off balance in the direction of motion, gravity tends to make it fall forward. Leg action is quickened to support the weight. Third, this position prevents the hips from being pushed forward from under the trunk, which would tend to make the trunk fall backward. Fourth, this inclination may reduce the air and wind resistance. This is of more significance in some situations than in others, depending upon the strength of opposing air currents and the speed of the gait.

The most economical gait is a natural, easy one in which the arm and leg swings approximate pendular movements. Since this is dependent upon the length and weight of the legs and arms of the individual it is apparent that the cadence and length of stride vary with individual builds. Two persons, one very tall, the other very short, find it almost impossible to keep in step, at least without a conscious effort on the part of each to adjust to the other. Each person has an optimum gait, at least from the standpoint of economy.

A gait which is slower than this optimum one becomes less efficient because the momentum of the part or of the whole body is being checked instead of being utilized. Balance must be maintained and is often more difficult than in a brisker walk. Muscular contraction for support and drive, although less at any one instant, is more sustained. This contributes to fatigue.

As the speed of the walk increases beyond the optimum several adjustments occur. At first the length of the stride is increased. This gives a greater angle to the driving leg and hence a greater forward component. At the same time the trunk can be inclined forward a little more, bringing it more nearly in line with the rear leg. The lengthened stride also lowers the height of the hips and of the trunk. In order to keep it moving with a minimum of vertical oscillation the supporting knee is kept slightly flexed as the weight passes over it.

The increased velocity comes from increased muscular force in the drive. More flexion is necessary in the swinging leg because the hips are lower. More force is necessary to accelerate the leg swing since it must cover a longer distance on each swing and do so more quickly. The greater angle on the forward leg slightly increases the restraint of that leg. This is partially overcome, however, by knee flexion and the speed with which the trunk approaches a position above the point of support.

As the speed continues to increase there is a limit reached beyond which the leg cannot be swung faster. Therefore, the length of the stride is reduced somewhat in order to make it possible to swing the leg forward rapidly enough, to keep a continual drive, to reduce the restraint of the forward leg, to reduce the hip swing, and to allow the knee to straighten and hence relieve tension there.

As the speed of the walk increases beyond the optimum the arm swing increases in extent and in speed. The elbow is bent more and more, principally to make it possible to swing faster because the lever is shorter. The hand tends on its forward swing to move more toward the medial line of the body, though the elbow points almost straight back on the back swing. The arm swing serves to check rotation of the trunk with the pelvis, and to keep the trunk pulled slightly forward.

RUNNING

The natural limits of the walk depend upon the length of the legs of the individual and the maximum speed possible for the swinging leg. When it no longer becomes possible to get the leg forward before the other finishes its drive, the natural adjustment is to push the body a little harder in its forward and upward direction. It is thus projected into the air; it continues entirely unsupported. The swinging leg has more time to make its excursion and the distance covered per stride is greater because of the distance traversed while neither foot is on the ground.

This period of nonsupport during each step is the first difference between the walk and the run. It characterizes the run just as the period of double support characterizes the walk. This is one of the distinguishing characteristics utilized in a walking race to eliminate contestants who are running.

Second, more force is applied by the extensors of the driving leg. This gives added forward momentum, and greater upward momentum so that the body will resist falling longer.

Third, the length of each stride is longer as a result of progress during nonsupport and of the greater angle of the driving leg with the vertical. The greater angle backward gives an increased forward component to the drive. The body weight rides lower so the supporting knee bends more as the body passes over it.

Fourth, both these factors, the bent knee and increased forward component, partially decrease the up-and-down bobbing which otherwise would occur. The amount of bobbing varies with the style of the run, being greater in a short loping gait than in a fast run. Because of the longer stride in the run the rise and fall on each step is less abrupt.

Therefore, the vertical oscillation appears to be less in the run. Actually it is more but it is spread over a longer distance.

Fifth, one thing which is peculiar about the run is the fact that the angle of the forward leg with the vertical does not ordinarily increase with the speed of progression or with the angle of the rear leg. In certain forms of easy running, which amount more nearly to a succession of leaps, the leg reaches forward for the longest possible stride and does not start down until the body is riding down the descent side of its flight parabola. Restraint is minimized by ankle and knee flexion. Usually, however, the run is not of this form. Instead of reaching forward for contact, the leg is swung forward and then started back just before contact is made. This, combined with the fact that the body is moving constantly forward, makes the foot contact the ground almost underneath the body. The extensors are already in action, there is practically no restraint, and the leg goes immediately into an angle by which it can impart forward momentum. This tendency to pull the leg down to the ground before contact becomes more pronounced as speed increases.

Sixth, the first contact of the foot with the ground is made with the ball of the foot rather than with the heel. This permits a slightly longer stride. It minimizes jar; the "give" comes first in the ankle and then in the knee. It allows for quicker extension of the ankle, since the weight does not have to ride from heel to toe. The heel is dropped down and may or may not go as far as the ground. Usually in very rapid running it does not touch the ground.

Seventh, the arm swing in the run is much more vigorous. The elbow is invariably bent. This shortens the lever and not only makes it swing more easily but makes it possible to keep the arms going rapidly enough to synchronize with the leg action. With the elbow always flexed during the arm swing the tendency to swing the arms across the body is emphasized. The hands reach, or may cross, the median line of the body on the forward swing.

Eighth, the angle of the body with the vertical becomes much greater, particularly in fast running. This greater slant of the body in the direction of the run makes the lengthened stride easier because the iliofemoral ligament does not stop the leg so soon at the rear end of the stride; it puts the trunk more nearly in line with the driving leg, and hence makes the forward component more effective. This body lean also serves to streamline the body and hence to reduce air and wind resistance.

The length of the stride and the rate are both factors in the efficiency of the run. These, of course, vary from one individual to another. The greatest economy in the run is ordinarily at a rather slow pace, but one which is somewhat faster than the fastest walk. For all individuals an easy run is more economical than a walk at the maximum limits of the walk. This is due to the difference in the swinging time of the legs. In the walk the leg is carried forward almost straight. In the run the knee is flexed, so that the heel is near the thigh; this means a shortened lever arm, which permits greater speed.

VARIATIONS IN THE WALK OR RUN

We have all heard someone say, while watching another at a distance or in indistinct light, "That is Mr. X, I can tell by his walk." That kind of guess is possible and the reason given is fairly adequate, although the general outline and build of the person also help to give the impression. There is, however, an individuality of gait which is very pronounced in some persons; that individualization is usually due to the accentuation of some part of the total movement.

A few examples should call to mind people whom you know who use these or other equally pronounced styles. Mr. A is a tall, thin, flexible man. His stride is long because of his long legs, and he exaggerates it somewhat. When his legs are spread in full stride, his weight seems to settle down as though his legs would give way. Then with a big drive from the rear foot he rises high over the supporting leg with the knee practically straight. The result is a long loping gait with a pronounced rise and fall on every step.

The opposite of this walk is that of Miss O, who is very restrained in all her movements. Her stride is short, there seems to be no movement of her hips, and the arms seem to be held immovable at the sides. The feet slide along the ground with very little thrust, and as a result the whole body seems to glide along almost as if on wheels.

Miss P too is restrained in her movements and uses a short step. She, however, uses more drive from the foot, and the general impression is one of a stiff, jerky, hurried progression.

Mr. B has a slow, relaxed style, and appears to settle down as if for a long rest on every step. But Mr. C gives an appearance of speed not only by the swiftness of his movements but by the angle and slight tension of the body.

The same type of individualization is seen in the run. There is the long, easy stride and the short one; the relaxed, disjointed gait and the tense, strained pace. Of course, many of the differences in the run depend upon the speed and the reason for the running.

Shirley[11] studied the development of the walk during the learning stage in infants. The babies seemed to follow the same general progression in learning, though at very different rates. The final state, in which they learned to walk without support of any kind, was in every case accompanied by certain changes, all of which tended to make the gait more like an adult walk. These changes were an increase in speed of walking and in the length of the step, and a decrease in the width of the step and the angle of the step. The "toeing-out" position which characterized almost all of the walks with support was corrected within a few weeks after the child learned to walk alone.

Shirley also states that each child showed individual characteristics in the pattern of the foot prints which persisted from the first test taken at a few weeks of age through the last test near two years of age.

In addition to individual characteristics and variations of the walk and run, adaptations are made for specific situations. On ice or a slippery surface the stride is shortened, the drive is greatly reduced, and the foot is often slid along the surface during the recovery phase instead of being swung free above the ground. These changes serve to keep both feet more nearly under the body weight at all times, and to avoid slipping of the driving foot due to lack of friction. The muscles of the hip may be tense to help in balance of the trunk. Tenseness of the trunk may occur also, especially if the person is really afraid of falling.

On a very soft surface such as mud, the steps are shortened to avoid slipping, the steps are taken very lightly, the foot is raised as quickly as possible to avoid sinking too far into the mud. The same general type of gait is seen in soft sand, but the stride may be longer since there is little danger of slipping as there is in the mud.

The slow processional walk is used to show dignity and grace. For that reason the step is taken slowly and kept at a reasonable length, the body weight is kept moving forward slowly but constantly. The swinging leg is brought forward slowly and with the foot close to the floor. This gives a long period of single support which requires perfect balance.

The military march is a brisk walk, which aims to give an impression of precision, poise, and efficiency. Its characteristics are chiefly exaggerations of certain phases and vary with the style of training. The arm swing is usually slightly longer and may be either an easy swing in a sagittal plane with slight elbow flexion at the end, or may involve a decided lower arm flexion across the front of the body. One hand is usually used to carry a gun hence it is an unsymmetrical arm action, with a minimum of trunk movement and a free swinging of the one arm. The leg swing is performed with a similar exaggeration. There is a little more pronounced lead of the thigh on the recovery, and a fast snap to the knee extension. The drive is made with firmness and a strong extension of the foot and flexion of the toes. This adds force to the movement. The swinging phase is the showy part, but the drive is also essential to the briskness and power of the gait. The mass performance and uniformity of action also add much to the effectiveness of such an exhibition.

The run is used in a great many sports and varies with the other movements required in connection with it. When the player is standing but expects to start running quickly certain changes in posture are made. The feet are spread, knees are slightly flexed, weight is forward on the ball of the forward feet, and the trunk is inclined slightly forward. This puts the weight as nearly as possible in line with the expected movement, puts the legs in a position for a quick drive, and puts the extensor muscles in a state for quick, strong contraction.

The ability to stop quickly is also essential in many sports. It is usually made by planting one foot forward in the normal running position while the leg is kept on an angle so as to offer restraint to body momentum. Of course, that must be preceded by a backward inclination of the trunk and shifting of the weight to the rear of the base. Flexion of the legs serves both to avoid jar and to provide a period in which momentum can be checked.

Sometimes a throw or stroke of some type must be made while the player is running. This requires perfect balance and proper use of body weight in the throw or stroke. Also, it requires smaller steps, weight perfectly controlled within the base, and often a change of step or cut step to get exact co-ordination with arm action and transfer of weight at the right time.

In many instances the run is used to aid in a jump. In the high jump the steps are kept fairly short so as to get maximum vertical lift, the legs are flexed a little to get more force from the extensors, and the final arm swing is more vigorous to aid in the lift. In the broad jump the steps are longer, but the angle of take-off is much more nearly forward. The forward momentum of the run is very important in this case.

The walk and the run are fundamental forms of locomotion which are varied and adapted to many other forms. The basic principles are common to all, hence largely explain the more complex specialized skills.

REFERENCES

1. Elftman, Herbert, Forces and Energy Changes in the Leg During Walking, *American Journal of Physiology*, 125, 1939, p. 339.
2. ————, The Function of Muscles in Locomotion, *American Journal of Physiology*, 125, 1939, p. 357.
3. ————, The Function of the Arms in Walking, *Human Biology*, 11, 1939, p. 529.
4. ————, The Work Done by the Muscles in Running, *American Journal of Physiology*, 129, 1940, p. 672.
5. Finley, F. Ray, *Kinesiological Analysis of Human Locomotion*, Microcard PH77, 1961.
6. Morton, Dudley J., *The Human Foot*, New York, Columbia University Press, 1935, Ch. 15, Locomotion; Ch. 16, Mechanics of the Foot in Walking; Ch. 17, Mechanics of the Foot in Running.
7. ————, *Human Locomotion and Body Form*, Baltimore, Williams and Wilkins Co., 1952, Ch. 10, Weight Distribution in Locomotion; Ch. 11, The Foot in Walking; Ch. 18, Postural and Locomotor Habits; Part II, Analysis of the Walking Stride.

8. Peszczynski, Mieczyslaw, Gait and Gait Retraining, in *Therapeutic Exercise*, 2nd ed., Sidney Licht (ed.), New Haven, Elizabeth Licht, Pub., 1961, p. 406.

9. Rose, Dorothy Lou, *Effect of the Obliquity of the Shaft of the Femur in Women upon Speed of Running and Vertical Jumping Ability*, Microcard PE442, 1959.

10. Sheffield, Fred J., Garsten, Jerome W., and Mastellone, Anisllo F., Electromyographic Study of the Muscles of the Foot in Normal Walking, *American Journal of Physiology*, 35, 1956, p. 224.

11. Shirley, Mary M., *The First Two Years: Postural and Locomotor Development*, Minneapolis, University of Minnesota Press, 1931.

12. Steindler, Arthur, *Kinesiology of the Human Body*, Springfield, Ill., Charles C Thomas, 1955, Ch. 37, Mechanics of the Gait.

13. ————, *Mechanics of Normal and Pathological Locomotion in Man*, Springfield, Ill., Charles C Thomas, 1935, Ch. 27, The Mechanics of the Human Gait; Ch. 28, Graphic Description of the Gait.

CHAPTER 15

Fundamental Manipulative Skills

THE FUNDAMENTAL MANIPULATIVE SKILLS include four types. They are clearly distinguishable in terms of use of force. In the first type are the small precision movements, performed principally with the fingers, usually dealing with small objects. Secondly, there are those in which force plays a more important part but the hands keep contact with the object, as in pushing or pulling. The third type includes those in which momentum is developed in an object and then released, as in all types of throwing. Finally, there are those skills in which momentum of a body part, or of a tool, is imparted to a stationary or moving object so that it is moved thereby. They all require the application of the proper amount of force, control of the direction of the object, and often also a control of body position or movement.

TYPE I. PRECISION SKILLS

The person who is good at these skills is said to possess a high degree of dexterity. Strength is never a factor, muscular endurance is seldom significant. It would appear that facility in this type of skill is dependent upon such factors as a clear concept of what is to be done, an acute sense of space relationships and small dimensions, and a dependence upon the kinesthetic sense for these small movements, co-ordinated with a keen sense of touch. The hand is the primary functioning unit, but these skills usually require positioning of the arm and sometimes of the trunk and head if the performer is trying to see what he is doing.

The hand and its potentials for work and the kinesthetic aspects of the hands will be discussed in Chapter 16. A brief statement will be given here to indicate the variety of these skills.

The most fundamental of the hand actions is grasping. The infant is born with a grasping reflex, and he exhibits an amazing amount of strength in his early grasp though it is merely finger flexion. For an adult also, whether the object grasped is round like a doorknob or long and slender like the chinning bar, the technique is similar. The fingers flex over the object, sometimes spread sometimes not, but always the thumb is on the opposite side to increase the strength of the grip and prevent the hand from slipping. The grasp may be for the purpose of turning the knob, for pulling on it (Type II), or for just gripping the object as in hanging from a bar.

The technique nearest to the grasp is "pinching." In pinching, the end of the thumb is brought in apposition to the end of one of the fingers, usually the second or third, sometimes both of them. This is done in picking up something small such as a pin or screw or a pencil for writing or something larger such as a piece of paper or a book. If the object is light and is to be placed somewhere, or the screw put into a hole, the hand is usually in a pronated position. If the object is heavy such as a book, it is apt to be held with the palm up, as the finger and wrist flexors are stronger than the extensors. When sewing, the length of the stitch is determined partially by a rapid succession of pronator-supinator actions. If one is attempting to turn the screw, it may be performed simply by a middle finger flexion, with the thumb pressing lightly on the other side for a clockwise twist, or finger extension for the counterclockwise turn. More resistance from the screw or a larger object to be turned requires pronation or supination of the forearm coupled with either the grasp of the hand or the finger pinch. This pronation-supination action is seen in its most pronounced form in something like wringing clothes.

There is another array of skills in which there is finger flexion or at least pressure. It may involve one finger only, such as pulling the trigger on a gun or pressing a needle through in sewing. More commonly there is a rapid succession of finger responses, such as in typing, playing the piano, or operating a calculator or punch-card machine. In some cases there needs to be a very light, rhythmical action by the fingers; in others it is more forceful and according to fixed patterns rather than a continuously repetitive action. The same action may vary according to circumstances; for example, the electric typewriter requires a much lighter and more sensitive touch than does the manual one.

Finally, there is another assortment of skills which might be called "hand balancing." This is characteristic of most of the acts in eating. One balances food on the fork or in the spoon. The food arrives at the mouth because of arm action, but it is kept on the spoon because of proper interplay between pronators, supinators, wrist abductors, and finger flexors. The same is true in balancing the coffee cup for drinking. Similarly, if one pours flavoring from a bottle into a measuring spoon without spilling or overflowing the spoon, one must be ambidextrous.

For all of the above actions there must be release, i.e., the fingers must loosen their grip or extend and perhaps even spread. However, these are relatively weak movements in comparison with most of the flexor actions. There are relatively few skills in which extension of the fingers is strong. To be sure, one may have the hand in a position for writing with a pen, and without moving the hand a quick extension of a finger may roll aside a pencil which is in the way. Perhaps the game of caroms is intriguing partly because it uses a skill seldom used otherwise. This predominance of flexor use and greater strength is as characteristic of hand manipulations as the similar characteristics of the extensors of the lower extremity for support of body weight.

TYPE II. PUSHING AND PULLING

Pushing may take place in any plane and apply to any type of object. If the object is light and hence requires only slight pressure, the hand is placed on it and extension of the elbow is sufficient. Elbow extension is accompanied by some movement in the shoulder, depending upon the starting position of the arm. Exactly where that force is applied and, to a certain extent, the direction in which it is applied depend upon the object and its possibilities for movement. For example, a window must move always in the same groove, and it makes little difference whether the force is applied at the center or to one side of center or at top or bottom, if it slides easily. Likewise, an object which is on a slippery surface or which has a very low center of gravity may be pushed at almost any point and still move along parallel to its supporting surface. But one which offers considerable friction between its base and its support, or in which the center of gravity is high and perhaps over a narrow base, is much more apt to rotate and fall. This may be the result desired, but at any rate the point of application depends upon the nature of the object and the purpose of the movement.

The optimum direction is clear. The nearly vertical push is in line with the only direction the window can move. The second diagram has too large a horizontal component, and if the window tends to stick a bit this effort will only make it bind more.

If the object is too large to be moved simply by arm action, then the mass of the body must be used, assisted by the force of leg extension. The force is always applied as nearly as possible in line with the desired movement and near the center of gravity. If the pushing is to be done upward, the body is placed as nearly under the object as possible, to give a vertical direction to the force. The knees are flexed so that leg extension can be added to arm force. If the push is to be forward, the hands are placed about in front of the chest with elbows flexed. The body leans forward with chest or shoulder against the object. The angle is as great as the friction between the feet and the supporting surface will permit. The force is created by leg extension. If the push is downward the weight is placed over the object. The weight of the performer may be put entirely on the object, but the force of the legs cannot be used as in the other two cases.

When the resistance moves but the force is continuous, the performer walks along behind adding sufficient force to keep it in motion. The body is leaning in toward it, and the trunk must be held rigid. If the trunk is in a somewhat vertical position, then the abdominal muscles must act to prevent hyperextension. If the trunk is in a nearly horizontal position, the back extensors must prevent trunk flexion. An alternation of these positions will help, therefore, to avoid fatigue in long continued activity.

If the resistance does not yield to any of these means, often a sudden application of force will start it in motion. This is true because the performer develops momentum as he moves into the object. This additional force may be sufficient to overcome the inertia which keeps the object at rest, and, when once set in motion, in can be kept in motion with less effort.

Pulling is similar in many respects to pushing.

If the resistance is light, arm action alone is sufficient. If the pulling is downward from shoulder level or above, there is arm depression at the shoulder and usually elbow flexion. Pulling in practically all planes requires elbow flexion, but shoulder action may vary considerably, being either elevation, depression, or in or approaching a horizontal plane.

When the resistance is greater, the force can be increased by leaning away from it. Leg extension may be brought into use also. If one is facing the object and moving backward, the back extensors fix the trunk. If one is facing the other direction, the abdominal muscles are active. When one is pulling downward the body weight may be suspended on the object by removing the feet from the floor.

In lifting, which is a form of pulling, the legs are used if the object is of any size. For example, in lifting a heavy suitcase, one stands close beside it and flexes the knees; then, after grasping the handle, one lifts by knee extension. Somewhat the same procedure should be followed even if the object is not large or heavy. Balance is easier when squatting directly over the feet and is, therefore, more economical of effort. When the trunk is carried forward by hip flexion and the hands reach down for the object, the amount of resistance becomes considerable because of the length of the trunk and the distance of the load from the hip.

The sudden application of force or the transference of momentum developed as the force is applied may also be effective in pulling on a resistance that does not otherwise yield.

In the carrying of loads, which is the balancing of objects that have been lifted, a few general rules can be applied which contribute to ease and economy of effort. The load should be carried as nearly as possible in line with the gravital line of the body in order to decrease the rotational moment. Otherwise, the effectiveness of the load becomes greater in direct proportion to its distance away. For example, a relatively light weight is difficult to hold at arm's length from the body. The feet should be used in such a way that there is a firm base. The load should be carried as a part of the body mass and not have a motion or momentum independent of that of the person carrying it. That is, swinging or swaying motions of an object may cause a disturbance of equilibrium or require gross adjustments by the performer.

Pushing and pulling may have other variations in work skills and operation of machinery. For example, a combination of the two may be seen in the turning of a crank or the operation of certain types of looms. Even the thrust on the "stick" gear shift and the pull on a crank for a motor are forms of pushing and pulling.

TYPE III. THROWING

The styles of throwing vary widely depending upon the size of the ball used, the distance and speed desired on the ball, and the game in which the throw is being used. There will be only two styles discussed here. They are the single underarm throw and the single overarm. Most other throws are similar to one of these.

Single Underarm Throw

Description: Right-hand Player. The single underarm throw is well illustrated by the underhand pitch used in softball. The player starts in a standing position facing in the direction in which the throw is to be made, with feet together. The ball is grasped in the fingers of the right hand, which is held just in front of the body. The right arm swings back at the same time the trunk is inclined forward and turned partially to the right. Then the arm is swung quickly forward at the same time a step is taken forward on the left foot. The release is made by straightening the fingers slightly and allowing the ball to roll off them. The ball is released at about the bottom of the arc described by the hand, i.e., when the arm is at right angles to the direction the ball is to go. The ball is aimed to travel for some distance in approximately a horizontal path. In the follow-through the arm continues somewhat higher on the swing; the weight is well forward over the left foot, and may even require a step forward on the right foot. The left arm swings easily in opposition to the right and ends near the side or is lifted out and backward when the throw is vigorous.

Muscular Analysis. The size of the ball relative to the hand will determine the manner in which the fingers are used in holding the ball. The regulation softball in the hands of most school children or women requires some spreading of the fingers. This is accomplished by the extensor communis digitorum as it slightly extends the metacarpal-phalangeal joints. It is assisted in this spread by the abductor minimi digiti, and abductor pollicis. With this joint and the wrist extended the last two phalangeal joints naturally flex. As an aid in grasping the ball this flexion is further emphasized by action of the flexors sublimis digitorum, and profundus digitorum, flexors longus pollicis, brevis pollicis, and opponens pollicis. With a ball which is smaller relative to the hand, there is flexion of the fingers with the thumb spread in opposition to the second and third fingers. These two fingers are in about the same position they are in for the larger ball, spread apart but extended at the articulation with the metacarpals and then flexed over the ball. Muscular action is the same. The fourth and fifth fingers are flexed along the side of the ball but do not grip it as firmly as the others do.

The right arm is swung back by action of the latissimus dorsi, teres major, middle and posterior deltoid, and long head of the triceps. Inward rotation is opposed by the teres minor and infraspinatus, which also help slightly in the backward movement particularly in the latter stage, when there is a little abduction. Accompanying the arm movement is adduction of the scapula produced by the rhomboids and middle portions of the trapezius. The elbow is extended at the end of the swing by the triceps.

The change in trunk position is due to flexion of the hip by the iliopsoas, and to trunk rotation produced by the left external oblique, right internal oblique, and right erector spinae, oblique rotators, and quadratus lumborum. There is, also, strong inward rotation of the right hip by the tensor fasciae latae and the anterior fibers of the gluteus medius and minimus. The weight is entirely on the right leg, which is held in extension by the vasti muscles.

The forward arm swing is made by the anterior deltoid, pectoralis major, coracobrachialis, and long head of the biceps. The serratus anterior and second part of the trapezius abduct and rotate the scapula. The release is made by a relaxation of the flexors and continued action of the extensors already in use.

The step is exactly the same as in the ordinary step, the right leg making the drive, the left swinging forward. The step is a little longer than normal for the walk and the weight is controlled by allowing the left knee to flex partially under control of the quadriceps extensor. After the drive, the right leg relaxes so that it finishes with the knee flexed.

Mechanical Analysis. The backward arm swing, rotation of the body, and the shifting of weight onto the right foot are all preparatory movement designed to give greater speed to the ball. The first two, arm swing and rotation, move the starting point for the ball farther back, and thereby increase the arc over which the ball is carried in the hand. This increased arc gives a longer time for acceleration; hence the ball is traveling faster at the time of release. This first shift of weight puts it over the right foot, where it may be easily thrust forward in the drive of the right leg, thus adding momentum to the ball. It also frees the left foot for the step. The forward slant of the body facilitates the backward arm swing and helps in balance. It also puts the weight more nearly in front of the right leg so that the force of the right leg drive is in line with the trunk.

The speed of the ball depends upon the speed with which the arm is moved. The speed of the arm may depend upon the size of the ball, being decreased if the ball is heavy. The arm is kept extended, and therefore speed is improved. Since the hand is traveling in an arc, the point of release of the ball is very important in relation to the direction of flight of the ball. It should be at the point where the desired line of flight is at a tangent to the arc of the hand. If the ball is to go in a horizontal direction that point is where the arm is straight down. A wrist snap may be used but it will affect the point of release very little and should be used before the release in order to increase the speed of the ball. The ball may be released over the fingers in such a way as to give it spin but the time of release does not vary.

The left arm swinging backward during delivery of the ball, helps in trunk rotation. The first part of the swing reacts on the trunk to draw it forward; the momentum of the last part continues the rotation. The extended position of the left arm at the end helps to counterbalance the forward trunk and right arm.

Single Overarm Throw

Description: Right-hand Player. The single overarm throw is a much more complex throw than the underhand one. The thrower stands with left side in the direction in which the throw is to be made. The weight is well back on the right foot, usually with the right knee moderately flexed and the left leg raised slightly or at least placed forward a little in a stride position with the foot easily touching the ground. The trunk is inclined well back. The left arm is raised forward.

The ball is grasped in the fingers. The right arm is raised with elbow bent and about shoulder high.

The arm is drawn backward, which brings the arm, palm down, past the chest out to the shoulder; then the elbow extends until the arm is out nearly straight. The arm is abducted so that it is about in a straight line with the shoulder, but the trunk is inclined sideward so that the right shoulder is lowered and the arm is inclined downward.

The throw is made by a quick reversal in all directions. The elbow starts forward with the hand trailing, then the hand is whipped on past it. At the same time the body is turned forward and to the left, and the weight is thrown forward onto the left foot. The ball is released when the body is facing approximately forward and the hand just in advance of the shoulder. In the follow-through the body finishes its turn, facing nearly to the left of the throwing direction, the right arm is extended and a step is usually taken forward on the right foot. The left arm is brought backward, stopping at the side or extended on backward, depending upon the purpose and style of the throw.

Muscular Analysis. The weight is supported on the right foot by the control of all the extensor muscles, which allow flexion in preparation for a strong drive. The left leg is abducted by the gluteus medius, gluteus minimus, and tensor fasciae latae. It is usually relaxed with the exception of ankle extensors (gastrocnemius, soleus, and peroneus longus). These hold the foot extended and the toes lightly touching the ground to aid in balance.

The trunk is inclined to the right; the movement is initiated by the following muscles in the right side: gluteus medius, gluteus minimus, tensor fasciae latae, quadratus lumborum, erector spinae, rectus abdominis, and external oblique. Gravity continues this action and, if the movement is slow, gravity is largely responsible for it. While the body balances momentarily in that position the trunk is kept from falling to the right by the left trunk flexors and extensors. The left arm is raised by action of the deltoid and supraspinatus and the scapula rotated by the serratus anterior and trapezius.

The ball is grasped as previously described for the underarm throw. The right arm is raised by the deltoid. The scapula is rotated upward by the serratus anterior and trapezius. The elbow is kept flexed with the forearm in a pronated position. This is accomplished by the brachialis anticus, pronator teres, and brachioradialis. The arm is drawn backward and downward by the posterior deltoid, infraspinatus, teres minor, and long head of the triceps. Strong trapezius action keeps the scapula rotated and also adducts it with the assistance of the rhomboids and relaxation of the serratus. The elbow is pulled into closer flexion with the help of the biceps, its supinating action being counteracted by the pronators. Then while the deltoid supports the shoulder in this abducted position the triceps swings the elbow into extension.

The forward movement of the arm starts at the shoulder with the pectoralis major, anterior deltoid, and coracobrachialis contracting. As it moves forward it is rotated strongly outward by the teres minor and infraspinatus. There the direction of the arm movement changes with trunk rotation.

The right leg is strongly extended by all the extensors and the left leg assumes the weight. This thrust gives momentum forward and some rotatory momentum. Most of the rotation is accomplished by the outward rotation of the right hip and by the left erector spinae, latissimus dorsi, quadratus lumborum, and internal oblique; and the right external oblique and rectus abdominis. The backward swing of the left arm also contributes to the rotatory movement. It is produced by the latissimus dorsi and teres minor while the deltoid holds the arm partially abducted and assists in the swing.

The right arm as it continues forward by the pull of the anterior shoulder muscles is suddenly rotated inward by action of the pectoralis major, teres major, and subscapularis, and relaxation of the teres minor and infraspinatus. While the rotation is still in progress the elbow is extended by the triceps. A vigorous flexion of the wrist (flexor carpi ulnaris, flexor carpi radialis) gives the final push as the finger flexors relax and allow the ball to go.

The follow-through is a continuation of the movements already begun, elbow extension and trunk rotation, and a step forward with the right foot.

Mechanical Analysis. The speed of a ball thrown by the overarm throw is largely dependent upon the distance through which the ball is moved while in the hand and the magnitude of the force applied during that time. The rotation of trunk to the right, the shift of the weight back, inclination of the trunk backward, and extension of the arm backward, each move the starting point farther backward than it would be otherwise.

During the throw the body acts as a single lever with the axis between the foot and the ground. The ball which is at the end of this long lever is carried forward rapidly by the leg thrust and trunk action, plus the snap of arm, forearm, and wrist. Rotation around the longitudinal axis also adds to this speed.

The greater accuracy usually shown in this style of throw over that of the underarm throw is due to several factors. The greater speed of the ball makes it possible to throw the ball in a straighter arc, particularly at distances of some length. The hand and the ball are moving throughout the throw in almost a straight line. Therefore the exact point of release is not quite so important, and there is less chance for the ball to go off at a tangent to the arm swing. The hand is also facing more nearly in the proper direction at the time of release. This follow-through is in the same direction and, therefore, has no tendency to affect the flight of the ball.

The right-arm extension in the preliminary movement puts the anterior muscles of the shoulder on tension for quick and strong action. Right leg flexion serves the same purpose for the leg extensors.

The left-arm movement serves two purposes, balance and increase of the speed of the rotatory movement. As the arm is brought backward, the reaction on the trunk swings the trunk forward. If the throw is used for pitching, or in any situation where a quick return of the ball is anticipated, the left arm stops at the side with elbow bent. Thus the pitcher finishes the pitch in a defensive position ready for quick action. If the throw is a hard, vigorous one, and the follow-through free, the left arm may continue on past the trunk. In that case the unchecked momentum of the arm adds a little to the rotatory momentum; but it is primarily an aid in balance, counteracting the forward position of the trunk and right arm.

The direction of the hand movement and the angle of release depend upon the purpose of the throw. If it is a quick throw over a relatively short distance, the ball will be aimed directly at the desired point and the path of the ball before release is in approximately the same line. If it is an easy ball or one thrown for maximum distance, it will be aimed upward at about a 45° angle. This change in direction is made by changing slightly the plane of the arm movement and by keeping the trunk inclined slightly backward for the higher arc. In any case, the ball leaves the hand at approximately right angles to the plane in which the arm is at the moment of release.

TYPE IV. STRIKING

The striking activities in sports represent a wide variety of skills. The tool may be the hand only, as in volleyball or handball; or the foot, as in soccer; or a short, solid paddle, as in darts, paddle tennis, or table tennis; or a racket, as in tennis or badminton; or a more solid stick or club, as in baseball, hockey, and golf.

The principles are the same for all. Assuming that maximum distance or speed of the ball are desired in each case, the performer attempts to carry the striking tool through as long an arc as can be properly controlled and in the least amount of time. This ensures maximum momentum of the tool, which in turn is imparted to the ball. The longer tool gives the possibility of increased speed.

The direction in which the ball travels is determined almost entirely by the direction of the striking surface at the instant of contact. The ball leaves it at a right angle to the surface; forward, up or down, right or left, according to the angle of the striking surface.

The other factor in determining direction is the rotation of the ball, usually caused by the way the striking surface moves over the ball at the moment of contact. Such rotation may cause it to curve to one side or the other or to soar higher or drop more quickly than it would do otherwise.

The reaction or counterresistance of the striking surface is also important, particularly when the ball approaches the surface at high speed. This is obtained by having a solid surface and by gripping the tool very firmly.

The simple underhand serve in volleyball and baseball batting will be described here as illustrative of this group of activities. The first is made with a stationary ball and with the hand only; the second involves contact between a moving ball and an elongated striking tool.

Underhand Volleyball Serve

Description. The player stands facing diagonally out to the right side of the court. The ball is held on the left palm a little in front of the body. The right hand is swung out, and the weight is shifted to the rear foot with the knee slightly bent. The ball may remain on the hand or be tossed gently into the air as the serve is made. The right arm swings forward, the hand striking the lower back surface of the ball. The ball leaves at approximately right angles to the arm. At the same time the weight is shifted forward. In the follow-through the weight continues forward, the player usually stepping into the court. The arm swing continues so that the hand appears to reach for about the top of the net, and the shoulders are turned facing the net.

Muscular Analysis. The ball is held in place on the left hand by elbow flexion, brachialis anticus, biceps, and brachioradialis; and by the wrist flexors, flexor carpi ulnaris, flexor carpi radialis, palmaris longus. Body weight is supported by the extensors of the right leg. The right arm is swung back by the posterior and middle deltoid and the supraspinatus and is sufficient to require action of the trapezius to rotate the scapula. Scapular action is reinforced by the serratus anterior or the rhomboids, depending upon the plane in which the arm is lifted. The triceps holds the elbow extended.

The forward arm swing is started by the lower pectoralis major, the teres major, and the coracobrachialis. The first two cease action and are replaced by the upper pectoralis and the anterior deltoid. The scapula is moved by the serratus anterior. The weight is shifted forward by ankle extension, gastrocnemius, soleus, and peroneus longus, and, if the feet are spread apart, by the adductors of the left leg. Trunk rotation comes from the left erector spinae, quadratus lumborum, internal oblique, and right external oblique.

Mechanical Analysis. The facing described ensures freedom of arm movement and use of the adductor action of the anterior shoulder muscles.

The preliminary arm swing serves to stretch the muscles, and to increase the arc through which the hand will move. Momentum of the back swing and triceps action swings the hand up and opposes the pull of gravity and elbow flexion. The shifting of weight is also most important in increasing the length of the arc, and the shifting with bent knees helps to keep the arm swing flattened out. The long arc of the swing imparts the necessary momentum to the hand and ball. The direction of the ball is dependent upon the direction of the arm swing and the point at which the ball is contacted. If the path of the swinging hand is circular, and the ball is held in the front part of that arc where the path is upward and the hand contacts the ball from below, the ball will be lifted high in the air and may not clear the net. If the arc of the arm swing is flattened out by the shift of weight with knee flexion, and by trunk rotation, the angle at which the hand contacts the ball will be more nearly horizontal. A ball which is hit squarely at the back tends to roll off the hand and does not have sufficient lift to go over the net. If the ball is hit below center and the striking surface of the hand is turned to approximate that of the ball, it will have the desired lift. Again the arm is approximately at right angles to the line of flight of the ball.

Ability to place the ball is much more important here than is force, since the distance to the net is not great and the rear line limits distance. Adjustments in line of arm swing and point of contact are very important.

Baseball Batting

Description: Right-hand Player. The stance is taken with the batter facing the plate and the left shoulder pointing directly toward the pitcher, face turned toward the pitcher. The feet are spread sideward in an easy stride with knees slightly flexed. The trunk is inclined forward a little by flexion at the hips. The bat is grasped by both hands, left hand nearer the end of the bat than the right. The position of the hands depends upon the weight of the bat, strength of the batter, and the batter's preference in use of the hands. The position varies from one with left hand near the end and right hand against it, to one with the left hand somewhat down the bat and the right hand a little beyond it.

The backswing is made by shifting the weight toward the right foot, rotating the trunk to the right about 20° to 30° and lifting the bat backward in nearly a horizontal swing until it is almost behind the head. It is supported all the time by the hands, and not allowed to drop toward the ground or onto the shoulder. The left elbow is kept practically straight throughout the swing.

In the forward swing the bat again travels in nearly a horizontal plane, unless hitting a low ball. The weight is shifted forward toward the left foot. The trunk is rotated back to the left with the arms swinging free from the body and practically straight. The bat is held back until just before contacting the ball. Then it is whipped through to meet the ball so that it is approximately at right angles to the path of the approaching ball. At the moment the ball is hit the left-shoulder is slightly nearer the pitcher than the right one. The arms are reaching forward slightly toward the pitcher and are about in front of the right shoulder.

The follow-through is a continuation of the forward swing and the transfer of weight. It is usually followed immediately by a step with the right foot diagonally forward and to the right. If a hit has been made the player checks the weight and steps out on the right foot, releases the bat first with the right hand, carries the left arm downward on the follow-through, and finally drops the bat as he starts into a run toward first base.

Muscular Analysis. The starting position is with legs abducted, gluteus medius and minimus acting. Most batters toe out, particularly with the left foot. This position is produced by the small outward rotators of the hip. The vasti control the amount of flexion at the knees. The erector spinae and quadratus lumborum assisted by the hamstrings at the hip support the trunk in its forward position. The head is turned to the left by the right sternocleidomastoid and the left splenius.

The bat is grasped firmly by the flexors of both hands (flexor sublimis digitorum, flexor profundus digitorum, flexor longus pollicis, opponens pollicis, and palmaris longus). The bat is lifted up and maintained in the same plane by the middle deltoid of both arms; and by the extensors carpi radialis longus and brevis and flexor carpi radialis, which hold the wrists firm and mildly abducted to support the weight of the bat.

The weight is moved toward the right by the extensors of the left leg and the adductors of the right one. The left leg is rotated by the group of small outward rotators and the right leg is rotated inward by the tensor fasciae latae and anterior part of the gluteus medius. The upper trunk is rotated by the right erector spinae, internal oblique, and the left external oblique. The right and left muscles co-operate sufficiently to keep the trunk from any lateral bending.

The arm action is dominated by the left arm, which is elevated and adducted by the anterior and middle deltoid, the upper pectoralis major, and the coracobrachialis. The right arm is drawn back by the posterior and middle deltoid, the infraspinatus and teres minor. The strong action of the pectoralis rotates the left arm inward somewhat and with a little pronation of the forearm the bat is guided in a flatter plane. The teres minor and infraspinatus likewise rotate the right arm outward. The left serratus anterior abducts and rotates the left scapula, while the right rhomboids and second and third parts of the trapezius adduct the right one.

The forward movement is more forceful but is almost a reversal of the back swing. The trunk rotation is to the left instead of the right so that the opposite set of muscles is doing the work. Rotation is inward in the left hip and outward in the right. Right leg extension starts the body moving forward and the adductors of the left leg help draw it forward. The deltoid supports the arms at the proper level and arm action is reversed. The wrist snap occurs as the wrists move from full abduction into adduction by the pull of the flexor carpi ulnaris and extensor carpi ulnaris.

The follow-through is a continuation of these movements with diminishing force. It is seldom checked by active muscular effort. If the ball is not contacted the wind-up is complete because of the momentum.

If the ball is hit, the force of the swing in the follow-through is greatly reduced. The flexors of the right hand relax. The left arm is brought down by the teres major and latissimus dorsi as the deltoid also relaxes. The weight is allowed to shift entirely onto the left leg. The right foot is swung forward and sideward for a step; the extensors and abductors of the left leg, by contracting, push the weight sideward so that it falls over the right foot. The right erector spinae, quadratus lumborum, and internal oblique, and the left external oblique check the trunk rotation which is in progress and turn the trunk to the right. The batter is now ready for the run toward first base.

Mechanical Analysis. The starting position with feet spread and knees easy is one to furnish a firm base, permit movement of the body mass, and make the pivot possible without disturbing balance. The forward inclination of the trunk makes arm action freer than when the trunk is erect. It also helps to lower the shoulders so that the swing can be more nearly horizontal and the bat approach the ball more squarely from behind.

Maximum swinging speed is attained by the combination of weight transfer, rotation of the body, and the swing of the extended arms. With the left elbow straight, the bat extended beyond the left hand, final extension of the right elbow, and wrist snap, the striking end of the bat acquires speed by virtue of the long lever set in motion by these various forces. The wrist action controls the exact level of the bat, preventing the head of the bat from dropping or from rising too high. Likewise the wrists control the facing of the bat, attempting to have the hands and the head of the bat in line when contact is made. Perfect timing is necessary if the maximum of accuracy and momentum are to be attained. Only if the grip is tight and the wrists firm will the proper reaction be given to the ball.

The free follow-through prevents interference with the swing. The reaction of the ball on the bat slows its swing. Momentum helps to carry the batter forward onto the left foot. This leaves the right foot free for a step but the motion must be checked before the runner is in a position for the dash to first base.

Further details of the placement of balls will be discussed in Chapter 17. This skill has many elements in common with golf, paddle tennis, aerial darts, badminton, tennis, and other striking activities. Some of these will be discussed in Chapter 17; the reader may make his own analysis of any which are not included.

REFERENCES

1. Smith, K. Maurine, *A Preliminary Investigation of "Intension Displaying Movements" in Tennis and Badminton,* Microcard PE132, 1953.
2. Steindler, Arthur, *Kinesiology of the Human Body,* Springfield, Ill., Charles C Thomas, 1955, Ch. 26, Mechanics of Shoulder-arm Complex; Ch. 28, Mechanics of Elbow Joint; Ch. 30, Mechanics of the Hand and Fingers; Ch. 32, The Arm as a Whole.
3. ————, *Mechanics of Normal and Pathological Locomotion in Man,* Springfield, Ill., Charles C Thomas, 1935, Ch. 23, The Mechanics of the

Shoulder-arm Complex; Ch. 24, The Mechanics of the Elbow Joint; Ch. 25, The Mechanics of Wrist and Fingers; Ch. 26, The Arm as a Whole.

4. Treanor, Walter J., Motions of the Hand and Foot, in *Therapeutic Exercise*, 2nd ed., Sidney Licht, (ed.), New Haven, Elizabeth Licht, Pub., 1958, p. 101.

5. Wild, Monica R., The Behavior Pattern of Throwing and Some Observations Concerning Its Course of Development in Children, *Research Quarterly*, 9, October 1938, p. 20.

CHAPTER 16

The Hand as a Functional Unit *

FUNCTIONALLY, OR KINESIOLOGICALLY, few if any parts of the human body have been studied less than the hand, or at least presented more sparingly in the literature. Anatomically, in terms of bones, muscles, and articulations, it is as well understood as any body segment. Physiologically, its performance is similar to that of the rest of the body mechanism for movement and co-ordination, touch, and kinesthesia. But the specific movement and peculiarities of the hand function have concerned few physiologists.

For the psychologist, the hand is often the tool of overt reaction, and to study this, tapping, tracing, and other manipulatory and discriminatory tasks have been used. It is not the hand with which the psychologist is concerned, however. It is the expression of reaction time, of attention, of co-ordination, of sensation, or other bodily function.

The orthopedic surgeon, facing the problems of repair and reconditioning of hand function has been more alert to hand dynamics than anyone else. However, he apparently is too busy to write, and if he does it is apt to be a presentation of one or a few cases of injury, surgery, retraining, and the like. The functional parameters are sometimes inferred.

In contrast, the foot, which is the counterpart of the hand in the lower extremity, has elicited pages; yes, volumes. Morton and others have written extensively on the morphological, evolutionary, and functional characteristics of the foot. Perhaps it is because it is the base of the human, structurally and functionally. But I am more inclined to think it is for other reasons. Perhaps it hurts more, we abuse it more, we clothe it more, we fatigue it far beyond the point where we would quit with the hand. And, perhaps, too, we have found no really satisfactory substitute for the foot. In some respects at least, the tongue can com-

* This chapter is in essentially the same form as a paper presented at a conference held by the Quartermaster Research and Engineering Command, U.S. Army, Natick, Massachusetts, April 1956. The conference was on the Protection and Functioning of the Hands in Cold Climates. The paper appears in the conference report. Reprinted by permission of Technical Information Branch, Technical Services Division, Quartermaster Research and Engineering Command.

pensate for hand deficiencies, and man has invented machines to do the things which the craftsman and mechanic used to do.

The kinesiologists have apparently followed like sheep in bypassing the highly complex co-ordinations of the hand. True, we build on the work of the others, but that is scarcely an excuse for the omission of such an important segment of the body. Steindler[7] has done a reasonably comprehensive presentation of the mechanics of the hand, in both normal and pathological states.

The artist is perhaps more sensitive to the use and the expressiveness of the hand than anyone else. Study of almost any piece of sculpture or painting will reveal the communicative power of the hand through its position or gesturing. In a home in Iowa City there is an unusual picture hanging above the fireplace, a spot where family portraits are often hung. It is a Grant Wood painting prized by the family but is probably unknown to most art collectors and critics. It is a portrait of the hands of Grant Wood's physician, a beloved doctor of the community who lived only a little longer than the artist himself. Both men have served mankind in very different ways through the use of sensitive and dexterous hands and fingers. Grant Wood appreciated hands and understood them from the standpoint of use, skill, and empathy.

The skills of the hands are as varied as the work of the surgeon, the artist, the musician, the jeweler, the machinist, the seamstress, the masseur, the baseball pitcher, and all the various craftsmen. The hand, as a structural and functional organ, is unique in the animal world. Its skill and adaptability controlled by the human brain have yielded endless products and satisfaction to man himself through methods of expression, work, and art. The hand can be a means of construction of minute or gross materials, or a weapon of destruction. So varied are its co-ordinations that it seems scarcely possible to talk of functions of the hand in general. The outstanding characteristic common to all hands is versatility. Perhaps there is no better place to start than with respect to the morphology and intricacies which permit precision of the finger functions.

The first digit is unique and is definitely the most important of the five digits. The first metacarpal is placed at an angle of 45 to 50 degrees with the other metacarpals. At rest, the wrist is slightly hyperextended and the thumb is in line with the axis of the forearm or the radius. The first metacarpal approaches a position parallel with the others only when it moves in snugly against the palm pointing, along the index finger. The thumb articulation is classed as a saddle joint, a type found only at this one point. Its movement is the same as any condyloid one: that is, flexion, extension, abduction, and adduction. However, the reciprocally curved surfaces produce a stronger joint than a condyloid one. In flexion, the finger tips converge toward a point in the wrist at the base of the thumb.

The shorter length of the thumb makes it possible to contact easily the pads at the base of the fingers as well as the tips. Grasping of knobs, balls, and other objects is possible by spreading the thumb on an angle with the plane of the palm. In such a grasp, the thumb tip is approximately equidistant from all finger tips. Holding or grasping with the total hand and the pinching type of grip of thumb and finger are both dependent upon the flexibility of thumb, and if the hand is clothed, upon the freedom of the thumb to move.

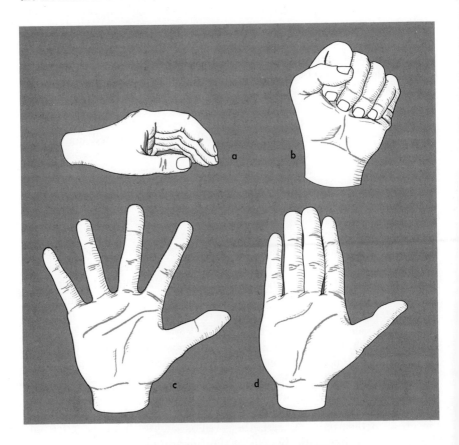

FIGURE 64: Positions of the hand
a—relaxed; b—flexed; c—abducted fingers;
d—adducted fingers, abducted thumb

The resting relaxed position of the hand is not a straight one. If the arm is supported with the wrist straight from the forearm or slightly extended the fingers are mildly flexed, the thumb is in a volar position to the second digit. If the wrist is flexed, the fingers are straighter. If the wrist is extended, the fingers flex more. The relaxed, cupped hand and accompanying variation in finger position are the result of tension of finger flexors and extensors. This flexion persists even if the arm hangs relaxed, so that gravity pulls freely on the dangling fingers.

The fingers are straight or hyperextended only if tension and postural rigidity are present or if external restraint is applied. Maintenance of extended fingers would be as fatiguing as a clenched fist. There would simply be a difference in the muscle group which becomes fatigued. Relaxation may occur if external restraint holds the fingers straight, but if pressure is applied continuously, circulation may be impaired.

The intrinsic muscles, that is, those located entirely in the hand, with one exception, are all muscles of the digits. This is in contrast to the foot, where the short muscles span the arch and are more important in its support than in toe flexion. The only digit with a significant number of intrinsic muscles and with significant cross section (indication of strength) is the thumb. The thenar eminence is simply an assortment of muscles operating the thumb. They number four in all. Likewise, the fifth digit has three short muscles giving that digit a more varied movement than the three middle fingers. The lumbricales are an important part of the extensor mechanism of the interphalangeal articulations.

The other muscles affecting the hand are located in the arm, most originating above the elbow. These fall into two groups: those stopping on the carpals and directly moving the wrist and those with tendinous extensions into the fingers, affecting both fingers and wrist. Both groups are more numerous and stronger on the anterior or flexor side of the arm. The forearm girth increases perceptibly when strong hand action occurs. Therefore, tight clothing or other limitation on the forearm interferes in the sense of comfort if not in actual strength.

In addition to the common extensor serving digits two to five, the index and fifth fingers each have a long extensor, providing relatively strong extension. This not only facilitates independent extension of these two digits but may indicate a complementary effect in sustained effort. Action potential recordings or tracings are used to determine the extent and duration of a muscle's contraction. Most muscles producing sustained effort show an increase in action during the period. This apparently means more motor units to produce the effect, even though it is usually an actual loss in strength output. Lippold[2] found that with the index finger in extension, the electrical activity decreases. He attributes this to initial action of the extensor communis digitorum and later substitution of the extensor indicis. This would be possible only in those fingers with two or more synergistic muscles.

Steindler[7] presents an estimate of work potential for the various muscle groups based on work of others for the most part. The kilograms of work listed are as follows:

wrist flexors	13.4
wrist extensors	5.4
ulnar abduction	1.3
radial abduction	0.9
finger flexion at 1st phalanx	3.8
finger flexion at 3rd phalanx	0.8

When force is applied with the hand, it should be done with flexor action, i.e., with the palmar side. This is true whether it is a pushing movement of sustained effort or an accelerated wrist movement such as striking or ball throwing.

In general, the size of the hand is not significantly related to the strength of the grip. Hand size is more nearly related to strength in the grasping type of grip (0.24 to 0.30) than it is in the finger or pinching type of grip (−0.01 to 0.03). For the thumbless grip, the relationship is similar to the normal grasp. In the wide grip, size becomes a little more important. Coefficients obtained were 0.35 and 0.33. It is assumed that the size of the hand itself is not the related factor. In general, the larger hand tends to have larger muscles to move it. However, the strength of the muscle depends upon the use which has been made of it, and therefore the size of the palm or length of digits may be misleading.

On another sample of 35 females, the r's with span and normal and wide grips were 0.38 and 0.54 respectively. This is in general agreement with a preliminary study, though the coefficients are slightly smaller in this study. For this group of women, thumb length gave an r of 0.40 with normal grip.[6] This would appear to be one of the more promising of the anthropometric measures, but unfortunately the measure has not been used with other samples.

Likewise, hand size is apparently unrelated to fast manipulatory skills if we can assume that a speed test on block placing is indicative of precision skills. For 364 male subjects, the r between span and speed was 0.12.

So far as relative strength of the fingers is concerned, there is consistent ranking. This rank order is third, second, first, fourth, and fifth digit. In a group of 50 female subjects measured recently by this investigator, the strength of the second and third digits of the right hand was approximately double that of the fifth, though not as markedly superior in the left hand. For this group, the thumb of the left hand was very weak. The length of the fingers apparently is unrelated to strength: r for the ten fingers of the same 50 subjects varied from −0.22 to 0.05. Finger span correlated 0.29 and hand width 0.39.

The hand is in its strongest position for gripping if the thumb is in apposition to the fingers, i.e., fingers and thumb on opposite sides of the object. The size of the object is also related; optimum size is apparently that with enough spread to keep the palm only slightly cupped, the metacarpal-phalangeal joint almost straight, but fingers well flexed. Too small an object requires marked flexion of fingers and cupping of the hand. The result is shortening of the long flexor muscles to the point of insufficiency, an ineffective pull, and fatigue in the small intrinsic muscles. In a recent study, the various grips were as follows on 364 male subjects, ranked in order of magnitude: normal grip, thumbless grip, wide grip, and finger tip grip.[6]

Normal grip is that just described as optimum. The wide grip is one in which metacarpal-phalangeal joints are straight, palm flat, and distal pressure is on the second or third phalanx rather than on the proximal phalanx. The thumbless grip uses the heel of the hand for opposition rather than the thumb. The thumb is placed in an adducted position beside the second metacarpal. The finger tip or pinch grip makes the contact with the distal phalanx of each of the five digits. Correlation between normal and thumbless grip was 0.58, between normal and wide grip 0.49 and normal and finger tip 0.24.

For a group of 364 male subjects, the t between normal grip and the others (for maximum effort) was as follows:

Thumbless	19.4
Wide	30.5
Thumb and finger	54.4

For endurance (measured as ability to hold it one minute) the ts between normal and the other grips were:

Thumbless	19.1
Wide	27.1
Thumb and finger	45.7

It can be seen that there is progressive and highly significant loss between each of these forms of gripping, whether it is for a single all-out effort or a sustained one. There would appear to be implications for the construction of tools, handles, knobs, etc., and for the hand gear which is worn in doing work.

In a recent study 50 subjects were given a test of maximum normal grip and then asked to grip an electronic dynamometer for one minute as hard as possible. One trial was with the normal grip, the other trial was the finger tip grip described above. Eight seconds of rest followed each trial and then maximum grip was determined. Significantly greater loss was shown after the normal grip than after the finger tip grip. This was true of both right and left hand, though the loss was greater in the right one (R, $t = 6.3$; L, $t = 4.4$). This again emphasizes that the muscles involved in the two forms are not entirely the same. Also, correlations between loss on the two grips were 0.45 right and 0.37 left, substantiating this observation of differentiation of muscles.

In another sample of 40 subjects, normal, thumbless, and wide grips were maintained for one minute each. The drop-off in strength exerted during each successive 15 seconds was studied. All three grips showed a significant loss from the first to second quarter-minute and moderate but insignificant declines from that time on.

In a sample of 364 subjects (the age ranged from 17 to 33, predominantly under 24) there was no apparent relationship between age and hand performance.

Many studies have been made on methods of developing strength in large muscle groups of the body. Enough is known of methods so that hand strength could be developed if needed. Musicians and typists usually expect their specific practice to do the job. Physical therapists are most apt to work with manual resistance. A study by Walters[8] on 27 female subjects attempted to develop general fitness and promote strength on a basis of minimum exercise per day. One exercise, used for 1 to 1½ minutes per day for 11 consecutive days, consisted of running in place and simultaneously forcefully and rhythmically squeezing on a firm sponge-rubber ball. Grip strength did not appear to improve during the 11-day period but did show significant improvement when measured a week after ceasing the training program. This and other studies on strength development would indicate that fairly rapid improvement in strength could be made.

Probably the most outstanding characteristic of the finger range is the great individual differences to be found. That fact you have observed, perhaps, in the hyperextended-abducted "thumbing a ride" position. The same exists in other digits. In one sample of 50 subjects, the mean flexion of the second metacarpal-phalangeal joint was 85 degrees and of the fifth was 90 degrees. However, the range was 70–100 and 70–113 degrees respectively. In extension, the fingers follow an interesting pattern.

	Right	Left
2nd	88	91
3rd	56	56
4th	33	31
5th	78	82

The least variability was found in the fourth finger and the most in the fifth as shown by both means and ranges. Ranges on extension in these digits follow:

	Right	Left
2nd	65–105	65–110
3rd	33–75	35–75
4th	16–55	17–65
5th	35–100	35–100

Hand mobility is a product of three kinds of movement. The first is in the flexion-extension movement of the articulations within the fingers. All digits except the thumb fold into a compact form as in the closed fist. Extension is usually only to straight alignment, except in the thumb which hyperextends.

The second important movement is the spread of fingers for increased range. This is dependent upon the interdigital webs. Of these the one between thumb and index finger is most significant. It is a fairly common source of injury which may lead to serious loss of function. For normal action of the hand, it is considered essential that the third digit be able to move both medially and laterally.

The third source of motion is in the cupping of the palmar segment of the hand. While all hands are built with a slight arch, some hands are rigid, others are extremely flexible. It would seem reasonable to assume from observation that the pliable palm goes with deft and flexible fingers, though there is inadequate evidence on this point.

Many grasping activities require a spread of fingers. This can be accomplished only if the metacarpal-phalangeal articulations are straight or extended. Flexed fingers tend to focus on a given point, frequently the last segment of the thumb. An extended finger may be adducted firmly or abducted to a wide point limited only by the skin and fascial webbing between the digits. The spread from end of first to end of fifth digit is referred to as finger span. It is highly variable and not too closely related to total hand size. For 50 female subjects the r between span and other measures of hand size were:

Palmar width	0.40
Length of 3rd digit	0.69/0.62 (right and left)
Length of 1st metacarpal	
and thumb	0.45

The apposition of the thumb at the base of fingers is apparently not related to thumb length. On the same 50 subjects, the correlation between apposition and sum of first metacarpal and thumb lengths was 0.26/0.09, right and left respectively. Thumb apposition has little relationship to second finger flexion; r is 0.23/0.34 (right and left). Also, there is little relationship between flexion and extension range in the fingers. For these subjects, the second finger gave relationships at 0.18/0.14 (right and left) and for the fifth finger 0.01/0.10 (right and left).

The anteroposterior facing of the vertical hand, hanging or elevated, or the superior-inferior position of the horizontal hand is not a hand function. The movement known as pronation-supination, is a rotatory one occurring between the bones of the forearm. The hand merely rides alone. There seems to be little if any restriction on this movement by sleeves or even tight wrist bands. Most of the screwing, twisting, wringing types of movement are forearm rotation rather than hand function. The flexor grasping action of the hand is all that is needed to hold on and transmit the torque to the object being turned.

When the twisting involves supination, or outward rotation, it is easier and actually more economical if pulling is also possible. This is due to the fact that the biceps is the strongest of the supinators and its primary function is elbow flexion. If the object being turned must be pushed, as in turning a screw, muscular rigidity is approached in the brachial segment of the arm. The triceps must match the pull of the biceps to prevent flexion and thereby permit strong supination.

It should also be apparent that most hand movements are not independent of the forearm, total arm or often total body. In almost all action that might come under the heading of the pushing and pulling type, the hand merely becomes the means of transferring the force from some other source. In pushing, the hand is placed most effectively in a flat extended position, frequently with hyperextended wrist. The flexors of the fingers may or may not work; the wrist flexors usually do function in order to give stability to the wrist. In pulling, however, flexor action must be considerable to maintain a grip. Friction will lessen the required flexor strength but only finger flexors can keep the fingers curled over the knob or handle. Why cannot some persons chin themselves? It may be a lack of arm and shoulder girdle strength, but it may also be lack of finger strength to hold on.

What is the explanation of the highly co-ordinated and varied skill of the human hand? Skilled co-ordination might be defined as a precise amount in each of a series of efforts, in perfect timing with each other. Obviously, this is the result of neural control of highly sensitive muscles. Enough is known of brain structure and function to at least determine the site of cortical control. Pfeiffer[3] presented an excellent statement with respect to cortical relationships of the hand. The motor units of the hand are very small, i.e., have very few fibers. Consequently there are many of them. Movements of the hand, therefore, require many motor units and control of more than twenty articulations. Therefore, the area on the cortex governing action of each hand is a very large one. The neural control and the integration of arm and hand action make it possible to impart a very heavy blow by hand or to finger with great delicacy in an unlimited variety of skills.

The skin on the dorsum of the hand is essentially like that of the rest of the body and is loose and pliable. On the palmar surface, it is highly differentiated. One of the best ways to appreciate this difference is to observe the hand of the Negro. The back of the hand is pigmented like the arms, trunk, or face. The palms are nonpigmented, almost a match in color for the white hand.

Palmar skin can take a great deal of abuse. The toughness of the palmar skin and horny calluses vary according to the use that has been made of the hand. In spite of this, the fingers are very sensitive to touch. The palmar skin consists of papillary ridges equipped with the special nerve receptors, pacinian corpuscles, in highly concentrated fashion. In fact, it is estimated that as much as one-fifth to one-fourth of the total number in the body dermis are located in the fingers. The palmar skin is laid on a substantial base of fascia which is padded with more fat than the dorsal skin and anchored firmly to deeper fascia and ligaments. The result is an insulated palm taking more pressure and abuse than would otherwise be true. The sense of touch is extremely acute, particularly in the finger tips. This is, doubtless, the source of success on intricate skills. External padding is known to decrease the force of a grip. Whether excess fat padding does the same is merely a matter of speculation.

The fascial anchorings also cause the skin to fold consistently in given creases and with the help of the two palmaris muscles to form a neat semi-domed palm for ease of grasping. This is, essentially, the same process as pinning down overstuffed furniture to prevent bulging and slipping of padding.

In an attempt to understand and measure kinesthetic perception, measures of precision have been tried on many different groups. Russell,[4] Scott,[5] and Witte[9] agree that specificity of function exists and that acuity of perception of hand and finger position has little relationship to any other kinesthetic measure yet used in the upper extremity or otherwise. A finger-spread test has been used in which the elbow is left stationary on the table, but the wrist elevated, and thumb and fifth finger are abducted to touch a double bull's-eye type of target which is spread under the metacarpal segment of the hand.

This function was found to improve from junior high school age, through senior high and on through the twenties and thirties. After that age, it appears to decline. The same is true of a wrist extension to a specified position.

It seems reasonable to assume that acuity in hand positioning, like other kinesthetic perceptions, is related to facility of motor learning. It is hypothesized by the author that further refinement of those tests or others of similar function might well lead to a satisfactory prediction of success in skills such as typing, keyboard, or machine panel manipulation of all types, where relative position of keys, knobs, and controls is important to rapid and successful work.

Jackson[1] reported a study on tapping speed for three groups: men typists, women typists, and women nontypists. Action centered at the wrist was faster than finger tapping for the nontypists; with the typists, wrist action ranked second. For all three groups fingers two and three were fastest, though not in the same order for all three groups. The little finger was always the slowest. Left and right hands were essentially the same. In a training period, only fingers three and four responded significantly. Finger four is considered by teachers of typing, Morse code, and music to be slower or less responsive to training. Experience has taught us that the fourth digit extending alone is extremely limited and may, therefore, account for some of its lesser effectiveness.

The nails are essentially protective devices for the end of the fingers, but persons engaged in handling small objects soon learn to use them for help in picking up these objects. One can readily appreciate this use if a nail is broken off next to the finger, or if the hand is gloved.

What are the things we don't know about the hand? They are numerous. Those who are concerned with high levels of skill and efficiency of the hand would profit by information on points such as the following:

How do we make the hand more flexible?

What are the minimum exercise or use requirements for maintenance of strength?

What is the recovery period following fatigue?

How can the hand be trained to use alternating muscle groups and thereby delay fatigue?

Can we develop sensitivity of touch and effort?

What is the optimum learning or practice arrangement for intricate hand functions?

How can we best measure kinesthetic perception of position and movement in the hand and arm?

How can we develop relaxation as a hand skill?

One of the screening tests for applicants to dental schools is a wood-carving assignment. Does such a measure offer possibilities for screening applicants for other jobs which require skilled hands?

How important is the dominance factor in the development of skill and sensitivity of touch?

Is the resting hand position the optimum preparatory position for work, or would a straighter position of the hand be more effective because of the stretching of flexor muscles?

What is the range of joint movement that allows effective application of effort?

Is circulatory restriction of the hand more or less important than in parts where larger muscles are involved in the work?

Is skilled co-ordination of fingers, the so-called handy man, the result of inheritance or experience? Can the regression of kinesthetic acuity be delayed or prevented?

When the answers to these and may more questions are forthcoming, then we shall know more of the potentialities of the hand and have the basis for better matching of a man to his job.

REFERENCES

1. Jackson, C. V., Differential Finger Tapping Rates, *Journal of Physiology*, 122, 1952, p. 582.
2. Lippold, O. C., Fatigue in Finger Muscles, *Journal of Physiology*, 128, 1955, p. 33.
3. Pfeiffer, John, *The Human Brain*, New York, Harper & Row, Pubs., 1955.
4. Russell, Ruth, *A Factor Analysis of the Components of Kinesthesis*, Microcard PH36, 1954.
5. Scott, M. Gladys, Measurement of Kinesthesis, *Research Quarterly*, 26, October 1955, p. 324.
6. ————, Kinesiological Parameters of the Hand, Conference Report on Protection and Functioning of the Hands in Cold Climates, Natick, Massachusetts, Headquarters Quartermaster Research and Development Command, 1957.
7. Steindler, Arthur, *Kinesiology of the Human Body*, Springfield, Ill., Charles C Thomas, 1955, Ch. 30, Mechanics of Hand and Fingers.
8. Walters, C. Etta, Effects of Prescribed Strenuous Exercise in the Physical Efficiency of Women, *Research Quarterly*, 24, March 1953, p. 102.
9. Witte, Fae, *A Factorial Analysis of Measures of Kinesthesis*, Microcard PH20, 1953.

CHAPTER 17

Selected Sports Activities

THE SPORTS SELECTED FOR DISCUSSION in this chapter are those which are most frequently included in the physical education and recreation programs. They are the ones which physical education students have learned and which physical education teachers are most apt to teach. The list is not complete. Some activities were omitted intentionally because it seemed wise for the student to make some analyses for himself.

The form of the analysis varies in the different sports. Many of them are treated according to the outline provided at the beginning of Part III. Others are limited almost entirely to a mechanical analysis or to a discussion of unique features. These are the skills which have been discussed in exact or similar form in some other chapter; only the details are added here which supplement the other discussion.

All analyses are in terms of a right-handed or right-footed performer.

ARCHERY

Archery is a sport which calls for precision of movement. It is largely dependent upon the kinesthetic perception of position and ability always to reproduce exactly the desired position. It demands static rather than dynamic precision, such as is found in throwing. Archery belongs to the same class of skills as throwing, but involves the projection of the arrow by mechanical rather than muscular force. However, the muscular force of the performer operates the bow.

Description

The archer stands in an erect position with feet slightly apart, left side squarely toward the target. The head is erect but turned straight to the left. The hands are in position on the bow as it hangs in front of the body. The bow arm is raised to approximately shoulder level; the bow pulls against the palm just inside the base of the thumb, with either a loose or a tight grip. The arm is rotated so that the front of the elbow is in a frontal plane and not facing upward. The elbow should be almost straight but not locked in extension. The second, third, and fourth fingers of the other hand are used to grip the string. Each is flexed, particularly the last phalanx of each finger. The right arm is raised upward and across

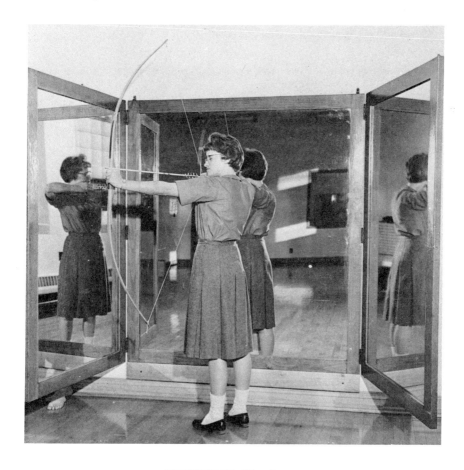

FIGURE 65: The draw

the body, and drawn sideward in a horizontal plane with hand close to
the left shoulder until the fingers are under the chin. The release is made
by extension of the fingers that are on the string, accompanied by a continuation of the draw with the right arm. The position is held until the
arrow hits the target.

Muscular Analysis

The muscles used in standing will not be repeated here. However, the
rigidity of the trunk must be increased. This calls for stronger action of
the flexors and extensors on the right side of the trunk, and corresponding control from those in the left side. The abductors of both hips are
used more or less, depending upon the width of the leg spread, but in
any case help to fix the upright position of the pelvis.

The neck is rotated so that the face is turned directly to the left. The right sternocleidomastoid and the upper right trapezius assisted by the left splenius and erector spinae (spinalis cervicis and longissimus cervicis) are responsible for this position.

The bow arm is raised by the whole deltoid, the anterior portion being weak in its efforts and the posterior portion being particularly active to resist the tension of the bow. It is assisted in this backward force by the teres minor and the infraspinatus. The rotation of the arm to adjust the elbow is accomplished by slight inward rotation by the teres major and subscapularis and pronation of the forearm by the pronator teres and pronator quadratus. The triceps holds the elbow extended or near extension, and the extensors carpi radialis longus and brevis and extensor carpi ulnaris hold the wrist firm, preventing flexion which would occur from the resistance of the bow and flexion of the fingers. The slight hyperextension of the wrist causes the fingers to flex easily. If a tight grip on the bow is used the finger flexors must be contracted.

The scapula on this side is rotated upward and adducted strongly by trapezius and rhomboids. The lower sections of the serratus anterior assist in the rotation of the scapula. The acromial point of the shoulder should not be elevated. In order to counteract this tendency, the upper part of the trapezius must not be used too strongly. The rhomboids counteract some of the extreme of upward rotation at the same time that they adduct the scapula. The pectoralis minor and subclavius help fix the shoulder girdle in front and hold the acromion down.

The right arm is brought into position across the chest partly because the bow is being lifted by the other arm and partly by the deltoid and upper pectoralis major. While it is being lifted and after it reaches the proper level, it is drawn backward exactly as the bow arm is pulled back. Similar movement of the scapula is also found. In order to prevent the hand from swinging out of line during this shoulder extension the elbow flexors must be used. The balance between supination of the biceps and pronation by the pronator teres keeps the forearm in straight alignment. The release is made by relaxation of the flexors profundus digitorum and sublimis digitorum, timed with contraction of the extensor communis digitorum to give a quick, smooth action of the string.

Mechanical Analysis

The preparatory movement in this case may be considered the draw, the release as the act, and the holding of position the follow-through. This is an excellent example of the way the follow-through may be used to prevent interference with the act itself before release is made. Good performers hold the position until the arrow reaches the target. The only exception is found with those using a loose grip of the bow. Their follow-through is characterized by the same holding of position, but the bow drops because the pressure no longer keeps it in contact with the heel of the hand.

The force necessary for the draw depends upon the weight or strength of the bow. The speed of the arrow also depends upon the bow strength, the construction of the bow, the kind of wood of which it is made, and whether or not the bow is fully drawn.

Methods of aiming vary but in general follow the same principles. The eye is above the line of the arrow. The point of aim is established by locating the point at which the eye looks down over the end of the arrow when the arrow is aligned for a flight directly into the gold. Obviously the greater the distance at which the shooting is done, the nearer the point of aim approaches the gold; and the closer the shooting, the nearer the point of aim approaches the archer.

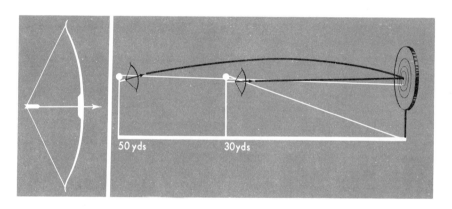

FIGURE 66: Point of aim

The other principal method of aiming uses a sight on the bow. It is used in much the same way as the sight on a gun is used. It must be raised and lowered on the bow as the distance varies. Such a sight is easily constructed of sponge rubber or plastic foam and a protruding pin which can be easily adjusted.

A smooth release is necessary in order to impart the full force of the string to the arrow and to prevent vibration of the string, which causes the arrow to "weave."

The flight of the arrow is determined by the law of projectiles, in common with all thrown objects. Its velocity, however, is much greater than gravital acceleration, and the standard shooting ranges are comparatively short, so that the flight is only slightly arched. As the range increases the arc of the arrow increases. In "clout" shooting and "flight" shooting, both being for greater distances, the aim is considerably higher, approximating the 45° angle of the distance throw. This requires an inclination of the trunk to the right, but otherwise the performance is the same.

If the bow is too strong or the arrow too long a complete draw is impossible. If the arrow is too short in proportion to the archer's arms serious injury may result from overdrawing.

REFERENCES

1. Ainsworth, Dorothy, *et al., Individual Sports for Women,* Philadelphia, W. B. Saunders Co., 1958.
2. Jaeger, Eloise, *How to Improve Your Archery,* Chicago, Athletic Institute, 1958.
3. Miller, Donna Mae, and Ley, Katherine L., *Sports for Women,* Englewood Cliffs, N.J., Prentice-Hall, Inc., 1955.
4. Purdue University, Physical Education Staff, *Physical Education for Women,* Minneapolis, Burgess Publishing Company, 1958.
5. Vannier, Maryhelen, and Poindexter, Hally Beth, *Individual and Team Sports for Girls and Women,* Philadelphia, W. B. Saunders Co., 1960.

BADMINTON

Badminton is a game involving striking techniques. It is similar in some respects to tennis but in the mechanics of performance it differs definitely. The equipment is largely responsible for this. The badminton racket is lighter in weight and smaller in size. This means that the racket lacks the potential force inherent in the larger moving mass. The lighter weight does mean, however, that it can be manipulated with more speed. Compensation is thus secured by increasing the second factor in momentum. The greater speed of the stroke creates a difference in the timing of the two games.

The other piece of equipment, the bird, is lighter than the tennis ball. This means that less momentum of the racket will impart correspondingly greater speed to the bird. The resistance offered by the feathers slows the bird and in general causes the bird to drop more abruptly than a ball of similar weight that started a similar course. The bird should be hit squarely on the cork. Usually any attempt to produce spin on the bird such as that secured in tennis results in either ruining the stroke or in fouling by "carrying."

From the standpoint of mechanics the strokes may be classified as either underhand or overhand. The serve belongs to the underhand strokes, as required by the rules. There is usually a short pause at the limit of the backswing in order to facilitate timing. The bird is dropped and the racket is brought forward in an arc to come behind and under the bird. The racket face is approximately at right angles to the direction the bird takes when it is struck. The radius of the arc described by the racket may be comparatively short if the action is limited to arm swing and the bird is to go high. The wrist snap just before contact adds considerably to the speed. The arc through which the racket travels may be much straighter if the weight is shifted forward at the same time as the swing. This is a shift of weight with the feet spread; no step is allowed in making the serve. The follow-through is lengthened and directed toward the net. This gives less arch to the flight of the bird because the racket face is carried through in a straighter line.

Any drive or underhand clear stroke follows essentially the same form as the serve. The force is obtained by arm swing and wrist snap, to some extent by transfer of weight and trunk extension, but there is usually less trunk rotation than occurs in most striking activities. The long, high, clear stroke resembles the tennis lob to some extent, but in many respects it would make a very poor tennis stroke.

The drop shot is played almost entirely with wrist action, as this reduces the speed and makes placement easier. It is a short, quick movement with no follow-through. Accuracy is of primary importance here, and direction is very obviously a matter of the angle of the racket face.

The overhead shots are very similar. They are played, preferably, at the height of the reach. The force imparted to the bird is secured from velocity of the racket swing, from vigorous wrist action, and to some extent by transfer of weight and trunk flexion. If a high clear is to be made, the racket face is turned upward a little. If a smash is to be made, the racket is moving down slightly to the bird, and wrist snap and trunk flexion add to the force.

Wrist flexion, which occurs in all strokes just before the bird is contacted, is responsible for most of the speed imparted to the bird. Wrist action is freest when the grip on the racket is loose. The grip tightens somewhat at the instant of contact but it need not be as tight as it is in most striking activities. Since the momentum of the bird is so much less than that of most balls, the reaction on the racket is less; therefore, the grip may be less rigid. Wrist action introduces an additional problem of timing to avoid misdirection of the bird.

Footwork is very important, since the player must cover a fairly large court with a very brief interval between strokes. The ability to start quickly and change direction quickly requires certain adjustments. While waiting, the player spreads the feet, one a little ahead of the other, keeps the weight forward and the knees slightly bent. This should facilitate a quick start. When moving, the player takes short steps and keeps the weight well balanced. The run may be made by ordinary short steps or by sliding steps sideward. The reach may be used effectively, although the player should not reach so far that he is off balance, or so far that he must continue in the same direction for another step or two before being able to reverse his direction.

See the analysis of tennis for the discussion of muscles used in this type of striking. Some differences will be apparent from the differences in form.

REFERENCES

1. Ainsworth, Dorothy, *et al.*, *Individual Sports for Women*, Philadelphia, W. B. Saunders Co., 1958.
2. Miller, Donna Mae, and Ley, Katherine L., *Sports for Women*, Englewood Cliffs, N.J., Prentice-Hall, Inc., 1955.
3. Purdue University, Physical Education Staff, *Physical Education for Women*, Minneapolis, Burgess Publishing Co., 1963.
4. Vannier, Maryhelen, and Poindexter, Hally Beth, *Individual and Team Sports for Girls and Women*, Philadelphia, W. B. Saunders Co., 1960.

BASEBALL, SOFTBALL

The four principal skills in baseball and softball are throwing, running, batting, and catching. The first three of these have been discussed previously, and hence they will not be considered here in any detail.

Pitching is a specialized form of throwing; the rules of the game prescribe whether it shall be overhand or underhand. It must be highly accurate. At its best the target may be considered about 18 by 36 inches. Actually, the possible variation is considerably less because the strategically good pitch is not the one nearest the center of the target but rather the one which is placed in the corners or near the edges of the area. Since the pitcher aims at these points rather than the center, the range of error must be very small.

The pitch must also be fast to be most effective. Moreover, the pitcher must be able to change the speed without giving it away by a change of delivery. The preparatory movement is the part which gives the batter most time to react to a change of form; therefore it should not be changed. Slightly less force may be put into the transfer of weight and the arm swing, though these changes also may be detected if they are too decided. Variations in wrist snap are probably most effective in changing the speed of the ball. Antagonistic muscles may slow down the arm swing just before delivery and hence help to camouflage the throw. There is danger in this case, however, of interfering with accuracy.

The good pitcher also makes use of the curve ball to deceive the batter. Spin causes the ball to curve just before reaching the plate. Therefore the batter is more likely to swing and miss, or to think the ball is not going to be good and let it go by.

Most of the other occasions in the game requiring throwing also demand speed. Therefore the "give" in the catch becomes part of the preparatory movement for the throw. The ball has been thrown fast, and the player receiving the ball requires considerable skill to avoid fumbling. The ball is thrown in as flat a path as the distance will permit. For example, a throw from base to base or from pitcher to baseman may be thrown almost straight. A throw down the base line from one base to the next needs a rise of three to four feet, or a little more if the ball is slower. A long throw from an outfielder will need more arch. In either case the throw is an overhand one in order to secure speed. Therefore it must have the same effort put into it that a throw for distance would have.

The running is the same as any fast dash; but the weight must be controlled in order for the player to stop on base or to turn the corner and continue to the next base. Stopping is mostly a matter of shifting the center of weight backward, getting the supporting foot ahead of the center of weight and slowing the pace. When the weight is shifted still further back, the player falls and slides on into the base and friction is mainly responsible for stopping him. When running two or more bases the runner should stay fairly close to the base line. This is necessary because too much time is required to run a large circular path. Knowing that it is impossible to turn a square corner at top speed the player swings gradually out of the base line before reaching the base, leans well in, and takes a circular path around the corner in such a way that he steps on the inside corner of the base. This inward lean enables him to keep up greater speed and to cut down the arc in which he runs.

The general principles of batting are the same as those of any striking activity. The body is turned beyond the position where it would face at right angles to the path at which the ball is coming. This permits transfer of weight and body rotation as well as a fuller arm swing than would be possible otherwise.

In most instances long hard drives are desired. Since the ball is coming to the bat fast, it has considerable momentum. Merely to counteract this momentum requires a real force. To send it back into the field requires still more. Since the bat is heavy, it also will have a great deal of momentum if it is swung with any speed. It is in order to develop this speed that the batter uses the back swing and long drive, the shift of weight and trunk rotation.

The ball is usually struck near the outer end of the bat. Since the bat is long, and is used as an elongation of the extended arms, the end of the bat is moving rapidly when it contacts the ball.

The difference between the reaction of the hard ball and the softball is due chiefly to the difference in effect on the balls at the instant of contact and the difference in elasticity or the recovery after flattening. The softball is flattened by the impact, and hence some of the force is absorbed. The hard ball more nearly retains its shape. Therefore, more of the reaction of the bat is imparted to it. Also, the hard ball is lighter, the bat is heavier; and therefore the same force will give it greater speed than would be given the softball. In addition to this the smaller ball moves through the air with less resistance.

FIGURE 67: Preparatory position for pitching

FIGURE 68: Beginning of the forward swing

The placement of the ball is very important in the game. Whether it goes in the direction of first, second, or third base depends upon the direction the bat is facing when it makes contact. This direction may be affected by the control of the bat at the wrist or the time at which the ball is hit. If the swing of the bat is timed so that the bat is parallel to the line across the front edge of home plate, the ball will go down the center of the field. If the hands are leading beyond the head of the bat, the ball goes more to the right. If the hands are retarded, the ball goes toward third base. Similarly, if the ball is hit squarely over the plate it is easier to send it straight. If the swing is too early and the ball is hit farther forward, it is carried toward the left. Or if it is hit too late near the back of the plate, it will go down the first base line.

The ball that is hit with the bat on an angle has spin which tends to make it curve still further to the right or left. Figure 70 illustrates this point. Thus the ball that appears to be fair down the first or third base line may suddenly curve outside. Cutting up under the ball or hitting down into it will also direct the ball in the direction of the swing and usually puts spin on it.

The shape of the ball and bat also affect the direction. A ball which is hit squarely behind its center by the center of the bat goes out straight. One hit above the center of the ball or below the center of the bat will be a grounder. However, a ball which is hit a little below its center or above the center of the bat rises sharply into the air. If the difference is too pronounced, that is, only the lower surface of the ball makes contact near the top of the bat, the ball rolls or slides over the bat for a foul tip. This is especially true if the ball has top spin.

The grip is an important factor in getting accuracy and speed. The hands must be near the end of the bat and together if a full swing is made. Obviously the grip must be very tight at the time of impact if the bat is to take the impact of the ball and also impart momentum to it. The timing of the wrist action determines whether the handle or the head of the bat leads.

The bunt differs from ordinary batting chiefly in the grip and the swing. The swing is slower and short. Usually the bat is not moving into the ball at the time of contact, but instead it is held in the path of the ball and may even "give" with it. This serves the same purpose as the relaxation of a player when catching a ball; the rebound is very short. The hands are spread far apart on the bat. This limits the swing and reduces the force, but makes it possible to direct the ball very accurately (Fig. 69).

The only new skill in fielding that has not been discussed is catching. Success in catching is dependent upon judging the motion of the ball and the proper place for contacting it and upon the ability to stop its momentum in such a way as to keep control of it.

bunt

FIGURE 69: Batting

full swing

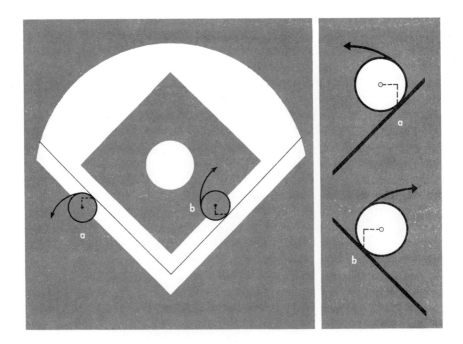

FIGURE 70: Rotation of the ball
a–drive down third base line rotates out; b–drive down first base
line rotates out

The first essential in judging the motion of the ball is to watch it. If the ball is bouncing, irregularities in the ground may cause the ball to change its course. Such balls should be played as a pick-up at the ground, or, if the bounce is long, they may be caught in the air. The speed of fly balls cannot always be estimated accurately at a distance. The fly ball may even change its line of flight because of the rotation or spin of the ball. A fly ball with back spin tends to be buoyed up in the latter part of its flight. Therefore it will be carried farther than it would otherwise. On the other hand, a ball with back spin, such as the foul fly behind the plate, tends to drop very abruptly. Only if the player watches the ball carefully can he adjust properly to the flight of the ball.

In stopping the ball, the catcher must apply resistance over more or less space in order to allow time to reduce the velocity of the ball. This accounts for the "give" in the arms and body during the catch. Without this the ball would rebound from the hands. In the case of baseball, and also many other sports, the "give" can be used as the beginning of the throw which must follow immediately. The footwork, body position, and arm action should be such that the catch and the throw are continuous.

REFERENCES

1. Bunn, John W., *Scientific Principles of Coaching*, Englewood Cliffs, N.J., Prentice-Hall, Inc., 1955.
2. Meyer, Margaret, and Schwarz, Marguerite, *Team Sports for Women*, Philadelphia, W. B. Saunders Co., 1947.
3. Miller, Donna Mae, and Ley, Katherine L., *Sports for Women*, Englewood Cliffs, N.J., Prentice-Hall, Inc., 1955.
4. Purdue University, Physical Education Staff, *Physical Education for Women*, Minneapolis, Burgess Publishing Co., 1963.
5. Race, Donald E., Cinematographic and Mechanical Analysis of the External Movements Involved in Hitting a Baseball Effectively, *Research Quarterly*, 32, October 1961, p. 394.
6. Seymour, Emery W., Comparison of Base Running Methods, *Research Quarterly*, 30, October 1959, p. 321.
7. Vannier, Maryhelen, and Poindexter, Hally Beth, *Individual and Team Sports for Girls and Women*, Philadelphia, W. B. Saunders Co., 1960.

BASKETBALL

Basketball is a sport consisting almost entirely of ball handling and body balance in running and jumping. In their basic forms these have already been discussed, but certain special problems will be considered here.

The first point to be considered is the size of the ball. The majority of players, at least girls, are unable to grasp the ball with the fingers of one hand, so that the throws must be made with two hands, or the ball allowed to rest on one hand without a grip. The use of two hands usually means a limited arc in the delivery and less effective use of the body in the throw, but better accuracy. The use of the one hand requires certain adjustments in form to keep the hand behind the center of weight of the ball and often results in lowered accuracy of throwing, particularly in the less skilled player.

Most of the passes made in the game are comparatively short, and therefore do not require great effort. Only as the players are forced to take long shots or choose to use a long pass is the problem of maximum force important. The hook pass is best suited for long passing. It has most of the advantages of the overhand throw that a smaller ball which can be grasped in the fingers has. The ball is back, balanced between the hand and wrist, the arm starts extended back and downward, weight is back, and the trunk is turned to the right. The force comes from swinging the extended arm upward and forward, shifting the weight, and turning the body. The fingers and hand are behind the ball so that some wrist snap may even be used just before the release.

The bounce pass and the dribble in the boys' game are similar in several respects. The angle of incidence determines the angle at which the ball rebounds. The distance the player can cover in time to catch the ball again or the length of the pass will regulate the size of the angles necessary. Spin may be used on the pass to vary the angle and length of the rebound and still place the bounce to the disadvantage of the opponent. The fingers or part of the hand giving impetus to the ball must be behind the center of gravity of the ball and in line with that center and the direction the ball is to take. For example, a ball cannot be sent forward if the hand is on top of the ball. In the dribble the player must keep the ball always within his range of vision. Therefore he plays the ball well out in front and leans forward toward it. His flexed knees and lowered center of weight also help him to move quickly and to change direction if necessary.

In order to protect the shot the ball is usually carried upward close to the chest and the face or by the extension of one arm from the shoulder upward. In either case the force of the arm is augmented by a jump. This adds the force of leg extension to the throw and lengthens the distance through which force is applied. Young players or girls often find it impossible to get the ball from the free throw line to the basket by the usual type of shot. Various adaptations are made which are more or less successful. They may turn and, with one hand behind the ball, push it up. This gives the advantage of trunk rotation and a slightly lengthened arc. A variation is the double underhand toss with a pronounced knee bend and leg extension. This greatly increases the arc through which the ball is carried and gets maximum use of the leg extensors. This is, of course, practically useless except when the player is entirely unguarded. It may be used for free throws by young players who do not have strength to get the ball up otherwise.

In general the most successful shots are those that are well arched and drop down into the basket. A ball coming down from above the basket has almost the full width of the basket in which it may fall and still go through. A ball coming toward the basket in a line more nearly parallel to the rim has only a narrow path in which it may travel and still go through (Fig. 71). Also, if too much force is used on the arched ball, the backboard may cause the ball to rebound into the basket. Too much force on the flatter shot merely causes it to rebound more nearly at right angles to the board, and the basket is missed. A two-handed shot cannot be arched if the elbows are spread wide and the upper arm is abducted. Beginning players frequently use this style—ball in front of chest, hands too far behind the ball—and most of the force comes from elbow extension. In this position the force is diminished and directed too nearly straight forward.

The proper use of the backboard is important in shooting baskets. A ball which is thrown straight into the backboard, or approximately at right angles to it, will rebound in about the same path. If it is rebounding with much force, it will not show any appreciable drop until long

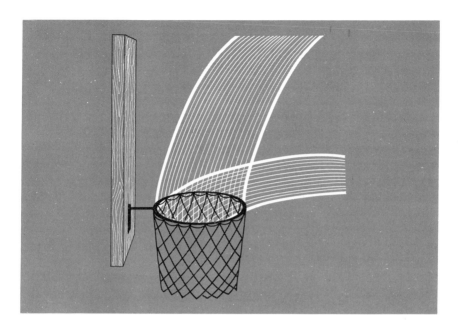

FIGURE 71: Comparison of width of basket in arched and flat shots

after it has gone beyond the width of the basket. Another type of shot strikes the board at a very small angle, that is, while moving in a path very nearly parallel to the face of the board. If this path is across the board, or down on it from a high arched shot, the ball will continue in the same general direction but will rebound at an angle approximating that at which it struck the board.

In the banked shot close from the side of the basket, the ball is moving upward toward the board at a relatively small angle and in toward the basket at a similar angle to the vertical. The rebound will be definitely downward, but the ball continues toward the basket at the same angle (beyond the vertical) as the one with which it approached the board. The toss should be easy so that most of the upward momentum is gone when the ball hits. The rebound will be slight and the ball will curve down into the basket with the pull of gravity.

An understanding of the law of counterforce, of gravital acceleration, and of the components of a force will simplify this problem. If the ball strikes the board at such angle that its total momentum is at right angles to the face of the board, then a duplicate counterforce is provided by the board, assuming that the air pressure in the ball is sufficient to minimize the "give" in the ball when it hits. If the ball is moving almost parallel to the surface of the board, only a very small proportion of the force (momentum which it has) is against the board. Consequently when the ball strikes the board it continues in the same direction except for the slight deflection due to the reaction of the board to this perpendicular force. When the ball is moving upward at a small angle to the board, the pull of gravity is sufficient to reduce the upward acceleration to zero. The ball starts downward, but its path is governed by the reaction to the other one or two components of the shot.

Gravital acceleration causes a ball to drop sixteen feet in the first second of fall or four feet in the first half second, when it starts at zero speed. It will be greater if it is already moving downward when it strikes. This is equivalent to a distance from three feet above the top of the backboard to the floor in one second or from the top to the bottom of the backboard in the half second. The distance from the backboard at the end of each of those intervals is determined by the horizontal acceleration imparted to the ball. This explains the fact that the ball must be played with the proper force for a given angle and a given arc if the ball is to fall into the basket. There is, therefore, no one spot that can be taken for the point of aim, although the range on the backboard is fairly limited for different players and for similar shots. An understanding of these factors should aid in determining the place and time at which rebounds should be recovered. These facts should also explain the reason for arching all shots from in front of the basket so they will drop in from above without the use of the backboard. Lay-up shots from close at the side of the basket may be more accurately tossed over the rim than dealing with the backboard and the problem of angles of rebound.

None of the discussion so far has taken into consideration the fact that the ball may be rotating when it hits the backboard. The exact results will depend upon the speed of the rotation. In general a ball which has top spin when it hits the board is a little slower in starting to fall; however, top spin does not occur very frequently. A ball with back spin drops very sharply. This is used to get the ball down into the basket and to counteract the effects if the ball hits a little too hard. Side spin causes the ball to jump to the side of the spin. This is used especially on short close shots. Even a player under the basket may be able to get the ball up to the backboard with enough spin toward the basket so that the ball will be carried over the rim and drop in.

Jumping in basketball is somewhat different from other forms of jumping, because of the purpose of the jump and the necessity of observing rules on fouling. The jump is usually for height of reach rather than height of the whole body, although the whole body must be lifted if the reach is to be successful. The poorly trained player too frequently jumps without fully extending the legs, thus reducing the force of the leg extension and of the jump. Girls frequently flex the knees again while in the air; this reacts on the body by pulling it down.

The player must have control of body weight while jumping, and must not fall forward or step forward. This requires a nearly vertical take-off and is accomplished by an erect trunk and weight centered over the feet rather than forward. If the player is facing the basket, the arm swing must be more nearly sideward than in the ordinary jump. If the player stands sideward to the basket the arms may swing forward in a more natural position and they may be kept straighter. Also, the arm not used for reaching for the ball may be brought down again while the body is in the air, thus reacting to lift the body up.

The jump may be necessary to intercept shots, rebounds, or high passes. In this situation the player usually can run or at least step into the jump. The forward momentum adds to the height of the jump. However, it tends to carry the player forward after the jump. If the ball was caught it must be passed immediately, or the player must check his forward motion before steps are taken.

REFERENCES

1. Hutton, Joe, and Hoffman, Vern B., *Basketball,* Mankato, Minnesota, Creative Education Society, Inc., 1961.
2. Meyer, Margaret, and Schwarz, Marguerite, *Team Sports for Women,* Philadelphia, W. B. Saunders Co., 1947.
3. Miller, Donna Mae, and Ley, Katherine L., *Sports for Women,* Englewood Cliffs, N.J., Prentice-Hall, Inc., 1955.
4. Purdue University, Physical Education Staff, *Physical Education for Women,* Minneapolis, Burgess Publishing Co., 1963.
5. Vannier, Maryhelen, and Poindexter, Hally Beth, *Individual and Team Sports for Girls and Women,* Philadelphia, W. B. Saunders Co., 1960.

BOWLING

Bowling demands extreme accuracy. This accuracy is dependent upon the ability of the performer to control and to co-ordinate perfectly all movements in the delivery and release of the ball. Balance is essential to a consistent arm swing. The arm swing determines the general direction that the ball takes. The manner of release determines the direction of rotation of the ball while it rolls down the alley. This rotation, the speed of the ball, and the surface of the alley determine whether the ball goes in a straight line or curves either right or left and how soon that curve takes place.

Description. The ball is held by the thumb and the third finger, or by the thumb and the third and fourth fingers. The bowler starts in a standing position, both feet together. Usually the ball is held in front of the chest, the fingers of the left hand helping to steady the ball. The approach may vary from three to five steps but always ends with the left foot forward (for right-handed players). The last step with the left foot is directly in line with the right one but the toes are pointing straight down the alley. All steps are approximately normal walking steps except that the last step is usually lengthened somewhat and the knees are flexed more in each of the last two steps, especially in the last one.

The arm swing is very similar to the underarm throw described in Chapter 15. The ball is held in front of the body, usually chest high. The ball travels straight forward by a forward thrust of the arm. It then drops downward with the first step. It is allowed to swing back to easy extension a little beyond the hip. The forward swing is approximately straight forward and reaches the point of release about parallel with the left foot or when the arm is approximately perpendicular to the floor. At the same time the weight is transferred onto the left foot. The knees, hips and ankles flex on the last two steps so that the ball is just off the floor when released. The trunk is inclined forward slightly. The weight is entirely on the left foot which is in place or sliding slowly forward. The right leg is back and the foot is behind or to the left of the supporting foot, resting lightly on the floor.

The follow-through shows a continuation of the arm swing forward, continued forward bending of the trunk, and a holding of balance over the forward foot. The left arm is swung easily backward and sideward.

Muscular Analysis. The arm swing uses many of the same muscles as the underhand throw. The anterior shoulder muscles must come into action sooner to prevent too much elevation on the back swing due to the inertia of the heavier ball. For bowling a straight ball the forearm is in a midposition between pronation and supination, with the thumb and second finger parallel to each other and to the line of the swing down the alley. In this case the fingers and the thumb release simultaneously. A straight ball may be bowled with the forearm a little nearer supination, which brings the thumb farther forward than the second finger. In this case the wrist must be adducted by the flexor carpi ulnaris and extensor carpi ulnaris to avoid the tendency to hold to the ball too long with the thumb. In either case the forearm position calls for fine adjustment between the pronators teres and quadratus, and the supinator and biceps. The first form is frequently used by women bowlers because of lack of strength in controlling wrist action. The latter form is used by many men.

The finger flexors are used both in bowling and throwing to grip the ball, but the holes of the bowling ball prevent flexion of the last segment. The position of the other segments depends upon the span of the holes in the ball.

The leg muscles involved are the same as for walking, with the responsibility of controlled flexion falling on the extensor muscles. The right leg is brought over more or less to the left by the adductor muscles; and it may be rotated inward more or less by the gracilis and the tensor. The two lesser gluteals and the tensor support the weight laterally on the left leg during the finish of the delivery. This action is stronger than in many activities because the weight of the ball in the right hand and the forward momentum of the arm swing tend to overbalance the body toward the right. The back and abdominal muscles of the left side of the trunk also prevent lateral bending to the right.

The trunk is inclined a little forward but the back is straight. Therefore the spinal extensors must be acting. The head may even be slightly hyperextended as the eyes are kept focused down the alley.

The left arm swings backward. It is an easy movement brought about by action of the middle and posterior deltoid principally, but they may be assisted by the teres minor and infraspinatus.

Mechanical Analysis. The approach should be a smooth, natural gait progressing straight to the foul line. The number of steps in the approach is somewhat dependent upon the length of the legs, how high the ball is extended initially, and therefore how far it travels on the backswing. In any case the steps and the swing should be perfectly synchronized so that the forward momentum of each action will complement the other and be imparted to the ball without loss or independent action.

The back swing puts tension on the anterior muscles and also increases the arc through which the force may be applied. Too long a back swing or a circular back swing changes the position of the trunk and the line of delivery. The forward swing is taken with the arm straight and movement centering in the shoulder. This gives a long lever and, with the combined action of the anterior shoulder muscles giving strength sufficient to move the long lever, the possibility of speed. The arm swing and the leg flexion should be timed so that the ball just misses the floor on the low point of the arc, and the ball is released immediately after this point so that it is at the floor and merely starts rolling. If the ball is not released soon enough it is started in the upward arc of the arm and drops to the alley. Such lofting is frowned upon by the managers of most bowling lanes, as the heavy ball dropping only a short distance has sufficient force to mar the alley. Lofting may also interfere with direction of the ball down the alley.

The left arm and the right leg are used for balance. The weight must be held over the left foot; but it should not be too far forward or the momentum of the ball on its forward swing may cause the bowler to lose balance. Leaning forward too far and too soon may also change the direction of the arm swing, and the ball will be thrown down into the floor rather than forward. Losing the balance to the right during the delivery usually results in the forward swing being aimed too far to the left, because the plane through which the swing is made is changed. Loss of balance a little earlier may even cause the swing to cut in so much that the ball will strike the right leg. If the shoes are slick, the bowler slides forward on the left foot because of his forward momentum. The bowler must start far enough back to allow for this slide without crossing the foul line.

If the ball is released in such a manner that it is rotating in a clockwise direction as it rolls down the alley, it will curve to the right. This clockwise rotation is usually due to a supination of the forearm during the forward swing or just at the instant of release. Such a movement may result from action of the supinator or of the biceps. In the latter, there is usually a little elbow flexion as well. This gives a slight lift to the ball or tends to draw the ball back just at the moment of release. This supination may also occur if the back swing has been forced and the whole arm rotated inward. It is a false correction which the bowler may try to keep the ball from going too far to the left. In other cases the bowler attempts to compensate in forearm movement for too strong adduction of the humerous during the forward swing. The effect of this rotation is much the same as a similar rotation of a ball sailing through the air. In this case it results from friction with the alley. The ball will curve in the direction of the least resistance, the right.

The delivery may also be made so that the ball rotates in a counterclockwise direction. Obviously, it will have the opposite effect to that described above and cause the ball to curve to the left. This rotation is produced by pronation of the forearm. This is done very easily by action of the pronator quadratus and pronator teres, without any effect on the elbow joint itself. The left curve is frequently used to carry the ball into the one-three pocket for a strike. Care must be taken, however, not to get too much rotation on the ball. This occurs if the second finger gets too far in advance of the thumb or if the release of the fingers is delayed too long.

In aiming at the pins one must consider the angle at which they fall. The inertia of the moving ball is so much greater than that of the pins that the direction of the ball is never appreciably affected by the contact. A pin that is hit squarely in front is carried straight to the end of the alley. A pin that is clipped directly on the side will slide sideward, but, of course, it may roll if it falls on the alley. A pin that is hit at some point between these two will go diagonally backward. This is, of course, the explanation for the aim in strike bowling. The ball is aimed through the pins so as to pick off pins 1, 3, 5, and 9. One moves diagonally back and takes down 2, 4, and 7; number 3 takes down 6 and 10; and number 5 takes 8. The same principle is followed in much of the spare bowling.

A ball that is moving with too much speed and does not hit at the precise angle may knock the pin off the alley without taking the others

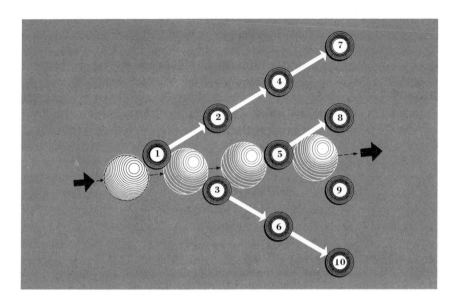

FIGURE 72: A strike from a ball hitting in the one-three pocket

with it. A ball with a little less speed may take down the first pins but leave them rolling on the alley and thus bring the others down.

This is essentially a form of striking, and in general the same factors controlling direction apply here. The difference is in the fact that the striking implement must be controlled at a distance of about sixty feet. It is a game primarily of skill and accuracy.

The same situation is found in another of the rather common recreational sports, shuffleboard. The cue is used to give speed and direction to the disc. The disc must be used to move others already on the target. The stationary discs will move in exactly the same direction as the bowling pins when hit in a similar position. However, the stationary disc has exactly the same weight as the striking one, and therefore will affect the direction of the latter. A disc hitting squarely in front may rebound slightly or take the place of the one already there or advance slightly depending upon the force with which it strikes. On the other hand, when it strikes on an angle both discs go off diagonally, and if it hits with much force both will go off the target.

REFERENCES

1. Ainsworth, Dorothy, *et al.*, *Individual Sports for Women*, Philadelphia, W. B. Saunders Co., 1958.
2. Greenlee, Geraldine, *Relationship of Selected Measures of Strength, Balance and Kinesthesis to Bowling Performance*, Microcard PE434, 1958.

3. Miller, Donna Mae, and Ley, Katherine L., *Sports for Women*, Englewood Cliffs, N.J., Prentice-Hall, Inc., 1955.
4. Purdue University, Physical Education Staff, *Physical Education for Women*, Minneapolis, Burgess Publishing Co., 1963.
5. Summers, Dean, Effect of Variations of Delivery and Aim on Bowling Achievement of College Women, *Research Quarterly*, 28, March 1957, p. 77.
6. Vannier, Maryhelen, and Poindexter, Hally Beth, *Individual and Team Sports for Girls and Women*, Philadelphia, W. B. Saunders Co., 1960.
7. Wilman, Joe, *Better Bowling*, New York, Ronald Press Company, 1953.

FIELD HOCKEY

Hockey is another of the sports in which striking is the predominant skill. The particular characteristics of this game result from the position of the ball, some aspects of the rules, and the construction of the stick. The rules aim to keep the ball entirely on or near the ground. Most striking aims to project the ball forcefully through the air; in hockey such a stroke is illegal. Occasionally the ball is lifted intentionally, but it is usually done with a scoop stroke which is not a hard hit.

The hockey stick is curved outward at the end, giving a horizontal blade of about six inches as the possible striking surface. The direction the ball takes is determined by the direction this surface is facing. The stick is round on one side and flat on the other. Only the flat side may be used for playing the ball. This means that in case the player has no time to change position and is forced to play a ball on the left side the stick must be turned over. This requires entirely different arm action from most games in which the reverse side of the paddle or racket is used for backhand strokes. Such a turn puts the stick on end so that the possible striking surface is greatly reduced.

Playing is usually done with the ball on the right side. The arm action is freest in this position; the shape of the stick facilitates play there and makes it difficult in other positions. There is danger of tripping over the stick when it is directly in front of the player. The player is in danger of fouling by obstructing an opponent if the ball is played on the left. Passing to a player on the left is fairly easy, however, but a pass to the right is difficult.

In most games the player uses a long backswing, often increased by cocking the wrist so that the striking tool is lifted high to the rear. The swing being hard and the follow-through free, the racket or club finishes the stroke very high. The hockey rules, for the sake of safety, prohibit such a stroke. The stick must be below the level of the shoulder at the beginning and end of the stroke.

The basic and most frequently used strokes in hockey are the dribble, the drive, and the push pass. The dribble is used to keep the ball under control, that is, to direct it and to keep it rolling easily within reach of the player's stick while he is running down the field. The contact is more of a tap than a stroke. In order to avoid a full swing of the arms and stick, the right hand is moved down the stick and the left hand is moved more nearly over the top of the stick. This results in movement of the stick only; speed and force decrease because of the shorter lever, but there is greater accuracy in playing the ball.

The drive is sometimes made with the ball stationary, but more frequently the player is forced to play it while the ball is moving slightly. The ball can be passed more accurately if it is brought under control and then played. A ball that is played while it is moving toward the player is apt to be missed if it is bouncing. The player is also more apt to undercut the ball and cause it to rise; it is difficult to judge the position of the ball and the timing of the swing so as to get the ball at the right point in the arc. A ball moving in toward a player may be stopped by putting the stick in the path of the ball and drawing the blade backward with the oncoming ball. The right hand is again down the handle so that the stick may be turned on an angle facing down toward the ground. This also facilitates the "give" on the stick just as the ball makes contact. If the shaft of the stick is in line with the ball, a ball that is bouncing will not escape as it might if the player attempted to stop it with the blade. This position of the stick traps the ball under the stick with very little rebound. The hands are then in position to go quickly into a dribble or to make a short pass. The right hand is moved if a drive is to be made.

The hand stop is used occasionally. Care must be taken not to allow the ball to rebound from the hand or to give it momentum in any direction with the hand. The rules require that the ball drop vertically downward if stopped in the air.

If a short drive must be made quickly as a pass or shot, particularly on a moving ball, it may be necessary to make it while the player is facing toward the ball. The position of the player thus limits the extent of the arm swing, particularly on the preparatory movement. Moreover, this is necessary since the stick must be kept low to avoid the possibility of an opponent's having time to secure the ball. If the drive is used for a free hit, or when the player has ample time to get ready, the position is the same as for most other forms of striking. The player is facing at right angles to the line of flight. The back swing is long but the stick is kept down by wrist control; the extensors of the left wrist and the flexors of the right hold the wrists straight. The right elbow must flex a little on the back swing, but both elbows are straight on the follow-through. The full swing of the straight arms and stick and the transfer of weight produce a hard hit. The momentum of the stick is checked on its follow-through principally by wrist action, a straight left elbow, and the posterior shoulder muscles at the right shoulder.

The push pass is used for a short, quick pass instead of a drive. It is useful when there is not sufficient time for a back swing or when a hard hit is not necessary. The stick is held very much as it is for dribbling, as this gives control of the ball. The stick is just behind the ball at the start of the pass, while the ball is carried briefly or pushed by the stick instead of being tapped as in the dribble. The lack of back swing makes it possible to play faster and to make the pass before the opponent has time to see where the player intends to pass. The action is performed chiefly by the wrists. The right foot is usually forward with the weight over it. The ball is close to the right foot so that it can be controlled with a short movement of the stick. There is always a little follow-through.

The stick is always manipulated with both hands except in the left-hand lunge. This stroke has very much in common with backhand strokes, but is made by the left hand. The stroke is made with a long, full swing which permits a great deal more force than is usually desirable. The stroke is flattened and low to ensure contacting the ball. The swing is also used to help the player turn, ready to run in the opposite direction after the ball is played.

Running and weight control are important throughout the game. They are necessary to enable the player to cover the field properly, to move rapidly, and at the same time to use the stick efficiently.

REFERENCES

1. Lies, Josephine T., and Shellenberger, Betty, *Field Hockey*, New York, Ronald Press Co., 1957.
2. Meyer, Margaret, and Schwarz, Marguerite, *Team Sports for Women*, Philadelphia, W. B. Saunders Co., 1947.
3. Miller, Donna Mae, and Ley, Katherine L., *Individual and Team Sports for Women*, Englewood Cliffs, N.J., Prentice-Hall, Inc., 1955.
4. Purdue University, Physical Education Staff, *Physical Education for Women*, Minneapolis, Burgess Publishing Co., 1963.
5. Vannier, Maryhelen, and Poindexter, Hally Beth, *Individual and Team Sports for Girls and Women*, Philadelphia, W. B. Saunders Co., 1960.

FOOTBALL

The basic skills in football are of four types: running, throwing, kicking, and tackling or blocking a standing or moving player. The first three of these have been discussed in considerable detail, though perhaps in simpler form. A few modifications are essential in each skill.

Running is almost always at maximum speed or at a speed calculated to fit in with the speed of the ball or of another player. The latter adjustment is dependent upon the player's perception of distance and speed of events about him and his ability to time his own movements with them. It is very often necessary to change direction quickly, either on the offensive or defensive. When a change of direction is imminent the steps must be relatively short. The weight is shifted quickly to the inside of the curve or angle which the runner is traversing. The turn may be taken in the regular stride with the adjustments coming in location of the weight center and the angle of the driving leg. However, some good dodgers place both feet more or less together and push with both feet when making a lateral change of direction.

The usual adjustments for a quick start are made. Seldom does the player stop voluntarily except in broken-field running or dodging. Usually he continues at top speed until brought down by an opponent. When anticipating being tackled he keeps his weight low, carries the weight well forward, and continues at top speed.

Throwing is usually of the overhand style with very strong arm and wrist action. Since speed is almost invariably a factor the throw is made in as straight a line as is possible. Only on the exceptional pass for maximum distance is the ball sent at or near the 45° angle. The ball is thrown with a spin on the long axis. This spin is imparted to the ball by pulling down with the fingers as the ball is released. This spin helps to keep the ball on its true course without the point dropping. It also makes it easier to catch without a fumble by keeping it on a straight axis.

Kicking may be done either as a punt or a place kick. The fundamental principles with respect to balance, aiming, and timing are the same for all kicks. The stance at the beginning of the kick has much to do with balance and with aiming. Watching the ball is essential both to aiming and timing.

In the punt the ball is held in the right hand with the long axis of the ball in line with the direction of the kick and the long axis of the foot. The left hand is used at first to steady the ball but is soon removed. The ball is almost placed on the instep by the right hand as the foot swings through. The player steps forward on the left foot and swings through with the right leg, with a strong knee extension. The ankle must be extended. The ball is contacted lower and the reach and follow-through of the leg are farther forward in a long kick than in a short one. However, in every case the follow-through is long and disturbs the player's balance.

In the place kick the ball is held on end so the toe can easily get under the center of the ball. There is not, therefore, the difficulty that is found in executing the place kick in soccer. The shoes afford protection to the toes, and the toe of the shoe is used for contact with the ball. This is also in contrast to most kicks in soccer. The adjustment of the stride is essential to bring the player at the point behind the ball where the leg

FIGURE 73: Dodging

FIGURE 74: The punt

swing will contact easily just at the beginning of the upward arc. The running approach gives momentum and permits a long leg swing. The knee is first flexed and then extended during the forward swing. The bent knee makes it possible to swing the leg faster, the final extension adds speed. Increased speed means increased momentum and if properly timed it can be imparted to the ball.

The ball may be held nearly upright for a short kick but is inclined back more and kicked nearer the center for a long kick. Height may be obtained either by tilting the ball toward the kicker or by striking it lower. For any given angle of the ball, the lower the contact point, the greater its rotation. Marshall[2] determined the optimum angle for the placement at 15° and the optimum point of contact for that and other angles. If the toe strikes too far below the center of the ball the rotation around the transverse axis is too great. This reduces the amount of the forward-upward force on the ball. Such a kick has more elevation, therefore it is more quickly out of reach of the opponents. This type of kick is frequently used in the kick for point following a touchdown. Distance is not important but a quick lift is essential. In a kick-off a ball rotating in this fashion is harder to catch.

Stopping another player is usually done in one of two ways. In one, the runner who is more or less in the open is tackled. In the other, the player in the line or backfield is blocked, often before he gets completely into a run. The most successful tackle is made by getting the player around the knees or lower leg. If the grip is firm he is unable to proceed further, of course. Even if the grip fails or is inadequate to hold him the application of force at such a distance from the center of gravity and near his point of support is very effective in disturbing his balance. It usually results in his falling.

Blocking in the line is effective only if the momentum of the player is equal to or greater than that of the opponent, and if he is properly braced to counteract the force of the opponent. Momentum is dependent upon mass and velocity. The members of the line are usually heavy. This provides the mass. However, speed is also essential. A player may be smaller than an opponent but if he can get into motion faster and have attained more of a driving position he may be successful.

The starting position for the linesman is a modification of the crouch start. The weight is low. The feet are spread laterally and also in an anteroposterior direction. The latter is necessary in order to get a good forward drive, or to move back out of the line and into the interference, and to get into motion quickly. The lateral spread is necessary to prevent being overbalanced by a push in that direction. In other words the player's position must be a stable one and also one permitting action forward or backward.

REFERENCES

1. Fitch, Robert E., *A Study of Linemen Stances and Body Alignments and Their Relation to Starting Speed in Football,* Microcard PE287, 1956.
2. Marshall, Stan, Factors Affecting Place Kicking in Football, *Research Quarterly,* 29, October 1958, p. 302.
3. Owens, Jack A., *Effect of Variations in Hand and Foot Spacing on Movement Time and on Force of Charge,* Microcard PE358, 1956.

GOLF

Golf is another striking game. All strokes are essentially alike, some employing longer clubs than others, some having longer swings than others, and the face of some clubs having more pitch than others. But in every case the various factors are adapted to the situation and the desired effect upon the ball. The great difficulty in golf is that the clubs are always long, the face of the club is small, and the ball is small. Very minute errors in technique may produce poor results or even cause the player to miss the ball entirely.

Drive

Description. The drive uses the longest club and the fullest swing. It is usually made with one of the wood clubs, the major difference between these clubs being in the pitch of the club face. The ball is teed up for the drive. The player takes a stance facing the ball, with left shoulder pointing in the direction the ball is to take. The trunk is inclined forward a little by flexion at the hip. The feet are spread about the width of the hips, the weight is evenly distributed between them, and the feet may be toeing out a little. The knees are in easy extension. The ball is played about in line with the left heel. The club is grasped by both hands with right hand below the left, but with the fingers of the right hand either overlapping or interlocking with those of the left. The fingers hold the club firmly. The hands are on the club in such a position that the "V" between the index finger and thumb of each hand points toward the right shoulder.

The club is carried back and up with the left elbow remaining straight. The right elbow is flexed but kept fairly close to the side. This puts the hands almost to the side of, and a little above, the level of the right shoulder. The wrists bend so that the club drops down behind the head with the club head pointing toward the hole. The weight has shifted toward the right foot. The whole movement is initiated by body rotation to the right, so that the left shoulder is now rotated toward the ball.

The down swing starts with the arms swinging back down the same path through which they came up. Then the wrists straighten out quickly during the latter part of the swing. At the same time the arms are swing-

a–back swing

b–contact

FIGURE 75: The drive

c–follow through

ing down, the weight is shifted to the left and rotation starts in the opposite direction, so that the player is again aligned with the ball when it is hit.

All of these movements are continuous after the ball is hit. The weight moves on and the body completes the pivot. The arms swing up to the other side, relaxing more at the finish than at the top of the back swing, and the club again drops behind the head.

Muscular Analysis. The preliminary arm swing, originating in the left shoulder, is produced by the left pectoralis major, anterior deltoid, and coracobrachialis. On the right the posterior deltoid, teres minor, and infraspinatus lift the arm up and back. The left serratus anterior abducts the left scapula and the right rhomboids and second and third trapezius adduct the other scapula. The left triceps holds the elbow extended and the right biceps, brachialis, and brachioradialis flex the right elbow. Bending of the left wrist is done by the extensors carpi radialis longus and brevis, with the forearm partially pronated by the pronator quadratus. The right wrist is abducted by the extensors carpi radialis assisted by the flexor carpi radialis.

The weight is pushed to the right foot by the abductors and extensors of the left leg; the extensors of the right leg support it with knee straight. Rotation occurs in the lower part of the cervical region, in the thoracic, and at the hips. Trunk rotation is the work of the right erector spinae, oblique extensors, latissimus dorsi, rectus abdominis, internal oblique, and left external oblique. Rotation in the left hip results from action of the six small outward rotators and the posterior parts of the gluteus medius and minimus. Inward rotation which occurs in the right hip is partly passive because of the fixation of the right leg and partly results from the action of the tensor fasciae latae and anterior part of the gluteus medius.

The downward swing again originates in the left shoulder with the teres major, posterior deltoid, and latissimus doing most of the work, assisted at the end as the arm swings up again by the teres minor and infraspinatus. The right elbow extends by triceps action and the arm is brought across the body finally much as the left arm was swung up in the preparatory swing. The wrist action just before hitting the ball is that of strong bending to the ulnar border by the flexors and extensors carpi ulnaris.

The rotation is exactly opposite to that for the preparatory swing. The final part of the follow-through is characterized by relaxation and the use of the momentum developed in the club head to carry it on up and to lift the trunk and head to a more erect position.

The fixation of the head and the localization of rotation between the neck and the feet is important in guiding the stroke in the precise arc necessary for a good contact. The forward inclination of the trunk requires support from spinal extensors the full length of the spine. Therefore, the posterior muscles of the neck are already acting. The right sternocleidomastoid lifts the sternum to the right and helps in forcing trunk rotation. The scalenus anterior helps in this movement and in fixation of the upper cervical region. The left posterior muscles are dominant over the other muscles of the cervical region in order to prevent turning the head as would naturally occur with the trunk rotation.

Mechanical Analysis. The preparatory movement is such as to secure as long an arc as possible for acceleration, to facilitate correct down swing, and to secure summation of movements in the successive joints and thereby obtain greater speed. The bending of the wrists, which makes the club drop behind the head, considerably increases the arc through which the club head moves. It also puts the wrists into position so that they may snap the club through quickly just before meeting the ball. This adds definitely to the momentum imparted to the ball.

The pivot increases the arc slightly and also uses the strong trunk muscles to strengthen the down swing. A good stroke requires perfect co-ordination of the swing, the pivot, and the transfer of weight.

In the good drive the ball is hit below its mid-point. The effect is not only to send the ball up at an angle, but to give it back spin. This causes the ball, just before it would normally start falling, to soar on up and hence cover considerably greater distance. However, it will probably not roll quite so far when it lands. The greater the loft of the club face the more easily it fits under the ball; the arc which can be expected from the ball becomes higher.

The good drive is made with the head of the club moving straight into the ball from the rear. If it is carried too far out and then brought in across the ball as it is hit, the ball develops a spin around a vertical axis, rotating clockwise. This develops high pressure on the left side of the ball in flight, so that it is pushed to the right for the familiar slice. The hook is made in a similar way by the club moving across the ball from the inside outward. The rotation developed is then counterclockwise, and the area of least resistance is on the left. Similar end results are obtained if the face of the club is turned on an angle. The ball will travel to the right or left depending upon the angle of the club face, but its path is much straighter.

The follow-through is a means of using up the momentum, of allowing gradual relaxation, of establishing a definite destination as a guide to the actual drive. The fixation of the head and eyes during the early part of the stroke is a means of controlling the path of the club and concentrating on the point of aim. Watching the ball, or the spot where it was throughout the swing is a means of avoiding lifting the head too soon. It also helps to control the down swing, to bring the arms and club down through the same path in which they went up, and therefore to ensure a more accurate hit.

Iron Strokes

The strokes with the other clubs except the putter are similar in basic form. The club heads are lofted to suit the needs for which the club is designed. The shaft is shorter than that of the driver or other woods, and hence the speed will be slightly less. The club head is heavy, however, and assuming sufficient acceleration the momentum imparted to the ball is practically the same as with the longer clubs. The greater pitch on the clubs lifts the ball in a higher arc. This greater height, plus the fact that the shaft is shorter, causes the flight to be shorter.

On a stroke such as that with a midiron, the aim of which is primarily distance, the preparatory swing and follow-through are practically the same as in the drive. On other strokes the back swing may be shortened to reduce speed and distance. Most of the approach shots aim for elevation and a drop with a minimum of roll after landing. This is achieved not only with a lofted club face but by a short back swing with a downward chop behind and through the ball at such an angle that a divot is taken in front of the point where the ball lay. This downward chop develops considerable back spin which helps the ball to rise, to drop quickly, and to land without rolling. This is due to the angle of the club face, which directs the ball upward, and to the spin on the ball.

Putting

The aim in putting is entirely different from that of the other strokes, all of which aim to lift the ball into the air. Putting is done on the ground and must take into consideration the level of the surface over which it is done and the resistance of that surface.

The face of the putter is nearly vertical so that the ball will be hit directly behind its mid-point. This pushes it directly forward but friction with the surface causes it to roll. The length of the back swing and force of the stroke depend upon the distance the ball must cover. The back swing is usually short and the club is kept close to the ground. The swing is a straight, horizontal one, instead of a circular one. This is accomplished by several adjustments in form. The feet are close together with the knees easy rather than locked in extension, as is natural when bending forward over the ball. A slight flexion of the elbows and hyperextension of the wrists helps to take the primary movement from the shoulders. The right hand may be moved a little to the right on the club and some players spread the right index finger down the shaft. This position of the hand gives a little better control for this short swing. The forearm is sometimes braced on the thigh in order to limit arm action

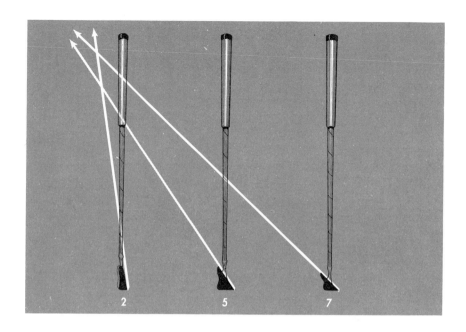

FIGURE 76: Angle of the iron club faces
2–#2, midiron; 5–#5, mashie; 7–#7, niblick

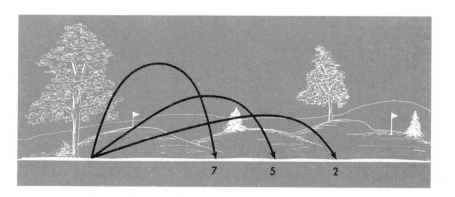

FIGURE 77: Flight of the ball from selected iron clubs
2–midiron; 5–mashie; 7–niblick

on short putts. Some players anchor on the right thigh, some on the left; in either case it helps to localize the action in the wrists. The hands are part way down the handle in order to limit the extent of the swing. The swing is mostly due to wrist action, although in longer putts the movement may be guided by an arm swing from the left shoulder.

The player bends forward so that the eyes are directly over the ball. This puts the eyes in a direct line with the desired putt. It makes it possible to check accurately on the position of the club as it addresses the ball. This position also brings the trunk down so that the grip can be shortened on the club. Thus, the arms and the club hang more nearly vertical, permitting a straight swing.

The force imparted to the ball must be perfectly matched with the amount of resistance offered by the surface. This depends upon the nature of the surface and the contour of the green. It must be just enough to carry the ball over the brink of the cup. If greater than that the ball is apt to hit the opposite side of the cup and bounce out again, or to roll over without dropping in.

REFERENCES

1. Ainsworth, Dorothy, *et al., Individual Sports for Women,* Philadelphia, W. B. Saunders Co., 1958.
2. Miller, Donna Mae, and Ley, Katherine L., *Sports for Women,* Englewood Cliffs, N.J., Prentice-Hall, Inc., 1955.
3. Purdue University, Physical Education Staff, *Physical Education for Women,* Minneapolis, Burgess Publishing Co., 1963.
4. Rehling, Conrad H., Analysis of Techniques of the Golf Drive, *Research Quarterly,* 26, March 1955, p. 80.
5. Suggs, Louise, *Par Golf for Women,* Englewood Cliffs, N.J., Prentice-Hall, Inc., 1953.
6. Vannier, Maryhelen, and Poindexter, Hally Beth, *Individual and Team Sports for Girls and Women,* Philadelphia, W. B. Saunders Co., 1960.

SOCCER

The kicking skills found chiefly in soccer and speedball will be considered because they represent another of the manipulative skills and are quite different in form. The ball may be played either while moving or when stationary. The kick is a form of striking, and follows the same rules already stated.

The *dribbling* type of kick aims merely to make the ball roll on the ground for a short distance. The kick must be easy and behind or slightly below the center of the ball. If kicked too far below center the ball is lifted and tends to bounce as it rolls. Control of the direction is easier if a broad surface of the foot is used rather than the toes. The leg is usually rotated outward so that the inside of the foot is used, but the outside may be used if desired. This form is always used when dodging with the ball.

There is no long back swing of the leg; this helps to keep the kick short. This kick is usually made in the regular running stride, with the foot giving impetus to the ball as it swings forward. Such a swing calls for stronger action of the psoas, pectineus, and adductors longus and magnus and less of the tensor fasciae latae and rectus femoris than in the ordinary run.

The *place kick* may or may not be preceded by a run. In either case the kicking leg starts in a preparatory back swing with the knee flexed. It is then swung forward to contact the ball slightly below center, the major point of contact being made with the top of the instep, approximately over the first cuneiform bone.

The force of the swing is produced by the hip flexors—iliopsoas, pectineus, tensor, and rectus—and knee extensors, the quadriceps. The supporting leg continues extension, thus throwing body weight into the force of the kick.

The direction of the ball and the lift in a good kick are dependent upon two factors. The first is the placement of the toes well under the ball so that the kicking surface on top of the foot is facing upward. If the foot is extended and the kick is made from behind the ball, the ball rolls or bounces along the ground instead of soaring. If the foot is flexed too much or if the toes are pointed directly into the ball, the ball will roll rather than rise. This is also apt to be injurious to the toes unless special shoes are worn.

When heavy shoes with toe protectors are worn, as in football and some forms of soccer, the place kick may be executed with the toes making contact instead of the instep. This makes it easier to get the foot under the ball so that it will be lifted. This is used especially in corner kicks. The placement of the football and the shape of the ball also make it easier to get under the ball.

The second factor in securing height is the proper placement of the ball in the path of the kicking foot. This path is an arc. Though this arc may be elongated somewhat by transfer of weight on the supporting foot, there is a limited range in which the toes will go under the ball and in which the proper angle of delivery can be made. In general, if the ball is to go low, the step with the left foot is fairly close to the ball, the body is inclined forward, and the right foot comes in behind the ball. If the kick is to go high, the left step is a little farther away from the ball, the body is more upright, and the foot comes in a little under the ball.

The *drop kick* and *punt* are practically the same, except that the ball is held in the hands and dropped in such a way that the ball is contacted on the front of the instep as the leg is swung forward. The kick is almost invariably taken with at least one long preliminary stride which gives body momentum and puts the kicking leg far back for a long swing. The punt is contacted higher in the air than the drop kick; and therefore, it may have certain advantages in the game. Also, it is not dependent upon the condition of the ground for the proper rebound and placement for the kick.

The force of the kick is dependent upon the length of the arc of the swinging leg, the speed with which it is moved through this arc, and the speed of knee extension.

Much of the kicking in the game must be done on a moving ball rather than a stationary one. In general, these kicks very closely resemble the place kick which is made with the top of the foot. Adjustments must be made to the direction the ball is moving, the direction it is to be sent on the kick, and the situation in the game.

If the ball is moving slowly on the ground, the player is coming in directly behind it, and the pass is to be straight ahead, the kick is made by leaning toward the ball and kicking from behind as in the place kick. The knee may remain partially flexed in this kick. Such a ball will stay on or near the ground. If the ball is bouncing high or is in the air, it may be kicked in a fashion similar to a punt, unless the player prefers to trap or block the ball and play it from the ground. A ball played in the air usually has a high arc and is used more by the backfield players. A ball which is to go to the side must be made by a side swing of the leg. Either the inner or the outer border of the foot may be used and the swing may be directed either medially or laterally. If the kick is very hard, a medial swing disturbs the player's balance less than a lateral one. In some cases the ball is almost out of the player's reach, or there is no time for a regular kick. In this situation the player leans slightly back, reaches forward with one leg, and "stabs" the ball with the toes. This is particularly useful for short, quick kicks at goal when the player is guarded, or for a quick pass around a guard; and at the same time it may help the player to avoid running into the opponent.

REFERENCES

1. Burdan, Paul, *A Cinematographic Analysis of Three Basic Kicks Used in Soccer*, Microcard PE312, 1955.
2. Meyer, Margaret, and Schwarz, Marguerite, *Team Sports for Women*, Philadelphia, W. B. Saunders Co., 1947.
3. Miller, Donna Mae, and Ley, Katherine L., *Individual and Team Sports for Women*, Englewood Cliffs, N.J., Prentice-Hall, Inc., 1955.
4. Purdue University, Physical Education Staff, *Physical Education for Women*, Minneapolis, Burgess Publishing Co., 1963.
5. Vannier, Maryhelen, and Poindexter, Hally Beth, *Individual and Team Sports for Girls and Women*, Philadelphia, W. B. Saunders Co., 1960.

SWIMMING

Swimming presents, in some respects, a very different problem from other activities since it takes place in a different medium. In all activities gravity pulls downward on the body. Ordinarily the muscles must be constantly active to prevent collapse of the segments. In swimming, however, the buoyant effect of the water is usually equal to or greater than the gravital pull. In fact, moving downward through the water is usually a problem requiring exact technique.

All progression is dependent upon the application of force against a resistant surface. The ground, floor, and most surfaces on which the person moves give sufficient reaction to make progress fairly easy and reasonably efficient. In swimming, however, the water offers less resistance; therefore, progress is slower and requires more effort. However, the swimmer usually uses both arms and legs to push against the resistance offered by the water instead of legs only, as in ordinary progression. Swimming strokes are among the least efficient of man's activities, as calculated on the energy input/work output basis.

On land, the air seldom offers enough resistance to be of much importance either in economy of movement or in speed. In the water, resistance is considerable. A surface of water, with the body at a given angle, offers as much resistance to progress of the body through it as a similar surface offers to a propulsive force. Streamlining and planing are, therefore, major problems in effective swimming strokes. Each tends to minimize resistance.

Buoyancy is the lifting force of a liquid on a body immersed in it. This lifting force is equal to the weight of the water displaced by the object. If the weight of the water displaced is less than that of the object, as in the case of a stone or coin, the object sinks. Such an object is referred to as being nonbuoyant. If the weight of the water displaced is the same as that of the object, it will remain suspended in the water. If the weight of the water displaced is greater than that of the object, then the object is lifted to the surface, and enough of it is pushed out of the water to reduce the displacement until the two forces are equal. This means that every buoyant object has its own floating position.

Since individuals differ so much in build it is evident that each will have his characteristic floating position. Heavy bones and solid musculature have weight and tend to make the person sink. On the other hand the person with a lighter frame, softer muscles, much adipose tissue, or a large chest floats easily at the top of the water. The buoyancy of some individuals is so great that they seem to be easily swept off their feet and find recovery difficult. Women are, in general, more buoyant than men because they usually have softer muscles and more adipose tissue.

Most swimmers apparently float higher on a face float than on a back float. This is explained by several facts. First, on the face float the swimmer usually goes under with a big breath and holds it, whereas on the back, he probably takes less air to start with and is more inclined to let some or most of it out. Second, the swimmer has the face under water all the time on the face float and does not, therefore, notice a slight drop until he is ready to breath with some stroke. By then, this lower position is partly overcome by the speed of movement and an upward planing of the body through the water. Third, the face float is frequently started at a vertical or semivertical position, but the back float is too frequently started in nearly a horizontal one or by kicking the feet as near to the surface as possible. Fourth, the swimmer in a face float almost invariably extends the arms beyond the head. This raises the legs in the water. However, this position is more difficult to assume on the back while the necessary position of head and chest is maintained.

It is wise for every swimmer to learn what his natural floating position is and how that is affected by changes in breathing and in position of arms, legs, and head. It is foolish for all swimmers to try to float like a "human cork"; but every swimmer should learn to make the most of what buoyancy he possesses. All swimmers who have any tendency to sink, or any tendency for the legs to drop below the surface of the water, should start the back float from a vertical or treading position. Then, without any attempt to kick or force the legs up, the head is laid back on the water. The feet will gradually rise to the natural floating position. They have an upward momentum from the lifting force of the water. If the swimmer starts on the horizontal, or any position above his natural floating position, the legs drop to that natural floating position and the downward momentum is often enough to drag the whole body on down. The less buoyant the swimmer is, the more important is this point.

If a part of the body is raised out of the water, the amount of water displaced is correspondingly reduced. The body is reacted on as a whole and it tends to sink because of the decreased buoying force of the water. This is frequently seen when the arms or head are lifted; the body begins changing position immediately.

An object has a center of buoyancy in the same sense that it has a center of gravity. This center of buoyancy is the center of gravity of the displaced volume of water. The easiest concept of floating considers the body as a first-class lever balancing around its axis, the center of buoyancy. The feet usually tend to sink because they are heavier for their volume than the other end of the body. The foot end of the lever may be raised by reducing its length or increasing the force on the upper end of the lever. This may be accomplished in several ways in the back float. Bending the knees until the heels are close to the thighs shortens the resistance arm, and, therefore, causes it to rise to some extent. Extending the arms beyond the shoulders and the head increases the length of that end of the lever. This is effective in raising the legs if the arms are moved in such a way that the chest is not compressed and the volume of air in the lungs is not reduced. With the arms in the extended position over-head, the wrists may be sharply flexed so that the hands project out of the water. The arms are thus caused to sink slightly but at the same time the legs are carried up, providing the swimmer is not in a vertical position.

The above positions may not be very comfortable to hold, but they are effective. However, if the swimmer remembers that keeping the mouth and nose above water is all that is necessary, fewer adjustments will need to be made. All adjustments of arms, legs, or head should be made gradu-ally, otherwise the reaction on the rest of the body or the momentum of the change and resistance of the water may cause the body to sink momentarily.

Again, we may consider the adjustment to floating or equilibrium more specifically, considering both the center of buoyancy and the center of gravity. The center of buoyancy has been defined as the point around which the upward buoying force of the water is equally distributed. The center of gravity is the same for the downward pull of gravity. The two forces are exactly opposite.

For convenience in this discussion, let us refer to the center of buoyancy as b and the center of gravity as g, as is shown in Figure 78. If the two centers coincide the swimmer floats in a horizontal position, if he is buoy-ant enough to float at all (see A in Figure 78). In most individuals b is

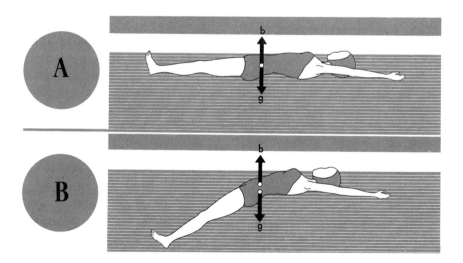

FIGURE 78: Floating positions

higher, that is, nearer the head than g; thus, the feet usually sink, unless the legs are buoyed up by some other force. This sinking is a rotation of the body around the center of buoyancy. Rotation will continue until g is directly beneath b. The farther these two points are apart, the greater must be the rotation to produce this effect. Adjustments in floating position are merely attempts to bring these two points closer. For example, bending the legs, raising the arms, or flexing the wrists raises the center of gravity. The actual distance between these two points is never very great; hence these adjustments can overcome the greatest part of that difference.

Various studies have been made from time to time concerning the factors affecting floating ability. It has been pointed out that this ability is largely dependent upon specific gravity. Specific gravity is determined by various factors. One of the most important is the amount of air or gas in the body and the amount of distention of body cavities, particularly the thorax. Hence, the person with the larger lungs who makes use of them by a maximal breath has an advantage. Positions of the arms and back also affect the expansion of the thorax. Likewise, the specific gravity of adipose tissue is the lowest of any of the body tissues. Therefore, a variation of adipose tissue affects directly the specific gravity of the whole body.

Since the body weight in relation to volume is the chief factor determining buoyancy, the body is equally buoyant in almost all positions. The position of the face is not, however, such that breathing is equally easy in all floating positions. When the body is in a vertical position, the same buoying force lifts the body until it gains a position of balance. The buoyant individual is lifted, when the hands are at the sides, until the head is almost entirely out of the water. Less buoyant persons have only part of the head out, and the very occasional "sinker" sinks entirely under water. If the arms are raised overhead, they will be thrust up out of the water and the body will sink correspondingly.

There are two main difficulties in the vertical type of float. First, if the body is not kept absolutely vertical, the lift on the legs will cause the swimmer to go into a face or back float. Second, there is always considerable bobbing unless the float is started very near the natural floating level. If support is removed with the head well above the water, the entire body drops and momentum carries it well below the natural floating level. Then the water lifts it up and the momentum again carries it past the proper level. Eventually balance will be reached but by this time the swimmer is probably out of breath.

Swimming Positions

Most swimming strokes make use of a horizontal or almost a horizontal position in the water, either on the face or the back. Movement keeps the legs higher than in the float; or they may be kicked toward the top. In this position, no part of the body need be out of the water, except as it is lifted by the water, or when the face is out for breathing. Many of the strokes keep the arms under water so there is no sinking effect during the arm stroke. This position is quite stable, with a broad base, so there is little danger of turning or loss of position. This position makes it easy to apply force for forward progression.

The side stroke is done in a horizontal position but lacks stability because of the narrow base, the tendency to hold the head high for air, and sometimes the uneven pull of arms or legs.

The vertical position, which may be used in changing direction or in treading, is a perfectly safe one, and an easy one, if the principles discussed above are observed. The head is above water, and the hands are often near the surface so there is a tendency to sink. However, if the swimmer does not attempt to stay any higher than necessary for breathing, it is usually fairly simple. The small base with the tall body above it makes it lose balance easily, but that factor is a help in returning to a swimming position. The drive of the arms and legs should preferably be a slight and constant force downward against the water. If the treading movements are made too vigorously, the body is lifted high out of the water but when the force is stopped or diminished the swimmer drops rapidly. If he is to stay on top, the downward momentum must be checked immediately; this requires greater force. The result is rapid bobbing in the water with continued vigorous strokes, and is typical of the beginner learning to tread.

Propelling Force of Strokes

Progression in any stroke is made by applying force against the resistance of the water with arms or legs or both. The counterforce and the direction in which the body is moved are exactly opposite to the direction in which the force is applied. For example, if the arms push vertically downward the body is lifted up or vice versa. Drives in a horizontal plane produce motion in a horizontal plane but in the opposite direction. In most strokes the push is toward the feet and the body moves head first.

However, the movement of arms and legs are rotatory ones, and hence the total movement is never in a straight line and never has a single component except for one brief instant during the pull. For example, the arm pull in the crawl has both a downward push and a backward one. This downward component which helps to lift the body will be called the supporting component, and the horizontal component which carries the body forward will be known as the driving component. Forces applied through a horizontal plane may also have two components, the one parallel with the long axis of the body and the other at right angles to the long axis. This is illustrated in the arm drive in an elementary back stroke. The first is what has been named the driving component.

The leg movement is limited in range so that it is impossible to get a flat push against the resistance of the water as is done with the arms in part of each stroke. The legs are always pushing through the water at an angle to the line of progress; the angle varies with the width of the leg kick. One component of that drive is in a transverse plane of the body. This increases with the width of the spread. Resistance to movement through the water also increases with the width of the spread. The other component is in line with the longitudinal axis of the body and is responsible for forward movement.

The general principle of leg action is the same as that in sculling. The foot and leg are adjusted to secure as large a longitudinal component as is possible on each drive, and then readjusted to recover with the minimum of resistance. The action of each leg is similar to the swing of the tail of a fish. This is seen most clearly in the simultaneous action of the legs in the dolphin breast stroke. In the crawl stroke, the legs work alternately in drive and recovery.

Resistance to Motion

Most of the resistance to motion is due to the tendency of the water to adhere to the body surface in contact with the water; this is skin friction. This friction affects any object regardless of shape and surface, although it increases with irregularities of surface. However, there are other sources of resistance which are sufficient to be considered.

As an object moves through the water, there is a tendency for the water to be pushed ahead of it. This is increased more as the surface presented to the water becomes larger and flatter. In a horizontal position, the top of the head and shoulders, and, in some strokes, parts of the arms and legs, are pushing against the water. For example, the wide leg spread of the side stroke and the wide arm spread of the elementary back stroke offer resistance. Similarly, the head carry commonly taught in life-saving technique presents the entire back of the trunk almost flat against the water. Likewise, a swimmer whose legs hang very low in the water finds that the legs drag against the water and hinder progress. Any adjustment to streamline or plane the body or to avoid holding the arms or legs out in a resisting position will facilitate movement.

Another type of resistance comes from actually pushing in the wrong direction. This may be seen in the beginner or the swimmer with faulty technique. In the side stroke, the arms may push on the recovery; or the elementary back stroke or back crawl arm recovery may be against the water. The spread in any of the leg kicks may be made with legs straight or with such force that the swimmer is pulled backward in the water.

This represents an error in technique and is not a source of resistance inherent in swimming.

A third type of resistance is offered by the water to any object passing through it. The layer of water against the object is subject to pressure in one direction from the object and to a retarding pressure from adjacent layers of water. The result is the development of eddies near the rear of the object. Wherever such a vortex exists much of the force creating it is wasted so far as progression is concerned. It is obvious that this effect increases with an increase in surface area presented against the water and with an increase in the speed with which the object moves.

In swimming, these eddies occur most regularly around the feet or hands or behind the arms. Obviously they are of greatest significance in speed swimming since the speed of the swimmer tends to increase their formation and since the swimmer is interested in achieving maximum rate of progress. "Streamlining" the body helps to reduce eddies; they cannot be entirely eliminated.

A fourth type of resistance is produced by the action of the eddies, which results in the formation of an area of low pressure in the water immediately behind the body part and between the two currents of water passing on each side of the body. This creates a suction on the feet or the rear of the hands and arms and tends to lessen speed.

An analysis of swimming strokes is simpler if they are divided into the recovery phase and driving phase of both arms and legs. The recovery phase serves about the same functions as the preparatory movement in other activities. The drive is the act itself. The follow-through is not necessary here as it is in most activities, though the very end of an arm drive may, in some strokes, be similar to the follow-through. The glide is a period of relaxation between strokes.

Elementary Back Stroke

Description. The swimmer starts in a back float with arms at the sides and legs together. The arms are raised with elbows bent and hands close to the sides, palms down. As the hands approach the shoulders, the arms are turned so that the elbows are brought in a little closer to the sides so the arms can be extended sideward with fingers leading and the arms sliding through the water. The arms are then pulled straight to the sides, and held at the sides while the body glides forward.

The kick is very similar to the arm movement. At the start of the leg movement, the feet are turned out so that heels are together. The knees and ankles are then flexed, with the heels close and the knees well apart. The movement at the hip is more abduction than flexion. Then the knees are extended with the toes leading so that the lower leg slides out easily into extension. The legs are brought together forcibly while straight with the ankles extending so that the soles of the feet push in against the water.

The legs are held together during the glide. The movements of the legs are the same as those of the arms and occur simultaneously.

Muscular Analysis. The arm action starts at the shoulder by action of the middle and posterior deltoid. The brachialis anticus, biceps, and pronator teres flex the elbow at the same time, and the latter also holds the forearm in pronation. The arm is turned so that the hand can lead out. The teres minor and infraspinatus produce this outward rotation and lower the elbow slightly at the same time the deltoid relaxes. During this time the scapulae are rotated upward and adducted, the amount of adduction depending upon the exact position of the arms and shoulders. If the arms and shoulders are held well back in the water, the trapezius does most of the work on the scapulae. If the arms are carried higher in the water and the elbows spread wider, the serratus anterior assists in the rotation.

The arm is extended by the triceps acting at the elbow and the middle deltoid acting at the shoulder. The triceps continues to hold the elbow firm, though the resistance of the water helps in this respect. The hand is held flat against the water if the forearm is in its natural position. However, fixation may be necessary by balance between the supinator and the pronator quadratus. The arm is brought down vigorously by the teres major, latissimus dorsi, the lower pectoralis major, and the coracobrachialis. The scapulae are rotated downward by the rhomboids and pectoralis minor. The wrist is held firm by the flexors carpi ulnaris and radialis and the palmaris longus. The fingers are adducted and mildly flexed by the flexor profoundus digitorum and palmar interossei, controlled by the extensor longus digitorum which keeps the fingers straight and localizes the flexion in the metacarpal-phalangeal articulation.

The toes are turned out by outward rotation at the hip due to action of the sextette of outward rotators. Their action is continued throughout the kick. This is further emphasized by the indirect action of the sartorius and iliopsoas as they help in hip flexion. The rest of the hip action is due to the tensor fasciae latae and the gluteus medius and minimus. The knee flexion results from the sartorius, the popliteus, and the hamstrings, although the action of the latter is partially passive due to the tension produced by the hip movement.

Knee extension is produced by the quadriceps extensors. The ankle is also gradually extended by the soleus, gastrocnemius, and peroneus longus. Both joints are held in this position until the end of the kick. The legs are brought together by the hamstrings, the gracilis and the adductors longus, brevis and magnus. The latter also help in outward rotation which brings the plantar surfaces of the feet rather than the inner borders toward each other.

The back, particularly the thoracic region, is held straight by the extensors. The head is held back by the splenius but is counteracted by the sternocleidomastoid, and the platysma, which pulls the chin in. This gives a straight cervical spine rather than a hyperextended one. The sternocleidomastoid and scalenus anterior help lift the chest when the head is fixed to resist their pull.

Mechanical Analysis. If the arms are brought up along the sides they do not disturb balance; if they are raised out of the water, they tend to sink the body. When they are too high, they may also produce an undesirable splash. The same is true of the legs. When they are flexed without being rotated, the knees are raised too high, the hips are forced down, and the water may be washed up over the face if the movement is vigorous.

Resistance is reduced by allowing the hand and foot to lead in extension. Rotation of the arm makes it possible to slide the arm out rather than force the forearm through the water. If the elbows are not spread too far from the sides while they are flexing, resistance is lessened. The arm reach sideward is only a little above the level of the shoulders. A reach which is longer than this tends to make the swimmer drop the chest. It also gives a very large lateral component to the first part of the pull; this is, therefore, partly lost effort. The lateral reach starts the arm pull with a larger effective component. If the wrists are firm, the hands present a flatter surface for pushing against the water.

Through most of the range of arm action there is a fairly large component of force downward toward the feet. As the arms approach nearer the side, they become less effective although it has been pointed out previously that there is a certain value to this part of the pull.

The arms or legs should not be left in the spread position any longer than necessary as they offer resistance to the water when they are out in this position. Resistance is reduced to its minimum when the body is straight.

The only forceful part of the stroke is on the arm and leg drive. The leg action can be very vigorous because of the combined force of the adductors and extensors. This stroke, as well as some of the other swimming strokes, is unique among activities in general in calling for strong action of arm depressors and downward rotators of the scapula.

Crawl

The crawl stroke is described here because it is taught so frequently. It is not the most economical stroke; and it is probably not the best adapted to the majority of swimmers who are seeking enjoyment, exercise, and safety in the water, rather than speed. Its value in these respects will be pointed out in the discussion.

Description. The swimming position is prone in the water with the head slightly lifted. The arm recovery starts when the arm is lifted out of the water from a position with hand about at the side of the hip. The arm is carried forward, swinging from the shoulder; the lower arm is relaxed and the palm is turned more or less upward. About the time the elbow is in line with the shoulder the arm is turned so that the hand comes forward quickly and is turned down toward the water. The arm is held so that the elbow is always a little higher than the hand. Therefore the fingers drop into the water first.

The hand may then continue its reach forward into the water with elbow extension, or the reach may be more toward the bottom with elbow slightly flexed. The arm action again centers in the shoulder. The palm and forearm are kept facing as nearly as possible toward the feet. The hand finishes at the side of the hip with the pull becoming less vigorous toward the finish. The arms work alternately, with one arm recovering while the other drives. In one version of the stroke the arm recovery is much faster, the forward reach is much shorter and more nearly vertical. In this stroke one arm starts the pull before the other arm has finished its pull.

The leg action starts as hip flexion. At the same time the knee bends a little and the ankle is hyperextended. Then the knee is extended quickly with the ankle flexing during the process. Motion again centers at the hip as the leg is lifted forcibly with the knee straight and the ankle extends quickly. The legs work alternately, with one leg moving downward while the other is kicking up.

The trunk position is one of easy extension. The head is turned on each stroke from the front to one side. At the same time that the head turns, the top of the head is lowered slightly in the water but the chin is raised so that the mouth will clear the water easily for breathing.

Muscular Analysis. The arm action starts by a lift of the posterior and middle deltoid and the supraspinatus. The inward rotation of the humerus is the result of action of the subscapularis, of the resistance of the water to turning of the forearm and hand, and to some extent of tension on the teres major and latissimus. This rotation changes just before the middle of the swing so that the arm is more nearly in its normal position. Relaxation of the subscapularis and brief contraction of the teres minor and infraspinatus cause this change and swing the hand forward so that it is leading rather than the elbow.

The elbow is slightly flexed throughout though its action is largely passive. Slight contraction of the pronator teres serves the dual function of controlled flexion and pronation. The fingers are adducted and flexed in the same way as in the elementary back stroke. They are very slightly flexed at the metacarpal-phalangeal joint to prevent hyperextension. This is the result of action of the flexor longus digitorum, controlled by the extensor longus digitorum, to prevent flexion of the phalanges.

Toward the end of the forward swing the anterior deltoid and upper pectoralis major come into action but the posterior deltoid is stronger

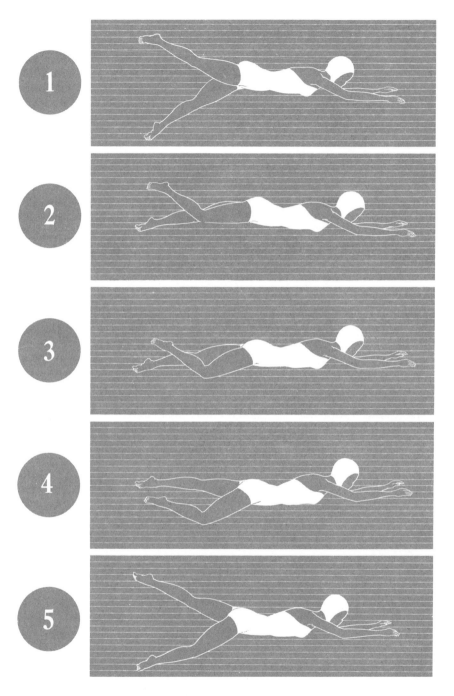

FIGURE 79: Crawl kick, showing recovery of right leg,
upward kick of left leg

in order to keep the elbow high. Throughout the arm action the scapula is being rotated upward and abducted. This is produced by the serratus anterior primarily. The trapezius is also used to help in the rotation and to fix the scapula. Without such fixation the deltoid action would be relatively ineffective on the arm.

If the long forward reach is used the triceps gradually completes extension of the elbow as the humerus is brought inward and down by the coracobrachialis, anterior deltoid, and pectoralis major. The latter also helps to give slight inward rotation of the arm again, which is a factor in keeping the elbow high.

If the catch is a little more nearly vertical, the elbow extension is delayed until later in the pull, and there is less adduction of the arm at the shoulder. The inward rotation is more pronounced, calling for stronger action from the subscapularis. The pronator teres helps in elbow flexion and also gives slight pronation. The latter is necessary to secure proper facing of the hand as a result of greater rotation in the shoulder.

The arm pull is produced by the lower pectoralis major during the first part of the stroke and by the teres major and latissimus dorsi throughout the pull. The scapula is brought back again by the rhomboids and third part of the trapezius. The wrist must be held firm to counteract the resistance of the water. This is done by the flexors carpi ulnaris and radialis and the palmaris longus as well as the finger flexors which have already been listed as being in action.

The kick starts in the hip by action of the iliopsoas, pectineus, and tensor fasciae latae. The knee action is partly passive, resulting from tension of the hamstrings and the resistance of the water to the lower leg. Neither factor will be effective unless the knee extensors are completely relaxed. Ankle extension is also assisted by the resistance of the water, but the soleus and gastrocnemius draw the ankle into complete extension. Then the quadriceps extends the knee, and finally the tibialis anticus and peroneus tertius flex the foot.

The forceful movement comes on the upward kick. The hamstrings are almost entirely responsible for hip extension, as the range of the kick used by most swimmers is too narrow to give the gluteus maximus much opportunity to function. Resistance of the water holds the knee extended but the vasti assist in order to counteract the effect of the hamstrings at the knee. The ankle is extended by the gastrocnemius and soleus, assisted by the tibialis posticus, which helps to pull the foot inward and invert it slightly.

The spinal extensors control the position of the trunk. The pelvis must be fixed to facilitate action of the hip muscles. This requires both anterior and posterior muscles, the rectus abdominis and external oblique, and the quadratus lumborum and the lower portion of the erector spinae. The head is raised by the splenius and the cervical parts of the erector spinae.

The turning of the head for breathing requires first of all relaxation of the extensors in order to allow the forehead to drop and the chin to rise in the water. At the same time the sternocleidomastoid and scaleni on the opposite side to which the face is turned rotate the head on a longitudinal axis. The platysma helps to flex the head and depress the lower jaw. This combination of movements raises the mouth out of the water sufficiently high for breathing. After the breath is taken the face is turned forward again by the sternocleidomastoid on the opposite side from the one which functioned previously. At the same time the head is raised slightly by the extensors.

Mechanical Analysis. The crawl is an adaptation of the four-footed animal's mode of swimming which is patterned directly after their process of locomotion on land. It involves a flexed recovery of the legs with a drive in the extended position. To this is added similar action of the upper extremity.

The flexion of the recovery phase is much less vigorous in order to avoid resistance to the water and yet serve to place the leg in a position to apply force in the proper direction. The extension of the foot in the kick adds force in much the same way that a wrist snap can add force to slapping, to a golf drive, or to any striking activity. The action of the lower leg and foot in the latter part of the leg spread adds an effective drive. It is the action of the ankle which closely resembles the whip of the fish's tail or the more familiar sculling action of the hands. Obviously, the feet must stay under water if they are to exert pressure against the water.

On the downward movement, the pressure of the water causes the knee to bend. This also means that the lower leg offers less resistance as it is in line with the progress through the water. There is no way of entirely avoiding resistance of the thigh to the water but it is not great unless the leg spread is wide.

The arm recovery should be made entirely above water, otherwise the arm offers too much resistance to the water. The hand trails from the hip to the surface of the water but offers very little resistance. Leaving the forearm relaxed shortens the length of the lever and therefore makes it possible for the deltoid to swing the arm forward with less effort, or to swing it faster if the stroke is being done for speed. The elbow must be a little higher than the hand in order to allow the arm to slide into the water. This position avoids the resistance of the water against a fully extended arm and the lift which would come from a straight downward pull.

When the straight forward reach is used, the beginning of the drive is almost vertically downward. Therefore, most of the effect is to lift the swimmer higher in the water. This will help to get the other arm above the water for recovery, makes breathing easier because the face is higher, and may help to reduce resistance slightly. This is important for a non-buoyant swimmer. It also gives the swimmer a chance for a momentary rest if the hand is allowed to float downward a little before starting the pull.

When the reach is deeper and approximately vertical the pull is more nearly straight for a longer time. This may help to add a little to the forward progress on each stroke.

The position of the head influences the position of the whole body. If it is too high, the feet tend to sink and resistance increases because more of the body surface is forward against the water. A very little drop of the feet, if the speed is adequate, helps to keep the swimmer riding upward in the water enough to keep shoulders high. It also helps to keep the feet under water in the kick without materially increasing resistance.

If the head is turned on a transverse as well as the longitudinal axis the mouth can be lifted out of the water for breathing. This avoids the necessity for lifting the whole head, which would cause the body to sink and actually give the swimmer less time to breathe.

The crawl stroke is one of the comparatively few activities in which breathing must be consciously regulated and co-ordinated with the rhythm of the rest of the activity. The breath must be taken in quickly, therefore the inspiration involves quick and active expansion of the thorax. The amount of air taken in must be gauged rather accurately. If too much is taken, discomfort is felt, and too much effort must be spent in exhaling it again quickly for the next breath. If too little is taken, the physiological demands of the body for oxygen are not met and the swimmer is exhausted. The exhalation should be fairly easy and gradual, caused by the elasticity of the thorax and the pressure of the water rather than by forced and fast expulsion.

The crawl stroke is a vigorous and not a resting stroke. However, if properly done, the stroke does permit the swimmer some rest and relaxation. The arm recovery is the resting phase of the arm action. The muscles should be relaxed except for those shoulder muscles producing the movement. The deltoid can relax through the arm pull, but otherwise the arm is fairly fixed. The same is true of the legs. Fatigue can be avoided by the alternation of flexor and extensor contraction and by a relaxed kick rather than a rigid one. One of the main reasons why swimmers fatigue so readily in the crawl is that they always swim it at their maximum speed. On land, one walks unless he is really in a hurry or in a race. Why not use a similar rate in the water for leisurely progression?

Diving

Without exception the dives consist of rotation around a transverse axis of the body. It may be only a half revolution as in the plain front dives and most of the simpler dives. In these dives, the body starts in an upright position and is inverted so that it enters the water head first. The position in the air during this process may vary. The number of revolutions may be increased to a full one, or more frequently one and a half, occasionally two or two and a half. It is also possible to add rotation on the longitudinal axis. Thus the different combinations of rotation and body positions make up the various dives.

A standing dive is dependent for height and direction on the body position and the diver's own ability to spring into the air. The starting positions were discussed in Chapter 12. Leg extension and arm elevation both contribute toward height of the dive. On a plain front dive, the body should remain straight. Angular momentum is given to the body by shifting the weight a little forward just before the take-off. Then the head is pulled forward slightly and lifted. The push-off with the weight forward gives angular momentum; the movement of the head and legs adds to this angular motion. The leg lift is performed by the extensors of the hip joint and fixation of the posterior part of the pelvis. The spinal extensors in the lumbar region are responsible for this. The body is held in a straight extended position for entry into the water.

The plain standing back dive shows exactly the same type of motion. The take-off is taken almost straight into the air by leg extension and arm lift. Angular momentum comes from shifting the weight backward just before the take-off and from a very quick and strong extension of the head and thoracic spine and the arm lift. The abdominals pull on the front of the pelvis strongly enough to limit hyperextension of the lumbar spine to a very slight amount. They also serve to keep the legs moving upward rather than hanging heavily. If the same position is held under water, the diver comes back to the surfacing facing the same direction in which he started. This is in contrast to the recovery which is most desirable for other dives where the position of the head is changed under water for the recovery.

Precise entry into the water on any dive is dependent upon proper timing of the upward momentum, angular momentum, and movements of body segments. This is comparatively simple in either of the two dives already discussed. Failure to use all the upward momentum and pulling the head down too soon, thus increasing the rotation, cause an overthrow of the legs.

On any dive from a spring board, the upward force is increased by the lift of the board. The upward lift depends upon the flexibility of the board, the location of the fulcrum, the force with which the diver jumps on the board, and the proper timing of arm lift and leg extension with the lift of the board.

Relatively simple dives such as a swan or front jack knife merely interpose other movements while in the air. The swan is a hyperextension of the whole body with arms extended sideward and backward. The jack knife dive requires flexibility and considerable strength of hip flexors and

a–front dive, trunk
forward too far

**FIGURE 80:
Position of take off**

b–front dive,
body inclined
too far

c–back jack, good angle

d–plain back dive,
body inclined too far

e—racing start,
angle good

f—racing start,
angle too low

a–pike

FIGURE 81: Diving positions in the air

b–tuck

c–layout

extensors in order to jack and to lift the straight legs quickly. This dive is made with a little straighter take-off. Therefore there is less rotation from the take-off. The leg lift in this dive is delayed and done quickly rather than steadily as in the plain dive. Both of these dives are dependent upon sufficient height, which gives adequate time for the movement.

A plain half-gainer involves the same type of movement. However, the rotation of the body is in the opposite direction. The body must lean slightly forward in order to clear the board. The toes give a forceful backward thrust as they leave the board. The feet are lifted forward and up while the head, back and arms are extended in much the same position as for the back dive.

Somersault dives involve more rotation of the body. They may be either forward or backward and they may be done with the legs straight or flexed or with the whole body straight. The straight leg position is known as a pike and the flexed one as a tuck position. When the whole body is straight, the position is termed a layout. The pike position calls for more flexibility, particularly elasticity of the hamstrings. For that reason the tuck position may be easier for some divers. The tuck position helps to permit faster rotation of the body because it is more compact. Time is required, however, for extending the legs again for the entry. The extension of the spine and legs tend to check rotation. Rotation is slowest in the layout dive. The greatest problem in the dive is to time the revolutions and the extension for a satisfactory entry into the water.

A twist dive involves rotation around the longitudinal axis. Provided the legs do not spread or the lumbar spine become hyperextended the twist can be done easily. The body parts are all fairly close to this axis and, therefore, turn readily. The twist is initiated by pulling one arm down and across the chest. The trunk turns toward the arm as a reaction to the arm movement. The diver helps the movement by leading with the head and lifting the opposite shoulder. This is the same type of movement by which the cat turns to land on its feet when dropped upside down.

REFERENCES

1. Alley, L. E., Analysis of Water Resistance and Propulsion in Swimming the Crawl Stroke, *Research Quarterly*, 23, October 1952, p. 253.
2. Armbruster, D. A., and Morehouse, Laurence E., *Swimming and Diving*, St. Louis, C. V. Mosby Co., 1950.
3. Councilman, James, Forces in Swimming Two Types of Crawl Stroke, *Research Quarterly*, 26, May 1955, p. 127.
4. deVries, Herbert A., A Cinematographic Analysis of the Dolphin Stroke, *Research Quarterly*, 30, December 1959, p. 413.
5. Duffner, G. J., and Lamphier, Edward, Medicine and Science in Sport

Diving, in *Science and Medicine of Exercise and Sports*, Warren R. Johnson (ed.), New York, Harper & Row, Pubs., 1960.

6. Groves, W. H., Mechanical Analysis of Diving, *Research Quarterly*, 21, May 1950, p. 132.
7. Heusner, William W., Theoretical Specifications for the Racing Dive: Optimum Angle of Take-off, *Research Quarterly*, 30, March 1959, p. 25.
8. King, William H., and Irwin, L. W., Time and Motion Study of Competitive Back Stroke Swimming Turns, *Research Quarterly*, 28, October 1957, p. 257.
9. Lanoue, F., Analysis of the Basic Factors Involved in Fancy Diving, *Research Quarterly*, 11, March 1940, p. 102.
10. Purdue University, Physical Education Staff, *Physical Education for Women*, Minneapolis, Burgess Publishing Co., 1963.
11. Robertson, David, *Relationship of Strength of Selected Muscle Groups and Ankle Flexibility to the Flutter Kick in Swimming*, Microcard PE499, 1960.
12. Thrall, William R., *A Performance Analysis of the Propulsive Force of the Flutter Kick*, Microcard PE501, 1960.
13. Vannier, Maryhelen, and Poindexter, Hally Beth, *Individual and Team Sports for Girls and Women*, Philadelphia, W. B. Saunders Co., 1960.

TENNIS

Tennis is another of the striking activities. It has great appeal to players partly because it offers great possibilities for variation in placement, speed, and spin. The basic strokes are the forehand and backhand drives, the serve, the volley, and the smash. These will be discussed here.

Forehand Drive

Description. The body is turned with the left side toward the net (right-handed player), and in this position the body should be well back from the line of flight of the ball. The weight is back almost entirely on the right foot, and the racket is swung back in preparation for the stroke. It may or may not pause there, depending upon the amount of time available for the stroke. The racket is then swung forward in a straight line rising gradually to about the level of the top of the net. The weight is carried forward at the same time, and the ball is contacted just beyond the left foot with the racket face at right angles to the direction the ball is to go. The swing continues somewhat upward in the direction of the net, and the arm is finally allowed to drop. The weight is forward and usually a step is taken forward on the right foot to save the balance. Thus, body rotation is a part of the follow-through but is at a minimum before that. The left arm is used forward and at the side for balance.

Muscular Analysis. The weight is supported on the rear leg with knee slightly relaxed but controlled by the extensors. The abductors, gluteus medius and minimus, tensor fasciae latae, and the muscles on the right

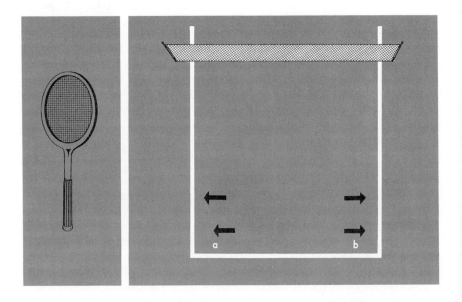

FIGURE 82: Foot positions in preparation for drives
a–ball approaching on left, stance for the backhand drive;
b–ball approaching on right, stance for the forehand drive

side of the trunk draw the trunk slightly to the rear with the weight over
the right foot. The arm is lifted by the posterior and middle deltoid, and
carried backward slightly by the teres minor and infraspinatus. The
triceps also assists at the shoulder, and it holds the elbow extended.

The forward swing is the work of the anterior deltoid, pectoralis major,
and coracobrachialis. The level of the swing is controlled by the middle
deltoid. The elbow is held extended passively, and the wrist is kept
straight by action of the flexor group. The grip is made tight by the
finger flexors.

The weight is shifted forward by the ankle extensors and the knees
flex to assist in keeping the swing flattened. This flexion is controlled by
the extensors, and the rear knee finally completely extends. The right leg
rotates outward, the left one inward. The adductors act, drawing the
trunk to the left with the stroke. The follow-through is merely a continuation of the forward swing, but with a decreasing amount of force being
applied.

Mechanical Analysis. The back swing and inclination of the body give
a starting position farther back and hence a longer arc for acceleration.
The racket is moved in a somewhat flattened arc at arm's length in front
of the body to enable the player to drive from directly behind the ball. A
common error is swinging the racket back into the primary frontal plane

of the body or even back of that, with the elbow straight and wrist hyper-extended. In this case the racket must travel in too much of a circular path. When moving in such an arc there is only one point at which the ball may be contacted to give the desired direction. It also creates a tendency for exaggerated trunk rotation and makes the co-ordination of the swing and the shift of weight more difficult. The flatter arc increases greatly the range in which the ball may be contacted with satisfactory results.

The forward drive is made as a swing from the shoulder and should carry the racket as a straight extension of the arm. This gives a long lever with the possibility of speed at the extremity of it. This possibility is realized by strong contraction of the shoulder muscles. Such a stroke is more powerful than one coming principally from the elbow because of the difference in length of the levers. The wrist position prevents the racket from hanging and thereby helps to improve placement of the ball. Wrist flexion whips the racket through at the same rate as the arm and may even be used to help give spin as the ball is contacted.

With a good transfer of weight the lever is really the whole body, rotating at the ground. The weight of the body and strength of the leg extensors carry this long lever with sufficient speed to give great momentum to the ball.

Bending the knees during the transfer of weight tends to flatten the swing and avoid the tendency to scoop or lift the ball. The angle of rebound of the ball is dependent upon the angle with which it meets the face of the racket. If the strings are tight and the ball is good, the ball acquires considerable speed from this drive. If the racket is drawn across the ball in any direction at the moment of contact, a spin is imparted to the ball. Spin affects the flight of the ball in varying degrees, depending upon the amount, the quality of the ball, the speed of the ball, and the wind resistance. The bounce is always affected by the spin and by the surface on which the ball falls.

The follow-through is a means of lessening the speed which has been developed and affording time for stopping, and avoids the strain which would result from an abrupt stop. The direction of the follow-through furnishes the majority of players a more observable check on the direction in which the stroke is made than is afforded by the position of the racket at the point of contact. This is extremely important for the beginner. The final step with the right foot not only saves balance but puts the player in position of readiness for the next play.

Backhand Drive

Description. This stroke is just the reverse of the previous one. The body is turned with the right side toward net, weight on the left foot, racket arm reaching back in front of the body. The hand is brought in on the racket, and in some cases the thumb is extended directly up the back of the handle. The swing should again be straight and along an upward incline. The weight is shifted forward with the knees slightly relaxed and with a little trunk rotation. The follow-through of the right arm is forward and upward toward the top of the net, finishing approximately in the frontal plane of the body.

Muscular Analysis. The preparatory swing is made by the action of the anterior deltoid, upper part of the pectoralis major, and coracobrachialis. The serratus anterior draws the scapula forward to facilitate this reach. The elbow is always flexed slightly, the biceps helping in both movements. The brachioradialis also helps flex the elbow. This flexion in turn helps the wrist muscles (flexor carpi radialis and extensors carpi radialis longus and brevis) to hold the wrist firm and slightly cocked, thus keeping the head of the racket up.

The forward swing is made with the middle deltoid supporting the level of the arm, and the posterior deltoid, teres minor, and infraspinatus pulling it quickly. The scapula is adducted to help this movement, the rhomboids and trapezius acting. The elbow is drawn into extension by the triceps. The wrist is extended by the extensors carpi radialis longus and brevis and extensor carpi ulnaris. This snaps the racket through for greater speed and holds it firm against the contact of the ball.

The transfer of weight is the same as in the forehand drive. The slight trunk rotation is partially passive, but with a little action particularly from the right extensors of the spine. The follow-through is a continuation of the drive, with lessened muscular force, pronounced rotation, and frequently a step for balance.

Mechanical Analysis. The points of mechanical importance are almost the same as in the forehand drive. However, the thumb is used up the back of the handle to brace the racket against the impact of the ball, and to avoid the natural tendency to allow the wrist to remain slightly flexed with racket trailing during the forward swing. With sufficient wrist strength this is not necessary. Most women use this grip.

Many players find it difficult to get sufficient backswing because of the arm crossing the body. On the other hand, the sweeping arm swing into abduction seems easier than the arm swing forward across the body. The full arm swing from the shoulder is more apt to be used, which means greater power to the swing.

Transfer of weight is equally essential for force. Direction is dependent upon the line of drive, angle of the racket, and timing. The most common error in line of swing is starting from a position of close arm adduction across the trunk, and swinging diagonally out from the body to the ball. Another error is in leading with too much trunk rotation, which results in a circular swing and poor placement of the ball.

Serve

Description. The tennis serve is the most individual of the tennis strokes. The one to be described here is relatively simple and basic in style. The stance is with the left shoulder toward the point to which the service is to be made. The racket is grasped as for the forehand drive, and the balls are in the left hand. The weight is back on the right foot.

The racket usually starts with the elbow flexed which brings the racket across the body about waist height. It is then dropped down, the whole arm is circled back and then upward. When the arm reaches almost right angles the elbow gives and the wrist relaxes so that the racket drops behind the back. At this instant the ball is tossed upward by slight arm and elbow flexion and a wrist snap.

The racket is then swung quickly up with full extension above the shoulder. As a continuation of that reach it is carried forward to contact the ball. At the same time the weight is shifted forward to the left foot and strong body rotation begins. The ball is contacted with the arm at full reach, just as the racket starts on the downward arc. The player is usually on tip-toe at that instant.

The follow-through is characterized by a continuation of the circular arm swing which usually ends with the racket near the left foot, by a continuation of the weight transfer; and by the completion of rotation. Almost invariably the player steps forward with the right foot to save balance and to be ready to move for the next play.

Muscular Analysis. The first extension of the elbow is mostly passive with gravity pulling the racket down. Then the arm is abducted by the middle and posterior deltoid, and assisted by the teres minor and infraspinatus, which keep it back and rotate the arm outward. On the upswing the triceps holds the elbow extended to keep the racket moving along rapidly. The wrist and fingers are firm. The scapula is adducted and rotated upward by the trapezius and lower part of the serratus anterior. The right quadratus lumborum, erector spinae, and internal oblique bend the trunk and rotate it slightly to the right.

Then the elbow is flexed by biceps, brachialis, and brachioradialis, and the wrist relaxes, allowing the racket head to drop. The ball is tossed from the left hand by action of the anterior deltoid, biceps, flexors carpi ulnaris and radialis longus, and the palmaris longus, acting on their respective joints with a quick, short movement. The flexors of the fingers must relax quickly in order not to interfere with the direction of the ball.

The lifting of the racket starts in the wrist by the flexor and extensor carpi ulnaris. Then the triceps extends the forearm with the pronators controlling the forearm just enough to keep the racket facing directly in the direction of the service. The wrist flexors are also necessary to keep the racket straight up, but the amount of their help depends upon the

FIGURE 83: Backhand drive

FIGURE 84: Serve (just before contact)

position of the racket at the pause. At the shoulder the middle deltoid pulls strongly with the anterior deltoid and upper pectoralis coming in to produce the forward movement. The coracobrachialis also assists and the lower pectoralis comes in later if the follow-through is done with any vigor. The scapular accompaniment is the result of the upper serratus anterior and finally of the pectoralis minor.

The shift of weight is of the same type as found in the drives but the feet are invariably closer together. The trunk movement is mostly rotation produced by the left erector spinae, latissimus dorsi, internal oblique and rectus abdominus, and the right external oblique. There is also some bending of trunk forward and to the left.

The follow-through is a continuation of all of these. Because of the strength and speed necessary for the serve, it must be vigorous. The left arm is usually carried back and up for balance, with the middle and posterior deltoid doing most of the work, the triceps acting if the elbow is held straight.

Mechanical Analysis. In many respects the mechanical considerations are the same as for the drives. The long lever and the resulting speed are provided for by the long arm swing and use of the body as part of the lever. Considerable force is put into it to secure the necessary speed. Flexion of the elbow on the upswing reduces the length of the lever and hence its speed. The pause permits closer timing of the swing and toss, and places the racket hand almost above the shoulder so that the racket can be extended upward very quickly into the striking position. The shift of weight and trunk rotation also contribute to the force of the stroke.

The direction is dependent chiefly upon the angle of the racket face. Unless the wrist is straight, the racket hangs back and the ball goes too high. The pause gives an opportunity to adjust the forearm so that the racket faces toward the point of aim.

The height of the ball on the toss and at the time of contact is extremely important. It should be as high as the player can reach, as this means swinging with a longer, straighter lever. It also makes it possible to hit the ball harder and still keep it in the service court. The position of the ball is important too. If it is too close over the head, arm action is cramped; if too far away, the player loses balance. It should be directly in an easy, swinging line. It should be at a point where the racket is just starting down on its arc. If it is contacted too far down on the arc it fails to go over the net; if too far back, it goes high and beyond the service court.

Volley

The volley resembles the drive in some respects. It may be either forehand or backhand, and the general form is the same. However, the volley usually has a very short back swing or lacks one entirely. The follow-through is always shorter than in the drives, even frequently omitted. The racket must be held very firm and placed in the line of flight in such a way as to give the desired direction. The racket head should always be as high as the wrist, or a little higher. The face of the racket must be turned up a little so that the ball will clear the top of the net. An exception to this occurs when the ball is played well above the level of the top of the net, fairly close to the net, and the return is aimed only a short distance across the net. The return with a volley is always comparatively short; therefore, the momentum of a long swing is not necessary. Also, time does not usually permit it.

Smash

The smash is so very similar to the serve that it will not be discussed in detail. Since the player frequently does not have much time to make the stroke, the back swing is usually started while he is moving into position. It may therefore be necessary to shorten the back swing. The important factors are again contact with the ball at the proper point and with sufficient force to give it the high speed characteristic of the smash.

Lob

The lob may be made from almost any position and as an adaptation of any stroke. It is a problem of direction and distance. The racket face must be turned up far enough to lift the ball, and the flight and speed so adjusted to the situation that it will be just out of the opponent's reach and allow the minimum amount of time for the opponent to recover.

The question of spin on the balls has not been discussed here. It may be of various types and added to any stroke. The basic discussion of spin appears in Chapter 11 and the reader may refer to this.

REFERENCES

1. Ainsworth, Dorothy, *et al.*, *Individual Sports for Women*, Philadelphia, W. B. Saunders Co., 1958.
2. Connolly, Maureen, *Power Tennis*, New York, A. S. Barnes, 1954.
3. Fraley, Oscar, *How to Play Championship Tennis*, New York, A. A. Wyn, Inc., Pub., 1954.
4. Johnson, Joan, Tennis Serve of Advanced Women Players, *Research Quarterly*, 28, May 1957, p. 123.
5. Kramer, Jack, *How to Win at Tennis*, Englewood Cliffs, N.J., Prentice-Hall, Inc., 1949.
6. Miller, Donna Mae, and Ley, Katherine L., *Individual and Team Sports for Women*, Englewood Cliffs, N.J., Prentice-Hall, 1955.
7. Sedgman, Frank, *Winning Tennis*, Englewood Cliffs, N.J., Prentice-Hall, Inc., 1954.

CHAPTER 18

Selected Activities in Stunts and Tumbling

ACTIVITIES OF THE STUNT TYPE are very commonly taught in the general program of the elementary and secondary school levels. They are also frequently used in specialized programs for developmental or corrective purposes. Certain representative activities will be analyzed here, primarily to indicate the principles of performance necessary to correct results and the muscles used in the performance of each.

Most of these stunts or activities fall into one of four types. A very large percentage of them are feats of balance. Another group is made up of stunts requiring rotation, usually around a transverse axis. Most of the others are dependent upon strength or flexibility and are, in a sense, measures of these two traits.

The balance events are simplified by an understanding of the rules of stability, dealing principally with the size of the base and the location of the center of gravity with respect to the base (see Chap. 9). However, since rotatory momentum is usually necessary to assume the position, this factor must also be considered.

The rotatory events may take place around a point of support or around an axis through the center of gravity. In either case, the important considerations are to use the rotatory forces effectively and to understand the effects of resistance of the body mass in various positions and the possible ways to reduce this resistance.

The strength events are usually governed largely by the weight of the performer or of the second person, who is being supported. However, certain variations may be possible to relieve the performer of part of the load. Such adaptations are made by variations of base and adjustments of position to reduce moments of rotation. These variations may be considered as an acceptable standard of achievement or as steps toward progressive development into the more difficult stunt.

The flexibility events may be localized in legs, back, or shoulders, though they very frequently involve total flexibility. Many stunts belong in one of the other categories but demand flexibility as well.

The stunts which are analyzed in this chapter represent these four types.

HEADSTAND

Description. The performer starts in a full squat sitting position with weight on the balls of the feet and trunk forward. The palms are placed on the floor about shoulder width apart with fingers pointing either straight forward or sideward. The forehead is then placed on the floor

FIGURE 85: The head stand
Right–tripod base for balance; *Left*–inverted stretch

far enough beyond the hands that the three points of contact, hands and head, form approximately an equilateral triangle. From this position the headstand may be attained by either of two methods.

In the first method, the legs are flexed and one knee placed on each elbow so that a balanced position is obtained. The legs are then extended upward either together or with one leading. As the legs extend, the spine also straightens and goes into more or less hyperextension in the lumbar region. In the second method, a push-off is taken by the toes and the legs are swung up, one ahead of the other, into position. At the same time the position of the back is changed from flexion to slight hyper-extension as before.

Muscular Analysis. The arms are brought forward partially as a relaxed drop as the trunk bends forward, and partially by action of the anterior deltoid, upper pectoralis major, and the coracobrachialis. If the fingers are turned outward a little, that movement must take place in the shoulder joint and is produced by the teres minor and infraspinatus. The wrist is hyperextended, the palms are flat on the floor, as a result of action of the extensor carpi ulnaris, extensors carpi radialis longus and brevis, and extensor communis digitorum.

The trunk is allowed to remain flexed chiefly by relaxation of the extensors. However, the splenius and the fibers of the erector spinae in the cervical region pull the head back so as to allow the upper part of the forehead to touch instead of the top of the head.

In order to place the knees on the elbows, the hips must be flexed more and rotated slightly outward, and the knees must be flexed. Flexion is produced by the iliopsoas, pectineus, and sartorius. These same muscles give most of the rotation, but when the arm spread is wide, greater rotation is required and the small outward rotators assist. In this case, the gluteus medius and minimus also assist, giving a little rotation and abduction. Knee flexion results from action of the sartorius, popliteus, short head of the biceps femoris, and tension of the hamstrings.

Hip extension comes from action of the gluteus maximus, semi-tendinosus, semimembranosus, and long head of the biceps. The gluteus loses its effectiveness as the thighs approach extension. During the early part of the leg lift the knees are kept flexed, then they are extended by the three vasti. The ankles are extended by the gastrocnemius and soleus.

Extension of the back is localized in the lower thoracic and in the lumbar regions and is largely due to the erector spinae in these areas. The quadratus lumborum assists in this extension and also helps to fix the pelvis for stronger action of the hip extensors. The body weight is shifted back toward the hands, and the trunk fixed over the arms. This requires action of the anterior deltoid and the pectoralis major. The brachialis anticus holds the elbow at right angles.

In the second method of assuming the headstand, the action is the same in the placement of hands and head. Then the leg lift is made by a push-off from the toes and by hip extension. The push-off results from contraction of the gastrocnemius and soleus, and the flexors digitorum and hallucis. Hip extension is attained, as before, by the gluteus maximus in the early part of the lift and by the hamstrings throughout. Knee and ankle action are the same. Trunk action is the same as in the other method, except that the momentum of the legs helps to produce the lumbar extension, and the reaction on the trunk helps to thrust it back over the arms. The leg swing may need checking, and this is done by action of the hip flexors and the abdominals. The momentum of the legs would tend to carry the whole body too far over.

Mechanical Analysis. The squat sitting position gets the body weight low so that it can be easily placed over the support. This position of the hands, particularly if the fingers are pointed out more or less, keeps the elbows in close to the sides during this preliminary stage and thus makes for a straighter position of the upper thoracic region, makes it easier to get hyperextension of the cervical region, and makes possible strong adduction of the scapulae. These all contribute to greater firmness of the upper trunk, to fixation of the posterior part of the shoulder girdle, and hence to better control of weight and to greater stability in the headstand. In this position, it is also easy for the performer to place the knees on the elbows.

Placing the forehead on the mat leaves the head still extended a very little when the body is inverted. This position is more comfortable and makes it easier to keep the weight back so it is partially on the hands. The triangular base allows some shifting of body weight in any direction without serious disturbance of balance. During leg extension, the weight shifts from hands toward the head; but, if the base is large and the performer uses all three points of contact, balance is relatively simple.

The beginner is apt to make one or two errors in this respect. The head may be placed nearly in a straight line with the hands. Momentum and shifting of body weight is at right angles to this straight-line base. Therefore the performer finds it practically impossible to hold this position. Hyperextension of the neck is also difficult with the head in this position. The other common error of the beginner is to shift all the weight to the head, usually with the head and spine not well extended. This gives a single point of support, and balance may be lost in almost any direction depending upon the momentum of the movement or location of body segments. Even if balance is maintained, this is uncomfortable for the head and neck because they have to support total body weight.

The first method of assuming the headstand seems preferable for the beginner, for those who do not have outstanding skill in co-ordination and balance, and for those who do not stay constantly in practice. The ease of maintaining balance is the chief advantage. In the second method, exactly the right amount of force must be used to swing the legs into the vertical position. If insufficient force is applied, the legs will drop back to the floor. If too much force is applied, it is difficult to check; and the balance is apt to be lost, causing the performer to go over on his back. Less force is required to carry the legs up in the first method because they are kept flexed.

HANDSTAND

Description. The performer starts in a standing position, one foot ahead of the other, hands raised forward with palms down. He then bends forward quickly, placing the hands on the floor a little in front of the toes. The hands are about shoulder width apart and the fingers point forward, or nearly so. At the same time, a push-off is taken from the feet and the legs are swung up one after the other into the inverted position. The head is held high in as complete hyperextension as possible, the back is arched, and the body is held in balance over the hands.

Muscular Analysis. The arms are raised forward by the anterior deltoid and the upper pectoralis major. They are then started down quickly by the lower pectoralis major and the latissimus dorsi. At the same time the trunk is brought forward and down. This is accomplished by abdominal action and momentum imparted to the trunk by arm and leg swing. The fingers are held in extension by the extensors longus and pollicis. They also assist the extensor carpi ulnaris and extensors carpi radialis longus and brevis in wrist extension. This permits the whole hand to be placed flat on the floor. The elbows are held firm by strong action of the triceps. This extension is reinforced by the stabilizing effect at the shoulder of the deltoid, upper pectoralis major, coracobrachialis, and supraspinatus. The shoulder girdle is fixed in its upward rotated position by the serratus anterior and trapezius. When the average person performs this stunt, there is considerable tenseness in the shoulder and shoulder girdle, and such additional muscles as levator angulae scapulae, rhomboids, subscapularis, and pectoralis minor come into action.

The leg action is simultaneous with that of the upper body. The push-off is by ankle extension, and hip extension is produced by all the hip extensors. As the legs finish the swing, the knee and ankle extensors contract.

As the legs go up, the spine is also hyperextended by a combination of erector spinae action and reaction from the leg swing. Tension of the abdominals holds the front of the pelvis firm and prevents the weight of the legs from giving too much curve to the back. The hyperextension of the head is a strong movement requiring the use of upper erector spinae fibers, splenius, and upper trapezius.

Wrist and finger flexors lift the palm and hence push the weight forward more toward the fingers. Wrist extensors shift the weight back toward the heel of the hand. This movement is helpful in maintaining balance.

Mechanical Analysis. The forward elevation of the arms is not essential but does aid in developing the rotatory momentum which inverts the body. Bringing the hands down close to the feet and forcibly lifting the legs instead of emphasizing the push-off will help give a rotatory movement. One common error is to reach too far forward, thus getting a forward drive from the push-off. The action of the arms and legs, both

**FIGURE 86: Hand stand
(same position whether
on floor or on support)**

moving in the same rotatory direction, complement each other in achieving the desired reversal of position. The movement of the head is in the
opposite direction and serves to check this rotation at the proper time.

The position of the head while the handstand is held is important in
distribution of weight, the head and most of the legs being on one side
of the gravital line, and part of the trunk and thighs on the other side.

Bending the knees lowers the center of gravity a little and makes it easier to hold the balance. However, this is not usually considered desirable form.

The base is narrow, just the length of the hands. If the fingers are pointed forward, they aid somewhat in balance, since the wrist is then extended to its full extent and the fingers can be used in pushing against the floor. This is a more difficult position than the headstand, both to assume and to maintain, largely because of the difference in the base. The base permits practically no variation of weight line in an anteroposterior direction. The weight is also held higher and supported by the arms, which offer at least two unsteady joints, the elbow and the shoulder. The position can be assumed only by a strong rotatory action that is at right angles to the line of the base. The problem is to get sufficient force to get the legs ups, but not enough to continue the rotation beyond a position of balance.

FORWARD ROLL

Description. The forward roll can be taken from several different starting positions. However, the simple form taught to beginners will be discussed here and variations suggested. The beginner starts in a squat sitting position with toes turned out at about a 45° angle. The arms are dropped in front of the body, between the legs; they are rotated inward and the hands are placed palms down just in front of the feet, with fingers pointed toward each other. This leaves the trunk bent forward. Trunk flexion is continued, and the neck is flexed as far as possible. At the same time, the weight is shifted forward over the hands. The elbows flex sufficiently to keep the weight low. The performer then rolls over, keeping the spine and legs in this same fully flexed position until the feet are again on the floor. Just before this time, the head is carried back. As the weight goes onto the feet, the body starts into full extension. The arms are often raised forward to aid in recovering the standing position.

The starting position in the above form puts the performer on his toes. Just as the forward motion is started, a slight push-off should be made with the toes. A more advanced form starts in the standing position. It differs mainly in that the push-off is more pronounced, it comes simultaneously with the forward leaning of the body, the hands make contact farther from the feet, the fingers point forward rather than inward, the body does not reach full flexion until it is going over, and there will be greater speed to the roll. A roll made with a running approach or following some other stunt which gives momentum to the body is essentially the same. The take-off is usually made by a jump from both feet.

If the roll is elongated or made over some obstacle, it is called a dive. It differs from the roll in stronger use of the arms and legs, take-off from the feet long before the hands make contact, and delayed body tuck.

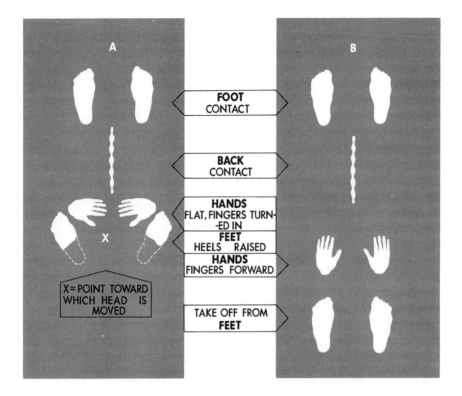

FIGURE 87: Base for a beginning forward roll

Muscular Analysis. The "toeing out" position is the result of outward rotation at the hip, produced by the gemelli, obturators, pyriformis, and quadratus femoris before the squat sitting position is assumed. In the squat sitting position the leg extensors should be relaxed.

As the legs are flexing the arms are brought together in front of the body by the anterior deltoid, pectoralis major, and coracobrachialis; the scapula is rotated upward by the serratus anterior. In order to get the fingers pointing in, the arm is rotated inward slightly at the shoulder by the pectoralis and subscapularis. The forearm is pronated by the pronators teres and quadratus. The wrist and fingers are extended by the extensor carpi ulnaris, the extensors radialis longus and brevis, and the extensor longus digitorum. The elbows flex gradually by controlled action of the triceps as the weight is taken on the arms.

The trunk drops forward first by relaxation of the back extensors and forward pull of the arms. Then it is flexed strongly by the abdominals, while the head is flexed by the sternocleidomastoid, scalenus, and platysma. As the roll is taken, the position is held by these same muscles and the legs are also held in position. The iliopsoas, pectineus, and sartorius flex and adduct the legs as the rotators relax; and the sartorius and hamstrings flex the knee.

Extension starts with the head and trunk, the erector spinae, splenius, and quadratus lumborum acting. Then comes leg extension, by hamstrings and gluteus maximus at the hip, vasti at the knee, and gastrocnemius, soleus, and peroneals at the ankles.

The arm swing, if used, is accomplished by anterior deltoid, upper pectoralis major, and coracobrachialis, and the serratus anterior assists with scapular abduction and rotation.

Mechanical Analysis. The squat sitting position for starting the beginner makes easier the complete flexion necessary for a good roll. Putting the hands close to the toes also contributes to maximum flexion. Such flexion is impossible if the knees are kept parallel. If the toes are turned out at the beginning, the knees are well spread when flexed.

Turning the palms down makes possible effective use of the hands in supporting the weight. Turning the fingers in to touch the finger tips gives two advantages. First, in this position, the weight rocks easily over to the outside border of the hands and then off. The hands will turn sideward with no resistance. When the fingers are pointed ahead, the hands act as a block to rotation; the long axis of the hands is in the direction of the movement, and the wrists resist hyperextension.

The second advantage is the position of the elbows and shoulder girdle. With fingers pointing in, the elbows point outward well away from the body, the whole arm is rotated inward and abducted, and the scapulae are abducted and rotated upward. In this position, relaxation more readily takes place in such muscles as the rhomboids, trapezius, and erector spinae; and such relaxation is necessary to complete flexion. On the other hand, when the fingers are pointed forward, the elbows are pointed backward and the arm moves backward in the sagittal plane as the roll is made. This must be accompanied by scapular adduction and downward rotation. This results also in a stiffening of the thoracic spine. With elbows and knees spread, the impediments to full flexion are removed.

When the head is pulled well under, the body starts rotating and the hips and weight line of the body are carried on beyond the hands. When this happens, the pull of gravity will carry the body on over. Momentum may be sufficient to carry it completely over, or far enough so that the arm lift will finish the roll. Otherwise, the push-off from the toes must be used to give the needed momentum.

The weight is supported entirely by the hands. The elbows control the height of the body and may allow the back of the head or shoulders to touch, but little weight is borne there. The roll is a rotatory movement around the point of contact of the hands. It is made quickly and easily because the body is tucked in so close to the axis.

The movement of the head and arms in the recovery is opposite to the direction of rotation and, therefore, helps to check the angular momentum of the roll. The reaction on the trunk also brings the lower part of the trunk and the hips forward. The recovery of the standing position is dependent upon accurate timing of the extension so that the weight is easily controlled over the feet without having to step into position.

In the more advanced forms of the roll, the push-off or the approach and push-off are used to give the momentum to carry the body over quickly, or often over longer distances. If the roll is lengthened even a slight amount, the take-off is from both feet, the knees may be kept together, leg flexion does not take place until after the roll is started and is not as complete. In this case, the hands are usually placed so that the fingers point forward. The momentum is sufficient to carry over the resistance of the hand. Also, the hand is in a better position to give a push-off from the fingers, and hence to add to the force of the movement.

BACKWARD ROLL

Description. The beginner's roll is described here again as the simpler form on which the more advanced roll is based. The beginner starts in a squat sitting position. The back is relaxed and the head is hanging forward. The performer starts the roll by sitting back as far as possible behind the heels. The legs are immediately brought up toward the body again with a hard pull. The trunk and neck are kept fully flexed. As the body rolls over, the hands are brought up to the shoulders with palms forward. The roll continues, supported by the hands when inverted. A final push from the hands is given in order to complete the turn to the feet.

Muscular Analysis. The balanced squat sitting position with head and neck flexed is achieved by relaxation of the extensors of legs and spine. The vasti muscles extend the knee, and the gastrocnemius and soleus straighten the ankle. The slight extension at the hip is mostly due to passive tension of the hamstrings. The legs are again flexed forcibly by hip flexors to bring them in close for the roll. The hands are brought to the shoulders by slight action of the anterior deltoid and upper pectoralis on the shoulder; flexion of the elbow is by the brachialis anticus and biceps, assisted by the pronator teres, which also holds the forearm in pronation. The actual turn is accomplished principally by the momentum gained by the original backward stretch, by that of the legs in flexion, and by the lift of the arms. During the instant of inversion, the elbows are partly extended by the triceps. The wrists are hyperextended in preparation for this support by the extensor carpi ulnaris, extensors

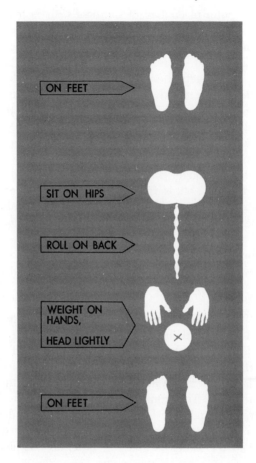

FIGURE 88: Contacts for a backward roll

carpi radialis, and the extensor communis digitorum. The final push is given by the further extension of the elbows, and by flexion of the wrist by flexor carpi ulnaris, flexor carpi radialis, palmaris longus and flexor profoundus digitorum. The standing position is regained by extension of the legs and spine.

Mechanical Analysis. The full squat sitting position is an aid to the beginner in that it puts the body in the position which must be maintained for a successful roll. Added momentum for the roll is achieved by thrusting the weight backward rather than allowing it to drop at the heels. The pull of the legs and arms also adds to the momentum.

The position of the hands at the shoulders is necessary to protect the neck, to aid in turning a straight roll, and it also enables the hands to give a very effective push to aid in recovery of the standing position.

The more advanced roll starts from a standing position, but the flexion and backward drop are a combined movement which adds somewhat to the momentum and speed of the roll.

The clown roll, done with legs straight and spread far apart, is mechanically very similar. The drop may be softened by complete trunk flexion and use of the hands on the floor between the legs. Jar may be avoided also by partial extension of the hips just before landing. This lifts the hips and serves as "give" at the moment of impact. It also reacts on the trunk in such a way as to force the shoulders backward, thus aiding the roll. The sitting movement starts the momentum and is supplemented by the lift of the legs. The push-off with the hands toward the end of the roll is more important in this roll because the straight legs make it difficult to get the trunk lifted and to regain balance.

FORWARD HANDSPRING

Description. The handspring may be made with a short running approach or from a standing position. The body is inverted by a process almost identical with that used in assuming a hand stand position. However, the legs are lifted more vigorously and the whole body rotates while slightly hyperextended, with the feet coming down to the floor only a little in advance of where the hands were. A push-off with the hands is used to help complete the turn.

Muscular Analysis. Muscular action is approximately the same as in the handstand. However, stronger action is used throughout. Hip extension is more vigorous. The neck, lumbar spine, and hips are kept extended during the turn. While the body is inverted, the elbows may be slightly flexed by control of the triceps. The final push from the hands comes from elbow extension (triceps), wrist flexion (flexor carpi radialis, flexor carpi ulnaris, palmaris longus, flexor profundus digitorum, flexor sublimis digitorum), and finger action from the two finger flexors. Body weight prevents actual flexion of the fingers but force is applied for a push-off. The shoulders are raised by action of the upper trapezius, levator scapulae and deltoid. The scapula is rotated upward by action of the serratus anterior.

Abdominal and hip flexor action is necessary at the finish to help straighten the body and recover balance.

Mechanical Analysis. The arms are usually raised forward and one leg is lifted forward at the start. The downward movement of the arms and the upward and backward swing of the rear leg starts the rotation. Momentum is secured because of the distance through which these parts are moving and because of the reaction on the trunk. The body is inclined forward a little at the take-off, which gives a rotatory effect to the push just as in the dive into the water.

If the knees are flexed during the turn, the legs are easier to carry over and the turn will be more rapid. If one leg leads, it gets over in a posi-

FIGURE 89: Front hand spring

tion for gravity to pull it down before the other leg has reached its height. This helps to keep the body rotating.

The performer will turn only if hyperextension is maintained. A little give at the hips or even pulling the head forward too soon will cause the performer to fall or sit down instead of landing on the feet.

If the center of gravity is not high, the handspring usually can be completed by flexing the hips sharply at the instant the feet strike the floor. This shortens the radius of rotation and accelerates the angular velocity. The center of gravity is permitted to slide downward and forward, instead of rising above the knees as a center of rotation.

This stunt is typical of many others in which the turn is made over some other base, or without support as a free turn in the air.

WORM WALK

Description. The performer starts in a standing position, bends down to place the palms on the floor in front of the toes, then steps forward one hand at a time until the body is in a straight position from head to feet (prone support). Then the feet step forward alternately, knees straight, until they are again immediately behind the hands. This is repeated over and over, usually at a fairly rapid rate.

(walk-over style)

Muscular Analysis. The trunk is pulled forward by very strong action of the abdominals and the hip flexors—iliopsoas, pectineus, and rectus femoris. The arms drop down into place; they are relaxed except for hyperextension of the wrist by the extensor carpi ulnaris, extensors carpi radialis longus and brevis. If the position is difficult to assume, arm action may be used to pull the trunk down. In that case, the arms are raised easily forward by the anterior deltoid, upper pectoralis major, and coraco-brachialis; the elbows are flexed by brachialis anticus and biceps. Then, as the trunk starts forward, the elbows are extended and arms are swung forcibly down. Elbow extension is by triceps action, speeding up the pull of gravity, and the shoulder extension is by the lower pectoralis, latissimus dorsi, and teres major. This action is brief and is checked by the deltoid. The serratus anterior and trapezius aid in scapular rotation.

As the trunk goes forward, the weight is pulled backward by the soleus. The knees are held firm by the vasti and rectus femoris against the tension of the hamstrings.

Then the hands move forward alternately by action of the deltoid. The body is stretched out more and more, with the weight of the trunk and hips pushing it forward over the hands. When in the nearly horizontal position, the weight is distributed between the hands and feet. The body is kept from collapsing by the extensors of the knees, and the abdominals. The arms are held firm by the triceps and the anterior deltoid, pectoralis major, and coracobrachialis.

The step with the foot is made by a slight drive with the toes. This is done by mild action of the gastrocnemius and soleus and flexion of the toes by the flexors longus digitorum and hallucis and flexor brevis digitorum. This lifts the hip and shifts the weight toward the other side so that the step may be made. The foot is flexed dorsally by the tibialis anticus. The hip is flexed by the iliopsoas, pectineus, rectus femoris, and tensor fasciae latae. The abdominals also continue action to flex the spine and hold the front of the pelvis firm for the hip flexors.

Mechanical Analysis. This stunt requires considerable flexibility of the joints and elasticity of muscles. The full flexion of the hip puts the hamstrings under tension and tends to cause the knees to flex. This requires antagonistic action to prevent flexion. Shifting the weight and hips backward helps prevent flexion of the knees. This shift, however, is more important in the maintenance of balance. It can be done without the shift only if the position is reached readily and the weight is taken immediately on the hands to prevent falling.

The arm swing which is used adds momentum to the downward movement, and hence helps to get the body farther down and to stretch the hamstring muscles. Gravity assists in bringing the trunk forward; but if extra help is needed, it must come from arm momentum.

Because of the long unsupported and segmented span from toes to shoulder, there is considerable effort necessary from the muscles. The abdominals are the ones which most frequently fail. The arms are held firm by the reinforcement of action at the shoulder and elbow.

This stunt is typical of many others which require hip flexion with the knees straight. Elasticity of the hamstrings is important. The prone fall position offers an opportunity to check the performer on the feeling of position. The hips are high if full extension is not reached, and the hips and lumbar spine sag if the abdominals do not afford support.

SINGLE SQUAT

Description. The performer stands with the weight on one foot. As the supporting leg is flexed so that the body goes down into a squat sitting position, the other leg is raised forward so that it does not touch the floor. The arms are carried forward for balance. The performer then rises to a standing position, still keeping the free leg from touching the floor. The arms move sideward quickly and then forward and up with a definite lift.

Muscular Analysis. The supporting leg is kept straight at first by the extensors of all three joints. Then flexion takes place by gradual relaxation of the extensors. They remain sufficiently in control at all times to allow flexion to continue or to stop it. Stronger contraction of the extensors is necessary either to hold a position of partial flexion or to reverse the direction of movement.

The free leg is flexed by the iliopsoas, rectus femoris, pectineus, and tensor. The knee is held nearly straight by the quadriceps. The trunk is inclined forward by the abdominals, which also fix the pelvis and facilitate action of the hip flexors. The arms are raised forward by the anterior deltoid, upper pectoralis major, and coracobrachialis, and the scapulae are rotated by the serratus anterior.

The body is lifted again by action of all the leg extensors. The erector spinae straightens the trunk. The arms are circled back by the deltoid, teres minor, and infraspinatus and then suddenly brought forward and up with the same muscles as on the previous occasion. This is a forceful movement which is checked about in front of the head by the teres major and the latissimus dorsi.

Mechanical Analysis. This is primarily a balancing stunt, the main difficulty lying in the smallness of the base. Leg strength is also necessary. Because of the shortness of the ankle extensors, it is impossible to keep the foot flat on the floor unless the lower leg is kept nearly vertical. This means shifting the center of gravity back of the foot unless the trunk is fully flexed over the knee and the head and arms are held far forward. The individual must decide whether it is easier for him to balance over the ball of the foot and keep the body more erect, or to use the whole foot and double up more.

The leg extensors must constantly control the position, even when near full flexion. If the weight is allowed to drop, with the supporting leg fully flexed and extensors relaxed, the performer usually finds that the muscles are stretched so much that their action is ineffective and the inertia of the body is too great to be overcome with that force.

Inclining the trunk forward with the arms raised brings the weight forward over the base of support. The strong upward movement of the arms on the rise, with their sudden checking, results in transferring of movement from the arms to the body and hence helps to lift it as well as keep it in balance as the other leg drops.

CHINNING

Description. The performer grasps the bar with both hands, palms toward the face. The body is freely suspended. The body is raised by flexion of the arms until the chin is over the bar between the hands; it may then be lowered to its starting position.

Muscular Analysis. The grip on the bar is maintained by the flexor profundus digitorum, flexor sublimis digitorum, and flexor longus pollicis. Elbow flexion is produced by the biceps, brachialis anticus, pronator teres, and brachioradialis. Arm depression is accomplished by the latissimus dorsi, teres major, and the lower pectoralis major. The accompanying movement of the scapula is by the pectoralis minor, rhomboids, and third part of the trapezius.

There is usually considerable rigidity of trunk in this movement, with the erector spinae, abdominals, intercostals, and diaphragm contributing to this rigidity. This is partly to give a firm origin so as to permit maximum effort from the shoulder muscles, partly to counteract the tendency toward hyperextension of the spine by the latissimus and the leg swing which would result from this hyperextension.

If the performer returns to the starting position, it is done by a more or less gradual relaxation of the same elbow and shoulder muscles that pulled him up.

Mechanical Analysis. There is a summation of forces in the two muscle groups, and each movement indirectly produces the other. This usually gives sufficient force to lift the weight. Resting inertia at the start sometimes makes it impossible to get started. Also, in this position, the muscles are fully stretched and their angle of application to the lever is extremely small. If there is any means of getting a slight push or boost it gives a little upward momentum, and relieves the muscles of the extreme tension. As the arms begin to flex, the angle of pull improves. Flexion of the elbow further promotes extension in the shoulder because of the tension on the long head of the triceps.

The weight should be kept as nearly under the bar as possible so that the lift will be vertical.

This position of the hands is preferable to one with palms away from the face because it facilitates action of the muscles. With palms turned away, the biceps tendon is wrapped around the radius, where it is less effective, and strong action tends to supinate the forearm. Also, in that position, the distance between origin and insertion of the pronator teres is considerably shortened, and hence that muscle reaches a state of insufficiency sooner. Rasch[4] conducted a study and reported others that had been done to determine the position of the hand for the strongest elbow flexion. The supinated position was consistently much better than the pronated one but a little poorer than a "mid-position." The latter position is not possible on the straight bar used for chinning. If the palms are turned away from the face, the hands must be spread wider on the bar. Movement in the shoulder is then adduction (nearly in the frontal plane) rather than extension (in the sagittal plane).

BALANCE

Couple or group balancing stunts are quite common. Rather than discuss any one, we shall consider the principles common to this type of stunt. First, the area of support should be broad, particularly if the top performer is to be high or is using much angular momentum to get into position. The only exception necessary is in events where the base must be in a position to move. The top performer should be so placed as to keep the weight line near the center of support.

When the base is on his back, the top performer must often be lifted by leg extension. The top should develop momentum himself so that the base does not have to do all the work. The base should time the extension so there is no great effort until near the point of extension. The movement should be rather quick, continuous, and complete. The top is easier to hold if the knees of the base are straight. The moment of rotation is too great if knees are partially flexed. Weight is easier to hold if the legs of the base are in a vertical position, except when he is standing; then the legs may be spread to widen the area of support. If the knees are kept straight, the legs may offer restraint and fairly easy support.

When the base is on hands and knees, the weight of the top should be on either the hips or the shoulders, if possible. This puts the weight directly over the points of support instead of causing hyperextension of the spine. Also, weight can be borne more comfortably on the flat spinous processes of the dorsal region or the short ones of the sacrum, than on the sharp, straight ones of the lumbar region. If weight must be borne through the central part of the trunk, as in the chest balance, the spine should be held straight and firm by the abdominals. If it is allowed to sag with the weight of the top performer, it is very difficult to straighten again while supporting the weight. Furthermore, lumbosacral and sacroiliac strains may occur.

REBOUND TUMBLING

Rebound tumbling includes all of that gymnastic work done on the trampoline type of equipment. It may be the large unit on which the performer does his stunt or series of tumbling stunts, or a small unit which he uses more as a take-off for mounting or vaulting other equipment or for performing over a mat. It is primarily work in the large unit which will be considered here, although much of what is said will apply to both types.

There are certain differences between tumbling on the trampoline and on a mat or the floor. These provide both the values and the problems derived from use of the trampoline.

Probably the most obvious difference is the fact that one may make landings which would be impossible in any other situation, even on entering the water from diving. This is because the downward drop of the performer is decelerated by the slow stretching of the "springs" of the trampoline. The body lands firmly on the bed, the trampoline provides the give which the ground tumbler would have to provide for himself by a give in his own body.

The second difference is that the performer has greater height from his point of take-off than he has from projecting himself into the air by his own efforts only. The concomitant of this greater height is the longer period of time in which to execute the stunt. This is really the significant point in making possible certain types of stunts. It is this period of flight in the air that is referred to by the subtitle of one text, *Two Seconds of Freedom*.[2] This increase in height and time of flight is a result of the recoil of the "springs." They have a limited range of action, but they lift the body for a period of time sufficient to accelerate it upward and project it into the air. In general the harder one drops on the bed and the further it is depressed, the longer the period of time in which it lifts and the higher the performer goes. Thus successive bounces on the trampoline may become higher and higher because the gradually increasing height contributes to a still greater height for the next lift.

And finally, there are very real differences in the feeling of effort put into a lift, in the reduced feeling of counterforce from the bed as one extends the feet for a lift, and in the feeling of more or less suspension because one is in the air longer than from the usual jump. Not only is there a changing kinesthetic sensation of performance, but for many new to the trampoline there are a thrill, an exhilaration, and a motivation which have both advantage and hazard.

The techniques of landing on the bed constitute the basis for coming down out of a stunt and also the means of transition from one stunt to another. There are seven of these landings which are usually considered to be different from the others in terms of contact surface and mechanics of rebound. These will each be discussed briefly. However, there are certain points that are applicable to all of them, and they will be discussed first.

1. The direction in which the performer goes into the air depends upon where his weight is with respect to his base as the bed lifts him. If the body is erect and the weight directly over the feet on a foot (or knee on a knee drop), then the body will go up straight in the air and come down again at essentially the same position. If it is off center with respect to the feet the performer will "travel" on the bed. For example, leaning forward a little or even dropping the head forward to look at the landing shifts the weight forward enough to project him forward into what may be not even a hairpin flight. Or landing with the weight mostly on one foot gives a lateral flight. Similar results are observed on other types of landings.

2. All parts of the body making contact on the bed must touch simultaneously. Otherwise the timing for the stretch and recoil of the trampoline is altered and the lift is ineffective. Very slight variations make a difference.

3. The body must be firm on the landing in order to get adequate

FIGURE 90: Trampolining
a—foot drop showing depression of the bed; b—erect elevation on
rebound

depression of the bed. Flexing at the knees or hips serves as the give
which the jumper ordinarily uses in landing on the ground. Flexion on
the trampoline does not properly "prime" the trampoline, that is, it fails
to stretch the trampoline springs continuously for a smooh recoil.

4. The performer must anticipate what he is to do in the air and initiate
turns during the latter part of the lift, just before being projected into the
air. This makes it possible to get counterforce from the base but it must
be done with weight still centered to prevent undue traveling.

Landings

The landing on the *feet* is the simplest. This is essentially the same
landing one would make in coming down from a vertical jump except
that the body is held firmly erect with the feet in position for a "flat-
footed" contact. The feet should be spread apart a little, not to exceed

the width of the hips. The weight must be centered for a straight lift. The height can be increased by extension of the ankles on the take-off and by lifting with the arms at the same time. The chief errors for the beginner are (1) bending the knees, which is the technique for "killing" the rebound; (2) shifting the weight off center; (3) landing with the feet together, thus making too small a base for easy balance.

The *knee* landing is very much the same in that the body is erect over the knees and hips are kept firm. The difference is in the larger base made by the lower leg and extended foot. This entire surface must contact simultaneously; an incompletely extended ankle or a leg which is allowed to drop will have a deceleration effect and kill the rebound. The only additional help that may be obtained is from the arm lift. The lower legs must be snapped down into extension while in the air so that the performer does not shift backward to get over the feet.

The *four-point* landing is on the same base as for the knee drop, plus the hands. It is the same as the so-called knee-hand position on the ground. The hips must be directly over the knee contact and the shoulder joint directly over the heel of the hand. Hands and legs must contact simultaneously. Most of the lift comes from precise timing of the landing, but some push can be obtained from the hands which is particularly helpful in returning to the erect position.

The *seat* drop should be a good erect, long-sitting position with the hands placed on the bed beside or slightly behind the hips. The hands are used to get an additional push for the lift. The surface from hips to heels must contact at exactly the same time. The most common error is in not holding the legs high enough. This leg position requires strong hip flexors and abdominals. The lever is long and therefore hard to lift and hold in this position. If the performer is unable to lift the legs straight he doubtless can get them up by flexing them into the tuck position and then extending them while on the drop, just in time for the landing. This technique may make it possible for him to perform the stunt, but it is not considered good form and he should be encouraged to develop adequate strength before he practices this technique sufficiently to build up a poor habit of executing the drop. During the rebound the legs must be dropped quickly for the next landing or the performer tends to lean forward to get over the feet, resulting in traveling.

The *back* drop is one which is a psychological hazard for many beginners because they cannot watch the mat or the usual point of focus which is set up for other landings. On the rise from the feet the body is inclined backward slightly, the legs are flexed and lifted forcibly which makes the body rotate on a transverse axis. The landing is made on the upper back while the body is kept flexed and the head forward. The rebound lifts the performer, and the legs are snapped down again which helps to achieve the reverse rotation. The feet should land where they were for the initial lift.

The *hand* landing is essentially a handstand, but the lift of the tramp is used to help get the feet into the air, and the push from the hands is helpful in reversing to the feet. As in the handstand, the hyperextension of the neck serves as a brake against forward rotation.

The *front* drop is simply a prone lying position with the head lifted and forearms contacting the bed just outside the shoulder line. Again the same clues to successful execution are simultaneous contact of all parts, rigid body position, and a press with the hands on the rebound.

These landings are used to project the body into the air so that other stunts may be done during the flight. These stunts are usually a rotation on the long axis of the body or a front or back somersault which involves rotation on a transverse axis, or a combination of both. The performer is then faced with the problem of inertia and forced to a solution through putting the body in a compact position around the axis or through getting more height to have time for the turns in more nearly a lay-out position. Trampolining becomes an individual matter of building a sequence of landings and intervening stunts which fit together continuously and show adaptation to individual abilities and build, and demonstrate some originality on the part of the performer.

Even small amounts of work on the trampoline have been demonstrated to yield increments in ankle strength and flexibility because of the repeated use of the foot in full extension. It also provides opportunity to demonstrate very clearly the components of force, principles of balance, moment of inertia, and other principles of mechanics. Because of the difference in sensations of movement, it can be used to teach concentration on the kinesthetic feelings of many different movements.

Maintenance of safety comes from practicing certain safety precautions and from following proper teaching progression. Under the former are such points as supervision of all performers, adequate numbers of competent spotters, instruction on spotting techniques and alertness of spotters when on duty, requirement that all performers attempt to stay on the center spot and kill the rebound when grossly off center rather than trying to rebound back, and short turns during practice to avoid undue fatigue and resultant danger of injuries.

Certain points on progression are significant here. The first thing the beginner should learn is to "kill" the spring, even before learning the techniques of really getting up and of using the feet. The knee bend serves to lower most of the body mass slowly onto the tramp and therefore to practically eliminate the rebound. A point of focus should be set up on the end of the trampoline to prevent dropping of the head to see the position on the mat and at the same time to provide a point of reference to help minimize traveling. This point of focus is built into the performance of every landing and stunt learned. The principles behind successful execution should be taught along with the actual techniques. Sufficient practice should be obtained on each of the successive stages so that the skills are really learned and kinesthetic control is established.

Variety can be used in practicing on the fundamental skills so that control is achieved. The teacher should reckon on the time spent on the tramp by the individual student rather than the number of lessons in which students have been on the trampoline. In the average class, each student is probably on the trampoline one to two minutes twice a week or less. In ten weeks time this is only ten to twenty minutes of practice. Probably in no complex skill can the learner arrive at an advanced level of performance with that amount of practice. Too many trampoline teachers have brought on injuries and disfavor for the program because they fail to plan a slow, developmental progression, and they rush the class along in an attempt to arrive at the showmanship stage at the earliest possible moment.

REFERENCES

1. Gustafson, William Frank, *A Mechanical Analysis of Selected Gymnastics on the Horizontal Bar, Parallel Bars, Side Horse, Still Rings, and Swinging Rings*, Microcard PE219, 1955.
2. Ladue, Frank, and Norman, James, *Two Seconds of Freedom: This Is Trampolining*, Cedar Rapids, Iowa, Nissen Trampoline Co., 1954.
3. Loken, Newton C., and Willoughby, Robert J., *Complete Book of Gymnastics*, Englewood Cliffs, New Jersey, Prentice-Hall, Inc., 1959.
4. Rasch, Philip J., Effect of Position of Forearm on Strength of Elbow Flexors, *Research Quarterly*, 27, 1956, p. 333.

CHAPTER 19

Selected Activities in Track and Field

THE TRACK AND FIELD EVENTS are forms of running, throwing, or jumping. The basic forms of these fundamental activities have been discussed in a previous chapter. However, since many of these events are adaptations in form, they will be discussed individually here to point out these changes.

HURDLES

The hurdle race is a variation of the sprint. The difference is due to the placement of the obstacles at regular intervals in the course. The hurdler aims to take these in his regular stride, making the necessary adaptation on the proper step so as to clear the hurdle. This adapted step is the only one to be considered here and will merely be compared with the normal one.

Description. In the ordinary run the leg is swung forward with the lower leg high but the knee is not lifted very much. The foot is brought quickly into contact for driving force. In order to clear the hurdle the whole leg must be lifted higher by flexion at the hip. The leading foot points over the hurdle as the other leg gives a powerful upward and forward drive. This lifts the total body some and projects it into the air for a longer period of time.

The body is inclined forward about in line with the rear leg. The arms are used vigorously in opposition to the legs. When the driving leg loses contact with the ground it is quickly flexed and abducted with the knee also flexed. In this position of suspension in the air the body sails over the hurdle. The forward leg is then snapped down quickly beyond the hurdle ready to start the next step.

Muscular Analysis. Flexion at the hip of the leading leg is secured almost to its full extent by the iliopsoas, rectus femoris, pectineus, and tensor fasciae latae. They also help to draw the trunk forward, assisted by the abdominals which give fixation to the pelvis and thus make the hip flexors more effective on the leg. With the spine extended, the abdominal muscles incline the trunk forward for its characteristic position above the hurdle. The vasti assist the rectus in extending the knee.

The drive in the rear leg comes as a strong extension at all articulations. The flexion of the trunk forward is sufficient to call the gluteus maximus into strong action in hip extension.

The forward arm swing is produced by the anterior deltoid, upper pectoralis major, biceps, and coracobrachialis. The elbow is flexed very slightly by the brachialis anticus, assisted by the biceps and pronator teres depending upon whether the hand is partially or fully pronated. The rear arm is usually flexed in the same way at the elbow and is swung back at the shoulder by the posterior deltoid, teres major, teres minor, and infraspinatus.

The rear leg is drawn up quickly with abduction by the gluteus medius and minimus and the tensor fasciae latae. It is flexed by the iliopsoas and pectineus, which also rotate the leg outward. The small rotator group assists in this rotation. The knee is flexed principally by tension on the hamstrings and inertia of the lower leg. Thus the leg passes over the hurdle in almost a horizontal position.

The forward leg starts extension at the hip as soon as the center of weight nears the hurdle. This is hamstring action. The knee and ankle are held extended to reach downward and the extensors relax very slightly just at the moment of contact in order to avoid jar. Contact is made when the weight is directly over the foot; the leg is ready to start immediately into its drive. The steps then return to a normal stride until the next hurdle is reached.

Mechanical Analysis. Maximum speed can be attained only when the hurdle is taken in regular stride and with the minimum of vertical lift. Otherwise force is wasted and the change in direction interferes with the forward momentum. This is easier on the low hurdle than it is on the high one. But in either case the stride must be regular.

The push-off must be harder than in the run in order to insure a longer period of float. The push-off is at considerable distance from the hurdle and directed forward to give the greatest possible forward drive. Both legs are carried as near to the hurdle as possible in order to keep the weight low. The trunk is inclined forward to get it in line with the driving leg and to keep the weight low. The arm swing serves to improve the body position, aids balance, and reacts on the trunk to keep it aligned.

The downward motion of the front leg serves to get that foot more quickly into contact with the ground for driving. It makes contact in a vertical position and is ready to drive instead of being in a restraining forward reach. The first step after clearing is very much nearer the hurdle than was the take-off.

RUNNING BROAD JUMP

Description. The running broad jump starts with a fairly long, running approach. The take-off is from one foot; the jumper is running at top speed and his body is inclined slightly forward. In the trunk type of jump both legs are quickly flexed after the body goes into the air. They may be kept in that position until the jumper is ready for the landing. In the "run in the air" type of jump the legs continue a running movement while in the air. The arms are extended forward during this time. When the body starts downward, the legs are extended forward in line with the line of flight. The trunk is kept inclined forward. Just before landing the arms are brought forcefully down and back. Just as the feet make contact the ankles, knees and hips flex so that the fall continues in the same direction. Then the arms are brought forward again. From this point the jumper may either continue on forward to finish on all fours or may go into complete extension and a standing position.

Muscular Analysis. The take-off is a strong extension of the whole leg similar to that of the driving leg on a run. The whole foot is allowed contact with the take-off board, in contrast to the run, so that the ankle extensors work more effectively. The flexion of the opposite leg is merely an increase in the normal flexion which occurs in the swinging leg. The iliopsoas, pectineus, and tensor flex the hip, and the tension of the hamstrings causes knee flexion. The other leg is brought up quickly in the same fashion with movement initiated by the hip flexors, and the recoil and tension in the hamstrings cause the knee to bend.

If the legs are held in this position the burden of the work falls on the hip flexors. If the "run in the air" type of jump is used it is the same as the run, except that antagonistic action is used to check the range of the kick, particularly the hip flexors to check the rear drive.

The abdominal muscles fix the pelvis and draw the trunk forward. The erector spinae holds the upper spine extended so that the whole trunk is inclined forward instead of there being total flexion of the spine from abdominal contraction.

The arms are swung and held forward by the anterior deltoid, upper pectoralis, coracobrachialis, and biceps. This action of the biceps in such strong movements tends to make the elbow flex. Slight flexion is usually permitted but it is controlled by the triceps. The feeling of reaching forward with the arms results in an extended wrist, usually rigid. This calls for action of both the flexors and extensors of the wrist.

When the knees extend the hips must still remain flexed. The vasti support most of the weight of the lower leg, and the rectus femoris helps at both articulations. The ankles may be in their natural position and held firm as the heels point forward for the landing. In broad jumping done on mats in the gymnasium, the performer frequently lands first on the balls of the feet. This avoids some of the jar which would occur from a heel landing. It also adds a little distance, since the heels do not need to drop completely onto the mat.

Flexion of the legs on landing is made possible by relaxation of the extensors. The arms are carried back by the lower pectoralis, latissimus, and teres major, then they are suddenly checked and brought forward again by inertia and the anterior muscles listed above.

Mechanical Analysis. The run preceding the jump gives forward momentum to the jumper, thus helping to gain distance. It also gives a chance to get the body aligned for the forward and upward thrust of the driving leg, and makes use of the natural drive in the run. The take-off is made flat-footed, even though it does cause some jar. Because of the larger area of friction, there is less opportunity for slipping. This position also starts the take-off with the ankle more fully flexed, which makes possible stronger action of the ankle extensors and action over a longer range. There is a little give in the knee which reduces the jarring effect and also results in stronger action from the knee extensors.

The leg lift during flight serves to make the body more compact. This facilitates balance, reduces air resistance, and in the tuck type of jump allows for relaxation of extensors, and is a position of readiness for the reach which occurs just before landing. When the legs are kept in motion they are effective in adding distance to the jump only when the rear drive is strong enough and is checked suddenly enough so that the forward reaction on the trunk is appreciable. It may also add to the reach in landing. If this form is done incorrectly it may have no noticeable effect, it may change balance, or it may interfere with the landing and actually shorten the distance.

The position of the trunk is forward throughout, coinciding with the thrust of the take-off, keeping the center of gravity well in front of the hips, and ensuring that the weight will not drop behind the feet in the landing. The reaction of the leg lift helps to draw the trunk forward. The first forward position of the arms helps to hold the trunk forward. Their backward snap on landing is to get a forward reaction on the body, and their final forward swing is again to carry the weight forward and assist in the landing.

The angle of take-off is important. The upward component to the drive must be sufficient to keep the body in the air long enough to gain distance from the forward momentum attained. The line of flight is similar to that of any projectile aimed for a maximum distance. The rise is at approximately 20° to 25° with the horizontal. The highest position is about midway on the jump and the angle of descent is the same as that of the rise. The legs are extended forward in the line of descent so that maximum distance may be gained. As the landing is made, flexion of the legs permits the hips and the center of weight to continue in this same line until over the feet. If the hips are allowed to drop below this line of flight the jumper sits behind his heels and shortens the jump. If the hips are kept too high the feet are forced down and the jump is shortened.

All the other broad-jumping events are variations of this form, but follow the same principles except that the take-off is about 45°. The standing broad jump lacks the momentum of the run. It must secure the force by strong action of the leg extensors. Both legs are used. A good preparatory movement gives stronger action and increases the range through which force is applied, hence it increases momentum. The use of the arms is also important in pulling the body forward. The line of flight is very similar to that of the running jump. The body is leaning far forward at the time of the take-off and the toes give a strong backward thrust just before they leave the board. Flexion of the legs in the air pulls the trunk forward.

The problem presented in the running high jump is to combine the forward momentum with sufficient upward thrust to lift the body almost vertically and allow it to cross the bar while at the top of the flight. Too much forward momentum is a handicap, although, as the jumper gains height, the take-off is a little farther away from the bar. Another problem is to reduce the amount of work done by keeping the center of gravity as close to the bar as possible when it crosses over. This is the advantage of the various rolls over the scissors style of jump. In a roll the body is approximately parallel to the bar, in the scissors the trunk is more nearly vertical. The height of the jump is dependent upon leg drive, arm lift, and the success of the layout in crossing the bar.

DISCUS THROW

Description. The discus is held in the palm of the hand with the fingers spread and the last segment of each finger is bent over the edge of the discus. The performer stands with the left side in the direction the throw is to take, or with the back toward the direction of the throw, with most of the weight shifted back on the right foot. The right leg is usually flexed a little. The right arm is swung forward across the chest, elbow moderately flexed and the discus resting lightly on the upturned palm of the left hand at about shoulder level. The right arm is then swung backward and somewhat downward with the elbow extending. This may be repeated a time or two before the throw actually begins.

Then with the right arm in the rear position the weight is shifted to the left foot, the body pivots rapidly over the left foot, a step is taken on the right foot, then on the left. Each step permits a half turn or, if the start is to the rear of the circle, the first step makes a three-quarters turn. When the left foot is in place the second time, the left side of the body is toward the direction of the throw. The weight is shifted forcefully onto the left foot and the pivot continues as before. At this stage the right arm which has been trailing is whipped forward as before but at a little more of an angle. The release is made just above the level of the top of the shoulder. The fingers straighten and the discus spins off the fingers, sailing in almost a flat position, but rotating in a clockwise direction. The angle of flight is approximately 30°.

The follow-through is merely a continuation forward and upward of the right arm, and a checking of weight by drawing the left arm and leg backward as a step is taken on the right foot.

Muscular Analysis. The discus is held in the fingers by the flexors profoundus digitorum, sublimis digitorum, and flexor brevis pollicis. The forward arm swing requires action of the anterior deltoid, upper pectoralis major, and coracobrachialis. The biceps and brachialis anticus flex the arm with the pronator teres assisting and checking against supination. The backward movement results from the posterior deltoid, teres minor, and infraspinatus, and the elbow is straightened by the triceps.

The weight is pushed to the right by the extensors of the left leg. The extensors of the right prevent too much flexion, and the adductors and the lateral glutei maintain the balance over the one leg. The trunk is twisted slightly by the right erector spinae, quadratus lumborum, internal oblique, and left external oblique.

The pivot requires extension and external rotation of the right leg, while the left leg is flexed and rotated inward. Rotation of the trunk is to the left by the opposite set of muscles. This is accentuated by a backward swing of the left arm similar to that of the right but with the elbow partly flexed. The right leg is then brought forward and to the left as normally for a step. This also increases the rotation, and when it is placed on the ground, the right side of the body is toward the direction of the throw.

The same movement continues for another half turn, which brings the thrower around ready for the final delivery. The extension and external rotation of the right leg is stronger. The rotation of the trunk is stronger, and is accompanied by a little trunk flexion produced by the abdominal muscles. The right arm is whipped forward as before but at a higher plane, which requires more action of the deltoid, particularly of the anterior and middle deltoid. The forearm is held fully pronated by the two pronator muscles; and a snap of the wrist by the flexor and extensor carpi radialis with pressure of the second and third fingers gives the discus the final push.

Mechanical Analysis. The discus throw is merely a variation of the throw which has been described in Chapter 11. As in all throws for distance the first problem is to impart sufficient momentum to the object. The discus is heavier than most balls, and therefore requires more force. The complete turn preceding the throw is a means of increasing the speed of delivery. Its effectiveness is dependent, however, on smooth, precise execution. A jerky, poorly co-ordinated pivot is useless. The trailing of the right arm during the pivot makes possible a final period of acceleration. The final whip of the arm and snap of the wrist also serve to increase speed. Body rotation and leg drive add force to the throw. The discus, being held in the extended arm, travels very rapidly during the turn. The limitations of the circle on the official throw prevent any considerable momentum from forward movement. It must be derived almost entirely from the turn.

The second problem in all throwing events is to secure proper direction for the missile. In this case the arm swing gives ample time for this adjustment. The preparatory movement serves the usual purposes of warming-up, stretching the muscles as a stimulus for action, and increasing the arc and then the speed. It also aids in direction, making possible a long sweeping movement from the beginning through the follow-through.

The special problem in the discus throw is air resistance. If the forearm supinates or the wrist is hyperextended, the discus presents a flat surface to the line of flight and is held back. The discus offers the minimum resistance if it presents its narrow edge to the line of flight. Also a little rotation around its short axis causes the gyroscopic phenomenon which adds to the stability of the discus in flight. The tendency of the discus to "sail" makes it possible to throw it in a flatter arc than most distance throws are made. The vibrating or weaving discus gives almost as poor results as the broadside flight because of actual resistance to forward motion and the downward resistance on the upturning edge. Such a throw will have a rather sudden drop.

The other throwing events present similar problems. In the shot-put, the weight of the shot makes the acquisition of momentum of importance. The forward movement across the circle is used instead of the turn. The body is inclined backward farther to increase the distance through which the shot is moved. The rotation of the trunk is used to acquire speed. The shot must be kept close to the shoulder at the start, not only to satisfy the rules of competition but because its resistance would be more effective if operating at the end of a longer lever. The total force may be derived as a summation of the following movements: hop and step across the circle, trunk rotation and flexion, leg extension, arm extension forward and up past the shoulder, and wrist flexion. All movements must be vigorous; arm action must be supported by scapular movement, trunk rotation is facilitated by a fixation of points of origin of rotating muscles, a solid nonslippery surface is needed for maximum leg drive.

The javelin throw is most like the overhand throw. The javelin is carried lower than a ball would be, but it is in such a position that it can be whipped forward through a very similar path. The running approach is used to gain momentum, but again its effectiveness depends upon continuity of movement and co-ordination of run, pivot, and arm swing. The wrist snap is important in all these events at the time of delivery. The javelin, being relatively light, is whipped forward out of the hand after the rear foot is off the ground.

REFERENCES

1. Bresnahan, George T., and Tuttle, W. W., *Track and Field Athletics*, St. Louis, C. V. Mosby Co., 1937.
2. Fischer, A., and Merhautova, J., Electromyographic Manifestations of Individual Stages of Adapted Sports Technique, *Health and Fitness in the Modern World*, Chicago, Athletic Institute, 1961, p. 134.
3. Herman, George William, An Electromyographic Study of Selected Muscles Involved in the Shot Put, *Research Quarterly*, 33, 1962, p. 85.
4. Myers, Earl, and Hacker, Rich, *Track and Field*, Mankato, Minnesota, Creative Education Society, Inc., 1961.
5. Vannier, Maryhelen, and Poindexter, Hally Beth, *Individual and Team Sports for Girls and Women*, Philadelphia, W. B. Saunders Co., 1960.
6. Zubovich, Frank M., *A Descriptive Analysis of Championship Pole Vaulting*, Microcard PE282, 1956.

CHAPTER 20

Special Types of Locomotion

UNDER THE HEADING OF SPECIAL TYPES OF LOCOMOTION several modes of travel will be discussed. All involve locomotion by means of some equipment, but each involves activity and skill on the part of the individual. These are included because they frequently are taught as skills in physical education programs and used as recreational activities. The forms of travel to be included are skiing, ice skating, roller skating, canoeing, and bicycling.

SKIING

Skiing is of three different types—travel on the level, downhill skiing, and ski jumping. These are different in many respects and will be discussed separately.

Progress on level ground is a cross between ordinary walking and the four-footed type of walk. Most of the real drive is attained by the use of the sticks. One foot is advanced in a stepping position with the heel lifted slightly in order to keep the ski flat and sliding easily on the snow. The knee is flexed. The stick on the opposite side is moved forward. Then the entire body leans forward far enough to throw the weight in line with the forward foot and stick. This puts the stick in position for a drive, and the foot in position for support. The rear foot does not carry weight and the heel must be lifted slightly.

Weight over the rear foot or carried too far beyond the forward one causes slipping and falling. Likewise a lateral spread of the feet may cause unnecessary resistance, difficulty in controlling the direction of the skis, and occasionally may cause slipping.

The skis must be kept pointing straight ahead. This requires more fixation of the hips than in ordinary walking. Normally the stride is accompanied by inward rotation of the rear leg and outward rotation of the forward leg. In skiing the drive comes partially from the arms; and the rotation which serves to lengthen the reach comes above the hips, in the spine and shoulders. The depressors of the arms, the teres major, latissimus dorsi, and the posterior deltoid, furnish the drive. Scapular accompaniment is the work of the rhomboids, pectoralis minor, and the third part of the trapezius. The triceps holds the elbow extended.

The total step is characteristic of any walk on a slippery surface, i.e., the feet are kept low and slide along the surface. The skis distribute the weight over what would otherwise be a nonresistant surface and make progress possible. The adjustments to loss of balance are always to try to get the feet under the weight, to flex the legs so as to lower the weight, and to use the sticks for support.

If sticks are lacking, then the skier resorts to more of a skating type of progression. There is more knee action, the drive comes from leg extension, the weight is carried a little lower. Control of the skis is more difficult.

In downhill skiing, the fundamental position is the natural slight crouch. That means some flexion in hips, knees, and ankles, with the lower leg at a greater angle with the vertical than the trunk; the ankles are flexed more than either the knees or hips. The hips are kept forward under the trunk. The weight line is toward the front part of the feet. This requires perfect control by the leg extensors to prevent too great flexion, and to make frequent adjustments to changes in the surface and in balance. The spinal extensors keep the trunk aligned. The arms are carried rather close to the sides, sometimes slightly forward for balance. This is largely the work of the anterior deltoid if the arms are forward. The elbows are usually flexed a little from action of the biceps and brachialis anticus.

In order to keep the skis close together and toeing straight ahead the hip adductors must work constantly, as well as the inward and outward rotators which must maintain control.

Balance is easier in the crouch position than it is in an erect position. Adjustments to the surface and to pace are made by varying the amount of crouch and by shifting the weight. If the speed is suddenly increased, the skier leans forward more; if the speed is decreased, the weight is shifted back. Likewise, leaning to one side, and shifting the weight onto one foot causes the skier to turn in that direction. The turn becomes more pronounced if at the same time the other ski is pushed out and turned to toe inward. Gravity and momentum are carrying the skier downward. This position of the outer ski causes resistance from that side making the turn continue. The radius of such a turn is large.

The speed attained on steeper slopes makes possible the Christiana turn. In this turn the weight is kept low but shifted inward. If the turn is to the right, the weight is on the right side of each ski with the right ski leading a little. Thus the force of downward momentum is met by the counterforce of the snow directed in such a way that the downward momentum actually turns the skier sharply uphill.

The skier may stop completely by spreading both feet and toeing skis in. This requires action from the lateral gluteals and tensor to spread the legs and turn them inward. If the ski is kept flat on the snow the anterior and posterior tibial muscles must invert the foot. On a very slick surface if the skis are turned to the inner edge the foot is everted by the peroneus longus, brevis, and tertius. The ankles straighten out somewhat and the knees are flexed, which brings them a little closer together. The weight is spread equally between the two feet.

Ski jumping is largely a feat of balance and is definitely a skill for advanced performers only. Momentum is gained by coasting down the approach much as on any downhill slope. The feet should be together. Just before the take-off is reached the knees flex and the trunk is bent forward. The actual take-off is made by a jump forward. The knees having been bent, the usual leg extension for a jump is possible. At the same time as the jump is made the arms are swung forward to help with the lift and to get the weight forward. The position in the air is with the whole body straight but inclined sharply forward.

The skis are held on an angle pointing downward at the rear and controlled by action at the ankles. The landing is made on a surface still somewhat downhill. This continuation of the glide helps to avoid a jar. This is further prevented by leading slightly with one foot and with the knees partly relaxed. The take-off and landing have much in common with ordinary jumping but the forward momentum attained by the approach makes the balance much more difficult.

Special exercises for skiing are always designed to strengthen leg, back, and abdominal muscles, to stretch the ankle extensors, and to encourage relaxation. The latter two are the main problems. The average person finds it very difficult to bend the knees and keep the foot flat on the ground as is necessary in skiing. Any exercise which gives strong dorsal flexion of the foot, particularly when the weight is supported, stretches the gastrocnemius and soleus. Some of these exercises are discussed in Chapters 18 and 19. The student of gymnastics will know other equally valuable ones. Relaxation is necessary in order to adapt to change of surface or to fall easily when balance is impossible.

ICE SKATING

The first problem in ice skating is that of balance. Ice skating is performed on a surface with the minimum of friction and the skate presents a very small, highly polished surface. The result is practically no friction. The weight must be kept constantly over the feet.

Progress is made by sliding either forward or diagonally outward and forward over one skate while pushing with the other. The knees are flexed more or less during the glide; and the trunk is usually inclined forward, the amount increasing with the speed. To prevent the rear skate from slipping, it is turned outward and the weight thrown on the inner edge.

The force is applied at an angle with the line of progress and hence has both a forward and lateral component. However, the drive is effective in causing the skater to move forward on the supporting foot.

The "toeing out" position is assumed by outward rotation of the hip by action of the small outward rotators, the gluteus maximus if the trunk is forward, and to some extent the lateral gluteals. The latter also assist the extensors in the drive by abduction of the hip. The skate is turned to its inner edge by eversion of the foot by the peroneus longus and brevis. The foot and leg are held in this position while the extensors of the leg act, first at the knee and hip, and finally at the ankle, giving the final push-off from the toe of the runner.

The knee of the supporting leg is partly flexed, maintained by the extensors. If the course taken is fairly straight, the alignment of the supporting foot is almost straight ahead. Very slight outward rotation is necessary to counteract the tendency toward inward rotation produced by the strong rotatory action of the driving leg. If the supporting leg is rotated outward more definitely, the skater deviates from a straight course in the direction of the forward foot.

There is tension of all muscles at the hip joint in order to keep balance. There must also be fine adjustment between the evertors and invertors of the foot. The tendency for lateral movement at the ankle is extremely pronounced because of the position on the narrow blade. The ankle joint has more range going from normal to inversion than it has into eversion. Also the weight seems to be thrust more naturally to the outside of the foot. Therefore, considerable strength is required from the lateral muscles, the three peroneals.

When the rear leg finishes its drive it is brought up beside the other by flexion and adduction at the hip. Muscles acting at the hip are the pectineus, iliopsoas, adductors longus and magnus, and gracilis. The latter also assists the hamstrings in knee flexion. The tibialis anticus and peroneus tertius flex the foot. The leg is held in this slightly flexed position during the glide, and the other leg partially extends, reducing the amount of flexion necessary.

The transference onto a new step must be done smoothly. The swinging leg moves on forward slightly and the supporting leg flexes again. The trunk leans forward more. Arm action varies. The arms may move in the direction of the feet, i.e., right arm and foot forward, left arm and foot back. This is most common in a slow, gliding style of progression. This results in a rotation of the trunk, but it can be used in pulling the weight of the trunk forward over the foot. Sometimes the arms work in opposition to the legs, as in the walk. This is more frequent in fast skating. Skating is often done without any use of the arms. In this case the trunk is inclined forward all the time and sways more from side to side.

If skating is for speed, the trunk may be inclined almost to the horizontal in order to reduce wind resistance. The arms are seldom used except in very short sprints. The strides are short and fast. The swinging leg moves on forward for a new step instead of pausing beside the supporting leg for a glide.

Stopping or turning on skates is much the same as in skiing. The skates are presented broadside to the ice, turned on edge, and the weight is shifted. If both skates are turned to the inner edges and toeing in, the skater stops rather abruptly. The turn may be made either by sliding around right or left on the respective edges of the skate with weight to the inside of the curve, or by advancing the outside skate and rotating that leg inward, skating on the inner edge.

Figure skating is done on a different type of skate, the rocker. This increases the problem of balance but permits different techniques because of the shorter blade in contact with the ice. The fundamentals of figure skating may be summed up in the abilities to glide either forward or backward on either the inner or outer edge of the blade of either the right or left skate. This makes at least eight basic movements which may be combined in various forms and sequences. Each is primarily a problem of weight control and differs considerably in form and in difficulty. The supporting knee is almost invariably flexed to lower the weight.

When the outer edge is being used, there is strong action of the tibialis anticus and posticus. The total weight of the body must be shifted to the outside. If the weight is forward the gastrocnemius and soleus support it, if it is backward the tibialis anticus and peroneus tertius must support it. Turning is the result of body lean and of twisting the trunk for a shoulder lead with only the very minimum of outward rotation at the hip. Balance is further controlled by the arm and free leg. For instance, the free leg is carried forward if the weight is forward and backward if the weight is back.

When skating on the inner edge, the skater must secure strong action of the evertors and the peroneals. The weight is controlled anteroposteriorly as before. Arm and shoulder action is antagonistic to leg action. This means a shoulder lead on a turn and better control of weight.

When the weight is carried in such a way that it is leading into the movement and the skate is turned so that the edge cuts the ice, slipping does not occur.

Safety in skating depends primarily on ability to fall properly if slipping does occur. The body should be relaxed, preferably in a flexed position, when going down. Flexion not only allows for more give when landing, but usually means a shorter drop and less momentum acquired in the fall. Landing should be made on the padded muscular part of the thigh rather than straight on the ischii and coccyx. Also if the body is turning when it falls, this will result in more or less of a roll, which aborbs some of the momentum and is less dangerous than a straight drop and rebound.

Tenseness causes jarring of the whole body and tension of muscles may sometimes cause fractures. Reaching with a stiff arm to break the fall is particularly hazardous. The sudden counterforce of the ice against downward momentum and inertia would ordinarily cause a falling object to bounce. In this case it is more apt to cause injury at one of the weak points, normally the wrist or shoulder.

ROLLER SKATING

The problem of balance on roller skates is much more simple than on ice skates. The supporting surface of each skate is larger than that of the ice skate. Also the skate can move only in an anteroposterior direction. This eliminates the danger of lateral loss of balance and the necessity for lateral checks on the foot and the ankle.

The momentum in straight skating is gained in much the same way as in ice skating. While the skater rides on one skate the other leg is used for pushing. The push cannot be straight because the wheels turn and the reaction is lost. Therefore some outward rotation at the hip is necessary. The timing is similar to that of walking, i.e., the swinging leg is brought forward and takes the weight as the other leg goes into the driving phase. The period of single support may be prolonged if the skater wishes to glide.

Just as the free leg reaches the floor ahead, the rear leg is rotated outward at the hips. This causes the skate to curve outward till it is almost at right angles to the line of progress. In this position the leg is extended and abducted, giving the driving power. As in ice skating, the drive has both a forward and lateral component but the effect of both is transformed into forward motion on the skate. The front leg is often flexed slightly at this stage but is extended again during the glide. There is less knee flexion during support than there is in either skiing or ice skating. Hence, the quadriceps muscles are used much less. If the knees are flexed and the trunk is inclined forward some as is done in fast skating, the gluteus maximus helps on the outward rotation and extension of the hip. In erect, easy gliding, this muscle does not work.

The arm action is usually in opposition to that of the feet, i.e., the left arm goes forward with the right foot, while the right arm and left foot are back. In slow skating the arms are used easily for balance and the trunk is often held steady with no rotation. In fast skating the arms help to pull the weight forward and trunk movement is more pronounced.

Turning may be accomplished in various ways, the shifting of weight being the important item. It may be done as a skating turn, in which the skater leans toward the inside during the glide, rotates the leg outward on the inside of the curve, and rotates the other leg inward as it is placed forward for a new step. A shorter turn may be made if this foot is placed across the gliding one; and the latter is quickly removed. Or the skater may coast on the inside leg, lean inward, and hold the free leg forward and across the other to carry the weight inward.

A complete reversal of direction can be made by rotating one leg almost completely outward as the weight is taken on that foot. The skater starts moving diagonally sideward. The other leg is rotated outward and placed with the heel beside that of the first foot. The weight is shifted so it is carried by both feet. This results in the skater turning in a small circle, leading with the toes of one foot and trailing with the toes of the other. The diameter of this circle is about equal to the distance between the feet. The turn may be facilitated by swinging both arms in the direction of the turn; though the turn will be faster if the arms are swung around close to the body than if they are fully abducted. It is for the same reason that the ice skater starts a spin with the arms abducted and then lowers them gradually as he begins to lose momentum.

This turn may be used for stopping, as the forward momentum is used up in the spin. The arms are then abducted during the turn in order to decrease the speed of the movement. Also, the "pigeon-toes" stop may be employed as in skiing or ice skating. The latter requires strong inward rotation of the hips, backward tension on the legs by the extensors and a shifting backward of the body weight.

Fancy skating is done by employing similar use of the weight and changes in position of the skates. Backward skating is similar to progress forward. The drive is made by rotating the leg inward as it is extended and abducted. This results in a backward, outward stroke with the skate on a definite angle.

Strong muscular action is limited almost entirely to the legs. The hip extensors and abductors and the flexors and extensors of the ankle are used most. The hip flexors and adductors function on the swinging leg. The peroneal muscles and intrinsic muscles of the feet get very little action, in contrast with their activity in ice skating.

CANOEING

Canoeing is more definitely a form of transportation in a vehicle than any of the other forms of travel discussed so far. However, it does involve some physical activity. It also is a common sport and one which physical education teachers are usually expected to be able to teach. It is included, therefore, in this chapter .

Description. The paddling position is a kneeling one with the hips resting against a thwart or seat rather than on the heels. The trunk is kept straight and fairly erect throughout the stroke. When paddling on the right side, the fingers and thumb of the right hand are around the handle just above the blade. The fingers of the left hand are flexed over the top of the grip.

The start of the straight stroke is made with the arms extended easily forward along the side of the canoe. The left hand is directly above the right, which means the paddle is in a vertical position. The arms are brought down so that the paddle dips straight down into the water. The stroke is made by pushing with the left arm on the top of the paddle at the same time that the right arm draws the paddle to the rear. When the paddle reaches approximately the plane of the hip and shoulder it is cut up sharply out of the water by drawing the top of the paddle directly across the front of the body.

The recovery starts with the lifting of the blade from the water. It is now in approximately a horizontal position. The left wrist is adducted so that the back of the blade is now facing directly up. The arms are extended forward and the left lifted up and across the body so that the

FIGURE 91: Paddling positions
Stern in foreground ready to start a straight away stroke. Other
paddlers doing draw stroke.

blade is again in a vertical position and ready to dip down for the stroke.

The arm action will vary slightly with the various strokes as the line of pull and the angle of the blade vary. The above description is the basic form.

Musclar Analysis. The paddle is gripped by the flexors longus digitorum, sublimis digitorum and flexor longus pollicis. The adductor pollicis of the left hand is also used to hold the base of the thumb firmly on the back of the grip. The paddle is lifted into the starting position by the middle and anterior deltoids. On the left the upper pectoralis major and coracobrachialis assist. Upward rotation and abduction of the scapula are very pronounced on the left side and require strong action of the serratus anterior. The elbows are in an easy extended position, with very little action from the triceps, particularly on the right arm where the position of the hand is such that the weight tends to extend it. The left triceps is more active, especially if the straight-arm syle of paddling is used.

The dip is started by allowing the deltoid to relax partially. It is continuous with the draw, which brings in the arm depressors. The teres major and latissimus dorsi are responsible for right arm action. In the left arm the pectoralis major and coracobrachialis pull the arm firmly across the chest and slightly downward. Both elbows are locked in extension by the triceps as soon as the stroke starts.

The abdominals and iliopsoas pull the trunk forward a little just as the dip is made and the stroke starts. This helps to lengthen the reach slightly, to drop the blade, and to make the body weight effective in the push on the upper end of the paddle. The erector spinae and oblique extensors control the extent of this trunk inclination and draw it back to the erect position, assisted by the hamstrings in hip extension. There is a slight rotation of the trunk to the right due to dominance of the right extensors and action of the laissimus dorsi.

During the draw the right scapula is strongly adducted by the rhomboids and trapezius. The left scapula is held abducted by the upper serratus anterior.

The cut out of the water is made by the flexion of the left elbow, if the bent-arm form is used. The left deltoid, teres minor, and infraspinatus also draw the left humerus sideward. The right arm is lifted a little by the deltoid so that the paddle is entirely above the level of the gunwales. The left wrist is adducted or flexed downward by the flexor carpi ulnaris and extensor carpi ulnaris.

The reach is then made by arm elevation as previously described.

Mechanical Analysis. Progress in the canoe is the result of the counterforce of the water, just as in swimming, and in the same way that progress in walking is due to the counterforce of the ground. The paddle must then be put into the water in such a way that the counterforce is in the desired direction. In paddling straight ahead the blade is carried straight back and the canoe is thrust straight forward. However, paddling must be done on one side; and the canoe moves straight provided there are both a bow and a stern paddler, and provided their strokes match each other in force.

The canoe is guided by changing the direction in which the blade applies force. This may be done by changing the direction in which the paddle is moved through the water or to some extent by changing the angle of the blade on an otherwise straight stroke. For example, a diagonal stroke may be made bringing the paddle back and away from the canoe and the effect will be to push the canoe slightly forward and away from the paddle. The same effect may be secured, though the

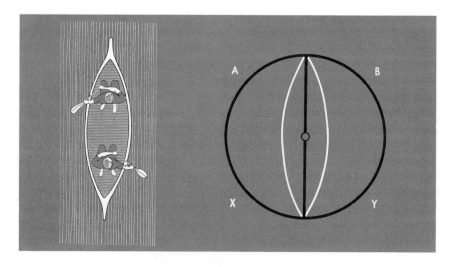

FIGURE 92: Effect of strokes in stern
a–push over; b–draw

turning will be less pronounced, by bringing the paddle back with the blade turned out slightly and a mild outward pressure exerted against the water. This modification of the end of the stroke is frequently necessary in the stern when the canoe is traveling in a straight course. This is because paddling is done to one side of the canoe and the paddle follows the inward slope of the canoe; therefore each stroke tends to make the canoe rotate around its center of weight. The necessity for adjusting the stroke in the stern is more pronounced if the bow paddler has a little stronger stroke than the stern paddler.

The canoe turns around the weight center, which is also the center of the canoe when it is loaded with keel even. When there is only a stern paddler, the center of weight is shifted backward.

The blade produces maximum driving force only when it is in a vertical position. A long stroke carried far to the rear loses practically all driving power because of the angle of the paddle with the water surface. Such a position may be useful in guiding, with the paddle acting as a rudder. However, if speed is desired, or if the canoe is traveling against current or wind, force is necessary and the guiding must be done with the blade in an effective propelling position.

The balance of the canoe is very important. It has a more or less rounded bottom and tapering ends. Obviously all weight should be over the keel (or center line) or evenly distributed on each side of it. Un-

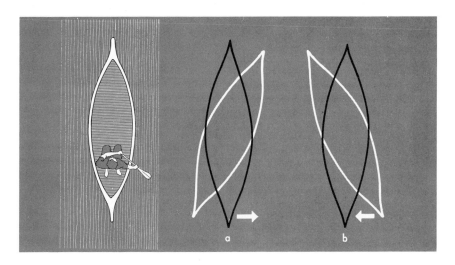

FIGURE 93: Diagram of paddling position

symmetrical loading makes the canoe very unstable. Also, sitting on seats or thwarts and standing in the canoe so raise the center of weight that the canoe is difficult to balance. If the weight is kept low and the paddle is not allowed to swing under the canoe on draw strokes, balance is not difficult.

The canoe is streamlined and, if not overloaded, draws very little water and hence offers very little resistance to progress. If the bow is heavily loaded, the weight center shifts forward, the bow dips deeper in the water, and steering becomes more difficult. If the stern is overloaded, the bow is lifted out of the water and is more subject to the effect of the wind.

Most of the steering of the canoe is done from the stern position. If the blade is forced through the water away from the canoe the stern end of the canoe will move in the opposite direction or away from the paddle. However, the canoe does not slide sideward as a whole, but rotates around its weight center. This means that the bow turns in the direction in which the paddle is moving (see Fig. 92). Likewise, when the blade is drawn toward the canoe, the stern moves in the opposite direction to the force, which means that it moves toward the paddle. The bow is then turning away from the side on which the stern paddle is being operated.

If an abrupt turn is to be made, the bow may assist. Of course, the same effect is produced on the bow end by the strokes, i.e., a draw toward the canoe brings the bow over toward the blade, and a push away from the canoe moves the bow away from the blade.

Confusion often arises in the mind of the paddler concerning steering. This is due to failure to account for the different effect on the total canoe of strokes taken in front and behind the center of the canoe or the axis of rotation, and on different sides of the canoe. The total problem of steering is illustrated in Figure 92 by means of a wheel. Points A and B represent the positions of the bow paddle; points X and Y are those for the stern paddle. The one pair of spokes in the wheel represents the keel or median line of the canoe. With paddles in positions A and Y, and the turn going to the left or counterclockwise, the keel must be drawn to positions A and Y by draw strokes. The same turn but with paddles in positions B and X would require a stroke with a push away as part or all of the stroke. The right turn, or clockwise turn, with paddles in A and Y requires the pushover stroke; but in positions B and X, the draw is used.

BICYCLING

Bicycling is another balancing activity. The cyclist, mounted on top of the bicycle, represents a distinctly topheavy unit. A base only one or two inches wide, rounded, and movable, creates a situation which defies all requisites of stability in a stationary position. It is only when forward momentum is secured that balance is possible. The unit is in this sense similar to the top, which can stand only so long as the rotatory velocity is sufficient to prevent lateral displacement of the center of gravity. The gyroscopic effect of the spinning wheels aids in keeping the bicycle upright. The bicyclist cannot depend entirely on forward momentum but must keep the gravital line fairly close to the wheel line. Greater forward momentum carries the bicycle forward and gives more time to readjust any lateral deviations in position. However, this same increased forward momentum causes the cyclist to fall harder if he does not successfully make the adjustment in balance.

Balance is maintained partly by the use of the front wheel of the bicycle. If the rider starts to fall to the right, the front wheel is turned slightly toward the right. At the same time the weight is shifted a little to the left. The result is that the bicycle tends to move under the center of weight of the rider and balance is recovered. If the fall starts to the left, the movement is reversed; the front wheel turns toward the left and the weight is moved slightly right. Care must be taken not to turn the wheel too far or to lean too far out.

The impetus furnished by the cyclist is obtained by full leg extension with the foot in contact with the pedal. The downward movement starts with leg extension from the vasti muscles; it is followed by hip extension from the hamstrings, and some ankle extension from the gastrocnemius and soleus. If the ball of the foot is placed on the pedal rather than the middle of the foot, ankle extension is more effective. The fixation of the foot on the pedal makes it possible for movement at any of the three joints to reinforce that at the adjacent joint. The result is considerable potential force. This may be increased by dropping the weight onto each foot as it starts downward. This does increase the problem of balance, however.

Flexion of the leg on the recovery is due to relaxation of the extensors. The foot then merely rides up with the pedal and passive flexion of the leg ensues.

The trunk is usually kept erect or inclined slightly forward to permit the hands to reach the handlebars. In racing, the cyclist inclines the trunk farther forward in order to reduce wind resistance and to secure stronger action of the hip extensors.

The pedals and their sprocket wheel are connected to the cogs on the rear wheel by the chain. The latter has a definite ratio of revolution to that of the pedal. The use of a bicycle with different gears makes it possible to pedal at the same rate but to get more revolutions of the rear wheel and hence more traction from the rear wheel. In most bicycles the driving and braking units are located in the rear wheel which puts them behind the center of weight of the machine. This is characteristic of the power in most machines, although braking power is usually distributed on cars today. Bicycles with hand brakes have both front and rear wheel brakes which work independently of each other. The cyclist must be careful to apply the rear brake first.

Turning is a fairly simple skill, if the turn is not made too sharply. If the turn is too sharp, forward momentum causes skidding of the front wheel and carries the rider on. The cyclist must lean to the inside of the curve to prevent centrifugal force from overbalancing him. The greater the speed the greater the curve should be, and the greater the lean that should be used.

The chief dangers in bicycling are falling sideward when speed is great enough to cause a hard impact and skidding after landing; or striking some obstacle with the front wheel so that the inertia of the rider carries him head first over the handlebars.

REFERENCES

1. Christensen, E. Hohwu and P. Höberg, *Physiology of Skiing, Arbeitsphysiologie,* 14, 1950, p. 292.
2. Elvedt, Ruth, *Canoeing A-Z,* Mount Holyoke College, 1946.
3. Miller, Donna Mae, and Ley, Katherine L., *Individual and Team Sports for Women,* Englewood Cliffs, N.J., Prentice-Hall, Inc., 1955.
4. Putnam, Harold, *The Dartmouth Book of Winter Sports,* New York, Thomas Yoscloft, Pub., 1939.

CHAPTER 21

Home and Occupational Activities

IT WAS POINTED OUT in an early chapter that the repertoire of man's activities is almost unlimited. In previous chapters the fundamental or basic skills have been analyzed. This analysis has also included the most common activities of the physical education program. There are still many types of activities which have not been considered, but the reader should now be able to make an analysis of any other movements in which he is interested. A few suggestions will be offered here on activities which constitute for many people daily life skills or occupational skills. Most of this discussion will be concerned with an understanding of the mechanics rather than a muscular analysis.

STAIR CLIMBING

Climbing stairs is a modification of ordinary walking. The work involved, or the energy necessary, is considerably greater than in straight walking because the total body weight must be lifted vertically upward the height of the step on each stride. This requires stronger contraction of the extensors of the legs.

The swinging leg must be flexed more than in the walk in order to place it on the next step. While it is being placed the rear leg has lifted the weight upward alone. However, as the forward leg begins to lift, the weight is very soon above the reach of the rear leg. The final drive comes from the big toe, and the opposite leg assumes the entire weight.

The trunk is inclined forward a little more on the stairs than in ordinary walking in order to keep the weight more nearly over the forward leg and to align the trunk with the rear driving leg. An extreme trunk flexion is sometimes seen. This is more frequently used by a person advanced in years or by one who is fatigued. This increased angle at the hip joint gives the gluteus maximus better opportunity to act. In this position the climber can drop the hands onto the knees or thighs and by pushing with them can use the arm depressors to assist the vasti in knee extension. The forward inclination of the trunk also makes it easier to use the hands for pulling on a hand rail if one is available along the stairs.

The foot is usually placed flat on the step, although the weight is apt to be forward toward the ball of the foot. The heel is raised as the weight shifts forward and upward, and the final contact is with the big toe. When the steps are deep, or the person is tired or is carrying a heavy load, the feet may be brought together on every step, the weight shifted, and the same foot used to lead out on each step. This is the typical form of stair climbing used by the small child after the crawling stage.

Early studies on locomotion showed lower physiological cost with the foot flat on the step rather than only the ball of the foot in contact. This evidence and experience indicate that the former position is more economical, but it is also associated with a slower rate of ascent.

Descending stairs is also a modification of the walk. Since it is a matter of controlling the rate at which gravity pulls the body down, the leg extensors perform most of the work just as they do in going up stairs.

As the swinging leg moves forward for the new step, its swing must be limited according to the width of the steps. The leg reaches for the next step with knee and ankle straight. The supporting leg is gradually flexing so that the body drops far enough for the free foot to make contact with the next step.

The ball of the foot is placed on the step first, but the ankle gives immediately to avoid jar and to help in lowering the weight. The heel may drop entirely to the step or it may be kept slightly elevated. This depends primarily upon the rate of descent. As the weight drops forward and the knee is flexed, the heel automatically rises again.

The trunk is kept more nearly upright in descent than in ascent. The weight is supported most of the time on the rear foot; almost as soon as the front foot takes the weight the rear one starts the forward swing. Therefore, the trunk is kept up and the weight shifted forward gradually.

Walking uphill or downhill shows about the same variations as stair climbing. The chief difference between the two activities is in the use of the feet on an inclined rather than a flat surface. The tension on the gastrocnemius and soleus is greater; the contacting surface is smaller and the possibilities of friction greatly reduced. The angle of the trunk is usually greater on the hill. Going down, the entire body may appear to be inclined slightly backward.

REACHING

Reaching is a very common performance and may be done from almost any position and in any direction. High reaching overhead is probably among the more difficult forms. In order to get the greatest reach the person rises on the balls of the feet; the feet are fairly close together or the weight is entirely on one foot. However, this is a very unstable position, and if any load is involved in the reaching, balance becomes almost impossible. The easiest position is with the feet spread a little in an anteroposterior direction. Then the body should be kept in straight alignment over that base.

Reaching forward to place or to obtain an object always necessitates flexion of the spine or hips. If the reach is long, and especially if the object is heavy, balance becomes very difficult. The work is done by the extensors of the spine, the extensors of the hip, and the elevators of the arm.

Reaching down or to the floor may be done either by bending the trunk forward or by flexing the legs. The first is not only more difficult for balance but is also more work. This is because of the length of the resistance arm, that is, the distance from the hips to the point at which the weight of the trunk, head, arms, and load, if any, is applying. The back extensors do practically all of the work in this case. If the legs are flexed instead of the back, balance is easier, the weight is kept more nearly centered over the base, and the leg extensors do the work. These muscles are stronger and the articulations less subject to strain than those of the back.

MISCELLANEOUS ACTIVITIES

Lifting is a work skill which can be costly in energy by the very nature of the activity. The foot-pounds of work depend upon the size of the load to be lifted, the distance through which it must be lifted, the range through which the body mass must be moved in doing the lifting, and the mechanical efficiency or lack thereof in performing the task. If the load can be divided it will be possible to perform the work with better distribution, little more cost, and greater safety. For example, if the farmer is buying 200 pounds of feed, it would be better to have it in 50-lb. sacks, or at most in 100-lb. units, so that they may be lifted easily without strain. The housewife at the supermarket should choose to have her groceries put into two or three small boxes rather than one large one, as she will doubtless have to move them herself when she gets home. Loads should be distributed to the two hands for counterbalance, rather than being all in one hand.

When lifting heavy loads, the back should be kept relatively straight and the knees should lift as much as possible. The load should be in as close as possible to the gravital line of the body without the load. The base of support should be broadened to help on the lift, and the body should lean away from the load to counterbalance it while carrying it. Movement through the range necessary from knee flexion to extension requires less work than bending the trunk forward and lifting the trunk and the load, transmitting its effect through the shoulders.

Much work can be planned ahead of time. Objects placed on the floor require too much bending. Energy will be saved if they are on shelves or platforms at convenient heights—on surfaces from which they can be pulled off without necessity of lifting them up over a side, as in taking something heavy from a box. Car manufacturers frequently err in designing car trunks. The high rear wall of the trunk may keep articles from falling out of the trunk if the lid comes open, but it is unnecessarily difficult in the much more frequent occasions when the spare tire or a suitcase must be lifted into or out of the trunk.

When one is trying to push on switches, gears, cranks, or similar devices it is desirable that the hand contact be somewhere between waist and shoulder level. If it is high enough that one can stand, this is desirable from the standpoint of force that can be applied and optimum position to delay fatigue in the upper extremity. Shoulder level or slightly below would be preferable in such a task, but effectiveness diminishes rapidly as the height of the handle goes above shoulder level. If the handle is low enough that one can sit, this will save energy but minimize the amount of force that can be applied in any single effort. The optimum level is, then, about waist level or slightly above so that the worker may lean into the action and use body weight. A handle or crank should be situated in line with the shoulder joint or a little outside that line rather than too nearly in the median line of the body. In some instances the worker can be taught to adjust his position accordingly; in other cases he must sit or stand at an exact spot in order to work various switches or controls, and the designer of the equipment is then responsible for such placement.

Foot pedals may be operated either with the foot as a functional unit or with the entire leg or total body entering into the action. For example, the pedal on the piano, the accelerator on the car, or the switch on the electric sewing machine is operated with foot action only. The heel should rest on some support. The body position should preferably be such that the ankle is in approximately normal position with respect to the lower leg. For example, the driver who sits too close to the wheel of the car not only finds the arm action cramped, but must sit with the lower leg so nearly vertical that the foot must be held in a dorsally flexed position on the accelerator. This may lead to an excessively "heavy" toe on the accelerator and certainly to fatigue on long drives. In all of these examples the range of action is small, and light contractions of the extrinsic extensors of the foot will give sufficient results.

When more force is needed the entire leg should be used, and the equipment usually provides for a greater range of action. For example, there is the pedal on the bicycle, the brake on the car, the rudder on the sled, or the foot pedals on the pipe organ. Each may have a light touch or a more vigorous one. Knee extension tends to be the most pronounced movement, though here too ankle extension may be used as well. In the case of the organ, toe or heel may be used for contact; the latter is then almost entirely dependent on leg rather than foot action. If this is an action which requires maximum strength, the angle at the knee should be about 120°. This is the position recommended by engineers[8] for both force and comfort. It has also long been recommended as the angle to be used in administering the leg extensor test in the strength and PFI batteries.

In pushing with either the upper or the lower extremity, the resistance should be far short of maximum if the task is to be prolonged. The lighter the resistance, the less fatigue will enter in. However, it should not be so light that errors will be made because of light contacts in moving a hand or foot past the lever. A long reach with the arm having to be held in readiness can increase the cost of the activity and bring on fatigue unnecessarily early.

Furniture for such tasks can either facilitate or inhibit the use of the arms or the legs. Chair arms can be very disturbing and also cause fatigue of the shoulders when the worker tries to hold the arms out away from them or to incline the trunk forward so that the arm rests will not be in the range of arm action. The chair or stool should provide some support for the back and promote erect sitting. If force is to be applied with the legs, there must be support provided posterior to the hips to help the worker brace for the action. The seat should not be so wide that the worker has to sit forward to use the legs and thereby forfeit the support for the back. Neither should the edge of the seat cut in on the posterior aspect of the thigh, which it will do if the seat is either too broad, too high, or placed too close to the pedals that the occupant is operating. Such pressure will interfere with circulation and help bring on fatigue. Likewise, a leg that must dangle without support and with little use will be handicapped with poor circulation.

The height of work tables, counters, and equipment panels will affect the mechanics of the worker and determine his efficiency. For example, the kitchen counters should be adjustable to the task to be done and to the height of the user. Designers of kitchen units have not yet come up with that convenience, though some contractors will install counters of different heights in different parts of a kitchen to help meet this problem. School desks are normally built so that they may be adjusted to the sitting height of the child, and the teacher should give attention to this detail. A proper fit will encourage good posture and work habits, provide better vision for work, and delay fatigue. Anyone who stands or sits behind a desk or work space will be affected with respect to posture, comfort, and fatigue. The college student who is annoyed by the lecturer who bends over the podium excessively should observe that this piece of classroom equipment does not fit the instructor. In most modern auditoriums the podium is adjustable so that every speaker may be comfortable and at ease. In fact modern engineering has provided the speaker's desk with a whole panel of buttons, and by pressing the right ones, the surface may be placed not only at the right height but at the desired angle and with the optimum illumination. This is but a minor example of the attempts of industry today to recognize the variations in human build and abilities and provide for the possibility of equal efficiency of all users. However, part of the job of education and of the supervisor in business and industry is to teach the principles of efficiency and how to make one's own adjustments in equipment.

Something like a long ladder must be carefully balanced if one person is to carry it. It would be easier for two, as this not only shares the weight but avoids the problem of an end suddenly overpowering the carrier by its length. If it is either a step ladder or an extension ladder it should be closed up and fastened closed before trying to carry it. A long ladder that is to be erected for work should be lifted into position while closed to its shortest length. Preferably there should be two persons raising it, one pushing from underneath, and the other lifting, after assuring that the ladder is anchored so it will not slip.

Ladders should be placed against a firm support and at an angle considerably less than 90° with the horizontal on which it is supported. When the worker is up on the ladder the weight center of the combined ladder and body mass should fall well inside the space between the foot of the ladder and the wall against which it rests. However, this is not an instance in which if some is good, more is better. Too much of an angle adds to the horizontal component of the weight, and the foot of the ladder is apt to slip with possibly disastrous results. Vertical or near vertical ladders should never be used unless they are fastened securely at the top.

The worker on the ladder should be extremely careful about leaning sideward from the ladder. His center of gravity must at all times remain within the bounds of contact made by the four corners of the ladder. Leaning too far to the side may cause the ladder to slip on its top support or to rotate on its two ends of the near side and so tip the man off. If reaching must be done at heights, a scaffolding type of structure providing horizontal platforms should be used. This permits the worker to move along as he works, avoids the tendency to overreach, and provides space over which to manipulate loads that he may need to have at this elevation.

It must be remembered that each and every one of the rungs in the ladder must be sufficiently strong to withstand the weight of the user plus any load he carries and the force which he exerts against it in extending his legs for mounting the ladder. The reader will recall the discussion in Chapter 14 on the force exerted on the ground in walking. In climbing the ladder all of this extensor force is exerted against the rung rather than being divided into components as in walking on a horizontal surface. To some extent the arms may do some of the lifting, but in actual situations they are seldom used effectively for this purpose. A flat rung is more comfortable than a round one since it presents a broader surface to the foot.

When working at a height, there should be something for the hand to guide by and support the worker if he slips or becomes overbalanced. This is even more important than in ordinary stair climbing. One has doubtless noted that in most public buildings signs are posted on the stairs asking patrons to use the hand rail. The ladder itself provides this support in climbing; sometimes the surface on which one works provides a hand grip. The platform for the window washer on tall buildings usually has an outside guard rail.

Focus on some close point is important in working at heights. There is always a certain amount of body sway whether standing still or walking. It is easier to control if a close point of reference is available. It is also psychologically disturbing for many persons to look downward where there is no visible support below them. This produces tension and interference with normal sensations of movement. It may interfere with balance; in extreme cases it may cause weakness, nausea, and disability to function normally in the basic skills of standing and walking. Also, when working at heights the weight should be kept as low as possible, standing rather than reaching, in some cases even sitting rather than standing.

There are many activities in which one is pushing equipment ahead of him. It may be the lawn mower, the plow in the garden, the scrubbing machine, the vacuum cleaner, or the mop. In each case the trunk should be kept straight and the forward lean should come from flexion at the hip joint. The lean should be no greater than necessary to push effectively. For example, the vacuum sweeper and the power mower usually take very little effort to keep them moving. The trunk will be fairly erect. The plow, on the other hand, may meet with considerable resistance. The stance will become wider, the rear leg on more of an angle and the trunk farther forward to be in line with the leg. In each case the worker should step forward with the equipment as it moves forward rather than lean off balance.

If one needs to get down to work at foot level as in gardening or scrubbing the floor, it is better to lower the weight than to bend over for any period of time. One may use a kneeling pad and get down on the knees with hips either up or resting on the heels. The four-point position, i.e., on hands and knees, may be restful. If the work takes some time, a variety of positions will be restful and minimize fatigue. This general principle applies in all work, even when simply standing for a long time. In that case shifting weight from one foot to another, permitting various amounts of body sway, changing height of shoe heel, and even thrusting the hips forward to ride the Y-ligament occasionally may reduce fatigue.

Hammering and chopping belong to the group of striking skills of which baseball batting, badminton, tennis, and golf represent variations. These two activities may also show gradation in force and hence differences in form. The lightest form of hammering is produced by wrist action only; the tool is lifted and gravity pulls it down. Wrist action may be used on the return to increase the momentum of the striking head. Increased force requires progressively elbow action, shoulder action, and trunk action. The trunk action may be merely flexion or may also involve rotation. Stronger action also requires a heavier tool, which gives greater momentum and greater effectiveness in overcoming the resistance of the point or surface being pounded. However, it requires greater force to lift the tool in the backswing.

Chopping is very similar but involves a sharp striking tool instead of a flat one. It is usually of the more vigorous type with trunk flexion and rotation in order to increase the range of action and to use the increased force.

Shoveling is a form of lifting that must be done at some distance from the body. The shovel is held by both hands, which are spread on the handle in order to control it accurately. The trunk must be inclined forward. The extensors of the back and hips do the work. The muscles of the arms and shoulders assist in the lifting and are responsible for the manipulation of the tool.

Wringing or twisting movements and the use of a screw driver are all forms of supination or pronation of the hand or rotation of the whole arm. Wringing a cloth taken out of water requires a grasp by the finger flexors. One hand is strongly supinated while the other is pronated in like manner. Manipulating a screw driver requires supination or pronation, depending upon whether the screw is going in or out. Also, the screw is helped in going in by pressure. This may be obtained by the extensors of the elbow as the trunk is held firm; or by holding the arm straight and allowing more or less of the weight of the trunk to rest on the tool; or by pulling the trunk forward by abdominal action and thus getting body weight into the movement. Twisting or turning the screw driver may be done in such a position that the turn is made by inward or outward rotation in the shoulder. Such a movement is usually less effective.

REFERENCES

1. Gagné, Robert M., and Fleishman, Edwin A., *Psychology and Human Performance*, New York, Holt, Rinehart and Winston, Inc., 1959, Ch. 8, Engineering Psychology.
2. King, Barry G., Measurements of Man for Making Machinery, *Journal of Physical Anthropology*, 6, 1948, p. 341.
3. Metheny, Eleanor, *Body Dynamics*, New York, McGraw-Hill Book Co., Inc., 1952, Ch. 9, Balanced Posture: Working.

4. McCormick, Ernest J., *Human Engineering*, New York, McGraw-Hill, Inc., 1957, Ch. 11, Human Motor Activities: Speed and Accuracy; Ch. 12, Human Motor Activities: Strength and Force; Ch. 13, Space Requirements; Ch. 14, Design and Arrangement of Controls; Ch. 15, Arrangement of Equipment; Ch. 16, Human Beings in Relation to Equipment.
5. Rasch, Philip J., Effect of Position of Forearm on Strength of Elbow Flexion, *Research Quarterly*, 27, October 1956, p. 333.
6. Vanderbie, Jan H., Metabolic Cost of Simulated Sled Pulling on the Treadmill, *Research Quarterly*, 27, March 1956, p. 111.
7. Wall, James, Tennis Elbow, *Industrial Medicine and Surgery*, 92, 1960, p. 264.
8. Woodson, Wesley E., *Human Engineering Guide for Equipment Designers*, Berkeley, University of California Press, 1960.

Part **IV**

APPLICATIONS FOR THE
PHYSICAL EDUCATOR

CHAPTER 22

Kinesthesis and Motor Performance

A SENSATION EXISTS as an impulse fed into an afferent neural path (sensory nerve) by means of an appropriate source of stimulation. It becomes meaningful through the interpretation and action that the organism makes to that impulse. The action is sometimes a reflex one, such as occurs if one puts the hand on something hot. The pain reflex is invariably a flexor-withdrawal response. The things one sees are reacted to according to what past experience has taught us. The traffic light tells by color whether to go or wait; the object coming at us tells us to move. We know ahead of the experience how a given food should taste or an object feel. If the new situation proves to be different, we can at least qualitatively differentiate.

Thus we live in our environment in terms of the things we perceive through our receptors and the interpretation the central nervous system puts on the inflow of impulses. Also, we each live with our own body in terms of sensations in its various parts. There may be a tickling in the throat, an itching of the skin, or a more generalized feeling such as hunger, fatigue, or nausea. In addition there are sensations of muscular effort or its release, of moving or stopping an arm, of being in balance or out of balance, of placing the feet firmly on the ground for support or having the knees buckle—all these and many others are experiences within the body which the central nervous system interprets and signals action consistent with past experiences.

Kinesthesis is the term given to the sensation by which one is aware of position and movement of the total body or its segments. It has been one of the hardest of the senses to study because it is entirely an internal sense, and much of the effect is in the form of reflex responses. Attempts at consciously feeling a movement are not always successful. In fact we are so accustomed to ignoring these sensations that popular terminology is largely lacking for the various aspects of kinesthetic function.

Occasionally one hears a beginner in some activity say, "That felt good that time" or "That felt easier." This recognition of movement sensations is one step in the learning process of discarding erroneous patterns and selecting the optimum one. On the other hand, the student being helped on posture is apt to say, "But that doesn't feel good," when told that an assumed posture is better than the habitual one. This is because the habitual one has been practiced for so long that anything else feels strange. These two incidents represent some of the situations arising out of kinesthesis when learning is taking place.

VALUES

The kinesthetic sensation provides us with several abilities which are crucial to our mode of living, yet they are completely unrecognized by the average person. When an individual is impaired in sight or hearing, it is immediately noted and he is taught compensations or given "aids." Yet if an equal degree of impairment occurred in the kinesthetic sense, he doubtless would be an invalid confined to bed. Furthermore, external devices corresponding to glasses or hearing aids cannot step up the sensitivity. Stevens[20] (p. 1185) says that kinesthesis "is the most important sensitivity man possesses." And it is not hard to agree with that judgment.

It is through the combined proprioceptive and labyrinthine stimulation that we are able to balance, i.e., to stand or sit upright, walk, work, and do the usual things of an ambulatory organism. The temporary disturbances in the vestibular apparatus are sufficient to make one reel, grasp for support, or even become nauseated. An experience as mild as turning a somersault can leave the novice momentarily unsteady when he tries to walk.

Balance is a part of our every act. There are times when the body position is a very precarious one, as walking on a narrow ledge, balancing on one foot or similar feats. Balance is achieved by precise control possible through kinesthetic information fed into the central nervous system and by integration of sensations and response. In some stunts such as walking on the hands or walking a tight rope the person acquires superb skill in balance. The average person exhibits far more balancing ability than he recognizes.

The ordinary skills of everyday living are executed largely through the "feeling" of the act. We don't have to look at our feet to put on our shoes and tie them. We find the zipper even though it is on our back, and then open and close it. We successfully balance food on the fork or in the spoon, and seldom spill a morsel, without looking at it on the way to our mouth. In fact conscious attention may actually interfere with the otherwise smooth functioning of the several muscles involved. We walk in a dark room where we have been before, successfully avoid bumping into furniture, and without hunting put our hand directly on the light switch. These are all acts we have performed a sufficient number of times that the nervous system has built a learned response into the succession of movements. We can refer to these as learned skills, even though we may not think of them as acts meriting practice.

There are certain skills that we may set out deliberately to learn. It may be knitting or typing, which are largely finger skills, or it may be a gross motor act such as rolling a bowling ball, standing on one's head, or hitting a golf ball, but we can set out deliberately to acquire the ability to perform it successfully (by standards of end result) and consistently. This is learning. Learning of a motor act is dependent upon several things: (1) ability to sense what forces one is exerting, (2) ability to detect differences in feeling from one trial to another, (3) ability to elicit a consistent pattern of performance. These are all largely kinesthetic perceptions. They may be facilitated by the cerebral cortex, but any amount of willing or planning could not produce a co-ordinated act without the kinesthetic sensation operating in its afferent-efferent interplay. Thus learning is an active process of the entire neuromotor mechanism.

Skills once learned are available for ready use. They are also long retained. It is in a sense like writing the "code for action" on a tape so that it can be played back at any time. One does not forget how to throw a ball, to skate, to swim, or to ride a bicycle, although these may have been childhood accomplishments not used in recent years. This permanent recording is in the nervous system with kinesthetic functions being basic.

We also learn to live safely in our environment not by deliberate control but by depending upon our sensation of movement. Knowing that steps are in front of us is all that is necessary to successfully go down them. We are sure enough of arm action that we dare reach for the handle of the pan over the hot burner without carefully watching the hand as it grasps the handle precisely where it should. We watch the oncoming car as we cross the street, and know whether our present rate of walking will get us out of the way in time. Poor perception leads to bumps, falls, and other injuries, but for the average person thousands of such responses are made accurately and safely for every stubbed finger, sprain, and fracture.

The sighted person does learn to co-ordinate visual and kinesthetic sensation and may even do so to the point where he is totally unaware of the kinesthetic cues. Yet one has only to watch the trained, blind person for a few minutes to realize that the blind substitutes other sensations for his visual deficiency. The kinesthetic sensation is one of the most important of his assets.

One of the instances when the person is most apt to be aware of kinesthetic sensations occurs when the learner or skilled performer watches another performing the familiar skills. The observer comes away from the swimming meet exhausted. This is because he has "participated with" the performer to the extent of marked changes in tonus. These changes follow the pattern of his own sequence of action in doing the strokes or dives if they are similar to those of the athlete. If they are different from those the swimmer is using the kinesthetic sensations of the observer are interrupted, and he no longer experiences muscular participation.

This ability to project oneself sense-wise with another is *empathy*. This means that though the situation outwardly appears to be exteroceptive (visual stimuli) it is in reality a combination. The exteroceptive stimuli are also activating the proprioceptive channels, and musclar response is high enough to be perceived by the person if attentive to the situation. It is also sufficient to produce the usual symptoms of fatigue.

The specific structure and function of the various receptors were presented in Chapter 6. Further discussion seems pertinent here.

The extensor or antigravity muscles of the body are activated by the sensations originating within their own structure. For example, the stretch reflex is exhibited in instances other than as a response to an isolated stimulus such as knee tapping. The moment of rotation at the successive joints produces enough stress within the muscle to activate it sufficiently to hold the segments aligned. The extensors are more generously supplied with muscle spindles than are other muscle groups, thus making them more sensitive to stretching of the muscle.

The plantar surface is a unique area of skin with its pacinian corpuscles. Light brushing of the surface usually produces a tickling sensation. However, body weight or other resistance transmitted through the foot evokes extension of the leg and increased pressure, rather than elimination of the sensation by withdrawal.

These receptors enable the person to understand and adjust to shifts of weight from one foot to another, or from one part of the foot to another. For example, raising the heels throws the weight forward, and the receptors in the metatarsal area indicate how far forward and whether it is in position for balance. It is this perception of weight placement which causes the reflex extensor action resulting in hopping to again achieve balance.

The extensors of the upper cervical area are also supplied with more spindles than other muscles. These make it possible to keep the head balanced, and they also elicit response from other parts of the body. It has long been known that the cat and the rabbit use the head position as a cue from which other body parts are oriented. Man also experiences a response to marked turning of the head; this response is not a product of acceleration. According to Hellebrandt,[7] a turn of the head to one side is associated with increased tension in the upper and lower extremities on the side to which the face is turned. It is a clue which may help to explain the frequency with which drivers deviate from their traffic lane into oncoming traffic or off the highway. A distraction within the car which causes the driver to turn the head markedly might cause an imbalance between the two hands on the wheel. Since so many of the activities that are taught in sports, dance, and aquatics emphasize the head lead or head position, it is possible that kinesthetic cues and adjustments may be more significant in the performance than merely the mechanical effects. At least it is an area in which research might be done.

In general, evidence points to the three-way control of the erect standing position. The proprioceptive sensations within the extensors and the related structures of joints and feet provide an important phase of control. No less important is information from the vestibular receptors and the eyes. Experience in trying to perform balance feats with eyes closed readily confirms the importance of the visual cues. All of this information is integrated, in part at least, in the cerebellum. Other brain areas may participate as further evidence may reveal.

The eyes also respond to stimuli from other receptors. The most obvious response is that known as *nystagmus*, which occurs in conjunction with rotation of the body and angular acceleration which stimulate the crista in the ampullae of the canals. As the person starts to spin, the eyes turn slowly in the opposite direction maintaining focus on some point as long as possible. They then turn quickly in the direction of motion to attempt to pick up a new point of fixation. If the body rotation continues the eyes will again move in reverse and again snap forward.

Skaters, dancers, and tumblers are taught to use this visual focus as a means of improving balance and also as a cue on space orientation. The latter will be discussed later. Beginners may have trouble keeping a focus, but to a greater extent they seem to have trouble keeping the eyes open. They unconsciously close the eyes, apparently trying to eliminate disturbing adjustments of eyes.

The semicircular canals respond to angular acceleration of the head providing it is above a certain amount. Guyton[5] (p. 578) quotes this threshold at 2° per second per second. It is probable that the stimulus is from the mechanical "pull" of the lymph moving over the crista. Some investigators doubt this method of stimulation, but few if any question the location of the receptors for angular acceleration. Since the three canals are in three planes at right angles to each other, acceleration is registered regardless of the plane in which it occurs. The stimulus in the canal appears to persist for some 15 to 20 seconds following the final obvious reason for stimulus, i.e., stopping or attainment of a constant velocity.

A very common accompaniment of such rotation is a feeling of dizziness. Probably most beginners in tumbling have experienced this. To the person affected, the room around him seems to move or sway. He feels as if he will fall, and his movements, even his walk, are in-co-ordinated for a few seconds. This effect can be minimized by standing erect and motionless, with the eyes fixed on a point straight ahead preferably at eye level. It takes only a few seconds to terminate the dizziness.

Practice on such events reduces the severity and duration of the dizziness for most persons. Apparently, the central nervous system "learns" to make adjustment to these stimuli rather than continuing a bombardment of sensations with diffused effector stimulation. Also, if the performer learns not to be emotional over the dizziness the central nervous system is able to act more promptly.

The receptors in the utricle play a somewhat different roll. The stimulus is a result of gravitational pull on the otoliths, creating varying degrees of pressure on the macula as the head assumes different positions. Again, though the exact process has not been clarified, the site of stimulation has been. The extensors are activated by changing positions of the head, so that weight is shifted and body parts aligned for equilibrium. The receptors in the ciliated cells of the macula are the locus of information for static balance and for linear acceleration. Linear movement may occur in either an anterior-posterior or a lateral plane, and the body adjusts to keep balance or a base under the body. Movement itself does not stimulate the macula but the acceleration-deceleration processes do.

In addition to acceleration in a horizontal plane, it may occur also in the vertical. It is in this direction that some persons experience difficulty. There are few persons who are not aware momentarily of the sudden drop of a high-speed elevator, or the quick upward thrust as it starts up. The latter is most apt to be felt in the lower extremity, causing the knee extensors to contract to resist flexion as the upward thrust on the feet opposes gravitational pull on the body. The sudden drop produces more widespread effect, usually including a sense of heaviness in the stomach and sometimes holding of breath momentarily.

The brief and single stimulation from the elevator ride has no particular effect on the individual other than the sensation and a tonic response which is relieved immediately. It is the starting and stopping of the elevator, not its steady progress, that create the stimulus. When acceleration is repeated, general malaise results. This is commonly referred to as *motion sickness*. As in many other things the name is not completely accurate, since it is acceleration and not the motion *per se* which is the causative factor. Ruch and Fulton[17] call it "acceleration sickness." It is most frequent in passengers on planes or ships, though it may occur when riding in cars, children's swings, roller-coasters, or other amusement rides.

Chinn and Smith[1] give an excellent summary of research and clinical evidence on cause and nature of motion sickness. There is apparently relaxation of the smooth muscles of the viscera as well as of skeletal muscles. The result is general weakness, which persists even after the source of the stimuli has been removed. Prolonged stimulation results in reverse peristalsis, retching and vomiting, and closing of the glottis which further interferes with breathing. The effect appears to be most pronounced when the vertical rise and fall are marked, when associated with "side slipping," when acceleration and deceleration are spaced, and when angular acceleration is also being experienced. It is also more pronounced when the head is erect than when the person is reclining.

While the situations in a physical education class produce much less severe reactions, there are some which need to be recognized. Reference was made previously to the dizziness resulting from rapid turning on either a transverse or a vertical axis. It is the beginner who is most affected. For example, in learning a somersault, he slowly gets more or less inverted, turns quickly, and then slows down to regain balance on his feet. Techniques for quieting the sensation were presented earlier. After he has learned the procedure for a safe somersault, his forward motion is acquired by a running approach, his movement is more nearly uniform, and therefore, there is less stimulation than from a more elementary roll.

The beginner on the trampoline is sometimes in-co-ordinated because of the stimulation of the "rise and fall" from being thrown into the air. Further evidence of the effect is found in the persistence of the sensation of floating and dropping after getting off the trampoline. Deliberate attempts to relax seem to exaggerate rather than relieve the after-effects. Repeated short practices are probably the best approach to habituation.

Likewise, the swimmer is apparently affected. The beginner may be learning where the only movement of water is that caused by other swimmers. In attempting to float he senses the slight rise and fall of his body with the undulations of the water. He usually interprets this sensation as rolling over, lack of support, and starting to sink, or just as an uncomfortable state associated with being in the water. Apparently interference with breathing exaggerates motion sickness effects, and his limited breathing may help to increase the sensations of the beginning swimmer.

Beginners in many different types of skills are sometimes described as having a psychological block. This may be partially based on sensations of dropping. Jumping down from heights, dismounts from apparatus, vaulting apparatus, jumping or diving into water, high jumping, and pole vaulting all have one element in common, i.e., dropping more or less vertically. First experiences in dropping do not add to the eagerness of a nonenthusiastic novice. It is even possible that one reason divers hold the head high and do not correct dives for a more nearly vertical entry is that the sensation of dropping is more pronounced in the completely inverted position than it is in a semiprone one during the drop.

It would be extremely difficult to verify some of the hypotheses outlined above because the performer is not adept at differentiating among the various sensations he experiences or of describing them objectively if he indentifies them. However, it should be an intriguing area for research with findings pertinent to the teaching-learning process.

Space orientation is more than a visual perception of objects and their locations. It is the feeling of where one is in relation to the objects, of how those objects are moving and how to catch, hit, or avoid them. Worchel[24] made a study of space orientation in blind subjects. This, like some of the other sensations, the blind person develops to a very high degree as a substitute for his visual deficiency. Movement through space, direction of walking, turning, and reaching all show differential abilities in spite of visual restrictions.

It is very probable that what we refer to as eye-hand or eye-foot coordination is a phase of space orientation. The softball player fails to catch the ball not because he can't see the ball or can't get to it but because he fails to judge the flight of the ball and where he is with reference to it. The tennis player is most apt to miss the ball because the perception of his own speed of movement is not related to that of the speed of the ball.

LEARNING BASED ON KINESTHESIS

Each time a given response is made to a stimulus the more likely it is that the response will follow a similar stimulus in the future. This is particularly true if that response does not lead to other undesirable sensations or results judged unsatisfactory by the person. Repeated use of these neural pathways leads eventually to uniformity of response. This may be called learning.

The beginner in a skill is more or less experimenting with making his movements match those in his concept (acquired from visual or oral cues) of what he is trying. He is apt to judge the result of his experiment in terms of obvious results, not in terms of his feelings of the movement. For example, the ball goes where he wants it to go, or he stays in balance rather than falling. One reason he is not apt to judge in terms of feeling of action is that he is trying so hard to perform accurately that he is creating excess tension. Beginners' tensions are well known to teacher and student. Success and satisfaction are largely the basis on which tensions are relieved. Could it also be that teaching is not done in such a way as to create awareness of the degree of effort?

Studies that have been conducted in an attempt to teach primarily through awareness of the movement have not yielded results indicating advantages over other methods of learning. Roloff[16] summarized some of these studies and others have been done since. However, certain guides to learning would seem to evolve from knowledge of the kinesthetic functions. Some of these follow:

1. New skills should be built on known ones if possible. This will avoid

some of the beginners' tension. It will permit performance of the general pattern so that attention may be devoted to new aspects.

2. The skill should be learned as a whole rather than in its component parts. This will permit the establishment of the chain of proprioceptive stimuli and responses, and avoid relearning through annexation of parts. Progressive part learning would also appear to be better than distinct part learning where the "total whole" is not feasible.

3. Learning should start with general form and rhythm of action rather than with details and emphasizing accuracy. This will provide for better feeling of action and serve as a base on which precision may be controlled.

4. Learning should proceed to nearly a normal tempo for the skill as soon as possible. This does not mean starting with maximum speed. Such emphasis usually leads to tension and interferes with perceptions necessary for accuracy. However, a slow-motion style of execution differs too much mechanically and is too hard to adjust to a faster rate later. A compromise on a more moderate speed would seem best.

5. Individual tempo should be established rather than imposing a fixed one on the entire class. This is desirable because of individual differences in length and weight of levers and in strength.

6. Skills should always be performed in optimum equilibrium for that skill so as to free the attention for details of hand or foot action.

7. Practice should be carried out with proper equipment and the same equipment each practice period. A racket with weak stringing makes the learner feel that too much force is needed. A heavy racket will create a time lag in acceleration for the swing and cause errors when shifting to a lighter one. A slight variation in size of handle or weight of the equipment causes distracting sensations and variations in effort. A ball that is too large cannot be gripped properly, and therefore the style of arm action in throwing is different from that needed for a smaller ball later.

8. Players of all levels should be taught to note differences in degree of effort at different points in the skill or game and to use the opportunities for relaxation to the maximum.

9. In the early stages the learner should not work past the point of mild fatigue when interference with movement sensations appears to begin.

Ragsdale[14] said that learning should proceed by employment of every sense. He specifically named the kinesthetic one as of extreme importance. Awareness of how one is moving can be developed by conscious attention. Awareness can be used to build empathic understanding of demonstrations and visual aids as a basis for clarification of concept or model of what one is attempting. Awareness is essential in retention of corrections in posture and basic movements. Awareness of kinesthetic sensations also provides a basis on which the person can become more independent and self-helpful in initiating learning of a skill or practicing on it.

Special learning problems are sometimes observed.

The teacher should be aware of inability to localize because that particular muscle has been in little use. Surface contacts over a muscle may substitute for proprioceptive stimuli within it.

The left-handed performer is handicapped many times in observing a demonstration because of the necessity to translate performance to the alternate side. Teaching to depend upon empathy rather than verbal cues should facilitate this process.

The student may fail to perceive details of performance in a film or demonstration because he has not had a sufficient background of experience in the skill or has not been taught kinesthetic projection in the observation.

The swimming teacher is often impatient with the novice because of tensions and in-co-ordination. It should be remembered that the swimmer is working in a different medium and a different position from those in which most of his skills occur. The receptors in the utricle are being stimulated differently. The water contact on the skin and sometimes in the ears produces different sensations. The knee extensors no longer carry the main responsibility for exerting force, but the hip extensors and adductors are substituted in many strokes. There is no longer pressure in the soles of the feet or in the articulations of the lower extremity. The arms take on new importance in locomotion. Gravity is fairly effectively counteracted and a new buoyant force seems to replace it. Relaxation will do much to facilitate the interpretation of the new sensations and building of desired co-ordinations.

The player who has already learned a technique similar to, but differing in certain details from, the prescribed pattern seems to have more problems of learning than the complete novice. If he has really developed his technique to the consistent stage he has a chain response built up which makes the changes feel strange, or they may completely distract from the execution of the skill. The teacher and student will have to decide whether the new form is worth the cost, and therefore whether he will learn the new one or continue the old.

COMPONENTS OF KINESTHESIS

From the above discussion it is apparent that kinesthesis is composed of sensations stemming from the various proprioceptive, vestibular, and visual receptors. This in itself represents a diversification of function. But it consists of many more specifics than appear from the grouping of receptors.

One of the most difficult steps in trying to analyze kinesthesis as a total has been the measurement of the ability or its parts. The usual processes of test construction and the identification of elements by face criteria may have partially accounted for the specificity of capacities that have seemed to emerge. Tests have been set up which have been validated after a fashion at least.[2,8,19,20] Factor analysis studies that attempt to determine those measuring a similar capacity and to differentiate those that are different have been in more or less agreement.[18,22,23]

Balance has been very clear but is of two types, static and dynamic. It appears possible that dynamic, at least, consists of subelements which might involve linear displacement, equilibrium in angular motion, speed of motion, and perhaps others.

Positioning of body segments also subdivides. Ability to position accurately in the upper extremity does not necessarily mean comparable ability in the lower, and vice versa. Positioning at articulations seems to be more similar within one extremity than between extremities. Positioning in the trunk has an insignificant relationship with that in the extremities. Perception of movement in one plane does not necessarily agree with that in another plane.

Precision of perception of movement is higher in the small muscles of the hand than in larger segments. This is probably due to more proprioceptors in the hands and fingers than in the larger muscles of the shoulders. Precision of response is due to the smaller motor units. Also, it may be partially a result of size of the segment and possible range of error.

Space orientation, which was discussed earlier, can be broken down into controlling direction of movement in walking or turning, knowledge of distance covered, awareness of effort in relation to movement, position relative to a starting point, reaching and pointing, and even simple weight transfer. These capacities probably involve integration of data from more than one type of receptor to a greater extent than most of the other factors.

In all of these measurements visual cues are eliminated or minimized. Research in the area of measurement, analysis of components, physiological process of integration in the central nervous system, and application to learning is still very incomplete. It would be helpful if all phases could be developed, as this sensation or some aspect of it is a vital part of every waking moment.

INTEGRATION IN THE NERVOUS SYSTEM

Sensations always enter the organism's nervous system via receptors. It is relatively simple to visualize the process of stretching a muscle and the corresponding contraction following (see Chap. 6). However, no muscle works alone. There is the total synergistic group producing the action. This may include numerous supporting and guiding groups, facilitating and controlling action. The antagonistic group is affected by the act, new stresses are set up by the momentum, and the rate of change in body status and its position are all detected within the labyrinth. The eyes pick up the effects of the movement through visual cues. All these in multiple registration are fed into the central nervous system simultaneously and in sequence for as long as the movement persists, and then cessation is registered along with the new resting position. The end result is not chaos, purposeless response, or general rigidity, but rather a finely coordinated act precisely suited to the situation and with the body in balance.

It is in the central nervous system that the integration and the control take place. The cord and brain serve as a very efficient, high-speed "computer" and "organizer." In its functioning rests the secret of use, appreciation, conditioned reflexes, learning, motor memory, and the potential for the endless variety of skills of which man is capable.

The bits we know about its functioning leave us in admiration. The great number of unanswered questions leaves us challenged. Tremendous advances have been made in these understandings in the last few years, the next few promise to be more productive.

REFERENCES

1. Chinn, Herman I., and Smith, Paul K., Motion Sickness, *Pharmacological Review*, 7, 1955, p. 33.
2. Clapper, Dorothy, *Measurement of Selected Kinesthetic Responses at the Junior and Senior High School Levels*, Microcard PE214, 1954.
3. Espenschade, Anna, Kinesthetic Awareness in Motor Learning, *Perceptual and Motor Skills*, 8, 1958, p. 142.
4. Gooddy, William, and Reinhold, Margaret, Some Aspects of Human Orientation in Space, *Brain*, 76, 1953, p. 337.
5. Guyton, Arthur C., *Textbook of Medical Physiology*, Philadelphia, W. B. Saunders Co., 1956.
6. Hellebrandt, Frances A., Houtz, Sara Jane, Hockman, Donald E., Partridge, Miriam J., Physiological Effects of Simultaneous Static and Dynamic Exercise, *American Journal of Physical Medicine*, 35, 1956, p. 106.
7. Hellebrandt, Frances A., Houtz, Sara Jane, Partridge, Miriam J., and Walters, C. Etta, Tonic Neck Reflexes in Exercises of Stress in Man, *American Journal of Physical Medicine*, 35, 1956, p. 144.
8. Henry, Franklin M., Dynamic Kinesthetic Perception and Adjustment, *Research Quarterly*, 24, May 1953, p. 176.
9. Kabat, Herman, Proprioceptive Facilitation in Therapeutic Exercise, in *Therapeutic Exercise*, 2nd ed., Sidney Licht (ed.), New Haven, Elizabeth Licht, Publisher, 1961, p. 327.
10. McCormick, Ernest J., *Human Engineering*, New York, McGraw-Hill Book Co., Inc., 1957, Ch. 10, Body Orientation and Acceleration Forces.
11. Metheny, Eleanor, and Ellfeldt, Lois, Dynamics of Human Performance, in *Health and Fitness in the Modern World*, Chicago, Athletic Institute, 1961, p. 282.

12. Mumby, H. H., Kinesthetic Acuity and Balance Related to Wrestling Ability, *Research Quarterly*, 24, October 1953, p. 327.

13. Phillips, Marjorie, and Summers, Dean, Relationship of Kinesthetic Perception to Motor Learning, *Research Quarterly*, 25, December 1954, p. 456.

14. Ragsdale, C. E., How Children Learn the Motor Types of Activities, in *Forty-ninth Yearbook*, Chicago, University of Chicago Press, 1950.

15. Rasmussen, Grant L., and Windle, William F. (eds.), *Neural Mechanisms of the Auditory and Vestibular Systems*, Springfield, Ill., Charles C Thomas, 1960.

16. Roloff, Louise, *Kinesthesis in Relation to the Learning of Selected Motor Skills*, Microcard PE148, 1952.

17. Ruch, Theodore C., and Fulton, John F. (eds.), *Medical Physiology and Biophysics*, Philadelphia, W. B. Saunders Co., 1955.

18. Russell, Ruth, *A Factor Analysis of the Components of Kinesthesis*, Microcard PH36, 1954.

19. Scott, M. Gladys, Tests of Kinesthesis, *Research Quarterly*, 26, October 1955, p. 324.

20. Stevens, Mildred, *The Measurement of Kinesthesis in College Women*, Microcard PE93, 1950.

21. Stevens, S. S., *Handbook of Experimental Psychology*, New York, John Wiley & Sons, Inc., 1951, Ch. 30, Somesthesis; Ch. 31, Vestibular Function.

22. Wiebe, Vernon, *Factor Analysis of Tests of Kinesthesis*, Microcard PE308, 1956.

23. Witte, Faye, *A Factorial Analysis of Measures of Kinesthesis*, Microcard PH20, 1953.

24. Worchel, Philip, The Role of the Vestibular Organs in Space Orientation, *Journal of Experimental Psychology*, 44, 1952, p. 4.

CHAPTER **23**

Relaxation

Teaching of relaxation is a necessary part of teaching by all physical educators. It is true that all may not do remedial teaching for the neuromuscularly hypertensive cases, but all must teach relaxation as a part of regular skills. Such teaching may serve as a preventive measure to avoid building up tensions sometime in the future. Relaxation also leads to more efficient work and play skills if incorporated as part of the basic form for such movement.

Neuromuscular hypertension may develop from situations either real or imaginery. These cases appear to be more numerous and more severe as a result of pressures in today's society such as economic demands; emphasis on success; expectations of increased numbers completing higher education; status seeking in occupation, location of home, or acquisition of luxury items; and keeping up with the Joneses in general. The immediate causes may be physical or mental, generated by emotions, habits or attitudes, or in the form of environmental irritations and stress.

The symptoms that will be observed by the teacher or leader in motor activities are numerous enough to serve as cross-checks: They include—

1. Tensions in face, particularly around eyes and mouth. Facial expressions of concentration, intensity of effort.
2. General tenseness and stiffness in movement, inhibiting free action; stiff and frequently poor posture.
3. Mannerisms in movement, frequently repeated and unrelated to movement needed at the time.
4. Restless, continuous movement, irrespective of situation; hyperactivity.
5. Incessant, high-pitched, and rapid talking.
6. Increase in reflexes, reaction time, and responsiveness.
7. Fatigue, chronic or induced quickly from activity.
8. Excessive tenseness when trying to learn new skills.

Relaxation is a conscious release of muscular tension in a general sense or in a differential sense. The latter implies localized lowering of tonus in relation to increased muscular activity for a particular movement. Relaxation skill is based on the kinesthetic awareness of feelings of tonus. It is a motor skill which must be learned in much the same way as any other motor skill.

GENERAL REQUIREMENTS

The first step is removal of the cause. The cause may be health of the individual which needs medical care. It may be attitudes or emotional reactions that have an overtone of urgency or seriousness of consequences. It may be outside demands or frustrations. The individual needs to differentiate between those factors which must be accepted, those which can be ignored, and those which must have some modifications put into effect.

To receive release from tensions the individual must want to achieve relaxation rather than continue to enjoy his tension. It must be an important accomplishment for him, and he must persist at it.

He must become aware of the feelings of tension and the right amount of effort, be able to differentiate between efforts and to localize effort.

He must attempt to arrive at a physiological state in which normal reciprocal innervation will be in effect.

Relaxation must be learned as any motor act by attention and concentration during the practice. The learner must advance from situations which are purely practice to other situations in which a relaxed state becomes part of the co-ordination and contributes to an increased efficiency.

And finally he must persist in his practice at all times, incorporating it into other skills. The only true measure of relaxation ability is the facility with which one can turn it on at will and at the appropriate time.

LEARNING GUIDES

The principles behind the various steps should be understood for best selection of practice activities.

1. Learning must proceed as in any motor learning. There must be a concept of the skill as a goal to work toward. There must be practice leading to development of correct neural pathways and inhibition in the ones leading to wrong responses. There must be practice to the point of fixation of neural connections, to cortical recognition of situations where the skill may be used.

2. Relaxation of the body as a whole is possible only when gravital stress is ineffectual in disturbing balance. This is true when the body is in either a prone or supine reclining position or a fully supported semi-reclining position. It is also true in swimming where buoyancy neutralizes the effect of gravity so the body either floats on or is suspended in the water.

It is because of this fact that remedial teaching almost invariably starts in a supine reclining position. In some instances the head is stabilized with pillows or sandbags to eliminate the feeling that it will roll.

3. Environmental stimuli should be conducive to relaxation. For example, the room should be comfortably warm. Chilliness tends to raise muscle tonus and to cause shivering—series of involuntary muscular contractions to stimulate circulation and to create warmth in the body. Cold water has an even more rapid effect on the swimmer. Contact with cold equipment or, in the case of practice while reclining, the cold floor raises tonus. Light should not shine directly in the eyes though darkness is neither necessary nor desirable. Likewise, sound should not be excessive, loud, or erratic. Someone pounding in the next room or loud martial music or jazz would be distracting and stimulating. Music may be used as helpful background, but it should be low and soothing and purely background.

4. The learner must become aware kinesthetically of the gradations of effort in the parts of the body. This is achieved through experience; perception becomes more alert, guiding cues at the right times from another may be helpful in sharpening perception. Basically, however, there is no substitute for experience.

Tonus is a state of readiness; therefore, the arm or leg tends to feel always poised and supported. However, as relaxation is practiced the extremity begins to feel very heavy, sometimes almost detached from the body, and if moved and released by someone else it drops again with a dull thud. Heaviness is the term most commonly used in trying to describe the sense of being relaxed.

5. The learner must concentrate during practice in order to achieve results. This is a means of inhibiting stimulating ideas from dispersing impulses from the cerebral cortex and thus producing a tonic rise for purposes of readiness or action. Concentration on awareness of muscle effort or lack thereof helps the individual to produce the appropriate amount of effort at any time.

6. There must be relaxation of some muscles while others are working. This is essential because there are few instances when we can completely relax. It also contributes in work and play skills to a higher degree of efficiency and a postponement of fatigue.

In understanding the physiological process of relaxation it is necessary to recall the manner in which neural impulses originate, are transmitted and directed through the nervous system, and controls are effected (see Chaps. 6 and 22). Certain general points are important to note:

1. All the sensory receptors of the body send impulses into the central nervous system. This means that at any moment the person is experiencing a multiplicity of environmental impacts. In relaxation learning some

of the outside stimuli may need to be removed, and the person must learn to understand the others and not be disturbed by them.

2. Associations are built up in the nervous system so that the person may misinterpret a sensation, or he may consciouslessly decide on an action or react emotionally with general physiological results.

3. The proprioceptive and vestibular apparatuses are constantly providing autogenetic impulses which affect muscle tonus in various parts of the body. Some of these facilitate and increase muscular reaction; others tend to inhibit it.

4. There are both mental and physiological adjustments to be made in developing relaxation. The mental are largely matters of attitude and perspective on situations, problems, and experiences. The physiological adjustments are principally in the nervous system.

TECHNIQUES USED IN REMEDIAL TEACHING

Almost universally the starting position is supine reclining. At no articulation should there be strain. For this reason the knees are frequently flexed slightly with sandbags or rolled towels under them. This removes tension on hip flexors and strain on the lumbar spine. The arms should be spread sufficiently that there are no contacts of arms with clothing on the body. The forearm may be pronated or supinated as seems most comfortable for the individual.

When the learner has assumed a comfortable position, movement and squirming should be kept to a minimum. A passive state is maintained for a long enough period of time to lower pulse and breathing rates and to reduce proprioceptive stimulation to a minimum. With few incoming stimuli from the receptors in either muscle spindles or tendon endings, there are few impulses to send out to the muscles (via the alpha fibers to activate the motor units). This passive state through deliberate prolonged experience becomes a "learned state" in which inhibiting neurons in the central nervous system form connecting paths by which response to proprioceptive impulses may be reduced.

Awareness of the relaxed state and voluntary inhibition of the motor nerves may be induced by contrast. A muscle group is put into high level of isometric contraction, then permitted to relax. Practice is done in progressive stages from total body stretching, to one-sided, to opposing upper and lower extremity, to a single extremity and finally to a part of a single extremity.

Mental imagery is sometimes used to acquire feelings of either general or differential relaxation. It is based on the principle of empathic projection of self into the object in mind. General relaxation might be achieved from "being" a very limp rag doll. Localized relaxation might be accomplished by imagining that the back is very straight and tall like a flag pole, but the arms dangle passively like a flag on a windless day. The greatest problem in this approach is finding images that will be effective and not stimulating. For example, even an adult might fail to respond to the rag doll if in her childhood someone had thrown away her beloved but worn doll and she had been much disturbed over it at the time. As an adult she may either revive those girlish emotions or translate them into present-day frustrations and disappointments. The image then becomes stimulating and a barrier to being the doll.

There is another effective process of visualization which differs somewhat from the imagery. The individual is asked to recall some scene which has pleasant memories for him. The requirements are that the scene be one of great space, few if any landmarks in it, and no action or slow repetitive action. Qualifying in this might be a large, quiet body of water with no swimmers or boats, unless the boat is a small one perched on the horizon. Another might be a great expanse of fields of long grass or grain, no buildings or people, no action except the slow swaying of the grass in the breeze. The learner is asked in this case to remain apart from it, more in the capacity of an observer, but to keep his attention on the scene or some part of it, on its color (soft blue or green being preferred). Apparently his detachment from the thing in view is the effective force, for the person may lose all sense of readiness, alertness, or response.

Action sometimes holds attention in visualization practice. If this is used it must be monotonous action. This is the principle behind the old folklore method of overcoming insomnia by counting sheep. Supposedly all sheep look alike, walk alike, and can be kept walking by in endless line in the imagination. The same could be true for the continuous roll of the small waves on the lake shore, or the regular drip, drip, drip of water from a leak in the gutter on the house. Each of these might be effective, providing that the idea does not alert the learner to action, as would happen if he owned sheep and saw them walking out of his field into his neighbor's, or he wished to go swimming but did not have time, or he owned a house with a leaky gutter and it reminded him that it needed fixing and he must get to it. The swinging of the pendulum on a clock may be relaxing if one's worries are not involved with use of time. The sound of soft music may establish a feeling of free rhythmic action as one listens unless there is also an association of unpleasant memories with that same music.

In visualization the eyes should focus on distant points in the scene rather than on near ones. Looking at distant points does not require the same degree of contraction from the muscles of the eyes as focusing on near points. Close focusing with the eyes is more apt to be accompanied by the tonus of attention and readiness than is distance viewing.

Relaxation of facial muscles is used to induce general relaxation. The frown of concentration or the set jaw of determination is accompanied by higher tonus as a part of the organism's preparation for work. Since these muscles are all made of motor units of relatively very few fibers there must be many neural connections in the brain. This makes for more ready spread of facilitation or inhibition effects. Conscious effort at relaxation of facial muscles helps in general relaxation. This means relaxing and drooping of eyelids rather than squinting, releasing all furrows on the forehead, and letting the lower jaw drop passively. The face in general becomes passive and expressionless.

Likewise, release of tension in the muscles of respiration seems to be associated with more general relaxation. Inspiration requires muscular effort, but expiration may be passive. One technique is to take a deep breath and let it out as a sigh or with an audible, uncontrolled rush of air. When the person has been reclining and relaxed for some time there is a very low level of oxygen need. Under these circumstances, with passive relaxation of the muscles the intervals between inhalation become longer, lasting for several seconds. Again the interrelationship of relaxation apparently indicates the general spread of inhibition in the brain.

The greatest fault in systems of remedial relaxation lies in the tendency to work too long and perhaps exclusively in the reclining position or in generally passive states. It is essential that the individual transfer this ability to lower tonus to situations other than siestas or bedtime sleep, though these may have merit. He must be able to use them to conserve energy at work and to permit the optimum of ease in motor skills; and to voluntarily relax when doing so will make for greater safety. Relaxation is really learned only when it too becomes a reflex response to certain stimuli.

APPLICATIONS TO TEACHING OF MOTOR SKILLS

Initial movements of a skill should be of a free swinging type, rather than precise, controlled, forced movements. Music at this stage may be helpful but less so later when the individual in the class is establishing his own rhythmic pattern.

The learner should be encouraged to concentrate on what he is doing without making his concentration obvious through tense movements and intense facial expressions. Make positive suggestions to him and minimize the reference to detail and criticism. One may even be positive with respect to pleasant facial expressions while working.

Encourage normal breathing while concentrating on a performance. The tendency is to hold the breath while trying to be highly accurate. This is one of the difficulties with swimmers. For many strokes in the practice stage, it is essential that the breath be held. The beginner is apt to take too deep a breath. The result is general tension.

Teach for general awareness of effort, sequence of effort, feelings of passiveness and action by momentum rather than muscle contraction.

Teach the feelings of position so that the player knows whether he has wrist action or an elbow is straight.

Encourage a reasonable speed for each individual. Speed and forced movements are produced by additional effort and general tension and rigidity. Speed and details of accuracy may be built later on a basic, continuous, appropriately relaxed pattern.

Watch for evidences of tension and try to help minimize them. For example, in the stunt of bending over with legs straight and touching the fingers to the floor, relaxation of spinal extensors is highly desirable. If the head of the performer is sticking out rather than hanging downward, there is tension in the upper back and probably throughout the back. The tennis or badminton player who complains that he cannot hold the racket properly because his hand is tired is doubtless not relaxing it when not actually stroking with it. Or, the swimmer floating on his back should exhibit an outward rotation of the legs. Otherwise when he starts an elementary back stroke he has trouble with knees too high out of water. If his toes point straight up, he is no more relaxed than if the ankle were fully extended; the muscular activity is just at a different joint.

When the swimmer is unable to relax while trying to perform a crawl, by some means find out whether his eyes are open. The tendency is to close the eyes because the face is under water. Squinting the eyes and holding the breath are sufficient to send the novice into a state of near rigidity.

Any activity that requires maximum flexibility or is attempting to increase flexibility must provide relaxation of the antagonistic muscles first. Limited range may be used as an indication of hypertension.

Teach to use the force of gravity rather than muscular effort to check movements which may safely follow-through. This means working more into ballistic action and may be achieved by correct timing of muscle effort and relaxation.

Movements that are alternating and rhythmical, such as a flutter kick, must be relaxed if the finning action is to be achieved and the minimum of resistance and the maximum of driving effect acquired. The fishtail type of whip is a highly co-ordinated one in which relaxation at the proper time plays an important role.

Teach the habit of relaxation at short and appropriate times. For example, the swimmer should relax between strokes when possible. This can be done in an elementary back stroke, side stroke, or breast stroke. Yet it is hard because the learner builds a chain of continuous action rather than with relaxing interludes. Similarly, the racket hand should be relaxed between tennis strokes; in fact the weight of the racket should be borne by the other hand. The bowler should relax between the rolling of balls.

Analyze individual problems and errors in performance. Many errors come from lack of relaxation. The golfer who cannot pivot fully or cannot drop the club at the top of the back swing is overly tense. The archer who hunches the shoulders on the draw is failing to let the shoulder girdle hang relaxed. The softball batter who stabs at the ball rather than taking a full swing and the bowler who takes extra steps or short steps on the approach are both victims of "intention tension." The swimmer who does not relax while trying to tread has no chance of getting smooth, steady support from arm action. The dancer who is not relaxed is heavy on the feet, apt to be off balance, and is impossible to lead. In fact in practically every activity tension characterizes the beginner. If he is not helped to relieve it, his problems and frustrations mount, and he goes round the cycle of increased tensions.

Excess tension and hurried movements often lead to injuries of one type or another. Study of the accident-prone individual usually indicates he does not practice relaxation at his work. In a case when the person falls, relaxation is practically essential to prevent fractures or other serious injuries.

Teach for an appreciation of relaxation as a high level of skill not as a sign of laziness as some people are apt to interpret it. Help them to understand that relaxation may accomplish more than rugged determination.

REFERENCES

1. Haverland, Lillian E., *The Effects of Relaxation Training on Certain Aspects of Motor Skill,* Microcard PE161, 1953.
2. King, Shirley, *Relaxation and Stress,* Microcard PE390, 1958.
3. Metheny, Eleanor, *Body Dynamics,* New York, McGraw-Hill Book Co., Inc., 1952.
4. Rathbone, Josephine, *Teach Yourself to Relax,* Englewood Cliffs, N.J., Prentice-Hall, Inc., 1957.
5. Roney, Phyllis C., *Some Factors of Kinesthesis and Relaxation,* Microcard PE418, 1960.
6. Zeiter, Walter J., and Lufkin, Bernardine, Progress in Relaxation in Physical Therapy, *Archives of Physical Medicine,* 24, 1943, p. 211.

CHAPTER 24

Problems Related to Posture Training

THE DEVELOPMENT OF GOOD POSTURE in students is one of the aims of the majority of physical education teachers. Good posture means more than merely the ability to assume an erect standing position when it is desired. It is the ability to handle the body easily, gracefully, and efficiently under all circumstances.

The values of good posture are recognized both in popular writing and in scientific discussions. Practically every magazine that carries articles on health topics, at one time or another presents one on causes or cures for poor posture. The values which are emphasized are largely health related. The effects in terms of added energy expenditure are seldom fully treated.

From the health standpoint certain facts seem evident. Some types of poor posture are due to poor muscular tonus. As tonus is developed in the muscles through activity and through diet or other supplementary treatment, posture improves. It is known that tonus is associated with circulation and with economy of action.

Poor carriage almost invariably results in additional muscular effort and strain, since it increases rotatory moments at the various articulations. If that excess muscular effort is sufficient to produce fatigue, it can eventually affect the health of the individual. In more severe cases the strain on the joints may be sufficient to alter structure. There is also evidence to indicate that chronic strain definitely contributes to the development of arthritic types of ailments in later life. Such alterations mean limited use of body parts and continued fatigue and strain.

THE UPRIGHT POSTURE

The upright standing position represents an interesting stage in the history of human structure. In a developmental sense this orthograde position is a distinct advantage over a four-footed or even a semierect position. The head is raised, the line of vision is higher and may be used to better advantage. Of no less importance is the fact that the upper extremity is free from the responsibilities of support and may perform any of the myriad of manipulative acts. The importance of this change is not fully appreciated unless one has had to climb or crawl on all fours and carry a load at the same time. A different type of gait and greater speed are also possible with our upright position.

Some of the results of the development into the upright position are a distinct disadvantage. This includes the raising of the center of gravity over a decreased base, and change in alignment of the spine and its relationship to the pelvis.

Other changes were evident in this development, some of them being such that they could not be considered as being either an advantage or disadvantage. Among these changes may be classed the change in the position of abdominal viscera; the depression of the sternal border of the thorax with the resulting alteration in chest diameters and in habits of breathing; the change in the circulatory demands; and the development of a highly sensitive mechanism of equilibrium.

Since the spine is the "keystone" of the structure it is necessary to consider some of its specific functions. First, it is a support for the weight of the trunk, head, and upper extremity. Secondly, it is the solid point of attachment for most of the muscles anchoring and controlling the pectoral girdle, as well as for the latissimus dorsi which moves the shoulder joint. Both of these functions require a strong, well-supported unit. The third responsibility of the spine is to enclose and protect the spinal cord and the nerves which lead to and from it. This requires a firm, carefully articulated, and not too flexible column.

The fourth function of the spine is the absorption of jolts and jars which come to the body even from such commonplace activities as walking, running, and jumping. Without the flexible, padded articulations of the vertebrae the effect would be transmitted to the brain.

Still another function of the spine is to aid in the various activities which demand flexibility. A person with a stiff spine is handicapped in many skills and also fails to get full value from the shock-absorbing arrangement of the spine.

It is evident, therefore, that there are two principal demands on the spine, strength and flexibility. These are contrasting properties, yet both requirements are met adequately. Flexibility is secured by the multi-articulated column, with each articulation supplementing the range of movement in adjacent joints. The range at any one joint is small, the total range is large. The elasticity of the muscles also permits range of movement with control. Strength is secured by the hardness of the bone, by increased size with increased weight down the spine, by bony articular checks which prevent slipping of the vertebrae, by ligaments which bind the vertebrae firmly together on all sides, and by many short sections in the extensor muscles which actively support the spine. This is another example of the adaptation of structure to functional demands.

An understanding of this development of spinal function should aid the teacher of posture and body mechanics. Postural variations usually center in the spine as a result of poor control of this flexible column. If the cause can be found and removed, the variation disappears.

POSTURAL DEVIATIONS

Each type of postural deviation has its particular cause and effect. A consideration of cause and effect simplifies the process of selecting proper activities for correcting these conditions. Only the muscular and mechanical factors will be considered here. This does not belittle the value of the psychological states of motivation, interest, and effort. An additional factor, the establishment of kinesthetic patterns of performance and posture, is also important.

Kyphosis is an exaggeration or increase in the amount of the normal convexity of the thoracic region of the spine. Such a condition may arise from various causes. Lack of strength or tonus of the extensors of the spine in that region may allow too much flexion. Continued positions involving flexion may cause a stretching of the extensors and a readjustment of the tonus of antagonistic groups until the flexed position feels more natural. The weight of body parts, such as forward head or forward position of the arms, may cause stretching of the posterior muscles. Also, excessive relaxation may allow gravital forces to flex the spine too much. An example of this is the tall, self-conscious individual who attempts to shrink by slumping. Kyphosis should not be confused with other conditions which give a rounded contour to the upper part of the back. For example, well-developed muscles of the athlete, particularly the gymnast, may pad the shoulders and scapula sufficiently to give an appearance of kyphosis.

The correction is fairly obvious. The extensors must be strengthened and tonus improved. Excess gravital stresses must be removed by realignment of head, arms, and shoulder girdle, or by variety in occupational positions.

Round shoulders is a term often connected with the condition described above as kyphosis. Round shoulders is in proper terminology a condition of the shoulder girdle in which the scapulae are abducted. This brings the acromial points of the shoulder in front of the normal gravital line. The condition very often accompanies kyphosis and the reason should be obvious. However, either condition may occur independently of the other since entirely different muscle groups are responsible.

The correction requires strengthening of the adductor muscles, the rhomboids, and the trapezius. In most cases this is sufficient but in the more severe case in which the shoulders are inflexible because of short pectoral muscles, stretching of the pectoralis major and minor may be necessary. Coppock[3] found that this occurs infrequently. The kinesthetic

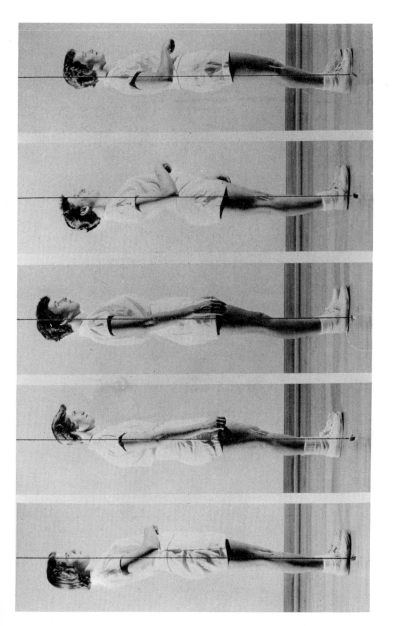

FIGURE 94: Postural variations

a–sway back; b–fatigue slump and round shoulders; c–good alignment; d–lordosis and hyperextended knee; e–forward head and hips, flexed knees

feeling of position is extremely important in correction of shoulder girdle position.

Lordosis is an exaggeration or increase in the amount of the normal concavity of the lumbar region of the spine. This state may occur as a compensatory adjustment to the deviations in the spine above this region. Relaxation and poor tonus of the abdominals may allow the curve to collapse. Also, if the hips are thrust forward, the curve increases in order to throw the upper trunk back into balance.

The correction may be dependent upon the development of abdominal strength or upon control of the position of the pelvis. The line of the pelvis varies with the lumbar curve. If the thoracic cage is fixed, the abdominals lift the front of the pelvis and counteract the tension of the hip flexors. A little additional tension in the hip extensors also aids in this change. Therefore it is essential that the individual secure proper coordination of the muscle groups and develop a feeling of position.

The *fatigue slump* is a fairly common condition in which the individual seems to relax almost completely. The spinal curves increase, the head and shoulders are forward, the hips are thrust forward, and the weight is back on the heels. This is a position of muscular economy because the weight is borne largely by the ligamentous tissues instead of by muscular contraction. At the hip, for example, the iliofemoral ligament prevents hyperextension and thereby supports the trunk. In the spine the curves are halted only by tension of muscles and ligaments, not by contraction. Such a position is temporarily economical and allows relaxation. As a habitual posture, however, it impairs balance and the tonus of muscles, and stretches the ligaments, which are not capable of repair as are the muscles.

The correction lies in strengthening of the leg extensors, spinal extensors, and abdominals. If these muscles are ineffective because of poor tonus, then the proper procedure is a careful, well-planned daily routine of activity. If the individual is generally fatigued and weak, then the activity must be preceded by rest, well-planned diet, and removal of any conditions detrimental to health.

Scoliosis is a lateral deviation in which the spinous processes do not appear in a straight line. The curve may be convex to either side in either the thoracic or lumbar region, or to either side through both regions, or to one side in one region and to the other in the adjacent region. This lateral flexion always results in rotation of the vertebrae since the pressure on the front and back of the vertebrae is already unequal by reason of the normal anteroposterior curves.

Scoliosis is usually due to asymmetrical weight bearing caused by poor habits or structural irregularities. Postural habits which may contribute to the condition are standing on one foot, thrusting the hip sideward until the weight is over one hip, or sitting with one shoulder or arm raised for

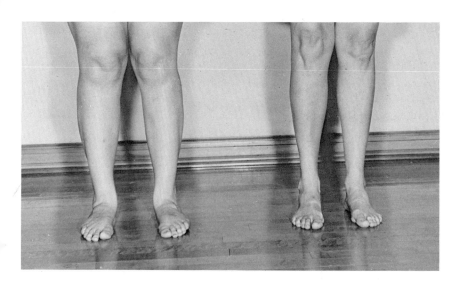

FIGURE 95: Normal and pronated feet

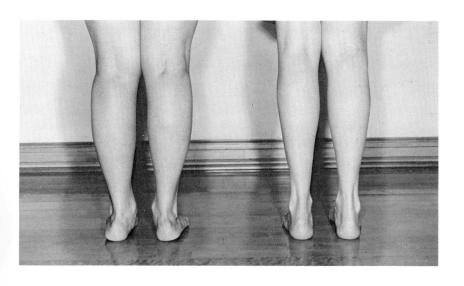

work. Structural causes include such conditions as unequal length of legs, foot deformities which cause lack of balance, or uneven form of the vertebrae. If support on one side of the pelvis is inadequate, that side drops, and a lumbar curve develops in order to help balance the trunk.

Pathological structure and muscle or nerve injury may give similar results but they are less common and require more highly specialized treatment and care. They will, therefore, not be considered here.

The correction of scoliosis varies. If it is a mild and flexible case, stretching of the spine by use of the extensors and by pressure from the abdominals may be sufficient. Suspension activities, using body weight, may cause stretching of the shortened muscles and stretching of the spine. Also, lateral bending to the side of the convexity, localized in the proper region, will help develop those muscles which have become relaxed and stretched. The latter treatment is ordinarily administered only under the careful supervision of the orthopedic physician. Correction rests first of all in removal of the cause, poorly balanced gravital pull. The next step is the development of strength in the spinal extensors. Kinesthetic sense of position is also vital.

Pronated feet occur when the tarsal bones are rotated inward. This causes some dropping of the tarsals and a tendency toward eversion of the foot with the weight being borne too far on the inner border of the foot. If the weight line crosses the longitudinal arch instead of running lengthwise through it, the strain is increased still more.

The principal cause is the weakness or stretching of the medial and plantar ligaments, and of the tibialis posticus, tibialis anticus, flexor brevis digitorum, and lumbricales. The tibialis anticus normally helps to lift the arch and invert the foot. But it cannot support it alone.

Correction lies in strengthening plantar structures and in realigning the foot to the optimum weight-bearing position by strengthening of the tibialis anticus, tibialis posticus, and lumbricales.

EVALUATION OF EXERCISES FOR POSTURE TRAINING

Some of the more commonly recommended exercises will be discussed here, as well as variations which may affect their value. This is only a small sampling of exercises available and others should each be evaluated in the same way before using. This list is not to be considered as the best collection of exercises. Each has been selected because it is used frequently, is representative of a type of exercise, or illustrates some point which seems important in the selection or use of the exercises.

1. Arms Swinging between Cross and Fly

The arms swing sideward and upward to a spread position diagonally above the shoulders. They are then dropped downward relaxed so that the elbows are near the sides, and the forearms are crossed in front of the trunk by relaxed elbow flexion.

The principal work is done by the deltoid muscles. The scapulae are rotated upward by the serratus anterior, and by the trapezius if the arms are forced back into and a little behind the frontal plane. This exercise is effective for round shoulders only if the trapezius is used. The downward movement is a relaxed one and therefore the rhomboids are inactive. It is effective in kyphosis only in so far as the momentum of the arms tends to encourage the subject to stretch taller; a certain amount of fixation of the thorax and spine is necessary to get the best swing and prevent the head from bobbing. It is not a good choice for this purpose.

2. Elbows Flexed, Arms Horizontal, Backward Movement of Arms in the Transverse Plane

This exercise is sometimes called "breaking chains." The middle deltoid holds the arm at the proper level, and the posterior deltoid, infraspinatus, and teres minor draw it backward. The scapula is adducted at the same time by the second and third parts of the trapezius and the rhomboids, which counteract each other's rotatory effect. The movement can even be localized in the adductors so that no motion takes place except by the gliding of the scapulae, but no stretching of anterior muscles can occur in such a case. This exercise is, therefore, excellent for round shoulders. It is also facilitated by an extension of the thoracic spine; and by indirectly encouraging an erect position it is good for kyphosis.

3. Elbows Bent and Close to Sides—Pull Elbows Down and Back Trying to Touch Them Together as Far Down the Spine as Possible

The action at the shoulder is unimportant from the standpoint of postural correction, except that very strong action can be obtained from the teres major and minor and from the infraspinatus. This would require fixation of the scapula by the adductors. The movement itself requires adduction of the scapula, which is taken care of very well by the rhomboids, assisted somewhat by the third part of the trapezius. This makes it particularly good for round shoulders. It is beneficial for kyphosis only if the spine is fully extended at the same time. Emphasis should, therefore, be placed on stretching the thoracic spine and keeping elbows close to the trunk.

4. Wand Lowering Behind the Shoulders

The arms start extended upward which means that the scapulae are rotated far upward. The downward movement, requiring that the stick stay behind the head and shoulders, requires strong adduction of the scapulae as well as downward rotation, which is too often partly passive in other exercises. Thus the rhomboids must act strongly. The best results are obtained if the movement is performed slowly and with some resistance from the arm elevators. At the same time the dorsal region of the spine must be stretched to make it easier to get the bar down. The head should be held erect by the cervical extensors and anterior neck muscles (scalenus anterior, rectus capitis anterior, and the longus colli). Hence the exercise is good for round shoulders, kyphosis, and forward head. Its effectiveness is increased by the resistance afforded by the bar when passing behind the shoulders. It calls for stronger action than simple arm lowering and stretches the anterior muscles if they are short. It also gives the performer an objective means of determining whether or not the exercise is following the described pattern and also of measuring improvement from time to time.

5. Prone Lying, Arms Extended Sideward Palms Down— Raising of Head, Shoulders, and Arms from Floor

This exercise when done properly is localized hyperextension of the thoracic region, with a little hyperextension of the cervical region. It is particularly valuable in developing the erector spinae in those two regions. The splenius also functions strongly because of the weight of the head. If the lowering is slow and controlled, these muscles work during movement in both directions. If the hands are raised more than the shoulders, then strong adduction by the rhomboids and third part of the trapezius also takes place. This is also more strenuous than an exercise such as "breaking chains" because of the weight of the extended arms.

Care must be taken to localize the action in the thoracic region. It should not be done with extreme hyperextension in the lumbar, which would elevate both the feet and the shoulders. Such an arch tends to increase the lumbar curve. This can be overcome by control from the abdominal muscles, which give fixation both to the ribs and pelvis. Few people need an increase in the lumbar curve. The exercise may be done with lumbar hyperextension however, if increased flexibility is desirable in the lumbar spine.

This exercise may also be done with the elbows straight and the hands clasped together behind the hips. Pulling toward the feet with the hands and drawing the shoulder blades together at the same time the performer tries to stretch tall helps to localize the movement in the upper back. This position of the arms reduces the amount of work performed because the weight of the shoulders is less and the range is slightly more limited. It does use the scapular adductors about as effectively as if the arms are extended sideward and left in line with the shoulders.

6. Relaxed, Flexed Trunk, with Extension Beginning in the Lumbar and Progressing Upward until Head and Back are Erect

This exercise may be very easy or strenuous depending upon how far forward the trunk starts and how much effort the individual wishes to put into it. The erectness of the final position also depends upon the amount of effort put forth and the performer's knowledge of and feeling for correct position. Its chief value probably lies in the development of that feeling and the ability to localize.

7. Hanging from the Horizontal Bar

In passive hanging the weight of the body is borne very largely by the capsular and ligamentous structures of the elbow and shoulder, protected somewhat by the elasticity of the muscles. The scapulae are abducted and rotated upward to nearly their full range, and the contact of shoulder girdle and thorax is maintained by such muscles as the rhomboids, trapezius, pectoralis minor, and subclavius. They are all being stretched. They are partially protected by similar tension of those muscles connecting arms and thorax, the latissimus dorsi, teres major, and pectoralis major. Such a position is economical of muscular effort but is not good for round shoulders, except to stretch the pectoralis major and minor if they are short. The exercise does permit stretching of the lumbar and thoracic spine. However, the weight of the legs rotates the pelvis forward and tends to increase the lumbar curve unless the abdominals are used to counteract this.

In active hanging, the muscles contract to hold the weight. The main difference is around the shoulder girdle where the rhomboids, the trapezius, pectoralis major, and subclavius depress and adduct the scapulae. This gives a firm point of origin for the deltoid, teres major and minor, triceps, and biceps. These muscles add their stabilizing force to that of the pectoralis major and latissimus for protection of the shoulder joint. This adjustment transforms an activity which is poor for round shoulders into one which is beneficial. A certain fixation of the spine is necessary also, and the extensors perform this function. The abdominals contract to support the front of the pelvis and furnish fixation for any possible leg action. The elbow flexors may be used to give support at the elbow.

Active hanging is necessary for other exercises and for apparatus events. It is better than passive hanging for shoulder girdle posture and for the development of spinal extensors; it is probably inferior for mere stretching of a flexible, scoliotic spine.

8. Back Lying, Shoulders over a Narrow Support, Arms Extended Sideward and Hanging

If the arms are out in line with the shoulders, good stretching of the pectoralis major and anterior deltoid will result, due to the weight of the

extended arms. If the arms are closer to the sides than shoulder alignment, they merely drop downward and rotate inward with tension only
on the deltoid. This is purely a passive exercise and has no developmental
effect.

9. Back Lying, Knees Bent with Feet on Floor—Contract and Relax the Abdominal Muscles Slowly and Rhythmically

The exercise should give the appearance of flattening the abdominal
wall, or even of making it concave during contraction. The individual may
have difficulty at first in localizing in the abdominals, and in continuing
to breathe normally while using the abdominals. If the hand is placed on
the lower abdomen it acts as a stimulus and usually helps to localize the
response. Abdominal contraction usually causes the lumbar spine to
flatten toward the floor. Complete flattening, in most cases, requires
action from the hip extensors to help turn the pelvis. If the pelvis and
thorax are more or less fixed, abdominal contraction may occur without
any movement other than compression of the abdomen. This exercise
should improve tonus and control of the abdominal muscles.

The bent-knee position relieves the tension of the hip flexors on the
pelvis and therefore relieves strain on the abdominals. Sitting positions
for the exercise provide the same situation. Similar control in the standing position is the ultimate goal, but this is more difficult since it involves
alignment of weight as well as control of upper back and leg positions.

10. Back Lying, Bend Both Knees Up to Chest, Extend Legs to Vertical Position, Lower Slowly to Floor

A little work is performed by the hip flexors and abdominals in bending
the legs, but a great amount is performed during the leg lowering. The
flexors control the drop if it is slow, but they can function only if the front
of the pelvis is fixed. Fixation is the duty of the abdominals. The tendency of the pelvis to tilt forward causes the lumbar curve to increase.
Strong abdominal action can counteract both of these effects. The quadriceps holds the knees extended.

The work is severe because of the length and weight of the legs. The
exercise can be made easier by allowing the knees to flex some and
thereby shortening the lever, by allowing the feet to drop when part of
the way down, by starting with the legs at an angle of about 45° instead
of vertically, or by lowering faster. In any case, however, the back should
be held flat and the pelvis firm. The exercise is even harder if the straight
legs are raised so that the heels are just off the floor and the legs are then
held in that position for a time. It is at this point that the downward or
rotatory component of the weight is greatest on the lever. At the same
time the angle of the hip flexors is smaller. The result is a very difficult
exercise.

This is not an exercise for those who have weak abdominals. They are unable to support the pelvis, the back extends and the muscles are stretched. It could be used in the later stages of developing strength in these muscles. At that time it might serve either as a developmental exercise or as a test of abdominal strength.

11. **Back Lying, Hands Folded on Chest, Legs Extended Vertically—Rock Up to a Sitting Position with Legs Straight on Floor and Trunk and Head Erect—Down to the Back Again**

The muscles working are very similar to those in the last exercise. The knee extensors hold the knee straight, the hip flexors and abdominals keep the hip joint at a right angle, the back extensors including those in the cervical region hold the spine straight. Action of the abdominals and anterior neck muscles avoids hyperextension.

The momentum to start the upward movement is gained by flexing the hips slightly more and then starting quick leg lowering by the hip extensors. This is checked almost immediately by the flexors and abdominals and the reaction on the trunk plus the little momentum gained tends to lift the body. Also a little pull with the arms through action of the anterior and middle deltoid and upper pectoralis major lifts the trunk and brings the center of gravity of the trunk more quickly over the pelvis. The weight and momentum of the legs, when the weight gets beyond the support of the hips, forces the body up unless the abdominals and hip flexors give way.

The return to position is easier, and accomplished by merely shifting the weight backward, dropping the head back a little, and lifting the legs very slightly to aid in overbalancing. The tendency in going in both directions is to hold the head forward. This is primarily an attempt to shorten the length of the lever and thereby reduce the work of the abdominals. In the upward movement the head lift may add a little momentum, and with the arms does help to bring the weight more quickly over the hips. Abdominal contraction which is strong enough to cause slight flexion of the trunk results in better development of the abdominals. If the exercise is used for strengthening abdominals, a little flexion of the trunk should be allowed; if it is used for extensor control and developing proper feeling of stretching, flexion should not be permitted.

12. **Standing with Feet Together, Lift Inner Border of Each Foot but Keep Heels and Toes on the Floor, Weight on Outer Borders of the Feet**

The lift is made by the tibialis anticus, the flexor longus hallucis, tibialis posticus, and flexor brevis digitorum. The main value is in strengthening these muscles, which support the arch along its medial border.

13. Toe Gripping

Flexion of the toes may be done against resistance, as over the edge of a step or chair; the edge should be under the metatarsals. The long and short flexors of the toes are used. The actual movement may be localized in the front of the foot, beyond the point of contact.

This exercise may also be done by grasping small objects with the toes. This requires strong toe flexion but also causes a lifting of the arch as a result of the strong flexor action.

14. Foot Circling

The direction of circling may be described as *in and up, out and down.* The first movement comes from action of the tibialis posticus followed by the tibialis anticus. The latter, assisted by the peroneus tertius, holds the foot up while it is moved laterally by the peroneus brevis. It starts down and into eversion by the peroneus longus; then the gastrocnemius, and soleus come into play. Finally, the foot is moved medially by the tibialis posticus and flexor brevis hallucis and this movement blends in with the dorsal flexion produced by the tibialis anticus.

If the toe extensors are used during dorsal flexion, they strengthen the movement and cause the toes to be lifted. This may cause stretching of the gastrocnemius and soleus but may relieve the tibialis anticus of part of the work and hence lessen the value of the exercise for this muscle. When the ankle goes into extension the toe flexors should be used. This prevents extension of the toes due to tension on the extensors longus digitorum and hallucis. The actual flexion of the toes will be very slight because of this tension. However, that resistance, which prevents shortening of the flexors, is helpful in developing the strength of the short and of the long toe flexors.

The value of the exercise is in strengthening all of the muscles, increasing flexibility of the foot, getting a strong lift on the inner border of the longitudinal arch, and strong flexion in the transverse one. The latter occurs only if toe flexion is included in the exercise. If the strength of the transverse arch is satisfactory, toe flexion may be omitted. If the whole foot is weak, toe flexion should be included.

FLEXIBILITY

It is impossible to state how much flexibility is desirable, principally because it depends upon the individual's build, muscular strength, and the activities in which he is to engage. However, the teacher who tries to teach a more erect posture, or modern dance, or stunts and tumbling, or hurdling, or high jumping may find students who are too inflexible for the necessary skills. Inflexibility is a condition in which there is a limited range of motion in one or more joints, and results from muscles which are short or do not yield to stretching, or from short capsular structures.

Flexibility can be developed by gradually increasing the amount of force used in elongating the muscle and at the same time gradually increasing the range. Antagonistic muscle action may be used, or it may be done passively by the weight of body parts, or by external resistance. Examples will illustrate these methods.

Sometimes women find it impossible to wear low heels with comfort because of the shortness of the gastrocnemius and soleus. Stretching may be achieved actively by strong dorsal flexion. However, these muscles are very weak in comparison to the posterior muscles and the results, therefore, will not be very great. Stretching may be achieved passively by having an assistant force the foot in dorsal flexion, or by putting a strap around the ball of the foot and pulling. It may be done more effectively and more strongly by using body weight. The subject may stand with the balls of the feet on a low block and lower the heels. The depth of the block may be increased as flexibility increases. The knees must be kept straight to stretch the gastrocnemius. Likewise, the subject may stand facing a wall a little more than arm's length from it. By falling forward to the wall, supported by the hands, and keeping the body straight and heels down to the floor, he can employ the body weight and its momentum to stretch the calf muscles. A strong antagonistic check is not essential in this case so that passive stretching is better than active contraction. The stretching should be done by slow, gradual movements rather than fast ones. A sudden stretch usually causes a muscle to contract and this would defeat the purpose of the exercise.

Short hamstrings are a handicap in many forms of stunts, track events, dancing, or diving. They can be stretched only by strong hip flexion with the knees straight. The trunk may be relaxed and dropped heavily forward; momentum is the important force in this case. In active bending, the abdominals and hip flexors draw the trunk forward. An arm swing may add to the momentum. Still greater force may be obtained by grasping the ankles and drawing the trunk down by elbow flexion and shoulder depression. Another form of forced stretching may be performed while either sitting or lying on the back. The toes of one foot are grasped by the opposite hand. The other hand is placed on the knee for pushing as the leg is extended.

The inflexible round back may be due to the structure of the vertebrae, which prevent extension. More frequently it is due to shortened ligaments on the front of the vertebrae, a rigid thorax, and unyielding intercostals. In suspension exercises the weight of the body causes an elongation of the spine. Strong localized action of the erector spinae is important to develop muscular strength and to stretch the spine. Exercises have been discussed for that purpose. Further stretching may be accomplished by an assistant who administers head suspension exercises or stretches the subject with pressure in the thoracic region. Some of the Bukh exercises are particularly adapted to this purpose.

A forward, rigid shoulder girdle requires stretching of the anterior muscles and strengthening of posterior ones. Many of these exercises have already been discussed. In addition to those, there are many forms of arm circling which strengthen shoulder muscles and use the momentum of the arm to increase its range of easy motion.

Some types of stunts and dancing produce increased range in hyperextension of the lumbar spine and hip. They probably develop sufficient abdominal strength to control the position. However, excessive stretching of the iliofemoral ligament on the front of the hip inevitably increases the muscular effort necessary for balance at the hip.

EVALUATION OF OTHER ACTIVITIES

In the field of stunts and self-testing activities there are many events which are useful in postural work and some which are definitely harmful. A brief analysis of some of these should make clear the means of evaluation.

The shoulder stand is basic to the inverted cycling exercise which is found on most of the popular "daily dozens." It requires support on the shoulders and neck, which gives an exaggerated forward head and thoracic curve. The exercise should be used very infrequently, if at all, by subjects with these conditions. The amount of work performed is not very great. The leg flexors are not used unless the leg action is very rapid; they would be used if a similar exercise were done in an upright position. The leg extensors are used, but they are required only to lift the weight of the legs and not that of the whole body. The inverted position may have a certain value for circulation, constipation, or dysmennorhea, but not for posture. The exercise does use the gluteus maximus if the cycling is vigorous and of fairly wide range, whereas it is sometimes not used in running in an upright position.

The rolls require so much back and neck flexion that they should not be done extensively by individuals with kyphosis and forward head.

Practically all the balancing events require strong extension of the spine. This is true of the head stand, hand stand, stomach balance, chest balance, and many others. If used specifically for correction of upper back, care should be taken to localize the action as much as possible in the upper back, rather than mostly in the lumbar region.

The wicket walk and the worm walk are merely forms of the hamstring stretching exercise.

Push-up and chinning are excellent measures of arm and shoulder girdle strength. They should be used as the final stage of a series of exercises which develop adequate muscular strength. A consideration of type of support and gravital pull will determine the proper progression of activities. Slow, controlled lowering of body weight uses the same muscles which are required to lift the weight. They may become progressively effective in such control through practice, whereas they may be too weak to even initiate upward movement if the total body weight is suspended on them.

Another modification of these two activities is to start the performer on an angle. Part of the weight is then borne by the feet instead of being supported entirely by the arms. This makes it possible to vary the difficulty of the exercise and usually to adjust it to a form which is easy enough for everyone to perform. The regular form of the push-up and chinning does not seem to develop the anterior deltoid; this modified form is better in that respect.

Much of the modern dance technique aims at the development of flexibility and the ability to localize. If the techniques are carefully chosen they should be extremely valuable. Practice is usually done to music or accompaniment of some type. The techniques are related to or used in dances and hence are apt to be more meaningful. Both of these facts tend to secure greater effort from the participant than exercises alone would do.

REFERENCES

1. Austin, Catherine, *What Do You Want for $1.98?* Philadelphia, J. B. Lippincott Co., 1938.
2. Billig, H. E., Dysmennorhea: The Result of a Postural Defect, *Archives of Surgery*, 46, 1943, p. 611.
3. Coppock, Doris, Relationship of Tightness of Pectoral Muscles to Round Shoulders in College Women, *Research Quarterly*, 29, May 1958, p. 146.
4. Flint, Marilyn, and Diehl, Bobbie, Influence of Abdominal Strength, Back Extensor Strength and Trunk Strength, Balance upon Antero Posterior Alignment of Elementary School Girls, *Research Quarterly*, 32, December 1961, p. 496.
5. Fox, Margaret, Relation of Strength to Postural Faults, *Research Quarterly*, 22, May 1951, p. 141.
6. Hines, Thomas F., Posture, in *Therapeutic Exercise*, 2nd ed., Sidney Licht (ed.), New Haven, Elizabeth Licht, Publisher, 1961, p. 486.
7. Lowman, Charles L., *Postural Fitness; Significance and Variances*, Philadelphia, Lea & Febiger, 1960.
8. Metheny, Eleanor, *Body Dynamics*, New York, McGraw-Hill, 1952.
9. Nader, Charles P., *Evaluation of Selected Postures in Relation to Muscle Tension by Means of Action Current*, Microcard PE126, 1953.
10. Ruch, Theodore C., and Fulton, John F. (eds.), *Medical Physiology and Biophysics*, Philadelphia, W. B. Saunders Co., 1955, Ch. 6, Reflex Regulation of Movement and Posture.
11. Walters, C. Etta, and Partridge, Miriam J., Electromyographic Study of the Differential Action of the Abdominal Muscles During Exercise, *American Journal of Physical Medicine*, 36, 1956, p. 259.

CHAPTER 25

Effects of Practice and Exercise

ALL TISSUES OF THE BODY develop and their capacity for functioning increases through proper use. It is a well-known fact that a muscle which is not used as the result of injury to the nerve, or even those involved when a joint is immobilized for a short time, will become flaccid and weak and lose much of the contractile power. Likewise, a muscle which is used regularly exhibits a healthy state of tonus, becomes firm, and may even increase in external measurement as well as in the maximum force which it can produce. The same evidence of capacity for work is shown in an active individual by improvement of all body functions.

Muscular activity requires co-operation of the circulatory and respiratory systems. Improved endurance is dependent upon improved functioning of these systems. Many studies have been conducted to show the results of intensive training. Some of these will be cited.

It is not the purpose of this volume to go into the physiological effects of conditioning. That is the province of the physiology of exercise. However, there are certain points of muscle selection and mechanics of action which will be outlined briefly.

WARM-UPS

There has been considerable discussion recently concerning the value of warm-ups. Evidence has been presented both approving and disproving value. Most of these studies have centered evidence entirely on the performance record which the subjects made. The production of maximum effort and the making of records are important considerations. However, there would appear to be other values to be derived, particularly for the learner or one preparing to concentrate on the acquisition of a skill.

Performance of easy, rhythmic movements, carefully selected in relation to the skill to be performed after the warm-up would appear to produce beneficial results. The person feels warmer and more comfortable in going into more vigorous action. Relaxation is promoted and can be incorporated easily into the skill to be performed. Relaxation should aid flexibility and if this is essential for the skill should facilitate learning. The warm-up should be specific to the skill, using at least the same muscles, in a similar fashion, and should build up to the intensity needed in the skill. Because they are of similar type this may be an opportunity to learn the feeling of differences in effort. The warm-up should be followed immediately by the practice session on the skill and concentration on performing according to predetermined style or on experimenting on the most effective one. There seems little question but that the average performer feels psychologically more ready for serious effort after a warm-up. Since this is a factor which will vary, it may have complicated the studies aimed at determining the value of the warm-up by means of maximum performance or even work output.

FLEXIBILITY

It is often desirable that the performer have a greater range of motion in a given part of the body than he exhibits ordinarily. The articulations are built with definite limitations to range. Attempts to go beyond the limits set up structurally are extremely doubtful. That means that stretching of ligaments and capsules to permit abnormal articular contacts should not be done. But the individual may have acquired further limitation through disuse of muscles, shortening of ligaments following injuries, scar tissue in muscles and fasciae, or excessive muscular hypertension. Working on these problems may be done safely.

The first step would appear to be an attempt to diagnose the cause. If it is tension, then relaxation learning will pay remarkable dividends. Relaxation must occur in the proper muscles to permit the desired movement, and any stretching which is to be done should be in the proper muscles. If strength is needed in the agonistic group it must be developed while the antagonists are learning to relax.

Stretching must be done as a long, slow, sustained stretch. The use of a fast, forceful, bobbing type of stretching will only induce the stretch reflex and further complicate the problem. It must be recognized that it will take a considerable span of time to accomplish a significant amount of increase in flexibility so that work should start well in advance of need.

Stretching should never proceed to the actual point of pain and subsequent soreness. There will usually be some discomfort, but the distinction between discomfort and pain is a subjective one. Therefore, the aftereffects should be noted carefully and aim to avoid tissue damage and give time for repair if it does occur. Flexibility once obtained can be maintained by occasional use to the full limits.

Lack of flexibility is one of the problems in the aging process. Shortening of fascia and ligaments does occur as well as frequent arthritic types of joint involvement. In cases not affected by the joint involvement, near normal flexibility can be prolonged for many years by regular use of maximum range. It is in this connection that certain work skills, regular use of gymnastics which require a wide range of movement, swimming, and certain other recreational activities are valuable to the person of middle age and advanced years.

STRENGTH

The building of strength is probably the most important problem of the therapist who is working with cases of physical rehabilitation and also of the coach of many sports. The basic principle that use causes hypertrophy and disuse results in atrophy is not adequate. The use must involve the muscle which is being strengthened; the exercise should not permit substitution of some other stronger muscle. Eliciting action from the right muscle will be easier if there is fixation of the part and the range of motion is not too great. In fact, isometric contraction appears to give as satisfactory results as isotonic.

The use must involve the muscle with a resistance near its maximum load and that resistance must be increased from time to time as the capacity of the muscle increases. The person must really go all-out in his efforts while exercising in order to draw on all motor units that can be used in the muscle group. Exercise for strength building must be done regularly, i.e., daily or even more frequently than daily if sufficient rest occurs between bouts. Strength increases rather rapidly under these circumstances. The daily time investment is low and the increase in strength becomes measurable within a few days. The point at which increased girth of the muscle occurs depends to a considerable extent on which muscle is being used, and on individual differences apparently reflecting the state of the muscle and fat deposits in and around the muscle. Increased girth is not an inevitable accompaniment of strength increment.

The therapist or physical educator is often confronted with the question of how much strength to develop in subjects or students. The usual criterion is strength to do the tasks which that person needs or wishes to do, plus some extra to delay fatigue in the performance of the task. For example, the person who is to be standing or on the feet a great deal needs sufficient strength to support the spine and shoulder girdle in optimum position and sufficient strength in the feet to avoid fatigue and pain in the feet and legs. The person who has had a knee injury or surgery needs sufficient strength in the quadriceps to keep the knee straight or support it when flexed to prevent further injury.

Strength of a muscle can be maintained with heavy work no more than once a week if the muscle is kept in good physiological condition by work of any type. Otherwise, disuse soon has its effect.

ENDURANCE

Endurance is a general state enabling the person to persist in work output over a period of time. It is primarily dependent upon efficiency of the cardiorespiratory systems. The term muscular endurance is frequently used, but refers entirely to the ability of the muscle to persist in work. This ability is dependent upon the capillary circulation in the muscle and indirectly upon the general condition of the body. However, it is more directly dependent upon the strength of the muscle. A muscle which has all motor units developed well has more strength; on submaximal tasks few motor units can do the work and many are left in reserve for a rotation into action, thus permitting tired fibers to relax before being needed again. A weaker muscle needs more of the motor units at any one time and therefore has less reserve for prolonged work. Increase in localized muscular endurance is, therefore, a matter of building muscle strength.

The process of building general endurance is not too dissimilar to that for building strength. The person must start at whatever level he is and push himself to the limit, and gradually increase the task as his capacity increases. The endurance training should be related to the activity for which the performer is preparing. For example, the sports person who is required to run a great deal, will develop through running, the swimmer through swimming. Any saving that can be effected will prolong the onset of fatigue. Better skills, less tension, and relaxation between spurts will produce economies.

Second wind is a phenomenon which has been experienced by most athletes who engage in vigorous sports. There is some disagreement on the physiological basis of second wind. However, it is known that it occurs only in the athlete who has undergone extensive conditioning, and only in activities which require fast and vigorous action.

THE LEARNING CURVE

The total learning curve on a complex motor skill is an S-shaped one. The initial plateau may be bypassed if the new skill is sufficiently similar to known ones that there is little or no early exploratory effort to find the general pattern of the co-ordination. The early stage is also characterized by excess muscle effort, near rigidity in some cases, in an attempt to be exact. This may persist with some cases as progress is made.

The role of the teacher at this stage is to clarify the concept of the task, to help prevent repetition of incorrect movements, and to encourage and call attention to details that will help still further. The role of practice for the beginner is to try to translate the concept of the skill into his own movements.

Then the learning curve goes up very abruptly. The movement pattern is taking form, the right muscles are functioning most of the time, and the mechanics and details of the skill are being improved. He begins to get satisfaction and thus is helped to relax.

As new elements are added there is apt to be a regression or at least lack of progress. Such plateaus are inevitable also at this stage as the total action is being integrated into the nervous pathways. It is at this stage that the learner becomes conscious of the differences between his successful and unsuccessful efforts. With patience on the part of the learner and help from some source he gradually continues to improve.

Practice does *not* make perfect. Practice does make for consistent performance, although this performance may be far below the standard expected for it. However, when the performer arrives at the stage that the skill is always performed the same way unless he is deliberately trying to change it, it is said to be learned.

Use films or demonstrations several times during the learning process, but use different cues for watching at the different times. The same film may even be used. On the first showing near the very beginning, emphasize the continuity and range of action. Try to point up similarities in the total movement to other skills already learned. Later, point out details of arm action or footwork which are still essentially gross movement. These muscles involve fewer motor units and synaptic connections than the hands have. Finally concentrate on detail when there is a basis for empathy and ability to see detail in the film and when the individual can cope with the feelings of action in the many motor units in the extrinsic and intrinsic muscles of the hand.

Success in any effort gives the performer a feeling of confidence. Usually confidence and self-assurance make it easier for the performer to execute highly co-ordinated and precise skills accurately. The beginner's uncertainty and anxiety increase his difficulties. They cause a tense, awkward, ineffective performance. The same thing is true of the skilled player if he is too anxious. Success in the skill helps develop assurance. The teacher's acknowledgment of success also builds confidence and is another direct responsibility for the teacher.

Fear is definitely known to have an inhibitory effect on the learning process. This is very evident in activities such as swimming, diving, skiing, skating, bicycling, horseback riding, apparatus usage, tumbling, and trampolining. It is probably of some significance also in sports such as soccer, hockey, and baseball. The way in which the activity is taught and the attitude built up in the student are partly responsible for preventing development of fear and for overcoming fear which may already be present. Careful supervision which builds on previously learned skills and which teaches activities within the ability of the group leads to success and confidence.

Practice on a skill always has some effect on the connections in the nervous system. It may have some effect on the physiological state and on the attitude of the person. Practice should be directed with full knowledge that changes are occurring in the performer. Skills that are well established are very difficult to change. If any attempt is made to make a change there is always a marked regression in skill. The learner should have the best and most satisfactory learning experience possible.

The role of the teacher in practice is to present the most economical form of practice, to analyze performance and make positive corrections at the right time, to help give meaning to the practice, and to maintain the general conditions conducive to learning. Practice is repetition of a constantly changing and improved form, understood by the performer and guided by the teacher. When this criterion is met, the amount of practice necessary will depend primarily upon the complexity of the skill.

REFERENCES

1. Cureton, T. K., Scientific Principles of Human Performance, *Health and Fitness in the Modern World*, presented at the Institute of Normal Human Anatomy, Rome, 1960, Chicago, Athletic Institute, 1961, p. 347.
2. Council for International Organizations of Medical Sciences, *Brain Mechanisms and Learning*, Springfield, Ill., Charles C Thomas, 1961.
3. Colville, Frances M., *Learning of Motor Skills as Influenced by Knowledge of General Principles of Mechanics*, Microcard PSY80, 1956.
4. Cratty, Bryan J., Comparison of Learning a Fine Motor Task with Learning a Similar Gross Motor Task using Kinesthetic Cues, *Research Quarterly*, 33, May 1962, p. 212.
5. Dillon, Evelyn, Use of Music as an Aid in Teaching Swimming, *Research Quarterly*, 23, March 1952, p. 1.
6. Forbes, Joseph, *Characteristics of Flexibility in Boys*, Microcard PE145, 1950.
7. Gagné, Robert M., *Psychology and Human Performance*, New York, Holt, Rinehart and Winston, Inc., 1959, Ch. 8, Motor Skills.
8. Harrison, Virginia F., Review of Neuromuscular Bases for Motor Learning, *Research Quarterly*, 33, March 1962, p. 59.
9. Karpovich, Peter V., *Physiology of Muscular Activity*, Philadelphia, W. B. Saunders Co., 1959, Ch. 3, Muscle Training.
10. Kingsley, Donald Bruce, *Flexibility Changes Resulting from Participation in Tumbling*, Microcard PE163, 1952.
11. Lyne, James, *The Frequency of Static Contraction Exercise Necessary for Strength Level Maintenance*, Microcard PE356, 1958.
12. McCue, Betty F., *Flexibility of College Women*, Microcard PE125, 1952.
13. Margaria, R., and Gualtierolti, T., Functional Fundamental Characteristics of the Nervous System in Athletes and the Effects of Performance, *Health and Fitness in the Modern World*, presented at the Institute of Normal Human Anatomy, Rome, 1960, Chicago, Athletic Institute, 1961, p. 162.
14. Mohr, Dorothy, Contributions of Physical Activity to Skill Learning, *Research Quarterly*, 31, October 1960, p. 321.
15. Nelson, Dale O., *Studies of Transfer of Learning in Gross Motor Skills*, Microcard PSY96, 1957.

16. Olsen, Barbara H., *An Investigation of the Relationship of Ankle, Knee, Trunk and Shoulder Flexibility to General Motor Ability*, Microcard PE251, 1956.
17. Purdy, Bonnie J., and Lockhart, Aileene, Retention and Relearning of Gross Motor Skills After Long Periods of No Practice, *Research Quarterly*, 33, May 1962, p. 365.
18. Riddle, Kathryn S., *Comparison of Three Methods for Increasing Flexibility of the Trunk and Hip Joints*, Microcard PE253, 1956.
19. Rodgers, Donald P., *Development of Strength by Means of Static and Concentric Muscle Contraction*, Microcard PE300, 1956.
20. Soares, Patricia L., *Relationship Between Selected Elements of Coordination and the Rate of Learning Complex Motor Skills*, Microcard PSY98, 1958.
21. Solley, William H., *Speed and Accuracy as Directives in Motor Learning*, Microcard PSY5, 1951.
22. Villa, Cynthia A., *Effects of Jumping Exercises on the Development of the Strength and Flexibility of the Knees and Ankles*, Microcard PE335, 1958.
23. Walters, C. Etta, *Effects of Prescribed Strenuous Exercises on the Physical Efficiency of College Women*, Microcard PE95, 1951.
24. Wiggers, Carl J., *Physiology in Health and Disease*, 5th ed., Philadelphia, Lea & Febiger, 1949, Ch. 53, Muscular Activity and Related Phenomena.

CHAPTER **26**

Mechanics Related to the
Prevention of Injuries

MANY OF THE ACTIVITIES of the gymnasium and playground have certain possibilities of danger. An understanding of these possibilities and the type of precaution to be taken can practically eliminate such accidents from the program. Some of these precautions may require the elimination of certain activities or equipment; or they may necessitate the teaching of safety facts or skills to the participants.

SPORTS

An understanding of momentum, of the comparative possibilities of momentum developed in angular and linear motion, of centrifugal force, and of the kinetic energy of moving objects is necessary for the solution of several problems.

A small ball coming at high speed has considerable momentum ($M = mv$) and small children or inexperienced players should not be expected to catch it. Even an experienced player should be provided with a catching glove to prevent bruises of the hand. A larger, heavier ball coming at a very much lower velocity may have the same or greater kinetic energy ($K.E. = \frac{1}{2}mv^2$). Play areas should be so arranged that persons will not be within the danger range unless they are part of the group, know what is going on, and are provided with proper protection.

The larger ball is less dangerous to the catcher and less likely to cause severe injury if it accidentally hits a player. Assuming that the two balls have the same momentum, the larger ball spreads its impact over a wider area and, therefore, is less apt to bruise tissue or break bones. However, the momentum may be such as to give the person a severe jolt or to cause him to fall. Ten pounds of force applied to one square inch of body surface would probably cause severe injury. However, if that ten pounds were spread over ten or twenty square inches, the amount of force per unit of surface area would be so low that the effect would not be serious. This principle will suggest safety measures. It is largely because of this distribution of force that the football pads are effective. The momentum of the oncoming tackler or blocker then reacts on the opponent's body mass more nearly as a whole instead of being localized at the point of contact.

Speed and momentum become very great at the end of a long lever. For that reason, practice with golf clubs, tennis or badminton rackets, baseball bats, or any long striking implement should always be conducted with ample space between all players. Also, the student should understand that he must not wander around aimlessly or without extreme caution among the practice group. As these games are ordinarily played, there is so much space between players that injuries from accidental blows are very rare during the game. However, every player should understand the length of his reach and the potential danger. This is particularly true of baseball or softball, where players frequently fail to decrease the momentum of the bat on the follow-through before dropping the bat.

Class organization is very important in the prevention of injuries in activities such as golf, softball, or the throwing events in track. Practice areas should be carefully spaced and divided. The striking activities in golf and softball and the throwing events in track involve more or less rotatory motion. Therefore, there is a large possible range in which the ball, discus, or javelin may sail when the delivery is poorly executed. The minimum spacing of participants should be that of the maximum possible range.

APPARATUS

Because of the angular momentum developed in moving apparatus, much of the playground or gymnasium equipment is dangerous. It should be carefully considered and, if the equipment is used, safety habits should be taught and enforced.

Any type of spinning equipment tends to throw the person off at a tangent to its arc. A merry-go-round type of apparatus is used principally by small children, and the speed which they can secure from it is usually not great enough to be particularly hazardous. However, other children or adults may start a faster rotation which the small child cannot counteract. The fact that he is usually sitting on such equipment or that he is standing and has a grip as well enables the rider to stay on. However, on an apparatus such as the giant-stride, the only contact is by the grip of the hands. Because everyone on the equipment runs to get started, considerable speed is created. As speed develops, the rider swings out above the ground. The pull increases with the speed, and finger flexors may not be sufficient to overcome it. This also takes more space than the eager observers along the side account for. Only children of similar age and size should use this equipment at any one time.

The to-and-fro swing of such equipment as the flying rings, the trapeze, and the playground swing represent somewhat the same danger. Throughout the arc there is more or less outward momentum; gravity also tends to pull the child off. If he is suspended by the hands, security is dependent upon the finger flexors. Sitting in the playground swing is comparatively safe. The height above the ground, in the event of a fall, is the greatest danger. The other major source of danger is the failure of children playing in the swing area to realize how much space is needed for the swings. On the horizontal bar, centrifugal force tends to pull the performer off on very fast swings. The grip must counteract this effect.

Rotating equipment frequently causes dizziness or disturbance of the sense of equilibrium of the rider. This may be a source of danger, since the rider is very apt to fall in dismounting from the equipment. Teaching children how to dismount forward with the line of swing, and how to focus the eyes on a point above the ground does much to help avoid this difficulty.

JUMPING AND LANDING

When a child drops off swinging equipment, comes down a slide, or lands from any type of jump, his movement must be checked without injury. Relaxation of the legs or flexion of the knees and ankles is essential, just as the "give" is essential in catching a ball. This provides time and distance through which the speed may be reduced. It is for the same reason that soft landing pits should be used for any type of jumping, or that mats should be used in the gymnasium for all forms of vaults or landings.

The landing surface should not be uneven or in any way cause the performer to turn or throw the weight sideward. The knee is flexed for the landing, and it is in this position that the knee can be twisted or pushed sideward, causing severe internal knee injuries. Ankle sprains may be caused in the same way.

TUMBLING

Safety in stunts and tumbling is also dependent upon an understanding of momentum and energy, of factors in stability, and of human anatomy. The "spotter" on headstands, handstands, and all couple or group balance events should be in line with the movement of the performer. In this position, momentum can be checked and the performer stopped in balance. The spotter must also know how to brace his own feet for checking this weight. In flips and somersaults, the spotter may be of real assistance if he gives support at the proper moment.

The responsibility should not rest entirely upon the assistant. The performer should work for a definite feeling of body position, of momentum, and of timing. On events such as cartwheels or dives, the performer is more or less on his own and dependent upon these kinesthetic reactions.

This feeling comes as a result of careful progression in the teaching-learning process. Safety equipment, properly used, will eliminate danger when errors are made during the learning period.

Stability in any position is dependent upon an adequate base and maintenance of the center of gravity over the base. Therefore the base should always be as large as possible, steady, and sufficient to resist the superimposed weight or any additional force exerted by jumping or turning.

Failure to understand anatomical structure and its limitations is responsible for another type of danger. Excessive hyperextension of the spine or of the hip joint, maintenance of weight in a hyperextended position, maintenance of heavy weight entirely by trunk muscles, or movements requiring flexibility beyond the normal range in any joint may cause severe strains. Such activities are usually of the exhibition or contortionist or "strong man" type, rather than primarily developmental. They can be eliminated with no great loss to the program.

The dangers in a stunts and tumbling program are due principally to falling, to poorly controlled momentum, or to strains from excessive weights poorly supported. Relaxation is the secret of safety in falling. When falling, a person develops kinetic energy. Relaxation allows parts of the body to be stopped more or less in succession and provides time in which to stop them. The stiff body is reacted on as a whole at the instant of contact. Falling is most dangerous when the performer is in an inverted position. If this happens, the performer should attempt enough support with the hands to protect the head, or to give time to get it out of the way or to tip the body over to the side. Landing may be made safely relaxed but on all fours, or the more skilled performer may even use a roll for recovery. In any event, relaxation is necessary to absorb the force of the drop. Specifically, one should avoid falling with the body stiff and flat on the floor; or on the hands with arms rigid, or on the head either directly or in such a way that the neck will be hyperextended. Mats should be used at all times to provide a less resistant surface for falling.

Poorly controlled momentum may result in falls, particularly in the balance events. In other instances, it may mean poor landings and faulty execution as in the rolls, somersaults, flips, vaults, and suspension stunts. These are, almost without exception, skills involving angular motion. Safety in these events depends upon several factors regulating that motion: the sources of rotatory force, the means of checking it. A careful progression in teaching activities will build up the necessary abilities as well as confidence; both contribute to success. Competent assistance should be provided all learners.

Strains come when performers attempt to lift loads that are too heavy, to lift loads in such a way that the back muscles must do all the work, or to continue heavy work when fatigued.

Tumbling on the trampoline creates some additional problems. The height of the rebound permits a very marked shift in position if the body goes up at other than a direct vertical. The size of the bed leaves little margin of variation in this respect. Focusing should be on the end of the tramp without lowering the head. This remains constant at all times while variations in placement of the equipment will produce variations in relative position of the focus from day to day if a point on the wall is used. The only landing in which injuries occur with any frequency is the front landing. Beginners often fail to get a single contact of all points simultaneously and thereby hyperextension of the back may occur. A student with a shoulder which is subject to dislocation should not work on the front drop, as the pressure on the hands is such that dislocation may easily occur. A safety belt should be used in learning front and back flips and similar events until the timing on the turn is learned. This will minimize the chances of landing on the neck.

SWIMMING

Dangers from swimming may be classed as drowning, sprains or fractures from water resistance, and physiological reactions to the water. The latter is certainly not of a mechancal nature. On the one hand, the membrane of the nose or ears may be affected so that germs already present may thrive and cause infections. Also, the water may cause the swimmer to be chilled with results varying anywhere from discomfort and lack of enjoyment to changes in breathing and heart action, muscle cramps, or inability to use the muscles for swimming. It is only this incapacity for muscular action that concerns us here. Cold and hypertension of the muscles are closely associated with muscle cramps. Massage may help to relieve the pain. Assuming a floating position takes care of the swimmer temporarily. Cold water is not a problem in most teaching situations, but swimmers should be taught to avoid extremely cold water, particularly if their tolerance for it is low. There is considerable individual variation on that point.

Drowning should be discussed here because of its relationship to the mechanics of breathing. Since breathing has not been discussed previously, a very brief description will be given first. Breathing is essentially dependent upon movement of the thorax due to muscular contraction and relaxation. This occurs by stimulus from the respiratory center in the medulla. This is a part of a total reflex action, the original stimulus coming from the change in carbon dioxide and oxygen content of the tissues of the body. In ordinary inspiration, the thorax is expanded by contraction of the diaphragm, intercostals, superior posterior serratus, and pectoralis minor. At the same time, the epiglottis, which is a musclar flap over the trachea, is lifted and the larynx expands. The pressure of air on the outside of the body causes air to rush into the lungs, resulting in an increase in thoracic volume. These muscles then relax, the diaphragm again moves up into the thorax, and the abdominal and intercostal muscles help in compression. The result is that most of the air is expelled.

This process proceeds more or less normally with certain modifications in rate, as long as the mouth or nose is above water at the time of the inhalation. The reflex mechanism controlling the opening to the larynx is usually very effective in permitting the entrance of air only. However, if water is taken in with the air, trouble begins. Experimental drownings of animals indicate certain facts concerning the process which follows the aspiration of water. In these experiments there was an immediate and reflex closing of the larynx; swallowing was rapid. This was accompanied by a struggle to get above the water. The animals sometimes died in this stage with no water in the trachea or lungs. In other cases, there was a period of relaxation of the larynx and a series of gasps during which water was inhaled. In either case, drowning was a process of asphyxiation due to the stoppage of the air passages by natural reflex action or by water and mucus.

When the swimmer is able to stay on top of the water after choking, he almost invariably coughs. Coughing is an attempt to clear the throat so that normal breathing may again be resumed. It may be effective or may not be, depending upon whether the mucus is cleared from the trachea and larynx. The coughing reduces the amount of air in the lungs, however, and thereby reduces the buoyancy of the swimmer. At the same time, the swimmer swallows more or less water. This may be sufficient to distend the stomach and somewhat decrease thoracic expansion toward the abdomen. This makes it harder for the swimmer to say on top of the water.

Another point is very important for the swimmer to remember, particularly for the swimmer with only a moderate amount of experience in the water. The body will float at or near the surface of the water if given a chance, but it is easier for the mouth and nose to be out of the water when the body is in a horizontal position than it is with the body in a vertical one. This horizontal position also facilitates the proper arm action for swimming. An arm pull in a horizontal direction is necessary for safety. When the swimmer is in a vertical position and attempts arm strokes, the pull is more apt to be in a vertical plane. This either causes bobbing or requires very rapid action to prevent sinking. It is on this fact that the old adage is based: "A swimmer gets just what he reaches for. If he reaches for shore he gets it; if he reaches for heaven he gets it."

Another safety factor with which the swimmer should be familiar is the value of artificial support in time of emergency. Practically all women and a large percentage of men have sufficient buoyancy to remain suspended in the water. A very little additional help should keep the head well above water. Sufficient help can be secured from a comparatively small piece of wood, such as would be available at almost all outdoor swimming sites. A little experimenting will soon show the minimum size which is adequate for the various sizes of swimmers.

Practically all the sprains in the water come from diving. The force with which the swimmer enters the water depends upon the height of the dive and of the board or platform. The entry of the hands first is designed to cut the water, and to allow the body to enter with the minimum of resistance. The water resists passage of any broad flat surface trying to progress through it. Such resistance may cause strains.

If the head is pulled back at the moment of entry, the neck may be hurt. Strains are most frequent in the lower back. This may be caused by hyperextended legs and flexed knees which drag in the water, causing further hyperextension of the lumbar spine, particularly if the diver attempts to make the dive shallow. The same effect may be seen on a dive in which there is a good spring or leg lift, but in which the diver turns too soon. This results in an overthrow of the legs and may strain the back, particularly if the abdominals are not holding the pelvis fixed. These lower back strains are usually in the lumbosacral or sacroiliac joints. Since the spine is fairly flexible in the lumbar region, far more hyperextension is possible than the standards of the dive would permit. It is the very poor diver who is in danger in this respect, and this danger can be avoided by the building up of control on simpler dives.

CANOEING

Canoeing safety is dependent upon proper methods of loading and unloading the craft and seating the passengers. All weight must be kept over the keel or evenly distributed over it. When a passenger must move in a canoe, he should hold the gunwales on both sides to assist in distributing weight more evenly; incidentally this keeps his weight lower. Passengers should be sitting or kneeling on the bottom of the canoe, not seated on the seats, which are always near the level of the gunwales. The proper height dock, and one against which the canoe can be brought broadside is a great aid in correct loading and unloading. When loading must be done from the beach, the canoe will tilt very easily if one end is supported on shore.

The only real danger in any of the strokes occurs in the draw stroke if the blade is allowed to pass under the canoe and the grip is retained. The paddle then acts as a lever to tilt the canoe.

Wind and waves are dangerous when hitting the craft from the side. The canoe turns on its long axis and capsizes. But if the canoe is moving into or with the waves, it merely rides with bow and stern alternately higher and lower. One should not canoe at all when the waves are large enough to break and drop into the canoe. In almost any situation, however, if the passengers lie in the bottom of the canoe, the weight will be low enough to keep the canoe from capsizing.

Statistics on the frequency of the various injuries in sports activities are extremely difficult to compute because of incomplete reporting and non-comparable diagnosis and terminology. However, it appears from various studies that have been done that the upper and lower extremity share about equally in injuries, and the two comprise the great majority of the total. In the lower extremity the knee ligaments or menisci suffer tears when the knee is bent or struck in such a way as to cause twisting when flexed. Ankle sprains are common from landing on uneven surfaces, and fractures in the feet from the same cause. In the upper extremity, chronic irritations are common. These take the form of bursitis, tennis-elbow, or Little League elbow. Shoulder dislocations may occur from forced hyper-extension of the arm, and fractures of the wrist from falls. Finger fractures occur most frequently from extending fingers firmly toward a ball in an attempt to catch it. The force of the ball hitting the end of the fin-ger results not infrequently in a splinter fracture in which one side of a condyle of a phalanx is sheered off.

Safety and enjoyment of activities without fear is the responsibility of both teacher and performer.

REFERENCES

1. Badgley, Carl E., and Hayes, John, Athletic Injuries to the Elbow, Fore-arm, Wrist and Hand, *The American Journal of Surgery*, 100, 1961, p. 432.

2. Badgley, George, Sports Injuries of the Shoulder Girdle, *American Medi-cal Journal*, 172, 1960, p. 444.

3. Bennet, George, Baseball and Other Injuries, *Medical Times*, 87, 1959, p. 302.

4. Broddon, M. B., Little Leaguer's Elbow, *American Journal of Roentgen-ology*, 83, 1960, p. 671.

5. Dayton, O. William, *Athletic Training and Conditioning*, New York, Ronald Press Co., 1960.

6. deVries, Herbert A., Prevention of Muscular Distress after Exercise, *Research Quarterly*, 32, May 1961, p. 177.

7. Henderschott, Robert, and Sigerseth, Peter O., Landing Force in a Collapsible Jumping Pit Compared with that in Conventional Pit, *Research Quarterly*, 24, December 1953, p. 410.

8. Hoar, Frank B., and Martin, Don B., Student Injuries in Secondary Schools in Oregon, *Research Quarterly*, 24, October 1953, p. 276.

9. Kantor, Leon, *The Etiology and Prevention of Shin Splints*, Microcard PE3, 1948.

10. Karpovich, Peter V., Water in the Lungs of Drowned Animals, *Archives of Pathology*, 15, 1933, p. 828.

11. Lewin, Phillip, *The Knee and Related Structures*, Philadelphia, Lea & Febiger, 1952.

12. Longheed, D. W., Jones, J. M., and Hall, G. E., Physiological Studies in Experimental Asphyxia and Drowning, *Canadian Medical Association Journal*, 40, 1939, p. 423.
13. Morehouse, Laurence, and Rasch Philip, *Scientific Basis of Athletic Training*, Philadelphia, W. B. Saunders Co., 1958.
14. Mosley, H. F., Athletic Injuries to the Shoulder Region, *American Journal of Surgery*, 98, 1959, p. 401.
15. Payne, Reginald T., Treatment of Drowning and Electrocution, *British Medical Journal*, 1, 1940, p. 819.
16. Quigley, Thomas, Knee Injuries Incurred in Sports, *Journal of American Medical Association*, 171, 1959, p. 142.
17. Rochelle, R. H., Kelliher, M. S., and Thornton, R., Relationship of Maturation Age to Incidence of Injury in Tackle Football, *Research Quarterly*, 32, March 1961, p. 78.
18. Ryan, Allan, The Role of Training and Conditioning in the Prevention of Athletic Injuries, in *Health and Fitness in the Modern World*, Chicago, Athletic Institute, 1961, p. 302.
19. Scherrer, J., and Bourgurgnon, A., Changes in Electromyogram Produced by Fatigue in Man, *American Journal of Physical Medicine*, 38, 1959, p. 153.
20. Slocum, Donald, The Mechanics of Some Common Injuries to the Shoulder in Sports, *The American Journal of Surgery*, 100, 1961, p. 394.
21. Smilie, Ian, *Injuries of the Knee Joint*, Baltimore, Williams and Wilkins Co., 1951.
22. Snively, George G., Kovacic, Charles, and Chichester, C. O., Design of Football Helmets, *Research Quarterly*, 32, May 1961, p. 221.
23. Steindler, Arthur, *Kinesiology of the Human Body*, Springfield, Ill., Charles C Thomas, 1955, Ch. 33, Sprains of the Joints of the Upper Extremity; Ch. 35, The Pathomechanics of the More Common Fractures of the Upper Extremity.
24. Zimmerman, Helen M., Accidents Resulting from Use of Trampoline, *Research Quarterly*, 27, December 1957, p. 452.

Appendix

Symbols and Formulas

a = linear acceleration
A = angular acceleration
cos = cosine of the angle
D = distance
F = force
g = gravity
I = inertia
m = mass
M = momentum
r = radius
sin = sine of the angle
t = time
v or V = velocity
ω = angular velocity

linear acceleration $= \dfrac{V_2 - V_1}{t}$

angular acceleration $= \dfrac{\omega_2 - \omega_1}{t}$

centrifugal acceleration $= \dfrac{V^2}{r}$

distance fallen in t seconds $= \frac{1}{2}gt^2$

angular distance $= \omega_1 t + \frac{1}{2}At^2$

force $= ma$

momentum $= mv$

kinetic energy $= \frac{1}{2}mv^2$

centrifugal force $= m\omega^2 r$

inertia of a particle $= mr^2$

inertia of a cylindrical object (on the long axis or the primary transverse axis) $= \dfrac{\Sigma mr^2}{2}$

inertia of a cylindrical object (on a transverse axis at one end of the object) $= \dfrac{\Sigma ml^2}{3}$

(l = length of the object)

distance of a projectile (to the same level, i.e., from the ground to the ground) $= \dfrac{V^2 \sin 2\theta}{g}$

(θ = angle)

distance of a projectile (to the ground, having started somewhere above the ground)

$$= \frac{V^2 \sin\theta \cos\theta + V \cos\theta \sqrt{V^2 \sin^2\theta + 2gh}}{g}$$

rotary component = force $\times$ sin of the angle

stabilizing component = force $\times$ cos of the angle

velocity $= \dfrac{D}{t}$

weight = mg

work = FD

Sines and Cosines

Degrees	Sines	Cosines	Degrees	Sines	Cosines
0	.0000	1.0000			
1	.0175	.9998	46	.7193	.6947
2	.0349	.9994	47	.7314	.6820
3	.0523	.9986	48	.7431	.6691
4	.0698	.9976	49	.7547	.6561
5	.0872	.9962	50	.7660	.6428
6	.1045	.9945	51	.7771	.6293
7	.1219	.9925	52	.7880	.6157
8	.1392	.9903	53	.7986	.6018
9	.1564	.9877	54	.8090	.5878
10	.1736	.9848	55	.8192	.5736
11	.1908	.9816	56	.8290	.5592
12	.2079	.9781	57	.8387	.5446
13	.2250	.9744	58	.8480	.5299
14	.2419	.9703	59	.8572	.5150
15	.2588	.9659	60	.8660	.5000
16	.2756	.9613	61	.8746	.4848
17	.2924	.9563	62	.8829	.4695
18	.3090	.9511	63	.8910	.4540
19	.3256	.9455	64	.8988	.4384
20	.3420	.9397	65	.9063	.4226
21	.3584	.9336	66	.9135	.4067
22	.3746	.9272	67	.9205	.3907
23	.3907	.9205	68	.9272	.3746
24	.4067	.9135	69	.9336	.3584
25	.4226	.9063	70	.9397	.3420
26	.4384	.8988	71	.9455	.3256
27	.4540	.8910	72	.9511	.3090
28	.4695	.8829	73	.9563	.2924
29	.4848	.8746	74	.9613	.2756
30	.5000	.8660	75	.9659	.2588
31	.5150	.8572	76	.9703	.2419
32	.5299	.8480	77	.9744	.2250
33	.5446	.8387	78	.9781	.2079
34	.5592	.8290	79	.9816	.1908
35	.5736	.8192	80	.9848	.1736
36	.5878	.8090	81	.9877	.1564
37	.6018	.7986	82	.9903	.1392
38	.6157	.7880	83	.9925	.1219
39	.6293	.7771	84	.9945	.1045
40	.6428	.7660	85	.9962	.0872
41	.6561	.7547	86	.9976	.0698
42	.6691	.7431	87	.9986	.0523
43	.6820	.7314	88	.9994	.0349
44	.6947	.7193	89	.9998	.0175
45	.7071	.7071	90	1.0000	.0000

Glossary

Abduction. Movement away from the median line of the body; or, when the reference is to the fingers and toes, movement away from the median line of the hand or foot.

Acceleration. Change in velocity. Velocity is expressed as distance covered per unit of time. Acceleration must also be expressed in units of time to indicate rate of change. Example: Gravital acceleration is 32 feet per second per second. It is sometimes written as 32 ft. per sec.^{2}.

Action potential. Electrical discharge accompanying muscular contraction.

Adduction. Movement toward the median line of the body; or, when the reference is to the fingers and toes, movement toward the median line of the hand or foot.

After loaded. Resistance applied only after contraction of the muscle starts.

Amphiarthrosis (*adj.* **amphiarthrodial**). An articulation with very limited movement.

Amplitude. The total range through which a muscle functions.

Anatomical position. An erect standing position with the feet parallel and arms at the side with palms turned forward.

Anatomy. Study of body structure.

Angular motion. Movement around an axis, rotatory motion.

Antagonist. A muscle which counteracts the pull of another muscle.

Aponeurosis (*pl.* -es). Connective tissue, similar to a fascia, which connects one muscle to another.

Arthrodia (*adj.* **arthrodial**). A joint which permits gliding movements.

Articulation. A connection between two bones, a joint.

Ballistic. A movement in which the motion is initiated by strong muscular contraction and it is then carried on by its own momentum.

Biarticular. Pertaining to two joints. Descriptive of those muscles which cross two joints.

Buoyancy. The lifting effect of a liquid on a body immersed in it.

Bursa (*pl.* -ae). A saclike structure found near articulations or between tendons and the bones to which they attach. It is filled with synovial fluid and serves as a cushion.

Capsule. An enclosure around a joint, constructed of fibrous tissue, and in some cases, ligaments of the joints. It is lined with synovial membrane.

Centrifugal force. Resistance or inertia of an object which opposes deflection from a straight line.

Cervical. Pertaining to the upper region of the spine. Ordinarily refers to the seven upper vertebrae, the neck region.

Circumduction. Movement of a part in which the extremity describes a more or less circular path.

Component. A constituent part.

Condyloid. Pertaining to an articulation with rounded, bulbous articular ends.

Contracture. A state of prolonged contraction of a muscle which persists even after the stimuli cease.

Deceleration. Reduction in velocity; negative acceleration.

Diarthrosis (*adj.* **diarthrodial**). A joint which has free range of motion.

Electromyograph. An electronic device for detection, amplification, and recording of action potentials.

Enarthrosis (*adj.* **enarthrodial**). A joint in which the spherical head of one bone articulates with a cuplike depression in another bone, i.e., a ball and socket joint.

End plate. The ending of a motor nerve fiber in a muscle.

Empathy. Projection of one's own feelings into those of another person.

Equilibrium. State in which the resultant of all forces acting on or in the object is zero.

Extension. Movement of a body segment by which the adjacent parts are brought into straighter alignment.

External work. Work in the mechanical sense, i.e., observable movement in overcoming resistance ($W = FD$).

Fascia. Connective tissue covering the outside of the muscle.

Fiber. Muscle cell.

Fibril. Filament within the muscle fiber.

Flexibility. Free range of motion in an articulation.

Flexion. Movement in a joint by which the two adjacent segments approach each other.

Float. Period of nonsupport in a run; suspension in the water.

Foot-pound. Unit of work.

Free loaded. Resistance applied so the muscle is stretched before contraction.

Friction. Resistance to motion generated when one surface is sliding or rolling over another.

Frontal plane. Plane running from side to side dividing the body into front and back weight halves; or any plane parallel to the primary one.

Fulcrum. Axis around which the part turns.

Gait. Walk or pattern of locomotion.

Galvanometer. A device for detecting and amplifying action potentials.

Ginglymus. Hinge joint, permitting movement in only one plane.

Give. Movement in the direction in which momentum carries a part, for purpose of deceleration.

Glycogen. A carbohydrate substance, frequently stored in the liver, carried by the blood to the tissues for use in the metabolic process.

Gravity. The magnetic attraction of the earth for all objects.

Hemoglobin. A substance found in the red blood cells. It combines loosely with oxygen in the lungs and gives up the oxygen to the tissues.

Hyper-. A prefix meaning "beyond," "greater than," or "above." Example: hyperextension is extension beyond straight alignment.

Inertia. Resistance to motion or change of motion.

Internal work. Contraction of muscles without motion.

Isometric. Constant length, applied to muscles when acting against a resistance greater than the force exerted.

Isotonic. Constant tension, applied to muscle when acting and part moves as a result of the contraction.

Kinetic energy. Form of energy due to motion of the object.

Kinesthesis (kinesthesia). Sense of movement and position of the body parts or of the body as a whole.

Latent time. Period of delay between the application of a stimulus and the beginning of the muscular contraction.

Lever. A simple machine used for the execution of work; it is a rigid bar rotating about an axis.

Lever arm. The parts of the lever between the axis and the points of application of force or resistance; the force arm and the resistance arm.

Ligament. Connective tissue tying bones together.

Linear motion. Translatory motion, motion in which all parts of an object move in the same direction, and each moves an equal distance.

Load. Resistance to be overcome by the muscle. The weight being held by a person.

Locomotion. Movement from one place to another.

Lumbar. Pertaining to the region of the spine just above the pelvis; ordinarily refers to the five vertebrae between the thoracic region and the sacrum.

Machine. A device by which the amount or direction of a force is changed in order to gain some practical advantage.

Moment. The tendency of a force to affect motion, or the quantitative value of that tendency.

Momentum. Product of the mass of the object times its velocity; "quantity of motion."

Motion. Changing of position, movement, in contrast to a state of inactivity or rest.

Neuron. Nerve cell.

Newtonian laws. Laws of inertia, acceleration, and counterforce.

Oscillograph. A device for measuring action potential.

Passive. Action produced by some force other than effort of the performer.

Pendular. Having the nature of a pendulum, having periodic oscillations.

Perpendicular distance. Distance between the axis of rotation and the line of force in such a direction that it is at right angles to the line of force.

Periosteum. The fibrous outer layer of a bone. It covers the bone except on the articular surfaces.

Physiology. Science which deals with the functioning of organisms.

Physics. Science which deals with the natural laws, properties, and phenomena of inanimate matter.

Plantar. Referring to the soles of the feet.

Posture. Position or carriage of the body for a given task.

Power. Time or rate of performing work.

Preparatory movement. First part of the movement for gathering of force or securing direction.

Projectile. An object set in motion by an external force, but carried in motion by its own inertia, and moving as a detached or independent object.

Pronation. Face down; used to refer to position of the total body, to hands and feet. In the case of the feet, it is rotation between tarsals and results in flattening of the plantar surface.

Proprioceptors (proprio- one's own). Receptor organs located within the body and receiving stimuli arising within the tissues.

Range. Total degrees or distance through which a part moves.

Reaction. Counterforce, a force which is opposite in direction from another force and equal to it.

Reaction time. Period of delay between the stimulus and response.

Reciprocal reception. A type of joint in which the condyle of one bone fits into a depression in the other bone in such a way that angular movement may take place in two planes at right angles, but that rotation around the long axis cannot occur.

Reflex arc. Simplest functional unit of the nervous system; connection within the nervous system which permits an automatic response to a given stimulus which has been experienced previously.

Relaxation. State in which muscle tonus is reduced.

Rest. Absence of motion.

Resistance. Anything which opposes motion.

Restraint. Force preventing or slowing motion.

Resultant. The combined or end result of two or more forces acting at different angles.

Rotatory component. The part of a force causing rotation.

Rotatory motion. Angular movement, movement around an axis.

Sagittal plane. Plane lying in the sagittal suture of the cranium; plane passing in an anteroposterior direction through the body.

Sarcomere. A unit in the protein filament of the fibrils.

Sine. The ratio of the side of the triangle opposite the angle to the hypotenuse.

Squat sitting. A position with the knees fully flexed, in which the performer balances on the balls of the feet.

Stability. Ease with which an object stays in place, dependent upon the amount of rise of the center of gravity if the object is tilted.

Stance. Position or posture of readiness for work or action.

Supination. Face up, applied to total body and to hand.

Symphysis. A class of joint, belonging to the slightly movable type, in which a cartilage is inserted between the two articulating bones.

Synapse. A connection between two neurons.

Synarthrodia (*adj.* **synarthrial**). An articulation which permits no motion, which is completely ossified.

Syndesmosis. A slightly movable joint in which a ligament or membrane is inserted between the two articulating bones.

Synergist. A muscle which co-operates with another muscle or group of muscles to produce a movement.

Tangent. A straight line leaving an arc, extending in the direction of the arc at the point at which the line departs.

Tendon. Connective tissue between a muscle and a bone.

Tempo. Speed.

Tetanic contraction or **tetanus.** A state of continuous muscular contraction due to very rapidly repeated stimuli.

Thoracic. Pertaining to the vertebrae to which the ribs attach; ordinarily refers to the twelve vertebrae between the cervical and lumbar regions; pertaining to the dorsal region of the spine.

Tonus. A state of continued slight contraction of a muscle.

Transfer of weight. Shifting of weight from one foot to another; shifting of gravital line from one base to another.

Translatory motion. Movement in which the object moves as a whole and all parts move an equal distance.

Transverse plane. Plane bisecting the body into upper and lower weight halves, or any plane parallel to the primary one.

Treppe. Increased contractions from repeated stimuli due to "warming up" of the muscle.

Trochoid. A pivotlike joint.

Velocity. Speed.

Vertex. The top of the head.

Work. Overcoming of resistance.

INDEX

Abduction, 25, 30, 32, 34, 36, 41, 59, 247
Acceleration, 155-157, 176, 177, 178, 184, 186, 191, 199, 380, 433, 434
Accuracy, 187, 189, 195, 199, 208, 225, 233, 236, 248, 258, 262, 265, 266, 269, 271-278, 313, 318, 337, 382, 383
Action potential, 176-178, 243, 433-434
Adduction, 25, 30, 32, 34, 36, 41, 433
Afterloaded, 433
Aiming: archery, 255; badminton, 256-257; baseball, 262; basketball, 266-268; bowling, 271-273; football, 280; golf, 285-286, 288, 433; soccer, 288-290; tennis, 313, 318, 319
Air resistance, 156, 184, 185-186
Amphiarthrodial articulation, 23, 433
Amplitude of muscle, 99-100, 171, 196, 433
Anatomical position, 17, 24, 58, 148, 433
Anatomy, 4, 7, 90, 422, 433
Antagonist, 49, 51, 53-54, 59, 62, 100, 114, 174, 176, 177, 178, 180, 199, 409, 433
Angular motion, see rotatory motion
Animals, 3, 4, 166
Apparatus: flying rings, 420; giant stride, 420; horizontal bars, 421; merry-go-round, 420; swings, 421; trapeze, 420
Aponeurosis, 94
Arch of foot, 45-47, 407-408
Archery, 252-256; point of aim, 255; stance, 208, 252
Aristotle, 5
Art, 3-4
Arthrodial articulation, 23
Articulations, 22-48, 433; classification, 23; ankle, 44-45; elbow, 25, 36-37, 426; fingers, 426; foot, 45-47; forearm, 36-37; hand, 40; hip, 40-42; knee, 42-44, 426; rib, 27, 31, 33; sacroiliac, 31, 48, 425; shoulder, 35, 423, 426; shoulder girdle, 34-35; spine, 27-31, 40; thumb, 25, 36, 40; wrist, 36-37, 426
Atrophy, 100

Axis: of a lever, 139-144, 148, 173, 185, 434; longitudinal, 170, 174, 176, 233, 305, 310; of motion, 25, 36, 58-59, 127-128, 139, 144, 157-158, 164, 174-175; second vertebra, 27-28; transverse, 158, 175, 304, 310, 320

Badminton, 188, 238, 256-258, 371, 394
Balance, 157-162, 164-168, 172, 194, 204, 206, 208, 210, 215, 222, 226, 370, 375, 378, 379, 384, 389
Ball and socket, see enarthrodial
Ballistic, 178, 394, 433
Baseball, 183, 187, 188, 189, 191, 234, 236-238, 241, 258-265, 415, 420
Basketball, 179, 180, 183, 265-269
Biarticular, see muscle
Bicycling, 131-132, 196, 362-363, 367, 377, 415
Bone: classified, 15-16; cancellous, 13, 15; compact, 12, 15; Haversian system, 13; landmarks, 17; ossification, 14, 30
Bowling, 205, 269-274, 377, 384, 395
Boxing, 176
Braune, 5
Breathing, see respiration
Bukh, 409
Bunt, 262
Buoyancy, 291-295, 384, 389, 424, 433; center of, 292-293, 433, 434
Bursa, 43, 152, 426, 433

Canoeing, 357-362, 425-426
Capsule, 23, 24, 35, 59
Cartwheel, see stunts and tumbling
Catching, 192, 258, 262, 264, 265, 415, 426
Center of gravity, see gravity
Centrifugal force, 174, 185, 415, 421, 434
Chinning, 225, 248, 335-336, 410, 411
Chopping, 176, 370-371
Circumduction, 25, 34, 35, 41, 434
Clarke, H., 14, 138, 153
Climbing: hill, 365; ladder, 369-370; stairs, 173, 364